Martin J Quinn
Ramunno Associates Inc
5 Pine West Plaza
— Suite 505
Albany NY 12205
(518) 456-2777

New York
Life, Accident, and Health Insurance

License Exam Manual

2nd Edition

KAPLAN FINANCIAL

At press time, this edition contains the most complete and accurate information currently available. Owing to the nature of license examinations, however, information may have been added recently to the actual test that does not appear in this edition. Please contact the publisher to verify that you have the most current edition.

This publication is designed to provide accurate and authoritative information in regard to the subject matter covered. It is sold with the understanding that the publisher is not engaged in rendering legal, accounting, or other professional services. If legal advice or other expert assistance is required, the services of a competent professional should be sought.

To submit comments or suggestions, please send an email to errata@kaplan.com.

NEW YORK LIFE, ACCIDENT, AND HEALTH INSURANCE LICENSE
EXAM MANUAL, 2nd Edition
©2006 DF Institute, Inc. All rights reserved.

Published by DF Institute, Inc.

Printed in the United States of America.

ISBN: 1-4195-3473-4

PPN: 5317-3302

06 07 10 9 8 7 6 5 4 3
J   F   **M** A M J J A S O N D

Contents

Martin J. Quinn
Ramomoo Associates Inc
5 Pine West Plaza
Albany NY 12205
(518) 456-2777

The topics addressed in this text are listed in this table of contents in their order of presentation by unit. Specific page references have been purposely omitted to discourage review of individual topics out of context. The state licensing examination requires candidates to obtain an in-depth understanding of the information presented in this text; this includes a recognition of the interrelationship of the topical information presented. If a topic warrants additional review, candidates are urged to cover the material immediately preceding and immediately following the topic targeted for additional study. This will enhance the individual's learning process and help retain the contextual integrity of the subject matter presented in each unit.

Introduction

Welcome to the New York Life, Accident, and Health Insurance License Exam Manual. This text applies adult learning principals to give you the tools you'll need to pass your exam on the first attempt.

Some of these special features include:

- exam-focused questions and content to maximize test preparation; and

- an interactive design that integrates content with notes and comments to increase retention.

PREPARING FOR THE EXAM

Are there any prerequisites to the licensing exam?

A number of states have prescribed specific prelicensing educational requirements that may require certification of completion before the candidate can take the licensing exam. These requirements typically involve attending an approved class or taking an approved self-study course on a correspondence basis. Some individuals may be exempt from the prelicensing requirement or even the licensing exam itself, usually on the basis of prior insurance education or experience. Contact your state's Department of Insurance to determine its specific licensing requirements and exemptions.

What topics will I see on the exam?

State insurance licensing exams cover a broad range of topics. Almost every state makes an outline of exam topics and content available through its test administrator. The licensing exam will include questions on the topics contained in the outline. These outlines also indicate the number of exam questions or the relative weight assigned to each main section of the exam. Contact your state's Department of Insurance to determine the test administrator in your state and obtain an exam outline from the administrator.

How is the License Exam Manual organized?

This manual is organized into specific units that reflect the main topics of a state's insurance exam. These units contain core content on basic insurance principles (life insurance/health insurance or property insurance/casualty insurance). Also included in this text is a unit covering the laws and regulations that apply to insurance in your state. At the end of each unit is a short quiz that covers the subject matter presented in that unit. Use these quizzes to gauge your understanding of the material presented in each unit.

In addition, take the Practice Finals that cover the core content and state law. Grade your performance with the answer keys provided.

In addition to the regular text, each unit also has some unique features designed to help with quick understanding of the material. When an additional point will be valuable to your comprehension, special notes are embedded in the text. Examples of these are included below.

TAKE NOTE

These highlight special or unusual information and amplify important points.

TEST TOPIC ALERT

These highlight content that is likely to appear on the exam.

How will this manual prepare me for the exam?

State insurance licensing exams are designed to test a candidate's knowledge and understanding of the broad principles and concepts pertinent to the specific line of insurance he plans to represent. This manual focuses specifically on those principles and concepts. Designed by insurance instructors and subject matter experts who are experienced with insurance licensing exams, the text plainly presents and explains the topics that are testable. As noted, Unit Quizzes and Practice Finals are included to help you gauge your understanding of the material.

SUCCESSFUL TEST-TAKING TIPS

Passing the exam depends not only on how well you learn the subject matter, but also on how well you take exams. You can develop your test-taking skills—and improve your score—by learning a few test-taking techniques:

- Read the full question

- Avoid jumping to conclusions—watch for hedge clauses

- Interpret the unfamiliar question

- Identify the intent of the question

- Memorize key points

- Beware of changing answers

- Pace yourself

Each of these pointers is explained below. Examples that show how to use them to improve your performance on the exam are also included.

Read the full question

You cannot expect to answer a question correctly if you do not know what it is asking. If you see a question that seems familiar and easy, you might anticipate the answer, mark it, and move on before you finish reading it. This is a serious mistake. Be sure to read the full question before answering it—questions are often written to trap people who assume too much. Here is an example of a question in which an assumption could produce a wrong answer.

1. Arthur incurs total hospital expenses of $8,300. His major medical policy includes a $500 deductible and an 80%/20% coinsurance feature. Assuming this is the first covered expense he incurs this year, how much will Arthur have to pay toward his hospital bill?
   A. $5,900
   B. $2,160
   C. $2,060
   D. $1,800

The answer is C. This is an easy question to answer only for someone who has read the full question, because this is the first application of the deductible. If you read the question too quickly, you might forget to account for the deductible.

Avoid jumping to conclusions

The questions on licensing exams are often embellished with deceptive distractors as choices. To avoid being misled by seemingly obvious answers, make it a practice to read each question and each answer twice before selecting your choice. Doing so will provide you with a much better chance of doing well on the test.

Watch out for qualifiers embedded in the question. (Examples of qualifiers include the words *if, not, all, none,* and *except.*) In the case of *if* statements, the question can be answered correctly only by taking into account the qualifier. If you ignore the qualifier, you will probably not answer correctly.

Qualifiers are sometimes combined in a question. Some that you will frequently see together are *all* with *except* and *none* with *except.* In general, when a question starts with *all* or *none* and ends with *except,* you are looking for an answer that is opposite to what the question appears to be asking. For example:

2. All of the following are excluded from the liability portion of commercial auto coverage EXCEPT
   A. expected or intended injury
   B. contractual injury
   C. insurer's cost of defense
   D. workers' compensation

If you neglect to read the *except,* you might select answer choices A, B, or D. The qualifier makes C the only correct option.

Interpret the unfamiliar question

Do not be surprised if some questions on the test seem unfamiliar at first. If you have studied your material, you will have the information to answer all the questions correctly. The challenge may be a matter of understanding what the question is asking.

Very often, questions present information indirectly. You may have to interpret the meaning of certain elements before you can answer the question.

3. Which type of authority does an insurer give to its agents by means of the agent's contract?

    A. Express
    B. Implied
    C. Fiduciary
    D. General

The correct answer is A. This question is asking you to apply knowledge of agency law in order to select the correct answer. It requires a knowledge of concepts such as express and implied agency.

This same content could have been tested in a different way, as illustrated by the next example.

4. An agent in XYZ Insurance Company, equipped with business cards, sample XYZ policies, and an XYZ rate book, informs a prospect that XYZ has given him unlimited binding authority. The prospect assumes this is true. Given the prospect's assumption, which of the following correctly defines the agent's authority in this case?

    A. Express
    B. Implied
    C. Apparent
    D. Binding

The correct answer is C. At first glance, the two questions appear very different, but in fact they test knowledge of the same principles of agency law. Be aware that the exam will approach a concept from different angles.

Identify the intent of the question

Many questions on licensing exams supply so much information that you lose track of what is being asked. This is often the case in story problems. Learn to separate the story from the question. For example:

5. Alan, age 39, is married and has one small son. He is employed as a sales manager by R.J. Links, a sole proprietorship that owes much of its success to Alan's efforts. He recently borrowed $50,000 from his brother-in-law, Pete, to finance a vacation home. Based on these facts, which of the following do(es) NOT have an insurable interest in Alan's life?

    A. His spouse
    B. His employer
    C. His brother-in-law
    D. His customers

A clue to the answer is presented in the last sentence—who does not have an insurable interest?

Take the time to identify what the question is asking. Of course, your ability to do so assumes you have studied sufficiently. There is no method for correctly answering questions if you don't know the material.

Memorize key points

Reasoning and logic will help you answer many questions, but you will have to memorize a good deal of information. Key points at the beginning of each unit indicate some of the most important points for memorization.

Mnemonic devices give you a shorthand way of remembering information with a single word or phrase. For example, the elements necessary for a risk to be insurable can be summarized as CANHAM:

C	Chance of loss must be **calculable**
A	Premiums must be **affordable**
N	Loss must be **noncatastrophic**
H	Large number of **homogenous** (similar) exposures must exist
A	Loss must be **accidental**
M	Loss must be **measurable**

Avoid changing answers

If you are unsure of an answer, your first hunch is the one most likely to be correct. Do not change answers on the exam without good reason. In general, change an answer only if you:

■ discover that you did not read the question correctly; or

■ find new or additional helpful information in another question.

Pace yourself

Some people will finish the exam early and some will not have time to finish all the questions. Watch the time carefully (your time remaining will be displayed on your computer screen) and pace yourself through the exam.

Do not waste time by dwelling on a question if you simply do not know the answer. Make the best guess you can, mark the question for review, and return to the question if time allows. Make sure that you have time to read all the questions so that you can record the answers you do know.

UNIT 1

Introduction to Insurance Principles and Concepts

KEY TERMS

Pure Risk

Speculative Risk

Law of Large Numbers

Elements of Insurable Risk

Hazard

Peril

Risk Pooling

Methods of Handling Risk

Adverse Selection

I. THE ROLE OF INSURANCE

We all have a compelling need for security, peace of mind, and freedom from worry. Unfortunately, achieving complete financial security historically has been elusive, in part because of universal problems such as death, sickness, accidents, and disability. These problems can strike at any time. The emotional stress they bring is increased by the financial hardships that almost certainly follow.

A. **THE NEED FOR ECONOMIC CERTAINTY AND SECURITY** When death takes the life of a family provider prematurely, surviving family members suffer when they are left without adequate income or the means to provide basic necessities. On the other hand, some people face the unpleasant prospect of outliving their incomes—retirement may be forced on them before they have prepared adequately for a non-income-earning existence. Sickness and disability also can leave economic scars, often more expensive than death. An accident or illness can easily result in catastrophic medical bills or the inability to work for months or years.

B. **INSURANCE AS A PRACTICAL SOLUTION** Insurance evolved to provide a practical solution to the problem of such economic uncertainties and losses. Life insurance, based on actuarial or mathematical principles, guarantees a specified sum of money on the death of the insured person. Annuities provide a stream of income by making a series of payments to the annuitant for a specific period of time or for a lifetime. Health insurance also evolved from scientific principles to provide funds for medical expenses because of sickness or injury and to cover loss of income during a period of disability. The true significance of insurance is its promise to substitute uncertainty with future economic certainty and to replace the unknown with a sense of security.

C. **INSURANCE CONCEPTS AND PRINCIPLES** Insurance involves the transfer of risk from one party to another through a legal contract that spells out the terms, perils covered, exclusions, and other special provisions.

1. **Life insurance** An insured transfers the risk of dying prematurely to the insurer by paying a premium and entering into a legal contract.

2. **Health insurance** An insured transfers the risk of falling ill or suffering injury to the insurer by paying a premium and entering into a legal contract.

3. **Risk** Risk is defined as the uncertainty concerning financial loss, the chance of loss, or the probability of loss. Insurance protects an insured against pure risk. **Pure risk** involves the chance for loss only. **Speculative risk** cannot be insured because it involves the chance for loss or gain (e.g., betting on a horse race is a speculative risk). The risk management techniques for handling risk are the following.

   a. **Avoidance** An individual may avoid the risk of a loss by not engaging in an activity or owning property. For example, a person can avoid the risk of having his auto stolen by never owning an auto. Avoidance may be useful, but it is not always practical.

   b. **Retention** Retention is considered to be the most common method of handling risk. Risks that are retained should be those that lead to small losses only. Owning a policy that includes a deductible is the most basic illustration of retention. In other words, the policyowner will pay for a smaller portion of the loss than an insurer.

TAKE NOTE

Purchasing insurance is a way to transfer risk. Through an insurance policy, the policyowner transfers the economic risk associated with a loss to an insurance company.

    c. Transfer One party transferring the chance of loss to another party is also a popular form of risk handling. The purchase of insurance is a form of risk transfer.

    d. Sharing Sharing risk distributes risk among a number of persons. Each person bears a portion of the risk in relation to what he has invested. A corporation is an example of this form of business where the investments of a large number of people are pooled.

    e. Reduction Risk may be handled better if it is reduced. Reduction may be accomplished through loss prevention and loss control. An example of control is where an insured installs a sprinkler system in a commercial building. If a fire breaks out, the sprinklers are designed to reduce or control the fire damage. Hiring a security guard to protect a business at night is an example of loss prevention that will reduce the risk of theft while the business is closed.

4. Measuring risk Risk is measured according to statistics of past losses. Measurement of the degree of risk determines whether a risk from a given peril is insurable. Risk management is a multistep process used to control, prevent, or reduce risk. Generally, risk management involves a four-step process of:

- identifying the possible risks present (exposure);
- determining what action to take in order to reduce or control risk;
- implementing specific action; and
- monitoring the action taken in order to make changes as needed.

5. Hazard A hazard is a condition that increases the chance of a loss occurring. A hazard may trigger a loss or may lead to the occurrence of a peril. There are two classes of hazards.

    a. Physical hazards Physical hazards are tangible, such as gasoline or other volatile chemicals stored in a garage, unsafe automobile brakes, or cracked sidewalks and driveways.

    b. Moral hazards Moral hazards refer to hazards that derive from the mental attitudes of individuals. This might involve dishonest acts (suffering a loss purposely in order to receive insurance proceeds), carelessness (losses due to apathy), or irresponsible activities (driving while intoxicated). Sometimes a distinction is made between **moral hazards** (dishonest acts) and **morale hazards** (carelessness or indifference).

6. Perils Perils are the direct happenings or events that cause a loss. Therefore, risk is the uncertainty we face that perils will occur and cause us to suffer losses. Common perils we are exposed to include:

TAKE NOTE

A hazard gives rise to a peril which gives rise to a loss.

- fire;
- windstorm;
- negligence;
- burglary;
- robbery; and
- flood damage.

7. **Economic loss** Economic loss is the decrease or disappearance of economic value. Pure loss is characterized by the actual destruction of property. Losses are caused by perils that are enhanced by hazards that, in turn, are the result of risk. Loss can be classified in two ways.

   a. **Direct loss** The loss from an insured peril must be a direct physical loss to the property insured. The property must be damaged or destroyed by the peril or perils insured against without any intervening cause. For instance, an auto colliding with a tree, lightning striking a house, or windstorm damaging a roof's shingles are examples of direct physical losses.

   b. **Indirect loss** Indirect loss is removed from the cause of direct loss but is related to it. This classification of loss is also known as consequential loss.

      1.) For example, assume a manufacturing plant suffers a direct fire loss. The indirect loss would be the loss of profit experienced by the business because it would have to cease operating because of the fire damage. The extent or amount of an indirect loss may exceed a direct loss as far as dollar value is concerned.

8. **Law of large numbers** An insurer is able to assume many risks with the reasonable assurance of experiencing a certain number of losses according to the **law of large numbers**. This is a mathematical rule stating that as the number of exposures increases, the more the actual results will approach the results expected for the event.

9. **Other methods of managing risk** Risk transfers may be accomplished by an individual purchasing an insurance contract. This may be referred to as an insurance transfer. Other forms of legal contracts are available that transfer risks involving noninsurance transfers.

D. **RATE MAKING (PREMIUM) CONCEPTS** Premiums charged on policies may not be excessive, inadequate, or unfairly discriminatory. The terms *rate* and *premium* are often used interchangeably. A **rate** is the price per unit of exposure; the **premium** is the entire (total) cost of coverage for a group of exposure units. Any rating system utilized must produce rates that are stable, are reasonably responsive to changes in loss exposures, and make adequate provisions for contingencies. A rating system must also be easy to understand and encourage loss control.

TEST TOPIC ALERT

With life insurance, insurable interest must exist at the inception of the policy. It does not have to exist at the time of claim. With property insurance, insurable interest must exist at policy inception as well as at time of claim.

1. **Types of rates** Several types of rates are in existence including but not limited to the following.

   a. **Manual rates** These are rates that are listed in a manual or rate book.

   b. **Class rates** These are rates that apply to large groups of homogeneous loss exposures.

   c. **Individual rates** Also known as **specific rates**, these are used when large numbers of homogeneous exposures do not exist. They involve an individual rate for each subject of insurance.

2. **Rating bureaus** A **rating bureau** is an organization owned by member insurance companies. The purpose of a rating bureau is to accumulate and analyze statistical data to develop rates, calculate rates for lines of insurance, and file rates with state regulatory authorities for approval.

   a. Rating bureaus may also develop policy forms and endorsements.

   b. Insurers are usually subscribers to, or actual members of, a rating bureau.

   c. The advantages of rating bureaus involve lower costs and expenses to insurers, standardizing policy forms and endorsements, and aiding small insurers who do not have sufficient rate making data.

3. **Independent filings** Membership in a rating organization is not always mandatory. Some insurers will file rates with a particular state by themselves. This type of action will be more expensive to an insurer. Insurers who wish to remain outside a rating bureau, file independently, and use rate cutting practices are known as **nonbureau insurers**.

4. **Adverse selection** Adverse selection is the tendency of persons whose exposure to loss is higher than average to purchase or continue insurance to a greater extent than those whose exposure is less than average. If an insurance company did not control adverse selection, it would go out of business.

   a. For example, an individual with a terminal illness has a greater desire to purchase life insurance than a healthy individual.

5. **Insurable interest** With life insurance, an insurable interest must exist at the time of application; insurable interest may be based on a business relationship (a partner insuring another partner) or on a relationship of love and affection (husband and wife). With property/casualty insurance, insurable interest is established when the insured would

suffer a financial loss if the property insured were destroyed or damaged (such as a homeowner) and must exist at the time of loss.

6. **Elements of insurance risks** Various types of risks are deemed to be insurable while others are not insurable. Risks or exposures that meet certain criteria may be insurable. If a risk does not meet certain requirements, then it is considered by an insurer to be uninsurable and other means must be utilized to manage any potential loss it holds. Some of the elements of an insurable risk include the following.

   a. **Economic feasibility** The premium charged for the coverage provided must be affordable to the insured. If the risk was so tremendous that the only way it could be covered would be to charge an extremely high premium, it would not be economically feasible for the insured.

   b. **Calculation of probability** The potential loss incurred must be calculable in order to be insured. An individual's loss of life is calculable utilizing the human life value or needs approach (both of which are reviewed in a later unit).

   c. **Sufficiently large numbers** For a risk to be insurable, there must be a sufficient number of insureds available with a similar potential loss who desire to purchase protection. This is similar to the law of large numbers.

   d. **Definite and measurable** The risk of loss must be definite and measurable in both time and place such as a death. The loss must also be such that it is difficult to falsify.

   e. **Fortuitous and accidental** The risk must also be unexpected and unintended. If it were expected and intended, it would not be insurable.

   f. **Less than catastrophic** Insurers do not desire to cover individuals who may all suffer losses at the same time because the insurer would suffer catastrophic losses. Insurers wish to spread the risk in order to combat against this.

E. **TYPES OF INSURERS** Insurance companies involved in the business of negotiating or soliciting contracts of insurance may be classified in several ways.

   1. **Domestic insurance company** A domestic insurance company is a company incorporated in, domiciled in, and organized under the laws of a given state and having its home office located in that state. For instance, the ABC Insurance Company of Boston is a domestic company in the state of Massachusetts because it is incorporated in and has its principal office in Massachusetts.

   2. **Foreign insurance company** A foreign insurance company is incorporated or organized under the laws of one state but is licensed and permitted to conduct the business of insurance in another state. For instance, Allstate Insurance Company of Oakbrook, Illinois is licensed to solicit the business of insurance in Wisconsin. Therefore, in Wisconsin, Allstate Insurance Company is viewed as a foreign company.

3. **Alien insurance company** A company incorporated or organized outside the United States but licensed in a given state is an **alien insurer** in that state. For instance, if Continental Reinsurance Company of London, England, incorporated in another country (England), is licensed to conduct the business of insurance in Texas, it is considered an alien insurer in Texas.

4. **Stock insurance company** A **stock insurance company** is owned by the holders of the company's capital stock. The main motivation of this type of company is to achieve profits. Policyholders of a stock company are not entitled to dividends or liable for any assessments which may be necessary.

5. **Mutual insurance company** A **mutual insurance company** is owned by its policyholders who share in the company's profits in the form of dividends. Some mutual companies issue assessable policies and others issue nonassessable policies.

6. **Reciprocals** These types of insurers combine some characteristics of a mutual insurer (owned by its policyholders) and a Lloyd's Association (individuals assume the risks). A **reciprocal exchange** (or interinsurance association) is a type of cooperative insurance. Under this form of insurance, each policyowner is insured by all of the others. Each insured is also an insurer, as contracts are exchanged on a reciprocal basis.

    a. A reciprocal exchange is not in the legal sense a mutual insurer because the individual subscribers assume their liability as individuals, not as a responsibility of the group as a whole.

    b. Reciprocals are managed by an attorney-in-fact.

7. **Fraternal insurers** A **fraternal benefit society** is a special type of insurer providing insurance benefits, particularly life insurance, for its members. The operations of the fraternal are closely related to and controlled by the bylaws of a large or nonprofit social organization (e.g., Knights of Columbus).

    a. Fraternal benefit orders are afforded tax exemptions.

    b. A fraternal order may assess a policyholder in case of financial difficulties.

8. **Private vs. government insurers** Private or commercial insurance companies are in the business to make a profit. Various plans offered by these companies include individual policies, group policies, industrial policies, and blanket policies. Government programs generally provide social insurance plans on a state or federal level. State plans involve programs such as workers' compensation and compulsory cash sickness plans. Federal plans include Federal Crime Insurance, Fair Plans, FDIC, Social Security, Medicare, and Medicaid. The purpose of government insurance is similar to that of private insurance where it helps to provide economic security against specific perils for the well-being of large groups of persons in our society.

TAKE NOTE

Insurance is offered through private or commercial companies as well as through governmental agencies at both the state and federal level. Social Security, Medicare, Medicaid, and state workers' compensation programs are examples of government insurance plans.

---

9. **Authorized (admitted) insurance company** An authorized (or **admitted**) **company** is an insurer that has received a certificate of authority from a given state and is thereby licensed or authorized to conduct insurance business in that state.

10. **Unauthorized (nonadmitted) insurance company** A nonauthorized (or **nonadmitted**) **company** is one that has not received a certificate of authority from a state and is therefore not licensed or authorized to transact insurance business in that state.

11. **Surplus lines company** Surplus lines companies are a common form of unauthorized carriers. When insurance cannot be supplied by authorized insurers, a surplus lines carrier (via a surplus lines broker) is utilized.

12. **Purchasing group** A purchasing group is composed of members whose businesses or activities are similar and has as its purpose the purchase of insurance on a group basis to cover the members' similar exposures.

13. **Risk retention group** Risk retention groups are composed of members who are engaged in similar businesses or activities. The group's primary activity consists of assuming and spreading all, or any portion, of the liability exposure of its members. The group may provide only liability insurance.

14. **Lloyd's of London** This organization is not an insurance company. It is a voluntary association of persons who agree to share in insurance contracts. All individuals (or groups of individuals) are responsible for the amount of coverage they write.

F. **INSURANCE AS A LEGAL CONTRACT** A contract is an agreement between two or more competent parties under the terms of which each promises to perform in a manner specified, for a consideration (promise or payment). Insurance policies are contracts and are held to the same legal standards as other contracts.

1. **Elements of a legal contract** There are four components required for a contract to be considered legal and enforceable.

   a. **Offer and acceptance (agreement)** One party must make an offer (applicant submits application and premium), and the other party accepts it, rejects it, or makes a counteroffer (the insurer).

   b. **Competent parties** Most parties to a contract are considered competent except for insane persons, those under the influence of drugs or alcohol, persons under duress or forced to enter into a contract, enemy aliens, and minors. However, minors who contract for food, clothing, shelter, and other necessities are considered competent.

TAKE NOTE

In all jurisdictions, insurance contracts are considered to have legal purpose.

c. Legal object or purpose To be valid, a contract cannot be against public policy. For example, a contract to purchase stolen goods is not legal because its purpose is not valid.

d. Consideration Something of value must be given in consideration of the coverage provided by the insurer. The insured's consideration is the premium paid and statements made in the application; the insurer's consideration is the promise to pay a valid claim.

2. Other contract features Insurance contracts may include one or more of the following features.

a. Aleatory contracts This is a contract based on uncertain events in the future where the value given up by one party does not equal that given up by another party to the contract. For example, a life insurance policy has an aleatory feature because the premium paid for it does not equal the amount paid by the company if a loss (death) occurs.

b. Contracts of adhesion This is a contract in which one party (insurer) creates the contract terms and the other party (insured) must adhere or comply with them. No bargaining or negotiating of the contract's terms or conditions is permitted. A contract of adhesion is sometimes referred to as a one-sided contract.

    1.) Policyowners are protected by the courts with regard to insurance contracts where ambiguities arise. In these cases, the courts will usually rule in favor of the party not involved in the development of the contract.

    2.) Under the Doctrine of Reasonable Expectations, courts interpret an insurance policy to mean what a reasonable policyholder would expect it to mean even though policy provisions may deny those expectations.

c. Utmost good faith Contracts must be entered into in good faith. When a party does not enter into an agreement in good faith, the other party may void the contract. Each party must rely on the fact that information supplied by the other party is true.

d. Executory contracts An insurance policy is an executory contract because some act prescribed in the contract remains to be performed by one of the parties (the insurer). For example, an insurer will not pay a claim until a specified event (the insured loss) takes place.

e. Unilateral contract In an insurance contract, only the insurer promises to perform. Therefore, under unilateral contracts, a promise is made by only one party.

TAKE NOTE

Timely payment of premiums is a condition of the continuance of a life or health insurance contract, as is providing proof of the insured's death, illness, or disability.

---

    f. Personal contract In a strict legal sense, life insurance contracts are not considered to be personal contracts. Legally, a personal contract requires some sort of personal performance on the part of the contracting parties (or concerns some kind of personal property). A life insurance owner does not have any personal performance requirements; the duty to pay premiums, for example, can be fulfilled by another and, in fact, the policyowner can even assign ownership of the contract to another. However, this legal concept is not to be confused with the fact that life insurance policies cover and protect persons, not property.

    g. Conditional contract Insurance contracts are considered conditional in that the obligation of the company to pay a claim depends upon certain acts, such as the payment of premiums and providing proof of loss.

    h. Indemnity Some insurance policies (casualty) stipulate that they will indemnify an insured in the event a covered loss occurs. Indemnifying means placing an insured in the same financial position following a loss that existed before the loss.

3. Insurance contract and the courts Insurance contracts are legal documents, and their performance will be upheld in the courts. Because of their adhesion characteristics, any ambiguities that arise will be ruled in favor of a policyowner by the courts.

4. Legal principles applicable to insurance contracts

    a. Waiver This involves the intentional or voluntary relinquishment (or abandonment) of a known right in an insurance contract. Insurers have the right to deny coverage for various reasons (e.g., an insured makes a material misrepresentation). The principle of waiver aids an insured in certain instances where an insurer attempts to deny a claim after making a waiver.

        1.) A waiver may be expressed (written or verbal) or implied.

        2.) It does not apply to perils that are not covered under the policy.

        3.) A waiver is contractual in nature.

    b. Estoppel This doctrine is utilized to protect an innocent injured party (the insured). It is a doctrine that an insured may use in certain situations when an insurer attempts to deny a claim.

        1.) For example, a salesperson was insured under a group life insurance policy issued to his employer. The salesperson had said at the outset that he was not interested in the coverage unless he could obtain $200,000 in life insurance. He was advised by his employer that he was eligible for only $75,000. However, after some negotiations with the insurer, it was agreed that a $200,000 policy would be issued, and a certificate was issued in that amount.

TAKE NOTE

An indemnity contract, which pays an amount equal to the loss experienced, can be contrasted with a valued contract, which pays a stated sum, regardless of loss incurred.

The salesman was then accidentally killed. His beneficiary (his widow) submitted a claim, and it was found that the deceased had been eligible only for the original $75,000 of life coverage. The insurance company paid $75,000 and refunded the premium paid for coverage over that amount. The court would hold that all the elements of estoppel were present. There was a false representation of a material fact, a reasonable reliance, and harm resulted. The company would be required to pay the additional $125,000. The required elements for estoppel to be present include the following.

a.) There must be a false representation of a material fact (the insurer issued the policy and stated that the insured was fully covered in the amount of $200,000).

b.) There is a reasonable reliance on the representation (the insured relied on the statement that he was fully covered).

c.) Harm will result (to the insured because the insurer does not want to pay the entire $200,000 claim).

c. Comparison of waiver and estoppel The concepts of waiver and estoppel are sometimes confused. They may be distinguished further as follows.

1.) Waiver is contractual in nature, whereas estoppel is tortuous in nature and rests upon false representation.

2.) Waiver provides effect to the intention of the party waiving whereas estoppel is enforced to defeat the inequitable intent of the party estopped (generally the insurer).

3.) Waiver is subject to the parole evidence rule and estoppel is not.

d. Parole evidence rule The parole evidence rule prevents the introduction into evidence of oral agreements made before the execution of a written agreement. According to this rule, when parties place their contract in writing, all previous oral agreements merge into the written contract.

1.) Life insurance (written) contracts are subject to this rule. Oral testimony may not generally be admitted to contradict the provisions of a life insurance contract.

2.) This rule does not become effective until a binding contract exists.

U N I T   Q U I Z

1. Which of the following insurance concepts is founded on the ability to predict the approximate number of deaths or frequency of disabilities within a certain group during a specific time?
   A. Principle of large loss
   B. Quantum insurance principle
   C. Indemnity law
   D. Law of large numbers

2. The owner of a camera store is worried that new employees may help themselves to items from inventory without paying for them. What kind of hazard is this?
   A. Physical
   B. Ethical
   C. Morale
   D. Moral

3. All of the following actions are examples of risk avoidance EXCEPT
   A. refusing to fly
   B. not investing in stocks
   C. paying an insurance premium
   D. refusing to drive

4. Which of the following statements is CORRECT?
   A. Only speculative risks are insurable.
   B. Only pure risks are insurable.
   C. Both pure risks and speculative risks are insurable.
   D. Neither pure risks nor speculative risks are insurable.

5. All of the following statements describe elements of an insurable risk EXCEPT
   A. the loss must not be due to chance
   B. the loss must be definite and measurable
   C. the loss cannot be catastrophic
   D. the loss exposures to be insured must be large

6. In the insurance business, risk can best be defined as
   A. sharing the possibility of a loss
   B. uncertainty regarding the future
   C. uncertainty regarding loss
   D. uncertainty regarding when death will occur

7. Buying insurance is a means of
   A. avoiding risk
   B. transferring risk
   C. reducing risk
   D. retaining risk

8. Which of the following best describes the function of insurance?
   A. It is a form of legalized gambling.
   B. It spreads financial risk over a large group to minimize the loss to any one individual.
   C. It protects against living too long.
   D. It creates and protects risks.

9. A tornado is an example of a
   A. physical hazard
   B. speculative risk
   C. peril
   D. moral hazard

10. An insured keeps a $50,000 diamond ring in a safe deposit box at a local bank. This is an example of risk
   A. avoidance
   B. reduction
   C. retention
   D. transference

ANSWERS

1. D	2. D	3. C	4. B	5. A
6. C	7. B	8. B	9. C	10. B

DISCUSSION QUESTIONS

1. How does life and health insurance protect policyowners from the uncertainty of economic loss?

2. Explain the concept of risk pooling.

3. Explain the principle of the law of large numbers and how it relates to insurance.

4. How does speculative risk differ from pure risk?

5. Distinguish between a hazard and a peril. Give examples of each.

6. What are the three types of hazards? Give examples of each.

7. What are the four ways in which one can treat risk?

8. What are the six elements of insurable risk?

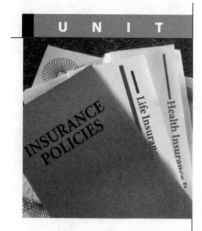

2

Introduction to Life Insurance and Types of Policies

KEY TERMS

Life Insurance	Law of Large Numbers	Aleatory
Risk	Rating Bureaus	Adhesion
Avoidance	Adverse Selection	Executory
Retention	Agreement	Waiver
Transfer	Consideration	Estoppel

TAKE NOTE

Life insurance can be applied for both personal and business uses.

I.   INTRODUCTION TO LIFE INSURANCE

Life insurance is a contract under which one party—the **insurer**—in consideration of the premium payment, agrees to pay an amount stipulated in the contract to a designated person, known as the **beneficiary**, upon the occurrence of a contingency defined in the contract, usually that of death.

A. PURPOSE OF LIFE INSURANCE One of the most important factors associated with life insurance is that it involves the immediate creation of an estate. The full amount of the estate is always created immediately, that is, at the precise moment when it is most needed: at the death of the insured. There are two parties involved in making the contract: the policyowner and the insurer. A beneficiary is not a party to the contract.

1. **Policyowner** This is the individual who pays the premiums and has other rights under the contract (receiving dividends, borrowing from the cash value, etc.). The owner of a life insurance policy may also be the insured, the beneficiary, or another third party such as a creditor or business partner.

   a. **The insured** This is the individual whose death causes the policy benefits (face amount) to be paid. The insured in a life insurance contract can also be the owner of the policy.

   b. **The beneficiary** This is the person, organization, or trust that will receive the benefits (face amount) payable upon the death of the insured. A beneficiary may also be the owner of the policy. A beneficiary is not a party to the contract, unless he is also the policyowner.

2. **Uses of life insurance**

   a. **Personal uses** These would include survivor protection by providing a death benefit to cover last expenses and a source of continuing income, estate creation to fund an estate for survivors, cash accumulation for retirement and other future needs, liquidity with the availability of cash values to the policyowner, estate conservation where the death benefit helps pay estate taxes, and viatical settlements that permit the sale of a life policy to a third party, allowing the insured to receive a portion of the face amount (typically 50 to 80%) while still alive if he is suffering from a terminal illness.

   b. **Business uses** These would include funding buy-sell agreements to ensure the continuation of a business, key person coverage that protects a business against the financial loss caused by the death of a key person, funding of deferred compensation plans, and providing split dollar plans to valued employees. (These topics will be presented in detail in Unit 5.)

II.   TYPES OF LIFE INSURANCE POLICIES

A. TYPES OF POLICIES Several types of life insurance policies are available to insurance consumers, including term insurance, whole life, endowments, and others.

1. Term life insurance A term life insurance policy may be defined as a contract that provides protection for a limited number of years, the face amount payable only if death occurs during the stipulated term, and nothing being paid if the insured survives the stipulated period. Term insurance has no cash savings value and has also been defined as temporary or pure protection. Since it provides pure protection only, it furnishes the maximum amount of insurance for the lowest price.

    a. Major types of term policies There are several types of term insurance policies available. The more common types include the following.

        1.) Level term This type of policy provides term insurance protection for a specified amount of insurance for the length or period of the contract. The premium in this contract will increase according to the age of the insured.

        For example, a one-year $100,000 level term policy may cost $200 for a 32-year-old male. Following that one-year period, if the insured wishes to continue the protection, his premium may increase to $215 and so on. For policies that are written for five-year periods, the premium will remain constant for those five years but will increase for a subsequent five-year policy period based on the age of the insured at renewal. **Annual renewable term** and **re-entry term** are examples of level term insurance.

            a.) Annual renewable term Also called yearly renewable term, this policy is issued for a period of one year and can be renewed, without evidence of insurability, for successive one-year periods. Premiums increase with each renewal, and most policies can be converted to a cash value type policy.

            b.) Reentry term Also called revertible term, renewal premiums are based on select mortality rates (lower rates) if the insured can periodically (reentry periods are generally every one to five years) demonstrate acceptable evidence of insurability.

        2.) Decreasing term This type of contract may be utilized as a rider for a whole life contract or written as a separate contract. It is characterized by a decreasing or declining face amount of protection from year to year. Because the face amount decreases, the premium remains constant throughout the life of the contract. At the end of the contract period, the policy face amount will be zero. This type of policy is best utilized to cover a decreasing obligation such as a home mortgage or an auto loan. The premium is very low because the face amount decreases as the rate per unit of insurance increases.

            a.) The most common use for this type of contract is in connection with a mortgage. For this reason, a decreasing term policy is known as a mortgage protection or mortgage redemption plan.

b.) The face amount of the contract decreases each year along with the principal amount of the mortgage (follows the amortization schedule).

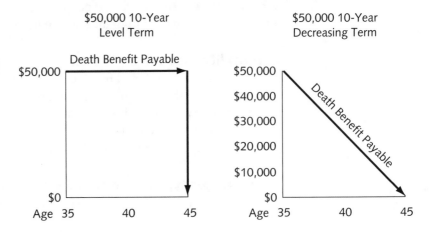

A level term policy provides a straight, level benefit amount over the entire term of the policy. A decreasing term policy pays a gradually decreasing benefit over the term of the policy.

3.) Increasing term This type of coverage is usually written as a rider but rarely as a separate contract. This coverage is characterized by an increasing face value with each succeeding payment of premium. In the majority of cases, it is primarily used in connection with a combination policy where increasing life insurance is added to an underlying contract.

   a.) For example, a return of premium policy illustrates this concept where increasing term insurance is used to offset the payback of premiums at the time of the insured's death. As a result, the insurer will repay all premiums paid while paying to the beneficiary the face amount of the policy upon the death of the insured.

4.) A jumping juvenile or junior estate builder is a type of policy that provides term insurance for juveniles. It is usually issued in $1,000 units for juveniles aged from one to 15 years. When the child reaches age 21, the face amount increases to five times the original amount with no increase in the premium.

b. Features of term insurance Most term life insurance policies have two major features that provide additional flexibility to an insured/policyowner.

   1.) Renewable feature Several forms of term protection provide renewal at the end of the term without requiring proof or evidence of insurability. In effect, the renewal of the policy is accomplished at attained age. If an insured purchased term insurance without this feature, he may be at a disadvantage once the policy period ends and they have developed a physical condition that might hinder the securing of insurance protection.

      a.) The cost of a term policy with this feature is higher because of the chance of adverse selection.

b.) Most renewable features are available to policies of one-, five-, and 10-year policy periods.

c.) Renewal premiums are based on attained age.

d.) Renewable term insurance protects the insurability of an insured.

e.) An age limitation is usually included in these contracts such as renewable to age 65 or term to life expectancy.

2.) Convertible feature This feature permits a policyowner to exchange a term policy for a whole life contract without evidence of insurability. This exchange is allowed at any time during the policy period and may be effected in one of two ways.

a.) Attained age method This involves the issuance of a whole life policy at the conversion date with premiums based on the current or attained age of the insured.

b.) Original age method This involves a retroactive conversion where the whole life policy being purchased bears the date and premium rate that would have been charged had it originally been purchased instead of the term protection. Many companies require that this option be activated within the first five years of the term policy or it will be lost.

c. Term insurance evaluation There are many uses, advantages, and disadvantages of term insurance.

1.) Uses and advantages Term policies are designed to provide protection against contingencies that require only temporary protection and necessitate large amounts of coverage for the smallest outlay of funds. Term insurance may be used:

- for families with lower incomes where some sort of protection is needed;
- to protect an individual's insurability;
- for protection on borrowed funds (mortgages, auto loans, education loans);
- as a supplement to cash value insurance where term is purchased as a rider to a whole life contract; or

■ as a way of hedging definitely known contingencies—for example, purchasing term coverage until the insured reaches age 65 when his pension plan begins to pay monthly amounts.

2.) Disadvantages There are also disadvantages that should be conveyed to the purchaser of term life insurance.

a.) Although the outlay of funds is low in the early years, premiums increase dramatically in the insured's later years.

b.) There may come a time when an insured has no protection after term insurance ends.

c.) Term insurance is actually more expensive (with no cash value return) than whole life if the insured survives a reasonable number of years (such as living to the end of the policy term).

2. Traditional whole life products In contrast to term insurance, whole life insurance provides protection for an individual's life. It is not limited in its duration. There are a number of variations of whole life insurance, including ordinary (straight) whole life and limited payment whole life insurance.

a. Ordinary (straight) whole life An ordinary, or straight, life insurance contract is one of the major types of life insurance policies. These contracts are based on the level premium concept where the assumption is that the premiums will be paid by the policyowner throughout the insured's lifetime. In many instances, an individual purchases a life insurance contract with no intention of paying premiums for his entire lifetime. His basic intention is to utilize dividends to pay up the policy in a shorter period of time, or to surrender the policy for a lesser paid-up policy, or surrender the policy upon retirement for an annuity. Therefore, an ordinary or straight life insurance contract is flexible and does not legally commit an owner to make premium payments for the rest of his life.

1.) Permanent protection combined with savings feature An ordinary or straight life policy provides permanent protection insofar as it never has to be renewed or converted. This type of contract provides the insured protection at a level premium rate throughout the life of the contract. In addition, these contracts are characterized by cash value buildup during the life of the contract. These are two primary advantages of whole life.

2.) Maturity at age 100 A straight whole life policy is designed so that its cash value accumulation equals the amount of the policy's face value when the insured turns 100 years old.

3.) Ordinary or straight life (also referred to as whole life) policies continue to be the most common type of protection sold, although interest in term insurance and universal life products have increased dramatically during the past several years. The **cash surrender value** in a straight life policy represents the savings element of this life insurance policy. One possible disadvantage of whole life is its cost, that is higher than that of term.

Consequently, insureds may have to purchase an amount of coverage that is less than they actually need because the cost is greater than term insurance in the early years. In addition, interest paid on the cash value of a whole life contract is traditionally lower (3 to 4%) than other forms of investments.

$50,000 Policy Face Amount

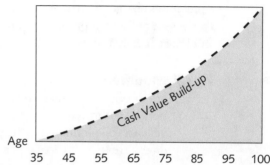

When the insured reaches age 100, the cash value of a whole life policy will equal the face amount and will be paid to the insured as a living benefit, if he is still living.

b. Limited-pay and single premium life policies

1.) Limited-pay policy Limited-pay life insurance policies emphasize savings more than straight life policies. These policies also make it possible for an insured to stop premium payments at the expiration of a specified period of time without any reduction in the amount of the insurance for as long as the insured survives. In other words, the policy becomes fully paid at the time of the last payment. The most common types of limited-pay policies are 10-payment life, 20-payment life, or life paid-up at age 65.

   a.) For example, a life paid-up at age 65 policy would be useful to an insured who desires permanent protection but does not want the premiums to continue beyond the end of his normal earning period (at retirement age). This type of policy also provides a larger savings element than a straight life insurance policy. If an insured purchases an adequate amount of protection under a policy with the premium payments limited to a short period of time, then he has the advantage of knowing that his insurance program will be completed at the end of that time and that a sizeable savings fund is accumulating.

2.) Single premium life policies A contract for which a single premium is paid at the inception of the policy and becomes fully paid is called single payment or single premium life insurance. Advantages of such a plan include:

   ■ tax-free buildup of cash value at desirable rates;

   ■ minimal sales commissions;

   ■ below market interest rates on borrowing;

   ■ use of cash buildup; and

   ■ gifting opportunities.

c. Modified and graded premium whole life These policies are useful compromises between straight life and convertible term insurance. The premium is less than that for straight life insurance in the early years. In addition, an insured is accumulating some cash values and the premium increase is not as great as it would be with convertible term insurance. Individuals who need whole life protection but cannot afford the premiums required would purchase these contracts because the premiums charged for these policies are lower in the earlier years. Both contracts involve a redistribution of premiums that is the actuarial equivalent of the regular ordinary life premiums.

1.) Modified life policies In many cases, insurers issue straight life insurance policies in which the premiums are not level over the premium paying period, but instead are lower than the normal premium during the early years of the premium paying period and increase to a fixed premium amount after a three- or five-year period.

a.) For example, a $200,000 modified life policy issued to a male age 30 may cost $1,500 per year for the first five years. After the five-year period has elapsed, the premium will then be $3,000 for the same amount of coverage for the duration of the contract's life. Again, this type of contract provides amounts of insurance to individuals who cannot afford the total annual outlay for the protection they need, but whose financial condition is expected to improve in later years.

2.) Graded premium whole life A graded premium contract is slightly different than a modified life policy, though it also has nonlevel premiums. The premium increases each year during the early years of the contract (usually five years) and remains the same after that time. The initial premium charged is usually less than the equivalent level premium for a straight life policy at the same age of issue.

d. Adjustable life insurance At any particular point in time, this policy is a level-premium, level-death-benefit policy. It may be of the limited payment or term insurance type. It is actually a combination of the two.

1.) This contract has all the usual features of level-premium cash-value life insurance. It possesses cash and other nonforfeiture values, dividend options, policy loan provisions, and so forth.

2.) This policy contains adjustment provisions that allow premiums to be increased or decreased, the face amount to be increased or decreased, and additional premium to be paid. Whenever these adjustments occur, the plan of insurance may also change, but with respect to the future only.

3.) An increase in premium increases future cash values and a decrease in premium reduces cash values.

e. Indeterminate premium policies These whole life contracts have maximum guaranteed premium rates specified in the policy, but initial premiums are generally set at a level well below the maximums. The benefits provided are the same as those for other policies, but these contracts provide a mechanism where insurers can adjust premiums to reflect changes in investment income.

1.) The company reserves the right to change the initial premium up or down subject to the specified maximum.

2.) The low initial premium is guaranteed for a specified period of time ranging from 2 to 10 years.

3.) The longer the guaranteed period, the higher the initial premium.

4.) Indeterminate premium term insurance is also available.

3. Endowments An endowment policy provides for the payment to the beneficiary of the face amount upon the death of an insured during a specified period or the payment of the face amount at the end of the specified period if the insured is still alive, whichever comes first.

a. Endowments are not as popular today as they once were, although they maintain a popularity in areas where saving is stressed. These contracts were originally designed to combine life insurance and savings elements.

1.) These policies may be issued for specified periods such as 5, 10, 20, 25, or 30 years or up to a specified age such as age 60 or 65.

2.) Once the specified period has passed and the insured is living, the face amount would be paid to that insured in a lump sum or in installments.

b. A **pure endowment** is a contract that promises to pay the face amount only if the insured is still living at the end of a specified period. Nothing is paid if the insured dies before the expiration of the specified period. These contracts are never sold separately because no one wants to risk losing all premiums if premature death occurs.

c. Endowments have been used for retirement, savings, and education purposes.

1.) Semi-endowments These pay half the face amount of the policy upon survival for the specified period. The full face amount is paid for premature death.

2.) Juvenile endowments These are available to cover children up to a specified age so that needed funds will be available for educational purposes.

d. Endowment premiums The cost of an endowment policy is greater than the traditional whole life contracts because of its savings nature and depends upon the endowment period chosen.

1.) For example, if a 35-year-old male purchases a $50,000 20-year endowment, his annual premium may be $2,200. A $50,000 whole life contract may cost

TAKE✔NOTE

Designating modified endowments as a class of life insurance policies enabled different tax rules to apply to contracts that quickly build cash values. If a MEC contract pays its values out as a death benefit, no tax penalty applies. If the values are accessed by loan or before the owner is 59½, they will be subject to income tax and a penalty.

$950. If the insured survives the 20-year period, he then is paid the $50,000 face amount since his contract has matured.

e. **Modified endowment contracts (MECs)** A modified endowment contract is a life insurance policy whose premiums exceed what would have been paid to fund a similar type of life insurance policy with seven annual premiums.

   1.) For example, if the total (aggregate) premiums paid at any time during the initial seven years of the policy's existence exceed the total premium that would have been paid on a seven-year level annual premium basis for the same period, the contract will not meet the required seven-pay test.

   2.) Previously, single premium life policies (and other types of limited-pay contracts) were taxed the same as other life insurance policies. A policyowner was able to borrow (make withdrawals, etc.) from the policy's cash value without paying tax.

   3.) Congress changed this with 1988 legislation including the new seven-pay test. Any policies issued before June 21, 1988 will be grandfathered and will not be affected by the revised tax law (unless they experience a material change). The objective of the tax modifications for MECs (those that do not meet the new test) is to discourage the use of life insurance with high premiums as short-term investments.

   4.) Therefore, this tax treatment will make the utilization of a high premium life policy as a short-term investment less attractive because it will be more costly (income tax on withdrawn amounts plus a penalty on withdrawals before age 59½). Because it is more costly, the return (on investment) experienced by the policyowner will be less. The revised tax law will not decrease a policyowner's return if policy funds are left with the insurer (and not withdrawn) and the policy was primarily purchased for its death benefit.

   5.) Once a policy is classified as a MEC, it will automatically make any policy subsequently received in exchange for it also a MEC (even if the new policy passes the seven-pay test).

   6.) Term life policies purchased before June 21, 1988, that are converted to cash value policies after June 20, 1988 will be treated as if originally entered into on the date of conversion. They must satisfy the seven-pay test at the time of conversion.

7.) Assignment or pledges of MECs with face amounts of less than $25,000 are exempt from taxation if the assignment or pledge is for funeral/burial expenses or prearranged funerals.

8.) A grandfathered life policy can become a MEC if it has a death benefit increase of more than $150,000. A grandfathered life policy will not become a MEC if it:

- remains in force with no policy changes;
- is terminated;
- is kept in force but the death benefit is reduced after the seventh policy year;
- has death benefit increases because of a cost-of-living provision linked to the Consumer Price Index (CPI);
- experiences death benefit increases because of interest or earnings of the policy;
- experiences death benefit increases from exercising the guaranteed purchase provisions in the policy; or
- experiences death benefit increases as a result of purchase options exercised when the insured has a newborn child.

9.) A policy entered into after June 20, 1988, that initially passed the seven-pay test may be subject to the test again if the death benefit:

- is decreased during the initial seven policy years; or
- increases because of premium increases after the initial seven policy years.

10.) MEC funds received under the policy will be considered taxable income first. Any amounts in excess of the gain in the policy are considered to be a tax free recovery of basis (the amount that the policyowner has paid into the policy). Therefore, the tax treatment of withdrawals from MECs is similar to the tax treatment of withdrawals in a deferred annuity during the accumulation (pay-in) phase.

11.) There exists a 60-day grace period for returned premiums to keep the premiums paid under the seven-pay net level premium amount. The insurance company may return excess premiums within 60 days after the end of the contract year.

12.) All MECs issued by the same insurance company to a policyowner during any 12-month period will be treated as one.

4. Nontraditional life insurance products

a. Universal life insurance Universal life insurance, also called flexible premium adjustable life insurance, is a variation of whole life insurance, characterized by considerable flexibility. Unlike whole life, with its fixed premiums, fixed face amounts, and fixed cash value accumulations, universal life allows its policyowners

TEST TOPIC ALERT

The mortality portion of a universal life policy may make it appear similar to an annual renewable term policy.

to determine the amount and frequency of premium payments and to adjust the policy face amount up or down to reflect changes in needs. Consequently, no new policy need be issued when changes are desired.

1.) Universal life provides this flexibility by unbundling, or separating, the basic components of a life insurance policy: the insurance (protection) element, the savings (accumulation) element, and the expense (loading) element. As with any other life policy, the policyowner pays a premium. Each month, a mortality charge is deducted from the policy's cash value account for the cost of the insurance protection. This mortality charge also may include an expense, or loading, charge.

2.) Like term insurance premiums, the universal life mortality charge increases steadily with age. Actually, universal life technically is defined as term insurance with a policy fund value. Even though the policyowner may pay a level premium, an increasing share of that premium goes to pay the mortality charge as the insured ages.

3.) As premiums are paid and cash value accumulates, interest is credited to the policy's cash value. This interest may be either the current interest rate declared by the company (and dependent on current market conditions) or the guaranteed minimum rate specified in the contract. As long as the cash value account is sufficient to pay the monthly mortality and expense costs, the policy will continue in force whether or not the policyowner pays the premium.

4.) At stated intervals (and usually on providing evidence of insurability), the policyowner can increase or decrease the face amount of the policy. A corresponding increase (or decrease) in premium payments is not required, as long as the cash values can cover the mortality and expense costs. By the same token, the policyowner can elect to pay more into the policy, thus adding to the cash value account, subject to certain guidelines that control the relationship between the cash values and the policy's face amount.

5.) Another factor that distinguishes universal life from whole life insurance is the fact that partial withdrawals can be made from the policy's cash value account. (Whole life insurance allows a policyowner to tap cash values only through a policy loan or a complete cash surrender of the policy's cash values, in which case the policy terminates.) Also, the policyowner may surrender the universal life policy for its entire cash value at any time. However, the company will probably assess a surrender charge unless the policy has been in force for a certain number of years.

TAKE NOTE

In UL policies, premiums payments must be large enough and frequent enough to generate sufficient cash values. If the cash value account is not large enough to support the monthly deductions, the policy terminates.

6.) Universal life insurance offers two death benefit options. Under the first option, the policyowner may specify the amount of insurance. The death benefit equals the cash values plus the remaining pure insurance (decreasing term plus increasing cash values). If the cash values approach the face amount before the policy matures, an additional amount of insurance, called the corridor, is maintained in addition to the cash values.

   a.) Under the second option, the death benefit equals the face amount (pure insurance) plus the cash values (level term plus increasing cash values). To comply with the Internal Revenue Code's definition of life insurance, the cash values cannot be disproportionately larger than the term insurance protection.

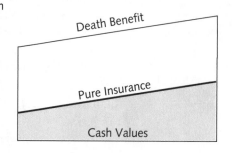

Level Death Benefit Option

Increasing Death Benefit Option

b. Variable life Variable life insurance (VLI) was designed to combine the protection and savings features of life insurance with the growth potential of common stocks. Variable life insurance is that form of life insurance contract under which the benefits, payable upon death or surrender, vary with the investment performance of an underlying portfolio of securities. However, premiums charged are fixed.

   1.) These contracts provide a guaranteed minimum death benefit. Benefits paid may actually be more depending upon the fluctuating market value of investments behind the contract at the time of the insured's death. The cash surrender value also fluctuates with the market value of the investment portfolio.

   2.) VLI has cash values that increase or decrease daily depending upon investment results, with no guarantee as to the amount of cash value.

   3.) Benefits will also vary with investment experience.

> **TEST TOPIC ALERT**
>
> The sale of variable contracts—including variable life, variable universal life, and variable annuities—requires the agent or producer to have both a life insurance license and an NASD securities license.

4.) Loan provisions are included so that the policyowner may borrow from the cash value if necessary.

5.) Nonforfeiture and reinstatement provisions are similar to those found in traditional life insurance policies.

6.) Variable life is also characterized by fixed premiums.

7.) An individual must secure a license from the National Association of Securities Dealers (NASD) before he can sell variable products. The license is granted by the NASD after the prospective licensee passes a Series 6 exam. All variable products are regulated by the Securities and Exchange Commission (SEC) including variable life insurance, variable/universal life, and variable annuities.

c. **Variable universal life insurance** Variable universal life (VUL), or flexible premium variable life, blends many features of whole life, universal life, and variable life. Premium flexibility, cash value investment control, and death benefit flexibility are key among these features. These features give VUL its unique characteristics and make it responsive to policyowners' needs.

1.) Every variable universal life insurance policy is issued with a minimum scheduled premium based on an initial specified death benefit. This initial premium establishes the plan, meets first-year expenses, and provides funding to cover the cost of insurance protection. Once they pay this initial premium, policyowners can pay whatever premium amount they wish, with certain limitations. Provided adequate cash value is available to cover periodic charges and the cost of insurance, they can suspend or reduce premium payments. Policyowners may even be able to avoid paying premiums indefinitely if their cash values realize consistently strong investment returns.

2.) Conversely, policyowners wishing to increase death benefits or take advantage of tax-favored accumulation of cash values can pay additional premiums into their plans. However, most policies contain maximum limits, and if the increase is above a certain amount, proof of insurability may be required.

3.) Cash value in a VUL plan is maintained separately from the rest of the plan. At the time of application, the policyowner elects to have the net premiums and cash values allocated to one or more separate account investment options. These accounts are usually mutual funds created and maintained by the insurance company and other investment companies. These funds are kept in separate accounts and function independently of the insurance

> ### TAKE ✓ NOTE
>
> These maximum limits are imposed to maintain the corridor between the cash value and the death benefit. This corridor must exist for the policy to qualify as life insurance and retain its tax-sheltered cash value accumulation status.

company's assets. Earnings or losses accrue directly to the policyowner's cash value, subject to stated charges and management fees. The policyowner can redirect future premiums and switch accounts periodically, generally once a year, without charge. The result is a life insurance policy that provides policyowners with self-directed investment options.

4.) VUL policies offer both a level death benefit, which provides for a fixed death benefit (until the policy values reach the corridor level) and potential higher cash value accumulation, or a variable death benefit, which provides a death benefit that fluctuates in response to the performance of investments.

5.) Under the level death benefit, the policyowner specifies the total death benefit in the policy. This amount remains constant and does not fluctuate as cash values increase or decrease. Instead, cash values build up within the policy until they reach the corridor, at which time the death benefit will increase to corresponding increases in the cash value. Until that point the cash value simply accumulates, with each increase replacing a corresponding amount of pure insurance needed to keep the death benefit at the specified amount.

6.) Under the variable death benefit, the policyowner selects a specified amount of pure insurance coverage that remains constant. The death benefit payable at any time is a combination of the specified (or face) amount and the cash value within the policy. Essentially, the cash value is added to the specified amount to create the total death benefit. Under this option, the emphasis is on the potential for both cash value and death benefit growth. This option is recommended for policyowners who want favorable investment results and additional premiums reflected directly in increased benefits.

7.) Like universal life, VUL policies permit partial withdrawals, allowing the owner to tap the cash value without incurring any indebtedness. Policyowners need not repay those funds, and no interest is incurred on the amount withdrawn. Withdrawals affect the policy's future earnings, and their effect on the death benefit depends on the death benefit option in force. Partial withdrawals taken in a policy's early years may be subject to surrender charges (when the insurer is trying to recover the costs of issuing the policy).

d. **Current assumption whole life (CAWL)** Considered a form of interest-sensitive whole life, current assumption whole life (CAWL) products use:

- ▪ an accumulation account (composed of the premium) less expense and mortality charges, and credited with interest based on current rates;

■ a surrender charge, fixed at issue, which is deducted from the accumulation account to derive the policy's net surrender value; and

■ a fixed death benefit and maximum level at time of issue.

1.) CAWL products may be classified into a **low premium** or **high premium** category. The low premium version includes a **redetermination provision** that states that after the initial guarantee period, the insurer can redetermine the premium using the same or new assumptions as to future interest.

2.) The high premium version possesses an optional payup that states that the policyholder may choose to cease paying premiums at a given point in time and actually have a paid-up policy. Incentive is provided to the policyowner to continue paying premiums because, unlike universal life, CAWL will lapse if the premium is not paid.

5. Combination policies Life insurance companies also make available special types of policies or combination contracts that may be purchased separately or added as a rider to whole life plans. The latter, however, has been the more common approach in recent years.

a. Family income policy (or rider) The purpose of this contract is to provide an income to the survivors of the family breadwinner who dies prematurely, in addition to a whole life insurance (face amount) foundation.

1.) Family income policies (FIP) involve a combination of decreasing term and whole life insurance.

2.) FIPs provide for monthly income payments to the beneficiary, starting at the death of the insured and continuing to the end of the policy period. Note that the payment period is measured from the policy inception date.

3.) The face amount from the whole life foundation policy may be either paid at the insured's death or held for payment when monthly benefits stop.

4.) For example, Mr. Smith purchases a $50,000 whole life policy with a FIP rider paying $500 per month for 10 years. After the policy has been in force for three years, Mr. Smith is killed in a hunting accident. His survivors will receive $500 per month for the next seven years ($500 multiplied by 84 months or $42,000). The beneficiary also receives the face amount of $50,000, either at the insured's death or when monthly income payments stop, depending upon the terms of the policy.

5.) If the insured lives beyond the specified period, only the face amount is paid to the beneficiary.

b. **Family maintenance policy (or rider)** This type of contract is similar to the FIP and is most commonly used as a rider to a whole life plan. Its purpose is also to provide additional income to a breadwinner's survivors.

1.) FMP policies involve a combination of level term insurance and whole life.

2.) The distinguishing feature between the FMP and FIP riders is that the family maintenance plan pays an income to the survivors for the specified period beginning with the date of the insured's death and continuing for the full policy period.

3.) For example, Mr. Smith purchases a $50,000 whole life policy but adds a family maintenance rider paying $500 per month for 10 years. Three years into the contract, Mr. Smith dies. His survivors will receive $500 for 10 years beginning at his death. His life beneficiary will also receive the face amount of $50,000 either at his death or when the periodic payments end.

4.) Just like the FIP, if the insured survives the specified period (10 years in this example), only the face amount is paid to the beneficiary.

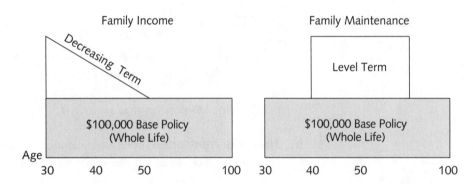

Family income and family maintenance plans are both designed to provide a period of monthly income following the death of the insured, if death occurs during the specified period.

c. **Family policy** These policies or riders cover the entire family under one contract. Whole life coverage will be purchased on the life of the father (or mother), and term insurance is provided on the spouse and children.

1.) All children in the family are covered even if born (or adopted) after the policy has been issued. Coverage is usually provided up to age 18.

2.) The most common family policy units provide $5,000 of whole life coverage on the breadwinner, $2,500 on the spouse, and $1,250 on each child.

3.) Premiums for family policies are based on the age of the primary insured (e.g., the breadwinner).

4.) A family with several children will receive a better (premium dollar) value than a single person or couple purchasing a family policy because more individuals will be covered for essentially the same cost (e.g., family of five versus a single person).

d. Multiple or double protection policies Many companies now issue plans that pay a multiple of the face amount if the insured dies within a specified period and only the face amount if he dies following the expiration of that specified period.

e. Multiple life policy This type of policy is also known as a **last-to-die policy** and is most often used to fund buy-sell agreements. It generally covers the lives of three to five people with benefits payable upon the death of each person except the last one to survive.

6. Other types of life insurance contracts

a. Joint life A joint life contract is one written on two or more lives. This contract promises to pay the full face amount in the event of the first death with regard to the two lives covered. Therefore, there is no coverage provided after the first person dies.

1.) As far as survivorship is concerned, if the policy is payable upon the death of the last of the two lives, it is referred to as a **last survivor policy**.

2.) Joint-life policies may be written on any whole life or term insurance plan.

b. Juvenile insurance Juvenile insurance is written on the lives of children. This coverage can be issued on the application of a parent or guardian.

1.) Juvenile insurance can be used to provide funds for funeral expenses, education expenses, or to guarantee insurability.

2.) A common form of juvenile insurance is known as a **jumping juvenile** or **junior estate builder**. These contracts are generally issued at ages one through 16 in $1,000 units with the face amount automatically increasing five times (i.e., to $5,000) when the child reaches age 21 (with no premium increase).

3.) Life insurance is also available at preferred rates for students (i.e., while in college).

c. Deposit term This is generally a combination of 10-year term with a modest endowment feature. The initial year's premium is higher than subsequent years. The difference between the first year and the subsequent years is the deposit.

1.) At the end of the 10-year period, the insured may renew the plan (with a higher first-year premium) or continue it as decreasing term life to age 100.

2.) If death occurs before the end of the period, the insurer pays the deposit premium plus interest as an additional death benefit.

d. Minimum deposit This type of plan is characterized by high early cash values. Cash and loan values are generally provided in the first policy year and are somewhat higher than normal cash and loan values thereafter. In most cases, this contract is sold only in high minimum amounts (e.g., $25,000 or $50,000).

1.) The higher early loan values can be used to pay a large portion of the premiums due in the initial and subsequent policy years. However, this procedure will decrease the face amount each time it is used.

2.) This plan is not advantageous for all individuals. It formerly allowed high tax bracket individuals to deduct interest paid on policy loans but this has been phased out. Presently it is only helpful to corporations.

3.) This type of plan may also be referred to as a high early cash value contract.

e. Split life This is a combination of two separate contracts including: 1) yearly renewable term insurance and 2) a retirement annuity. It offers an alternative method for combining savings (i.e., annuity) with life (i.e., term) insurance. The annuity begins pay out at the insured's age 65. The life insurance is renewable to the age specified in the policy.

f. Deferred life This policy pays the face amount only if the insured dies after surviving an initial period. The primary purpose is to protect the policyowner's insurability. If the insured dies during the deferred period, his survivor will receive a return of premium (plus any interest accrued). The premium will be discounted to reflect the decreased liability of the insurer.

g. Credit life This type of life insurance coverage is available to protect a borrower and a lender. For example, if the borrower dies, the amount of the loan is paid by the insurance proceeds. In addition, the lender (creditor) will not be left with an uncollectible debt if the borrower (debtor) dies.

1.) The creditor may not require that coverage be purchased by the borrower. In this case, the creditor may purchase coverage on the life of the borrower.

2.) Credit life insurance may not be written for an amount greater than the total indebtedness.

3.) Credit life insurance is available on an individual and group coverage basis.

h. Enhanced ordinary life (economatic or extra ordinary life) This is a type of participating whole life policy that uses dividends to provide some form of level constant coverage. The purpose is to provide a whole life participating policy with a low premium. Typically, the face amount is reduced after a few years and dividends are used to purchase deferred paid-up whole life additions to fill the gap when the reduction in face amount occurs. The result is that the face amount remains at least equal to the original face amount.

i. Indexed whole life insurance The face amount of these policies increases with the Consumer Price Index (CPI). The company agrees not to require evidence of insurability for the increases as long as each year's increase is accepted by the policyowner.

III. ANNUITIES

An annuity is said to be a mirror image of life insurance because it is designed to provide income to a person (the annuitant) while he is alive, whereas life insurance provides income to survivors when an insured dies. An **annuity** can be defined as the liquidation of a capital sum or the liquidation of an estate. It makes regular periodic payments over a fixed period of time or for the duration of a person's life. It can ensure a steady stream of income for as long at the contract owner wishes.

A. ANNUITY PRINCIPLES Despite the difference in function, annuities and life insurance are based on the same fundamental principles. Both employ a pooling technique and premiums are computed on the basis of probabilities of death and survival as reflected by a mortality table.

1. An annuity may be defined as a series of periodic payments made over a fixed period of time or for the duration of the annuitant's life. It may also be described as the systematic liquidation of an estate.

2. Annuities are often utilized by individuals to provide additional income at retirement and are also used to fund pension plans. Annuities, like life insurance, may be purchased on an individual as well as a group basis; the basic principles underlying both products are essentially the same.

B. CLASSIFICATION OF ANNUITIES Annuities come in many shapes and designs and may be classified according to how premiums are paid, according to the time when benefits begin, according to the source of income, or according to the number of lives covered.

1. According to premium payments

a. Single premium plans The insurer agrees that, upon the receipt of a lump-sum payment (a single premium), it will pay the annuitant (the person receiving the benefits) benefits in installments. Installments may begin immediately as with a single premium immediate annuity or at some later date as with a single premium deferred annuity. Payouts may be made monthly, semiannually, or annually.

b. Periodic premium plans These plans may be either level (scheduled) or flexible premiums.

1.) Level premium deferred annuity The insured agrees to pay the same premium per year to the insurer to a specified age. The purpose of level

TAKE NOTE

In contrast to the accumulation period in an annuity, the **payout period** or **annuitization period** is when the contract's values are converted into income payments payable to the annuitant.

(scheduled) premium annuities is to create a specified amount of annuity funds. At the designated age, the annuity fund is annuitized and converted into a stream of payments to the annuitant.

2.) Flexible premium deferred annuity Under this plan, the annuitant/insured will pay a periodic flexible premium from the date of purchase until the plan matures. The premiums paid may vary from year to year. In other words, the insured may pay whatever he wishes each year. Most of these plans have a minimum premium requirement, such as $100. The amount of the annuity benefit will depend upon the size of the accumulated funds when payouts begin.

2. **According to when benefits begin (annuity period)** There are two basic classifications as to when annuity benefits begin.

a. **Single premium immediate annuity** This is an annuity under which the first benefit payment is due one payment interval from the date of purchase. In other words, the first benefit payment to an annuitant would be made at the end of the initial income period following the purchase of an annuity. These annuities must always be purchased with a single premium. Therefore, no benefit payments are ever made until the entire purchase price of the annuity is in the possession of the insurer.

b. **Deferred annuity** This type of annuity may be purchased with either a single or periodic premium. Under this annuity, there must be a period longer than one benefit payment interval before payments begin. The longer the deferred period, the more flexibility may be allowed in premium payments. In most cases, several years must elapse before benefit payments begin.

1.) **Accumulation period** During the accumulation period, the company is required to return all or a portion of the annuity cash value if the purchaser dies (a death benefit). Minimum cash values are defined by nonforfeiture laws in most states but are equal to the contributions made to date, less withdrawals and expenses, plus interest earnings. If a deferred annuity is surrendered prior to benefit payment, a surrender charge is subtracted from the cash value (nonforfeiture value) unless the annuitant is receiving care from certain types of health care facilities (such as skilled nursing, extended care, convalescent care, etc.), in which case surrender charges are waived. The surrender charge percentage commonly decreases with contract duration.

3. **According to source (units) of annuity income** Some annuities may also be classified by the source of the income payments made, in other words, according to the units in which the payout benefits are expressed or the amount of the monthly benefit.

TEST TOPIC ALERT

For a given annuity sum, the life annuity provides the largest periodic benefit payment, compared to other forms of annuity payments that are based on a lifespan.

---

a. **Fixed annuity** This type of annuity guarantees a specified number of dollars that will be paid each month (level benefit amount) once the payment period commences. With a fixed annuity, the annuitant knows the exact (fixed) amount that he will receive each month. Most premiums paid for these annuities are invested in fixed dollar investments such as bonds helping to guarantee the fixed benefit. Fixed annuity investments are held as general account assets of the insurance company providing a guaranteed return.

    1.) **Interest rate guarantees** A current rate of interest is guaranteed for a specified number of years (usually from one to 10 years) during the accumulation period. After the guarantee period expires, the interest rate may be changed but is subject to a guaranteed minimum rate.

b. **Variable annuity** This type of annuity provides monthly benefits to an annuitant based upon guaranteed unit amounts rather than specific dollar amounts that characterize fixed annuities. The exact value of a unit is determined each time the benefit is to be paid. Because premium payments are invested in common stocks and other equity investments (held as assets in a separate account), the value of the units generally vary each month and cannot be guaranteed. The sale of variable annuities, like variable life insurance, requires a securities license (i.e., Series 6, NASD).

    1.) **Separate account assets** The separate account is maintained solely for the purpose of making investments for the variable annuity contractholder. Unlike the general account which provides interest and principal guarantees, values in the separate account fluctuate according to the performance of the underlying investments. All profits and losses are passed along to the contractholders.

4. **According to number of lives covered** Annuities may be classified according to whether premiums are paid by an individual covering a single life or more than one life. If an annuity covers one life, it may be referred to as an individual annuity. If it covers two or more lives, it may involve a joint life annuity or a joint and survivor annuity.

5. **Forms of annuities** The manner in which annuity payments are made can be matched to meet specific needs.

a. **Straight life annuity** This form of annuity provides payments to an annuitant from a specified date and for the rest of the annuitant's life. Payments cease upon the annuitant's death with no refund to survivors. This type of annuity has the potential for providing the maximum amount of benefits per dollar of outlay (assuming the annuitant lives beyond life expectancy).

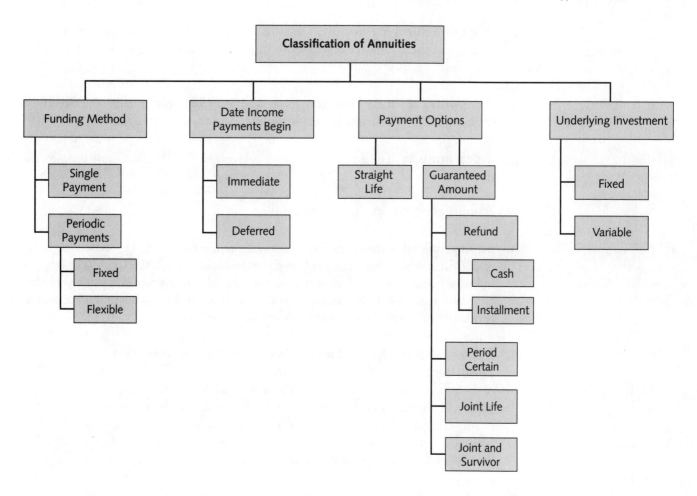

b. **Period certain annuity** These annuities pay installments for a fixed or specified period only. However, payments continue even if the annuitant dies before the end of the benefit period. This type of annuity provides a guaranteed minimum of funds. For example, if an annuitant is to receive $1,000 per month or 10 years certain and dies after the third year, the beneficiary will receive $1,000 per month for the next seven years.

c. **Installment refund annuity** The annuitant is guaranteed a specified amount to be paid out in installments. The amount is guaranteed, not the number of installments. If the annuitant dies before the guaranteed amount is paid out, the remainder is paid to a designated beneficiary.

  1.) **Cash refund annuity** This is another form of fixed amount annuity certain that promises to pay, in a lump sum, the difference between the amount paid into the annuity and the benefits received prior to the annuitant's death. The lump-sum payment will be made to the annuitant's beneficiary or estate.

d. **Joint life annuity** This type of annuity is designed to pay benefits to two or more annuitants at the same time. However, all benefits will terminate when the first annuitant dies.

e. **Joint and survivor annuity** Benefits under this type of annuity are paid throughout the lifetime of one or more annuitants. Therefore, payments continue until the last annuitant dies.

f. **Temporary annuity** This annuity pays benefits for a specific number of years or the annuitant's death, whichever comes first.

g. **Index annuity** The annuity purchaser is given an initial interest rate guarantee (usually one year or less), and each renewal rate is tied to a published index such as 10-year Treasury notes. This provides the consumer with protection against arbitrary profit-enhancing renewal rates.

h. **Equity-linked annuities** These annuity products are linked to some sort of stock market-related index such as the Standard & Poor's 500 Index. Equity-linked annuities have a short or nonexistent initial interest rate guarantee period. Normally, the contractholder is obligated to remain in the contract for a minimum period of time (such as five years) to earn the equity-index return.

i. **Market value adjusted annuities (modified guaranteed annuities)** The market value adjusted annuity shift some of the investment risk of the product from the insurer to the contractholder in that the annuity account value will fluctuate as market interest rates fluctuate. These annuity products usually contain a floor as to how low the asset value can go. The amount at risk is normally limited to amounts in excess of the premiums paid plus interest accrued at the minimum guaranteed level in the contract.

6. **Uses of annuities** Annuities are useful in both qualified (i.e., tax qualified) and non-qualified markets whether for business or personal use. Annuities are used to provide tax deferred retirement income to individuals or to supplement other income received from pensions or Social Security. Annuities can also be utilized to fund pension and profit sharing plans, individual retirement accounts (IRAs), provide funds for a child's education, public employee deferred compensation programs, 401(k) plans, and types of unfunded deferred programs. (These topics will be discussed in Unit 5.) In recent years, annuities have also been used to provide income to lottery winners (e.g., $50,000 per year for 20 years) or to recipients of lawsuit awards.

7. **Withdrawal provisions** If an early withdrawal of funds from an annuity is effected, penalties may be imposed. Partial surrenders and withdrawals before the annuity starting date (i.e., at retirement) will be taxed on earnings withdrawn. A penalty is assessed if an early withdrawal is made (before age 59½). No penalties are imposed if the contract owner becomes disabled.

8. **Income taxation of annuity benefits** Annuity benefit payments are a combination of principal and interest. Accordingly, they are taxed in a manner consistent with other types of income. The portion of the benefit payments that represents a return of principal (i.e., the contributions made by the annuitant) is not taxed. However, the portion representing interest earned on the declining principal is taxed. The result, over the benefit payment period, is a tax-free return of the annuitant's investment and taxes on the balance.

TAKE NOTE

A 10% penalty tax is imposed on withdrawals from a deferred annuity before age 59½. Withdrawals after that age are not subject to the 10% penalty but are still taxable as ordinary income.

a. **Exclusion ratio** An exclusion ratio is applied to each benefit payment the annuitant receives:

Investment in the contract ÷ expected return = exclusion ratio

The investment in the contract is the amount of money paid into the annuity. The expected return is the annual guaranteed benefit the annuitant receives, multiplied by the number of years of his life expectancy. The resulting ratio is applied to the benefit payments, allowing the annuitant to exclude a like percentage from income.

For example: Joan purchased an annuity for $10,800. Under its terms, the annuity will pay her $100 a month for life. If Joan is 65 years old, her life expectancy, as taken from the Internal Revenue Service's life expectancy tables, is 20 years. Her expected return is $24,000 (20 × 12 × $100). Her cost ($10,800) divided by her expected return of $24,000 equals 45%. This is the percentage of each annuity payment that she can exclude from her taxable income. Each year until Joan's net cost is recovered, she will receive $540 (45% of $1,200) tax free. She must include $660 ($1,200 – $540) in her taxable income.

b. **Deferred annuities** Deferred annuities accumulate interest earnings on a tax-deferred basis. While no taxes are imposed on the annuity during the accumulation phase, taxes are imposed when the contract begins to pay its benefits (in accordance with the exclusion ratio just described). To discourage the use of deferred annuities as short-term investments, the Internal Revenue Code imposes a penalty (as well as taxes) on early withdrawals and loans from annuities. Partial withdrawals are treated first as earnings income (and are thus taxable as ordinary income). Only after all earnings have been taxed are withdrawals considered a return of principal.

U N I T   Q U I Z

1. Which of the following provides guaranteed unit amounts rather than guaranteed dollar amounts?
   A. Fixed annuity
   B. Deferred annuity
   C. Variable annuity
   D. Flexible annuity

2. A policy that provides life insurance protection during a specific period of time or the payment of the face amount if the insured lives best describes
   A. a family income policy
   B. universal life
   C. adjustable life
   D. an endowment

3. Mr. James borrows funds from a bank to make improvements to his home. The bank suggests that he purchase life insurance that will pay off his loan amount in the event of his premature death. Which of the following would best help him achieve this objective?
   A. Level term
   B. Decreasing term
   C. Increasing term
   D. Convertible term

4. Which of the following statements regarding variable universal life insurance is TRUE?
   A. It offers a combination of investment options and a guaranteed death benefit.
   B. It provides pure protection only.
   C. It is characterized by fixed premiums and a decreasing death benefit.
   D. It offers a combination of pension and retirement benefits.

5. The contract that provides at issue the maximum amount of insurance protection at the lowest outlay of funds best describes
   A. term insurance
   B. whole life insurance
   C. universal life insurance
   D. endowments

6. A contract that is characterized by an increasing face value with each succeeding payments known as
   A. level term
   B. decreasing term
   C. convertible term
   D. increasing term

7. When an insured purchases a decreasing term life insurance contract, which of the following elements decreases each year?
   A. Cash savings value
   B. Loan value
   C. Premium payment
   D. Face amount of coverage

8. Anna, 65 years old, wants to ensure that she receives the largest possible monthly benefit from her fixed annuity contract. Which settlement option should she select?
   A. Life annuity
   B. Life and 10-year certain
   C. Life and 20-year certain
   D. Joint life

9. All of the following types of life insurance policies are characterized by having a cash value accumulation element EXCEPT
   A. universal life
   B. whole life
   C. term life
   D. variable life

10. The premium charged on a family policy is based on the
    A. age of the primary beneficiary
    B. age of the primary insured
    C. collective ages of all covered persons
    D. original age of the survivors

ANSWERS

1. C   2. D   3. B   4. A   5. A
6. D   7. D   8. A   9. C   10. B

DISCUSSION QUESTIONS

1. Define life insurance.

2. Briefly describe some of the characteristics of an ordinary life contract.

3. List some advantages of a single premium life policy.

4. Discuss the advantages of a universal life policy.

5. Discuss the basic characteristics of a variable universal life policy.

6. Contrast level and decreasing term insurance.

7. Compare and contrast a term contract's renewable and convertible features.

8. Describe how an immediate annuity works.

9. Compare the characteristics of a fixed and variable annuity.

10. Briefly describe the following:

    A. Cash refund annuity
    B. Installment refund annuity
    C. Endowment
    D. Family income policy
    E. Family maintenance policy
    F. Double protection

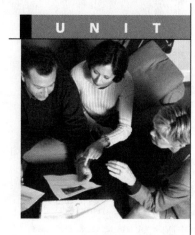

3

Life Insurance Policy Provisions, Riders, Options, and Exclusions

KEY TERMS

Waiver of Premium

Guaranteed
  Insurability

Accidental Death

Cost of Living

Accelerated Benefits

Viatical Settlements

Entire Contract

Insuring Clause

Free Look

Primary

Contingent

Tertiary

Common Disaster

Spendthrift Clause

Revocable

Irrevocable

Grace Period

Reinstatement

Policy Loan

Cash Surrender

Extended Term

Reduced Paid-Up

Dividend Options

Incontestability

Assignment

Settlement Options

War Exclusion

TAKE NOTE

Common riders to life insurance policies include waiver of premium, guaranteed insurability, payor benefit, accidental death benefit, term additions, coverage for others, and accelerated benefits.

I.   POLICY BENEFIT RIDERS

Supplemental additions called riders are frequently included or made a part of a life insurance policy. A rider may be used to add more life insurance or add a different type of insurance, such as disability or long-term care coverage, to the base policy. A rider may also specify conditions that could affect the coverage.

A.   WAIVER OF PREMIUM The **waiver of premium** provision found in a life insurance contract states that if an insured becomes totally disabled during the term of the policy, premium payments will be waived during the period of disability. The contract will remain in force just as if the insured continued to pay the premium. An additional premium is charged for this benefit, and it is subject to a waiting period (typically 90 days). If the insured is still disabled after this period, premiums are waived retroactively from the date of disability. For example, if an insured has his premium deducted on a monthly basis from a checking account and he satisfies the waiver of premium requirements for total disability, he will receive a waiver of the monthly premium deductions.

   1. Some life insurance contracts stipulate that disability must occur before a specified age such as 60 or 65.

   2. The additional premium paid for this benefit does not increase the face amount of the policy.

   3. A waiver of cost of insurance rider provides waiver of premium type coverage for the guaranteed death benefit (the mortality and expense charge) provided by life insurance contracts that have a variable death benefit (such as a variable/universal life policy).

   4. Disability income rider This rider provides both a waiver of premium and a supplementary income benefit if the insured becomes disabled. The definition of total disability is the same as that used for the waiver of premium rider. Generally, the disability benefit is expressed as a percentage (commonly 1%) of the policy's face amount.

B.   GUARANTEED INSURABILITY Many insurance companies offer a **guaranteed insurability option (GIO)**, also known as a **guaranteed insurability benefit (GIB)**, which allows a policyholder to purchase specified amounts of additional insurance without evidence of insurability. Additional characteristics include the following.

   1. The new insurance is issued at standard rates on the basis of the insured's attained age when the option is exercised.

   2. In most cases, this benefit allows an insured to purchase additional insurance coverage at three-year intervals beginning with the policy anniversary nearest his 25th birthday and terminating with the anniversary nearest his 40th birthday.

3. The amount of additional insurance that may be purchased on each of the specified dates is equal to the face of the original policy (or $10,000, whichever is less).

4. Some insurers provide additional option dates at other important periods in the insured's life such as marriage or the birth of a child.

5. This benefit is available for an additional premium.

C. **PAYOR BENEFIT** This rider or provision may be added to a life insurance contract that provides for the continuance of insurance coverage on the life of a juvenile in the event of the death or total disability of the individual responsible for the payment of premiums (a parent or guardian).

1. This benefit may be added for an additional premium and is also referred to as the **payor clause**.

2. This benefit provides that premiums will be waived until the insured child attains a specified age or the maturity date of the contract, whichever is earlier, in the event that the payor dies or becomes disabled.

D. **ACCIDENTAL DEATH** An **accidental death benefit clause** or **rider** may also be added to a life insurance policy. This benefit is sometimes referred to as **double indemnity**. It provides double (or sometimes triple) the face amount of the policy if the insured dies because of an accident.

1. An additional premium will be charged for this benefit.

2. To be covered, death must occur within 90 days of an accident. The purpose of this restriction is to ensure that the accident is the only cause of death.

3. Payment may not be made by an insurer if death results from illegal activities or other causes such as war; aviation activities, except passenger travel on scheduled or commercial airlines; or where an accident was involved in conjunction with illness, disease, or mental infirmity.

4. Accidental death or double indemnity coverage is usually limited to age 60, 65, or, in a few cases, age 70.

5. **Accidental death and dismemberment** AD&D insurance also provides benefits for death because of an accident or for the loss of one or more bodily members such as hands, feet, arms, legs, or sight.

E. **RETURN OF PREMIUM** Contracts or policies with a return of premium feature differ from the more common forms of life insurance contracts because they promise to pay upon an insured's death not only the face amount of the policy but also an amount equal to all or a part of the premiums paid.

1. The premiums returned may equal the entire amount the owner paid during the life of the contract. However, in most cases, the return is limited to the premiums paid during a limited period (such as the first 10 years of the contract's life).

2. This feature represents an increasing death benefit (e.g., if a term policy, it represents increasing term insurance).

F. RETURN OF CASH VALUE Some contracts offer a **term rider** to provide a return on an amount equal to the policy's cash value. Policies with this feature are similar to the return of premium contract except that the increasing insurance amount is somewhat different.

G. COST OF LIVING A cost-of-living rider increases or accelerates the face amount of a life policy each year by a specific percentage (such as 3 or 4%). This percentage is generally compounded annually. Its purpose is to increase an insured's life insurance coverage to coincide with inflationary considerations. This is another use of increasing term insurance coverage. The cost-of-living (COL) rider automatically increases the policy death benefit in accordance with the Consumer Price Index (CPI). No evidence of insurability is required and insureds are billed for the additional coverage.

H. ACCELERATED (LIVING) BENEFITS This rider allows an insured to utilize a portion of the policy's death benefit while he is still alive if the insured has been diagnosed with a terminal or catastrophic illness or is facing permanent confinement in a long-term care facility. For example, if the insured is suffering from a terminal illness and his $100,000 policy includes a 50% accelerated benefit, he may withdraw up to $50,000 to pay for medical expenses. Whatever amount is withdrawn will be deducted from the face amount when death occurs. Accelerated benefits are paid free from federal income taxation if the insured is terminally ill.

1. Many companies offer this rider without an additional premium but, any benefit amounts advanced are discounted to reflect the time value of money. The face amount of the policy (the death benefit), cash values if any, and premiums are reduced after the payment is made.

2. Benefits are paid free from federal income taxation if the insured person is terminally ill. Proceeds paid to a chronically ill insured are also not taxable if they are used to pay the cost of qualified long-term care that is not covered by insurance.

I. VIATICAL SETTLEMENTS A viatical settlement firm is a for-profit company (not an insurance company) that purchases an insured's entire life insurance policy with the objective of receiving the death benefit at the insured's death.

1. Viatical settlement firms The firm purchases the policy (typically for two-thirds of the face value) with the expectation that a profit will be earned on the purchase price. Viatical settlement firms make all premium payments after the purchase of the insured's life policy. When the insured dies, the firm collects the death benefit as the sole beneficiary. Some viatical firms purchase policies from people with cancer, but the vast majority of the business is AIDS-related.

2. Benefits of viatical settlements Viatical settlements are generally a higher percentage of the death benefit than the accelerated death benefit offered by life insurers. Viatical settlements are received tax free by the insured if he meets the definition of terminally ill. Under most conditions, **terminally ill** is defined as expected death within 24 months.

3. Viatical definitions A **viatical settlement provider** is any person who enters into an agreement with a person who owns a life insurance policy (viator) under the terms of which the provider pays compensation to the viator in return for the transfer, assignment, or sale of the policy. (A viatical settlement provider does not include banks or life insurance providers.) A **viatical settlement broker** is any person who, for a fee or commission, offers or attempts to negotiate viatical settlements between a viator and one or more providers. A viatical settlement broker does not include an attorney, accountant, or financial planner.

J. TERM RIDERS Term riders may be attached to whole life insurance to provide greater amounts of protection while reducing costs. For example, it is less expensive to purchase a $50,000 whole life policy with a $100,000 term rider than to purchase $150,000 of whole life.

K. ADDITIONAL INSUREDS Coverage for a spouse (spouse's term rider) or a child (children's term rider) may be obtained as an optional benefit via a term insurance rider to a permanent form of life insurance policy. This type of term insurance rider may also be used to protect dependent parents.

L. OTHER RIDERS Other riders available for an added premium that provide additional coverage include the long-term care rider and the war clause rider. The long-term care rider provides health care coverage generally for not less than 12 consecutive months if the required health services are provided in a setting other than an acute care unit of a hospital. A war clause rider may be added to a policy that would provide coverage if the insured person dies while in the military and during a war. However, the face amount of coverage may be limited because the risk is greater.

II.   COMMON POLICY PROVISIONS AND OPTIONS

From insurer to insurer and contract to contract, there are certain provisions that are included in virtually every life insurance policy. Specific wording will vary, but the content and effect of these provisions are fairly constant across the industry.

A. ENTIRE CONTRACT The entire contract provision is also referred to as the entire contract clause. This provision states that the policy and a copy of the application constitutes the entire contract between the insurer and the insured. A copy of the life insurance application is attached to the policy.

1. The life insurance contract provides that all statements made by the insured in the application will be considered as representations and not warranties.

2. The basic purpose of the clause is to provide assurance to the policyowner that he has in his possession all necessary documents with regard to his life insurance coverage.

3. The clause also prevents the policyowners and the producer from unilaterally amending the policy.

TEST TOPIC ALERT

The free look period begins when the policyowner receives the policy, not when the application is taken.

B. INSURING CLAUSE The insuring agreement or insuring clause states that the insurer agrees to provide life insurance protection for the named insured that will be paid to a designated beneficiary when proof of death is received by the insurer.

   1. The insuring clause states the party to be covered by the life contract and names the beneficiary who will receive the policy proceeds in the event of the insured's death. If no beneficiary is named in the contract, the policy proceeds will be paid to the insured's estate.

   2. The face page of the life insurance contract expresses the promise of the insurer and lists the name of the company, insured, amount of insurance carried, the mode and amount of premium, and when coverage is effective.

C. FREE LOOK This policy provision permits the policyowner to take a specified number of days after purchase to examine the life insurance contract. If the new policyowner decides that the purchase was unneeded or unwise, the contract may be cancelled with the entire premium refunded by the insurer.

   1. The free look laws vary in each state and range from 10- to 30-day periods.

   2. The free look period begins when the policyowner receives the policy.

   3. For the applicant to receive a premium refund, the policy must be returned within 10 to 30 days from the date he receives it.

D. CONSIDERATION CLAUSE This provision in a life insurance policy provides that the insurance coverage is granted in consideration of the application and the payment of the initial premium. The payment of the initial premium is necessary to place the insurance coverage in effect.

   1. The insured's consideration is the premium paid and his statements in the application.

   2. The insurer's consideration is the promise to pay the face amount of the contract to the named beneficiary upon the insured's death.

E. OWNER'S RIGHTS The owner of a life insurance contract is usually the applicant, the insured, or the premium payor. The owner of a policy has several stipulated rights in the contract. These include the right to change the beneficiary, receive dividends if any are paid, borrow funds against the cash value if they exist, and assign some or all the rights of the contract to another party.

   1. Third-party ownership Ownership will be in existence when a party other than the insured is the owner of the policy. For example, third-party owners could include a wife who is the owner of a husband's policy, a parent who is the owner of a child's policy, or a corporation which is the owner of a director or officer's policy.

F. PRIMARY AND CONTINGENT BENEFICIARIES

1. **Primary beneficiary** The **primary beneficiary** is the person designated by the applicant to receive the face amount of the proceeds upon the insured's death.

   a. The primary beneficiary may also be referred to as the designated recipient.

   b. In most cases, spouses designate each other as the primary beneficiaries of their policies.

2. **Contingent beneficiary** The **contingent beneficiary** is the individual who will be paid the policy proceeds if the primary beneficiary predeceases the insured. In other words, this secondary beneficiary will receive the face amount of the contract if the primary beneficiary is not living at the time the insured dies.

   a. Contingent beneficiaries may also receive installment payments that were being paid to the primary beneficiary if that person dies.

   b. The most common type of contingent beneficiary designation includes children of the insured.

   c. A **tertiary beneficiary** is the third party in line to receive policy proceeds if the primary and contingent beneficiaries predecease the insured.

   d. If no contingent beneficiary is present, proceeds are left to the insured's estate.

   e. Primary, contingent, and tertiary beneficiaries involve the succession of benefits under a life insurance contract.

   f. **Beneficiary designation options** Proceeds from a life insurance policy may be designated to any person or organization that the contract owner wishes. The surviving spouse is the most common designee of life insurance proceeds. However, other designation options are available, including the following.

      1.) **Individuals** Individual entities may be designated as a beneficiary by the policyowner. While the majority will name family or relatives, some will involve friends or associates. Some individuals have even left insurance proceeds (and their estates) to their pets.

2.) Naming minors as life insurance beneficiaries can present some legal and logistical complications. For instance, the minor may not have the legal capacity to give the insurance company a signed release for receipt of the policy proceeds. (Some states have adopted special laws that allow only minors of specific ages, such as 15 years, to sign a valid receipt.) If an insurer were to pay the proceeds and not receive a receipt, the minor could legally demand payment a second time upon reaching the age of majority. Furthermore, the minor may lack the judgment or expertise to manage the proceeds properly. Nonetheless, insurers recognize that policyowners may want minors to benefit from an insurance policy. In those cases, and in accordance with the laws of the state, insurers may:

- make limited payments to an adult guardian for the benefit of the minor beneficiary;
- retain the policy proceeds at interest and pay them out when the minor reaches majority or when an adult guardian is appointed; or
- place the proceeds in a trust for the present or future benefit of the minor, as determined by the trustee.

3.) Trusts A form of nonindividual designation where life insurance proceeds may be designated. Funds are left to the trust which, in turn, manages and distributes them according to the trust agreement.

4.) Estates Life insurance proceeds will be left to the deceased's estate if the policyowner does not designate a beneficiary or if any of the designated beneficiaries predecease the insured. It is not advantageous for policy proceeds to be left to an estate because of the various tax implications involved.

5.) Class designations Care must be taken when describing beneficiaries as members of a class. It may be difficult to determine the intent of the policyowner when designations such as "children," "minor children," "dependents," "relatives," or "heirs" are used. Per capita or per stirpes designations may be used to further clarify the intentions of the policyowner.

a.) For example, "children of the insured" and "my children" are class designations.

g. Distribution by descent When life insurance proceeds are to be distributed to a person's descendants, a per stirpes or a per capita approach generally is used.

1.) The term *per stirpes* means "by way of branches." A per stirpes distribution means that a beneficiary's share of a policy's proceeds will be passed down to a living child or children of the beneficiary in equal shares should the named beneficiary predecease the insured.

2.) The term *per capita* means "per person" or "by the head." A per capita distribution means that a policy's proceeds are paid only to the beneficiaries who are living at the time of the insured's death and have been named in the policy.

a.) For example: Arthur makes the following designation with respect to the proceeds of his life insurance policy: to his four children—Amy, Brian, Charlie, and Denise—as co-beneficiaries to share equally in the proceeds, and to the surviving children of any deceased children of Arthur, per stirpes. Brian predeceases Arthur, leaving two children, Xavier and Yolanda.

1. The per stirpes distribution means that the surviving co-beneficiaries—Amy, Charlie, and Denise—will each receive a quarter share of the proceeds. Brian's quarter will be shared between Xavier and Yolanda, who will take their share by their father's representation.

2. On the other hand, Arthur could have made the following designation: to Amy, Brian, Charlie, and Denise in equal shares if they survive him, and to the surviving children of his children who predecease him, per capita. When Brian predeceases Arthur, Brian's children—Xavier and Yolanda—would be counted among the surviving beneficiaries to take an equal share. Consequently, the proceeds would be divided among Amy, Charlie, Denise, Xavier, and Yolanda, with each beneficiary taking a one-fifth share.

3.) In short, the per capita beneficiary claims proceeds in his own right, while the per stirpes beneficiary receives the proceeds through the rights of another. Today, the per stirpes method of distribution is by far the more common approach.

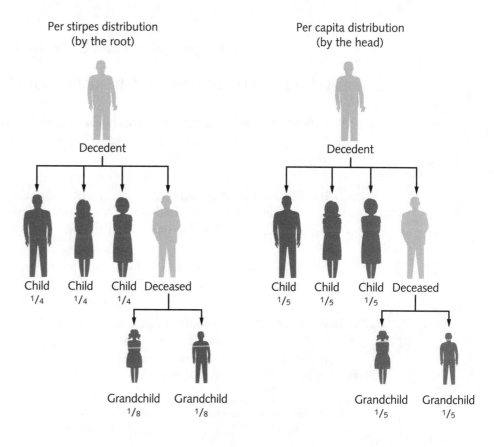

Per stirpes distribution (by the root) — Decedent — Child 1/4, Child 1/4, Child 1/4, Deceased — Grandchild 1/8, Grandchild 1/8

Per capita distribution (by the head) — Decedent — Child 1/5, Child 1/5, Child 1/5, Deceased — Grandchild 1/5, Grandchild 1/5

h. Common disaster clause This clause states that in case of death in a common accident (disaster) the insured shall be presumed to have survived the beneficiary. This prevents the payment of the insurance proceeds to the estate of the beneficiary and thus permits the proceeds to be distributed to any contingent beneficiaries or wherever else provided for by the policy. This clause helps to reduce estate taxes because the proceeds will not be taxed in both estates.

   1.) The Uniform Simultaneous Death Act has been enacted in most states. This law stipulates that if the insured and the primary beneficiary are killed in the same accident and there is not sufficient evidence to show who died first, the policy proceeds are to be distributed as if the insured died last. This law allows the insurance company to pay the proceeds to a secondary or other contingent beneficiary. If no contingent beneficiary has been named, the insured's estate will receive the proceeds.

i. Spendthrift clause This clause may be included in a life insurance contract and will protect the policy proceeds from the claims of the beneficiary's creditors.

   1.) This clause takes away all rights of the beneficiary to change the time of payment or amount of installments. The beneficiary is unable to borrow or assign any of the proceeds as well (which protects the beneficiary from his possible negative spending habits).

   2.) This clause may be attached to the contract as a rider or in the form of an endorsement.

   3.) It prevents proceeds from being attached by creditors.

G. REVOCABLE AND IRREVOCABLE BENEFICIARIES

1. Revocable beneficiary A revocable beneficiary is one that may be changed by the policyowner. The policyowner may change revocable beneficiaries without their knowledge or consent.

2. Irrevocable beneficiary The policyowner may also designate an individual to be an irrevocable beneficiary. In this case, the beneficiary designation cannot be changed without the consent of that named beneficiary.

   a. The policyowner retains all other ownership rights even though he selects an irrevocable beneficiary.

H. CHANGE OF BENEFICIARY Changing a designated beneficiary is an ownership right of the policyowner. If the policyowner desires to change the beneficiary, he must fill out an appropriate change of beneficiary form and return it to the insurer. The change of beneficiary form will stipulate the party or parties to be named as the new beneficiary.

1. As mentioned previously, if a beneficiary has been named irrevocably, his permission must be secured before the policyowner can make any beneficiary change.

I. **PREMIUM DETERMINATION** Life insurance premiums are based upon three basic elements: mortality, interest, and expenses. Mortality (or the average rate of death) in a given year is indicated by the 1980 Commissioner's Standard Ordinary (CSO) mortality table used by the majority of life insurers. The interest that an insurer earns on all premiums collected will affect premiums. Last, expenses such as the payment of death claims will also impact premium determination.

1. **Gross annual premium** The **gross annual premium** is the amount the policyowner must pay each year for the coverage. It is based upon mortality, interest, and expense calculations plus a specific provision for profit (or contribution to surplus).

2. **Net single premium** The **net single premium** is a sum that, if paid when the policy is issued and is augmented by compound interest, will pay the policy's benefits as they come due. This concept is used to compute periodic premium payments for all long-term policies.

3. **Modes of premium payment** The premium paying provision in a life insurance contract provides that all premiums (after the initial premium) shall be payable in advance to the home office of the insurance company or to a producer designated by the company to collect the premiums. Life insurance premiums may be paid annually, semi-annually, quarterly, or monthly. If a policyowner pays the premium in any other mode but annual, an extra charge will be assessed.

   a. Annual premiums are the least expensive of any mode, while monthly payments are the most expensive.

   b. Monthly premiums may be paid to the company or withdrawn from the policyowner's checking account (check-o-matic or pre-authorized checking plans).

   c. Premiums are based on mortality, interest, and expenses. Different mortality tables are used for life insurance and annuities.

J. **GRACE PERIOD** Every life insurance contract contains a grace period. This is the period of time, following the date that each premium is due, during which the insurance policy remains in force and coverage is provided, even though the premium has not yet been paid.

1. Since the policy remains in force during the grace period, the face amount of the contract will be paid to a named beneficiary should the insured die during the grace period.

2. If proceeds are paid out during the grace period, any outstanding premium owed to the insurer will be deducted from the face amount of the contract.

3. Generally, the grace periods in life insurance contracts are 31 days or one month.

K. **AUTOMATIC PREMIUM LOAN (APL)** The APL provision may be added to a life insurance contract that protects the policyowner against the inadvertent lapsing of the contract. As long as the cash value is sufficient, a loan in the amount equal to the premium due is made against the cash value to pay the premium.

> **TAKE NOTE**
>
> Most insurers impose certain requirements and limitations on the exercise of the reinstatement provision, and the policyowner may be asked to prove insurability.

1. In most instances, this provision must be requested by the policyowner at the time of application. Many companies do not allow it to be added once the policy is issued.

L. REINSTATEMENT A policy may lapse due to an intentional or negligent failure to pay premiums. If a policyowner wants to reinstate a lapsed policy, the reinstatement provision allows him to do so, with limitations. With reinstatement, a policy is restored to its original status and its values are brought up to date.

1. Requirements Most insurers require the following to reinstate a lapsed policy:
- all back premiums must be paid;
- interest on past-due premiums may be assessed;
- any outstanding loans on the lapsed policy may be required to be paid; and
- the policyowner may be asked to prove insurability.

2. Time limit There is a limited period of time in which policies may be reinstated after lapse. This period usually is three years but may be as long as seven years in some cases. A new contestable period usually goes into effect with a reinstated policy, but there is no new suicide exclusion provision.

M. POLICY LOAN A policyowner has the right to borrow against the cash value. Interest is assessed by the insurer for these borrowed funds, and the interest rates are determined by each state. Currently, most life insurance contracts issued today change a fixed rate of about 8% on some contracts and on others a variable interest rate is charged. (The variable rate is normally based upon Moody's corporate bond index.)

1. Any outstanding policy loans that exist at the time of the insured's death reduce the policy proceeds. The outstanding loan is subtracted from the face amount of the contract, and the remainder is paid to the named beneficiary.

2. Interest on policy loans is payable annually at the rate specified. However, interest that is not paid when due shall be added to the loan and bear interest at the same rate. If the total indebtedness equals or exceeds the cash value of the contract, the policy will terminate (subject to 31 days' notice to the insured or other policyowner).

N. NONFORFEITURE OPTIONS These options or provisions provided by a life insurance contract are available to a policyowner who wishes to cease paying policy premiums. In situations where the policy premium is not paid, the nonforfeiture options prevent the loss of the investment in the life insurance policy because the cash value is not forfeited if the premium is not paid. These options may go into effect automatically or, as stated, if desired by the insured. There are three basic nonforfeiture options: cash surrender, extended term insurance, and reduced paid-up insurance.

1. **Cash surrender value** The first option available to the policyowner is to surrender the policy for its cash value. All types of permanent life insurance contracts may be surrendered to the company for the amount of cash which has accumulated. This cash surrender value increases each year that the policy remains in force. Therefore, the cash surrender value forms the basis of all the other surrender or nonforfeiture values.

   a. When an insured exercises the cash surrender value option, the policy is returned to the insurer and the company has up to six months to pay the cash surrender value to the insured. However, in the majority of instances the insurer will send the cash surrender value payment to the insured within 30 days.

   b. Besides a complete policy surrender, some policies provide for withdrawals or partial surrenders. This feature is common in universal life policies, and some companies offer this feature with traditional cash value contracts. Traditional policies will have the face amount reduced by the amount of the withdrawal to minimize the effects of adverse selection.

2. **Extended term insurance** The second nonforfeiture option available to the policyowner involves extended term insurance. Under this option, the policyowner may request that the insurance company use the existing cash value to purchase term insurance equal to the face amount of the original policy. The term insurance will remain in effect for as long a period of time as can be purchased with the cash value available.

   a. Permanent type insurance contracts include a table that demonstrates to a policyowner the duration of the term period if this option is exercised.

   b. If a policyowner fails to select one of the nonforfeiture options when premium payments cease, this option generally goes into effect automatically.

Extended Term Option

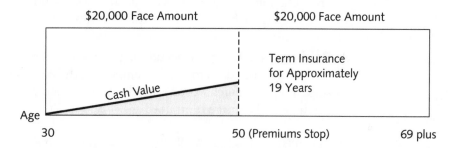

3. **Reduced paid-up insurance** With this option, the insurance company uses the cash value of the contract to purchase a single premium insurance contract of the same form as the original policy. The amount of coverage will be much less than the original policy, but no more premium payments will be required.

a. Thus, the policyowner will receive a paid-up policy that is paid in full for life.

Reduced Paid-Up Term Option

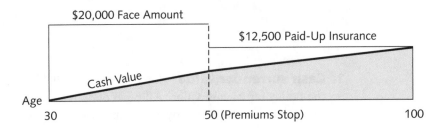

O. DIVIDENDS AND DIVIDEND OPTIONS Life insurance policies that pay dividends are referred to as **participating policies**. Life contracts that do not pay dividends are referred to as **nonparticipating policies**. A participating policy refunds a portion of the premium to the insured in the form of an annual dividend. The dividends cannot be guaranteed by the insurer but when paid are based on the difference between the gross premium charged and the actual experience of the insurer. The experience of an insurer is determined by its ability to meet current obligations such as paying policy proceeds to a named beneficiary, maintaining sound insurance company operations on a solvent financial basis, and other management and administrative expenses. There are several types of dividend options available to a policyowner, including the following.

1. **Cash payments** Dividends credited to a policyowner may be paid in cash to that individual. The insurer simply sends a check to the policyowner. Dividends paid in cash are not considered taxable income.

2. **Accumulation at interest** The policyowner may leave the dividends with the insurer to accumulate at interest in much the same fashion as a savings account. The interest earned will be at a rate no less than the minimum rate specified in the contract. Dividends left with an insurer may be withdrawn at any time.

   a. If the insured dies, the insurer will add the dividends that have accumulated at interest to the face amount of the contract (which is paid to the named beneficiary).

   b. The interest earnings on dividends are considered taxable income when paid, even though the dividends themselves are not.

3. **Paid-up additions** Dividends may be used to purchase additional amounts of insurance, which are added to the face amount of the contract. Paid-up additions are actually single premium purchases of as much life insurance as the amount of the dividend will purchase at the insured's attained age.

   a. These additions will be paid up or paid in full for life and actually increase the insured's death benefit.

   b. The paid-up additions of life insurance provide the same protection and possess the same characteristics as the base policy.

4. **Paid-up option** Dividends may be used to pay up a policy earlier than otherwise expected thus suspending premium payments. For example, when the cash surrender value of the policy plus any (yearly) dividend equals or exceeds the net single premium for the attained age of the insured for an amount of life insurance equal to the face amount of the policy, the insurer will endorse the policy as fully paid. The policyowner, however, must request this endorsement.

5. **To reduce premium payments** A policyowner may utilize dividends to reduce future premium payments. In this manner, the policyowner will pay the difference between the premium due and the dividend amount.

6. **One-year term insurance option** With this option, the policyowner may use a dividend payment to purchase additional one-year term insurance up to the amount of the cash value of the policy. The cost is based on the attained age of the insured. This particular option may be advantageous to a policyowner/insured whose life insurance needs fluctuate from year to year.

   a. Another type of dividend included in some life insurance contracts is known as a **terminal dividend**. Sometimes referred to as **interpolated terminal reserve**, this dividend is paid in the event that a policy terminates for some reason (e.g., insured's death, surrender of policy, etc.).

   b. Some insurers use this dividend to make the policy look more (cost) attractive. It is generally payable only if the contract has been in force for a minimum length of time.

7. If dividends are left with the company using the paid-up, interest, or additions options, the policyowner may convert the basic contract into a fully paid-up policy at an earlier date than that called for in the contract. For example, an endowment at age 65 purchased at age 20 might become paid up at age 50 (acceleration of endowment).

P. INCONTESTABILITY The incontestable clause of a life insurance policy states that, after a specified period of time, the insurer may not dispute or contest the validity of the contract or the statements in the application. After the contract has been in effect for a specific length of time, the insurance company agrees not to challenge any statements made by the applicant on the application.

   1. The existence of this clause is unique in insurance contracts because it is contrary to general fraud laws. It simply indicates that an insurer, following the contestable period, may not claim that any misstatements in the application were made with the intent of the policyowner/insured to defraud.

TAKE ✓ NOTE

Settlement options are the ways in which the death benefit proceeds from a life insurance policy can be paid to the beneficiary.

---

2. The incontestable clause also assures that a named beneficiary will not have to substantiate any statements that were made on the application several years after the policy has been issued. In this situation, it would be extremely difficult for the named beneficiary and others to supply or substantiate information if the insurer contested the contract at the time of the insured's death.

3. The period of time after which the insurer can no longer contest a policy is, for most contracts, two years from issue.

Q. ASSIGNMENT An assignment of a life insurance contract involves the transfer of the policyowner's legal rights under the contract to another party. The policy provisions concerning assignment do not usually grant the insured any rights to assign but do set out the procedures by which assignments may be made. When these assignments are effected, the insurer must be notified. The party receiving these rights is known as the assignee. The person transferring these rights is known as the **assignor**. There are several types of assignments available including the following.

1. Absolute assignment Under this type of assignment, the assignor transfers all rights to the assignee. It generally involves the securing of a debt.

2. Collateral assignment This type involves the assignment of some but not all of the policy rights to an assignee. A lender may wish that a life contract be collaterally assigned to it so that it may draw upon (one of the policy's rights) the cash savings value if loan payments are not paid promptly.

R. SUICIDE CLAUSE When this clause is inserted in a life insurance contract, death by suicide is not covered during the first two years of the policy's existence.

1. If suicide occurs during this initial two-year period, premiums are refunded but no face amount is paid.

2. Following the two-year period, full coverage, including suicide, is provided.

S. MISSTATEMENT OF AGE OR SEX Under this provision, the policy provides for an adjustment of benefits payable if it is discovered that, after an insured's death or at the time of the claim, his age was misstated on the application for insurance. Specifically, the benefit payable will be adjusted to an amount that the premium would have purchased at the correct age or sex. A benefit adjustment is involved whether the age was misstated higher or lower than it actually was or whether the sex of the applicant was misstated.

TAKE NOTE

For a given amount of insurance proceeds, the pure life income settlement option provides the largest periodic benefit payment compared to other forms of payouts that are based on a life span.

T. SETTLEMENT OPTIONS A policyowner should consider, at the time a life insurance contract is purchased, the manner in which the proceeds of the policy will be paid when it matures or when the insured dies. Any failure to adequately prepare for these contingencies may defeat the purpose for which the insurance was purchased. The policyowner may use any of several settlement options to have the policy accomplish for the insured what he would like it to do. Death benefit settlement options are usually designated in the insurance contract and are used to define how the policy proceeds will be paid to the named beneficiary or the insured's estate. Several settlement options are available.

1. **Lump-sum payment** Under this option, the proceeds of the policy are paid in a lump sum unless otherwise directed by the policyowner/insured during his lifetime. A lump sum settlement is not really an option because life insurance contracts usually provide for a lump sum settlement in the event of an insured's premature death. It is the most common form of policy proceeds distribution.

2. **Fixed-amount option** This settlement option allows the policy proceeds to be left at interest with the insurance company and to be paid out in installments of a specified amount until all funds are exhausted. Under this type of option, the amount of income is the primary consideration rather than the period of time over which the proceeds and interest are to be liquidated.

   a. In most cases, this settlement option is more advantageous than the fixed-period option, since it is much more flexible. Insurers allow the insured to specify varying amounts of income at various times, and the beneficiary has the right to withdraw the proceeds at any time.

   b. The amount of each installment is the controlling factor under this option as the dollar amount to be paid is established and not the length of time that installments are to be paid.

3. **Fixed-period option** This settlement option involves liquidating the proceeds and interest over a period of years, without reference to a life contingency. It provides for the payment of policy proceeds in equal installments over a definite period of months or years.

   a. The amount of proceeds, the period of time, the guaranteed rate of interest, and the frequency of payments determine the amount of each installment.

   b. The fixed-period option is valuable where the most important consideration is to provide income for a definite period of time.

    c. Many insurance companies allow the beneficiary the right to discontinue all remaining installments and receive a lump sum. The fixed-period option is generally not as flexible as the fixed amount option.

4. Life income options This option distributes policy proceeds and interest with reference to life contingencies. Life income options are a form of life annuity and serve the same functions.

    a. The amount of each installment paid depends upon the type of life income selected, the amount of the proceeds, the rate of interest assumed, the age of the beneficiary when the income begins, and the sex of the beneficiary.

    b. Several life income options are available.

        1.) The **pure life income** option provides installment payments for as long as the primary beneficiary lives, with no return of principal guaranteed.

        2.) **Refund life income** options may take the form of a cash refund annuity or an installment refund annuity.

        3.) In **life income with period certain**, installments are payable as long as the primary beneficiary lives, but should this beneficiary die before a predetermined number of years, the insurer will continue the installments to a second beneficiary until the end of the certain period. In the **joint and survivorship life income option**, if at the death of the first beneficiary and the second beneficiary is still living, installments are continued during the latter's lifetime.

5. Interest only Under this settlement option, the policyowner may leave policy proceeds with the insurer to earn interest. The proceeds are left with the insurer, and the interest is paid to the beneficiary on an installment basis.

    a. This type of settlement option is generally selected when the policyowner wants to provide for contingent beneficiaries (such as children) after the death of the primary beneficiary (such as a parent).

    b. This option may also provide additional flexibility for the beneficiary since the proceeds are retained by the insurer until needed. For example, funds earmarked for a child's education could be retained until the child reaches college age; meanwhile the interest could supplement the family's income.

    c. The beneficiary may be granted withdrawal rights where part or all of the proceeds may be withdrawn.

U. MODIFICATION PROVISION Numerous life insurance policies contain a provision that gives insureds the right to change the policy they currently own to another type of contract. In the majority of cases these policy modifications or changes of plans can include only alterations involving a higher premium rate.

1. Changes involving higher premium rates do not usually require evidence of insurability.

2. Changes to lower premium rates generally require proof of insurability. In this instance, the incontestability clause may also be reinstated.

V. CONVERSION OPTIONS Policyowners have the ability to convert a term plan to a whole life plan if so desired. The most common conversion involves converting from a group term life policy to a whole life policy. (This will be discussed in a later unit.)

W. FACILITY OF PAYMENT CLAUSE This clause states that if the beneficiary fails to make a claim under a life insurance policy within a specified period (e.g., 15, 30, or 60 days) after the insured dies, the insurance company may make payment to anyone who is entitled to the payment by blood or marriage. This provision is generally found in industrial life contracts (but may appear at times in other forms).

X. CHANGE OF INSURED PROVISION Some insurers include this provision in a life insurance policy involving corporate-owned life insurance. When an employee is insured for the benefit of the corporation (i.e., key employee life) and he retires or is terminated, the business may change the name of the former insured employee to that of the new employee taking his place. The new employee is still subject to insurability requirements, however. Therefore, a new policy need not be sold and issued, and no front-end load (i.e., commission) is payable.

III. COMMON POLICY EXCLUSIONS

Most life insurance contracts contain exclusions or named circumstances that would not be covered if death occurs. Some of the more common exclusions are as follows.

A. WAR EXCLUSION This exclusion normally provides for the return of premium with interest in the event death occurs under conditions excluded in the policy. This clause is generally included in a life insurance contract that is issued during wartime or in time of impending military action. The purpose of this clause is to control adverse selection against the company by those individuals entering military service. Especially during wartime, an individual entering the military may purchase more insurance than he normally would. There are two basic types of war clauses.

1. Status type clause If this clause is included in a life insurance contract, the policy will not pay in the event of death while the insured is in the military, regardless of the cause of death. This would hold true even if the insured were home on leave and his death had nothing to do with military action.

2. Results type clause This type of clause is much less restrictive than the status type clause. A contract that includes this clause would not provide coverage for a member of the military if he were killed as a result of military exercises or service in general. However, if the individual was home on leave and fatally injured in an accident or died as a result of a nonservice-related illness, the insurer would pay the face amount of the contract to a named beneficiary.

B. AVIATION EXCLUSION This exclusion restricts coverage in the event of death from aviation activities except when the insured is a fare paying passenger. This exclusion is generally found in double indemnity provisions as well.

1. This exclusion generally restricts coverage for military pilots and crew members. In addition, aviation deaths as a result of military maneuvers may be excluded. Aviation-related deaths of test pilots, stunt pilots (e.g., air show), crop-dusting pilots, or student pilots are not covered (although coverage for these may be added for an additional premium).

2. Commercial airline pilots and crew members are normally covered at standard rates.

U N I T   Q U I Z

1. The typical waiting period that must be satisfied before premiums are waived under a life contract is
   A. 1 month
   B. 2 months
   C. 3 months
   D. 6 months

2. The payor clause in a life insurance policy states that premiums will be
   A. waived until the insured child reaches age 30
   B. increased upon the death of the premium payor
   C. decreased upon the activation of the automatic premium loan provision
   D. waived until the insured child reaches the age of majority

3. Which of the following is not an example of a dividend option available to a policyowner?
   A. Cash payment
   B. Paid-up addition
   C. Life income
   D. Accumulate at interest

4. John Jones purchases a policy on September 1 and it is delivered 14 days later. The 10-day free look would expire on
   A. September 11
   B. September 15
   C. September 24
   D. September 25

5. The form of assignment where all rights are transferred to another person is known as
   A. collateral assignment
   B. absolute assignment
   C. consignment assignment
   D. homework assignment

6. Gladys is listed as her husband Ben's named beneficiary. After a lengthy illness, Ben dies three years after his wife. To which of the following are the policy proceeds left?
   A. Gladys
   B. Ben's heirs
   C. Ben's estate
   D. The state

7. Which of the following deaths would normally be covered by a life insurance policy?
   A. A student pilot is killed in an auto accident
   B. A navy pilot is killed during military maneuvers
   C. A commercial airline pilot is killed while flying his private plane
   D. A 20-year-old soldier dies in battle

8. Which of the following is the least expensive mode of premium payment?
   A. Annual
   B. Semiannual
   C. Quarterly
   D. Monthly

9. All of the following are types of nonforfeiture options EXCEPT
   A. fixed period
   B. extended term
   C. paid-up insurance
   D. surrender for cash

10. Which of the following insurance settlement options provides for the payment of proceeds over a specified time?
    A. Life income option
    B. Fixed amount
    C. Fixed period
    D. Interest only

ANSWERS

1. C	2. D	3. C	4. D	5. B
6. C	7. A	8. A	9. A	10. C

D I S C U S S I O N   Q U E S T I O N S

1. Discuss how the waiver of premium option functions.

2. Identify the two major components that make up the entire contract.

3. When does the free look period begin?

4. Contrast the primary and contingent beneficiaries and a revocable and an irrevocable beneficiary.

5. How does the automatic premium loan work?

6. What will occur when a policy loan is outstanding at the time of an insured's death?

7. Compare and contrast the three nonforfeiture options.

8. Discuss the concept of incontestability. Why is it important to an insured?

9. How would an incorrect age of the insured affect the policy proceeds of a life insurance contract?

10. Discuss the difference between the status and results clauses.

4

Application, Underwriting, and Policy Delivery

KEY TERMS

Producer/Agent	Representations	Medical Information
Errors and Omissions	Materiality	Fair Credit
Producer Authority	Binding Receipt	Standard
Application	Conditional Receipt	Substandard
Warranty	Insurable Interest	Preferred

I. PRODUCERS, SALES PRACTICES, AND COMPLETING THE APPLICATION

Life insurance is sold by a variety of companies through a variety of methods. Most consumers purchase their insurance through licensed producers or agents who present insurers' products and services to the public via active sales and marketing methods.

A. CATEGORIES OF PRODUCERS There are several categories of insurance producers.

1. **Producer/agent** A **producer**, also referred to as an **agent**, is an individual who represents a company. Under contract law, the company is considered the principal; actions of the agent are considered actions of the principal. This type of producer generally is able to bind coverage. A producer licensed and residing or having his principal place of business in a given state is considered a resident producer in that state; a nonresident producer resides in and has a principle place of business in another state but is licensed in the first state as well.

    a. **Independent producer/agent** **Independent producers** own their books of business that are generally placed with several different companies.

    b. **Captive producer/agent** A **captive producer** generally represents a single company that actually owns the business placed by the producer with that company.

2. **Surplus lines broker** A **surplus lines broker** places business with unauthorized insurers. Generally he must post a bond with the state and must report transactions to the state's Department of Insurance by filing affidavits.

3. **Types of marketing systems** There are many types of marketing or distribution methods available to insurers. Insurance may be distributed from insurers to policyholders in a variety of ways. One of the most common is the **agency system** of representatives who operate under the authority given them by insurers to make legal transactions with consumers of insurance. **Direct-selling systems** are the exception to the general rule that insurance is sold mainly through producers. Under these systems the insurer deals directly with the insured, without producers, through employees of the insurer (e.g., placing specialized or limited lines such as airport vending machines for accidental death and dismemberment protection). Direct selling may be accomplished utilizing mail or telephone without a producer. There are two major agency systems of marketing used to distribute various types of coverage.

    a. **Independent agency system** The **independent agency system** is a system in which the producer may represents several insurers. The producer is independent in the sense that business is placed with any one of a number of insurers that the producer represents. The producer is not an employee of the insurers and sells on a commission or fee basis as an independent contractor. These producers have the authority to bind the insurer immediately for many of the kinds of insurance written for his policyholders. Insurers recognize the independent producer's ownership, use, and control of policy and expiration records. Independent producers own the business that they solicit.

    b. Exclusive agency system Under an **exclusive agency system**, the producer normally represents only one company, as in the case of the typical life insurance producer. Business sold by an exclusive (controlled) producer is owned, used, and controlled by the insurer.

        1.) In marketing some types of insurance, insurers normally use producers who represent only one insurer. A producer will sell insurance for one insurer and therefore is restricted to its rule, rates, and policy forms.

    c. General agents General agents, or GAs, often provide field and sales supervision in a given territory for the insurer and are in a position similar to that of a wholesaler of manufactured products who distributes goods for one major producer. The general agent works under the authority of an insurer and hires, trains, and directs the activities of the life producers working for a given general agency office.

    d. Branch managers Many insurers also have **branch managers** instead of general agents. The branch manager usually operates more as an employee of the insurer than as an individual entrepreneur and is likely to be paid largely by salary.

    e. Group insurance Another marketing system involves group insurance. Marketing to consumers in this system (groups of employees) is usually accomplished on a group basis through an employer or some type of industry association, with payroll deductions as the convenient method of paying premiums. While life, accident, and health insurance is the most common form of group insurance, some insurers are involved with group property and liability insurance as well (e.g., mass merchandising).

4. Evaluating insurer financial status Consumers must be aware of the various criteria available with which to evaluate an insurance company's financial status. The most important criteria involve the insurer's management quality and philosophy. Because these areas are difficult for the consumer to understand, other avenues are available such as the insurer's financial status, its claim policies, service provided, and rating publications. All of these can aid the consumer in his purchase of insurance.

    a. Two areas that the consumer should review when choosing an insurer involve the company's solvency and its liquidity. **Solvency** involves total assets exceeding total liabilities, and **liquidity** means the ability to pay off liabilities as they become due.

    b. A consumer may investigate an insurer's claim history. In other words, when choosing an insurer one should attempt to determine if the insurer pays its claims.

    c. The consumer should also attempt to determine if the insurer provides prompt and adequate service to policyowners.

d. Best Insurance Reports A.M. Best, a financial publisher, provides insurance publications (one for property and liability and the other for life and health insurance) that contain information on insurer history, investments, operating results, personnel, underwriting results, and other financial data. This information is reported for all types of insurance companies. In addition, ratings are assigned to insurers that are based upon an analysis of their financial statements. Insurers may be rated A+ for excellent, B+ for very good, B for good, C+ for fairly good, and C for fair.

5. **Reinsurance** The process of reinsurance involves the transfer of insurance from one insurance company to another insurance company. In other words, it is insurance purchased by insurers. The purpose of reinsurance involves the spread or diversification of exposures and losses. Because catastrophic losses could financially impair an insurer, reinsurance is utilized to allow an insurance company to underwrite higher limits of coverage in a single contract without retaining the entire limit of liability.

   a. Reinsurance may also be used to improve an insurer's own financial and surplus position while meeting the demand for its policies.

   b. The utilization of reinsurance may allow for more rapid growth on the part of an insurer by having a reinsurer take over from that insurer part of the requirements for maintaining reserves, which permits the insurer to increase its writing of more business.

   c. From the reinsurer's standpoint, the normal purpose or motivation for reinsurance is to achieve profits.

   d. There are two principal forms of reinsurance agreements.

      1.) Specific or facultative This type of reinsurance is optional to both the insurer and the reinsurer. No formal agreement exists between the parties. Each contract under facultative reinsurance is written on its own merit and is a matter of individual bargaining between the original insurer and the reinsurer.

      2.) Treaty or automatic This type of reinsurance exists when the insurer agrees in advance to cede or offer some type of risk and the reinsurer agrees to accept that risk. In this situation a formal agreement exists between the insurer and the reinsurer. Quota share is a form of automatic or treaty reinsurance.

6. **National Association of Insurance Commissioners (NAIC)** The NAIC is a voluntary organization that was formed to achieve uniformity in state insurance laws. This organization studies legislation, contacts industry representatives, and prepares model bills that state insurance commissioners or directors may present to their respective legislators.

   a. The NAIC has a number of task forces that consist of members from the insurance industry and the public.

TAKE NOTE

Agency is a legal concept and refers to any commercial or business relationship in which one person acts for or represents another by virtue of the latter's authority.

---

b. These task forces study a broad range of insurance regulatory issues including early detection of possible insurer insolvencies, the role of investment income and rate making, price comparisons, certification of loss reserves by qualified professionals, and so forth.

7. Potential liabilities of producers (E&O coverage) A producer may not exceed the authority given to him by the insurer. Any misconduct of a producer makes him personally liable to the insurer (principal) for damages incurred.

    a. Exceeding binding authority, failing to transmit funds properly, and binding unacceptable risks are some examples of misconduct.

    b. Errors and omissions coverage is generally purchased by insurers in case of the failure of a producer to perform his duties competently and responsibly in the negotiation or solicitation of life insurance.

        1.) Producers have the duty to act in a fiduciary capacity in their dealings with insurers and insureds. This is a relationship requiring a high degree of trust and confidence. The information disclosed by a client may only be utilized for the use intended by the client and may not be disclosed by the producer or the insurer to any unauthorized individuals. Many of these kinds of responsibilities and duties will be discussed in Unit 11.

8. Producer/agent authority In order for an insurer (principal) to be liable for transactions entered into by a producer, an agency relationship must exist. In other words, a producer must have the authority to act on behalf of an insurer. The authority of producers may be classified in several ways.

    a. Express authority Express authority refers to what an insurer specifically instructs a producer to do. Such authority may be spelled out in a legal agreement between the insurer and the producer acting on its (the insurer's) behalf.

    b. Implied authority Implied authority may be established by custom (prior experience) or the conduct of an insurer indicating the intention (implying) to provide the producer with the authority to act on its behalf.

    c. Apparent authority Apparent authority is a type of authority not specifically given to a producer by the insurer. It is based on another person's belief that the producer has authority. In other words, apparent authority involves the type of authority that members of the public can generally expect a producer to possess.

B. THE APPLICATION FOR INSURANCE AND THE PRODUCER'S ROLE The sales practices engaged in by a producer involve many activities, including the application process. As mentioned previously, the life insurance application poses many questions that are relevant with regard to the underwriting of the risk. The age of the proposed insured is important because the older the proposed insured is, the higher the premium charged. The sex of the proposed insured is also important because females are charged lower rates than males. For example, a 30-year-old female will be charged a lower premium rate than a 30-year-old male, all other things being equal involving the plan applied for.

The medical sections of a life insurance application and the producer's report are also extremely important. Regarding the former, the underwriting department will be able to determine how much the insurer may issue to a life insurance applicant depending upon his medical condition. Situations may arise where the underwriters require that a physical examination or an attending physician's statement (given by a physician who has treated an applicant for a medical condition) is necessary to underwrite the risk. Generally, the back page of the application provides space for the producer's comments. The producer usually must state how long he has known the applicant and if the proposed life insurance will replace existing coverage. Other relevant information that must be disclosed on a life insurance application includes:

1. **Required signatures** Several signatures are required to complete a life insurance application. If any of the required signatures are not included, there will be a delay in the issuing of the policy. Required signatures include the applicant, the insured if different from the applicant, and the producer soliciting the insurance. In situations where a corporation is the policyowner, one or more of the partners or officers must sign the application.

    a. If a replacement of life insurance is involved, the applicant must usually sign another form stating that he realizes that a replacement is taking place. In addition, the producer must also sign such a form.

    b. When consumer reports are required or additional medical information is needed, forms authorizing this action must also be signed by the applicant and the producer. Any information solicited from the applicant's personal physician or hospital must also include appropriate signatures.

    c. If an individual is to pay premiums on a monthly basis and wishes to use a check-o-matic plan (premiums being withdrawn from a checking account), the applicant must also sign the appropriate documents.

2. **Changes in the application** Any changes made to a life insurance application after it is completed must be initialed by the applicant. It is permissible to change information but the insurer wishes to make sure that the applicant is aware of any change. Thus the requirement that an applicant initial the changes.

    a. Some insurers require that the producer initial application changes as well.

    b. The reason that an insurer would require initialing is to protect itself in case the applicant or producer does not recall these changes.

3. **Consequences of incomplete applications** Because the application is a critical tool used by the company in its underwriting process, the producer has the responsibility to see that an applicant's answers to questions are recorded accurately and completely. Any incomplete applications sent to the underwriting department will be returned to the producer so they may be filled out completely. This delay in the underwriting process will require the applicant to wait to have the proper protection issued. It behooves a producer to make sure that applications are filled out completely to avoid embarrassment and unnecessary inconveniences. In some cases, if delays occur, the applicant may simply withdraw his application for coverage.

4. **Warranties and representations** Statements made by an applicant for life insurance are considered to be **representations**. These statements, whether made on the application or to a physician or other medical examiner, are not considered to be **warranties**. The applicant must act in good faith, and if the information given is false or incomplete, the insurer may be in a position to rescind or cancel the contract. Obviously, if the applicant was involved in any concealment or the providing of false information, the insurer could rescind the contract because of the material misrepresentations. The difference between a warranty and a representation is as follows:

   a. **Warranty** Warranties are statements that are guaranteed to be true; they are promises that propositions of facts are true.

   b. **Representation** A representation is a statement made to the insurer for the purpose of giving information or inducing the insurer to accept the risk. Representations will be deemed as misrepresentations if the information provided is incorrect. Misrepresentations will not have much of an effect on a life insurance contract unless they are of a material nature.

      1.) A **representation** is substantially true to the best knowledge of the individual (applicant) making the statement.

      2.) Neither party to a contract may conceal facts that would have affected the formation of the contract. The doctrine of concealment requires the applicant to disclose all pertinent information pertaining to the risk.

   c. **Test of materiality** Simply stated, would the insurance company have taken a different course of action had the truth been known? If the answer is "yes," then the statement is material. If "no" is the answer, it is not material.

      1.) **Fraud** Fraud is closely related to the doctrine of concealment and is the intentional misrepresentation of a material fact that may void a contract.

5. **Collecting the initial premium and issuing the receipt** Generally, a prospective insured is given a receipt at the time the application is completed and an initial premium is paid. A receipt verifies that a payment has been made and stipulates when coverage will be effective if the proposed insured is deemed insurable. Insurers issue two kinds of receipts: binding and conditional.

a. Binding receipt If an insurer issues a **binding receipt**, coverage becomes effective as of the date of the receipt and will continue until the insurer rejects the application. In other words, coverage begins immediately when the premium is paid and the receipt is given to the applicant. If the application is underwritten and the company determines that coverage may not be extended, the premium will be returned and the applicant will be notified that coverage may not be provided. However, if a binding receipt is given to an applicant and he is killed in an accident the next day, coverage is effective and the claim will be paid even if it may be denied after the underwriting process.

b. The conditional receipt Under the terms of a **conditional receipt**, insurance coverage becomes effective as of the date of the receipt, provided that the application is approved for the plan applied for, the amount of coverage applied for, and the premium rate applied for. Coverage may also depend on the results of a medical exam that, if acceptable to the insurer, mark the effective date of coverage. This receipt is given to an applicant when he pays the initial premium at the time of application.

1.) Explanation of the conditional receipt The producer must explain how this type of receipt functions. He should inform the applicant that coverage is immediate, or when the medical examination is completed (if an exam is required), provided the insurer determines that, at the present time (or at the time of the medical exam), the applicant qualifies for the policy as applied for. If the applicant qualifies, he does not have to wait for coverage until the policy is issued and delivered; protection starts immediately.

2.) Coverage and the receipt If the applicant fills out the life insurance application and pays the initial premium to the producer, he will be issued a conditional receipt. If the applicant dies after the date on the receipt and before being issued the policy, the application will still be considered. If, based on the application, the applicant is found to be insurable, the insurance will have been effective on the date of death and the claim will be paid.

II. THE PRODUCER'S RESPONSIBILITIES

A producer has many fiduciary responsibilities (those requiring a high degree of trust and confidence) to both an insured/applicant and an insurer, especially during the replacement of life insurance. This information will be also be discussed further in Unit 13 as it relates to state laws and regulations.

A. **DELIVERING THE POLICY** One of the most important procedures involved with the sale of a life insurance contract is policy delivery. When the producer delivers the policy, he should again review the applicant/insured's original goals and needs with relation to the policy. In this way, the delivery process involves more than just "dropping off" the contract. Also, the insured may have additional questions with regard to the policy. Some of the more important aspects of this process are as follows.

1. **When coverage begins** Coverage provided by the insurer will be dictated by the type of receipt provided to the applicant following the completion of the application (and payment of premium).

2. **Obtaining a statement of good health** In many cases, the initial premium is not paid until the policy is delivered. Therefore, most insurers require that when the producer collects the premium, he must also obtain a statement signed by the insured attesting to his continued good health (before leaving the policy with the insured).

   a. The producer then turns in the signed statement and the initial premium to the insurer.

   b. The purpose of this requirement is to make sure that the applicant/insured has remained in good health during the underwriting period.

B. **EXPLAINING THE POLICY AND ITS PROVISIONS, RIDERS, EXCLUSIONS, AND RATINGS TO THE CLIENT** The majority of applicants/insureds will not remember everything about the life insurance contract after they have signed the application. This is the basic reason why a producer should deliver the contract in person. During policy delivery, the producer may again explain the policy and its provisions and exclusions. In addition, the producer will also discuss any possible riders attached to the contract and any change in premium rates that may have occurred.

1. Explaining the policy, its provisions, and exclusions to the policyowner will help to alleviate any future misunderstandings or policy lapses.

2. If the applicant/insured turns out to be a substandard type risk, the producer will have to explain any change in the policy rating. The producer must also provide the reasons why the policy has been rated in such a manner.

3. Any rider that has been attached to the contract because of adverse health conditions or for any other reason must also be explained to the insured. In many cases, an insured must sign and return to the insurer a statement verifying that he understands that a rider is attached and what restrictions are involved.

C. **MAINTAINING RECORDS** A producer must maintain up-to-date records and be available to aid an insured during a time of loss. A client's account should also be reviewed before each policy renewal date. At that time, the producer should again review the client's needs and coverages, making appropriate modifications where necessary. For this reason, it is very important for the producer to stay current with new developments in the insurance industry.

III. LIFE INSURANCE UNDERWRITING

The process of underwriting life insurance policies involves reviewing the background information and medical history of the proposed insured. This information allows an insurance company to determine whether to accept or reject a proposed insured for coverage. Field underwriting completed by the producer is important because he is the main link between the insurer and the applicant. The producer, in this case, is the underwriting arm of the insurance company underwriting department. In addition, this information also determines whether the insurer will charge standard or modified premium rates. There are several underwriting conditions involved in the issuance of life insurance.

A. **INSURABLE INTEREST** Each and every life insurance contract is subject to the doctrine of insurable interest. This doctrine states that the individual purchasing insurance coverage must have a direct and identifiable interest in the individual to be insured. It must be clear that the party purchasing insurance coverage has an economic interest of some sort in the insured. The purpose of this doctrine is to prevent individuals from profiting from the purchase of life insurance on the lives of others.

1. Insurable interest, in a life insurance contract, must exist at the time of application. It does not have to exist at the time of claim. In property and casualty insurance it must exist at the time of loss.

2. A beneficiary generally need not possess insurable interest (initially) in an insured except in a situation where that beneficiary is the owner of the insurance policy.

3. The doctrine of insurable interest is closely connected with the principle of indemnity or indemnification. Under the theory of indemnity, the insured (or in the case of life insurance, the insured's survivors) are placed in the same financial position as that which existed before the loss. This topic will be discussed later when the concept of human life value is addressed.

4. The most common areas involving acceptable insurable interest include blood relationships such as fathers, mothers, sons, and daughters but generally not nephews and nieces; marital relationships involving husbands and wives; and business relationships.

5. A company may refuse to honor a death claim if it proves that no insurable interest existed at the time of application.

B. **THE APPLICATION** The application for insurance is the basic source of insurability information. This is the first source of information from which the insurer will evaluate the risk. Thus, it is the producer's responsibility to see that an applicant's answers to application questions are recorded fully and accurately. There are three basic parts to a typical life insurance application: Part I—General, Part II—Medical, and Part III—Agent's Report.

1. **Part I—General** Part I asks general questions about the proposed insured, including name, age, address, birth date, sex, income, marital status, and occupation. The insurer will want to know about hazardous hobbies, foreign travel, aviation activity, or military service. Whether the proposed insured smokes is indicated in Part I. Also required here are details about the requested insurance coverage:

  ■ type of policy;

  ■ amount of insurance;

TEST TOPIC ALERT

In a typical life insurance application, the applicant signs Parts I and II but does not see Part III, the agent's report.

- name and relationship of the beneficiary;
- other insurance the proposed insured owns; and
- additional insurance applications the insured has pending.

2. **Part II—Medical** Part II focuses on the proposed insured's health and asks questions about the health history of the proposed insured and his family. Depending on the proposed policy face amount, this section may or may not provide all necessary medical information. The individual to be insured may need to take a medical exam.

3. **Part III—Agent's Report** Part III is often called the agent's report. This is where the producer reports personal observations about the proposed insured. Here the producer provides firsthand knowledge of the applicant's financial condition and character, the background and purpose of the sale, and how long the agent has known the applicant. The agent's report usually also asks if the proposed insurance will replace an existing policy. If it will, most states demand that certain procedures be followed to protect the rights of consumers.

C. **MEDICAL INFORMATION AND CONSUMER REPORTS** Life insurance companies may draw upon a number of sources to compile information on proposed insureds for life insurance coverage. As stated previously, the primary sources of information include the application, medical questionnaires and examinations, laboratory tests, inspection reports, and the producer's report. One of the more modern sources of information available to insurance companies is the Medical Information Bureau (MIB).

1. The MIB is an intercompany clearing house that provides a resource information bank and allows member insurance companies to check applications against the bureau's record of medical impairments. The MIB serves as an aid to underwriting because it will attempt to guide an insurer toward other sources of information if some medical impairment is detected.

2. **Consumer reports** A consumer report may be oral or written and involves a consumer's credit, reputation, character, and habits. A report is usually used to help determine an applicant's eligibility for insurance, employment, or credit. Every insurer has the option of verifying or acquiring additional information regarding an applicant for life insurance.

3. **Other sources of information** In addition to the application or MIB or consumer reports, underwriters can acquire information from medical questionnaires, attending physician's statement (from a doctor who treated an applicant in the past for a prior medical condition), physical exams, blood samples, or other tests.

D. **FAIR CREDIT REPORTING ACT** According to federal regulations that apply to life insurance transactions, each insurer and its producers are obligated to satisfy the terms of the federal Fair Credit Reporting Act with regard to information obtained concerning the applicant from a third party.

TAKE NOTE

Sources of insurability information include the application, MIB, consumer reports, and producer/agent report.

1. The Fair Credit Reporting Act states that when an applicant is denied coverage because of information obtained from a third-party source, the applicant will be informed of the source.

2. The insurer is obligated to allow an applicant to refute any adverse information.

3. Insurance companies may use consumer reports, or investigative consumer reports, to compile additional information regarding the applicant.

4. If the applicant feels that the information compiled by the consumer inspection service is inaccurate, he may send a brief statement to the reporting agency with the correct information.

5. A *Notice to the Applicant* must be issued to all applicants for life insurance coverage.

Notice to the Applicant

Section 14: Authorization and Signatures

I hereby authorize any licensed physician, medical practitioner, hospital, clinic, or other medical or medically related facility, insurance company, the medical information bureau or other organization, institution or person, that has any information (records or knowledge) of me or my health (all medical information, including psychiatric, drug, or alcohol use history), to give any such information to _____ corporation and its reinsurers for use in the processing and evaluation of my application for insurance and claims for benefits thereunder.

I also authorize _____ corporation and its reinsurers to release any such information to the medical information bureau and to other life insurance companies to whom I may apply for life or health insurance or to whom a claim for benefits may be submitted, for use in the processing and evaluation of such applications or claims.

This authorization also covers such information pertaining to my children proposed for insurance; their names are: (insert "none" if no minor children are proposed for insurance.)

I understand _____ corporation will provide me with a copy of this authorization at my request. I agree that a photographic copy of this authorization shall be as valid as the original, and that this authorization shall be valid for a future period of 2½ years from the date shown below.

I (we) have paid $_____ (if none say none) to the agent in exchange for the conditional coverage receipt and I (we) acknowledge that (we) fully understand and accept its terms.

Dated at city_____state_____this_____day of _____, 20_____.

E. RISK CLASSIFICATION The majority of life insurance companies have established certain basic requirements to obtain a desired level of business. Most insurance companies attempt to write a large percentage of standard risks. **Standard risks** are those insurable at standard premium rates. Almost all applicants for life insurance are in the standard risk category. **Preferred risk** is another form of risk classification used by insurers. It refers to the type of risk that the underwriting department prefers be submitted. For instance, life underwriters prefer that nonsmoker type applications be submitted because the potential for heart and lung diseases are less for these individuals. An additional risk classification involves **substandard risks**. These risks present the insurance company with additional exposures to loss due to adverse health conditions, moral hazards, or hazardous occupations or avocations. These applicants are usually issued "rated" policies. If an insurer feels that a particular risk is not acceptable, the applicant will be declined.

1. There are various methods insurers use to "rate up" a policy including assessing a flat additional rate charge that may vary depending upon the risk involved; applying a rate-up or step-up in age, which means that the insurer may treat the applicant as a 40-year-old for rating purposes even though the applicant is age 30; applying tabular rating according to a rate table used by the insurer; and using a limited or graded death benefit method (i.e., only a return of premiums if death occurs in the first two years after issuance).

2. There are numerous selection criteria that influence the classification and the underwriting of a life insurance risk including age and sex, occupation and hobbies, family health history, physical condition, moral character, personal history and habits, the type of insurance applied for, financial condition, aviation or military involvement, or the amount of travel outside the country.

F. OTHER UNDERWRITING CONCEPTS Additional concepts with regard to underwriting include but are not limited to the following.

1. Field underwriting As previously mentioned, it is imperative that producers conduct proper field underwriting because the underwriting department's decision—whether to insure the risk or not—will depend upon the accurateness and completeness of the information compiled by the producer "in the field."

2. Loss ratios Various types of ratios (e.g., loss ratio, expense ratio) may be utilized by an insurance company in order to analyze its success or failure. Through these means an insurer will be able to determine its underwriting profit.

3. Life insurance vs. annuities Underwriting annuities is generally a more liberal process than that of life insurance. Life insurance protects against premature death (and thus takes health status into consideration) whereas annuities take into consideration life expectancy for the most part.

U N I T   Q U I Z

1. A man would have an unquestionable insurable interest in the lives of all of the following EXCEPT his

    A. wife
    B. son
    C. nephew
    D. daughter

2. Which of the following is provided by the Fair Credit Reporting Act?

    A. The availability of credit life insurance on an impartial basis
    B. Protection to debtors against credit collection agencies
    C. That the applicant for insurance be informed that a consumer report may be requested regarding his application
    D. Information concerning the previous applications submitted to insurers by an applicant

3. Which of the following best describes the existence of insurable interest in a life insurance policy?

    A. Insurable interest must exist at the time of loss.
    B. Insurable interest must exist at the time of application.
    C. Insurable interest must exist during the explanation of policy provisions by the producer.
    D. Insurable interest must exist at the time of the insured's death.

4. Which of the following is TRUE concerning warranties?

    A. A warranty is a statement that is guaranteed to be true.
    B. Most statements made on an application are considered to be warranties.
    C. A warranty is the intentional relinquishment of a policy right.
    D. A policyholder is assessed an extra premium for a warranty.

5. Which of the following would be a preferred risk in the opinion of a life insurance underwriter?

    A. An applicant with heart trouble
    B. A 59-year-old man
    C. A nonsmoker
    D. A 20-year-old male with diabetes

6. Which of the following most closely defines a representation?

    A. A statement guaranteed to be absolutely true
    B. A statement that is true to the best of the applicant's knowledge
    C. A statement that is material to the risk involved
    D. A statement pertaining to the substandard nature of the risk to be insured

7. Which of the following is a risk classification involved in life insurance underwriting?

    A. Substandard risks
    B. Named beneficiaries
    C. Transferred risks
    D. Increased risks

8. A premium receipt that extends coverage immediately once the premium is paid and the receipt is given to an applicant best describes

    A. exempt receipt
    B. constructive receipt
    C. binding receipt
    D. insurability receipt

9. All of the following are factors that an underwriting department will consider in its decision to accept or reject a life insurance risk EXCEPT

    A. health of the applicant
    B. applicant's avocations
    C. beneficiary named
    D. applicant's age and sex

10. Which of the following is NOT a primary source of information available to a life insurance company's underwriting department?

    A. Medical Information Bureau
    B. Application
    C. Agent's report
    D. The applicant's financial records

ANSWERS

1. C   2. C   3. B   4. A   5. C
6. B   7. A   8. C   9. C   10. D

DISCUSSION QUESTIONS

1. Discuss the importance of completing a life insurance application completely and accurately.

2. What are the signatures required on the life insurance application?

3. Compare the terms *warranty* and *representation*.

4. Contrast a binding and conditional receipt.

5. Discuss the concept of insurable interest. What other principle does this doctrine follow closely?

6. What is the primary purpose of the Fair Credit Reporting Act?

7. How will standard or substandard risks affect the rating of an applicant for life insurance?

8. Why may a statement of good health be required from an applicant during the policy delivery process?

9. Why is it important that the producer explain contract provisions and any riders involved to the newly insured individual?

10. What type of information is provided to an applicant in the notice left with him by the producer?

5

Taxes, Retirement Plans, and Other Insurance Concepts

KEY TERMS

Insurable Interest	TSA	Social Security
Group Life	Defined Contribution	Fully Insured
Conversion	Defined Benefit	Currently Insured
Contributory	401(k) Plans	1035 Exchange
Noncontributory	Key Employee	Human Life Value
Credit Life	Buy and Sell	Needs Approach
Fraternals	Split Dollar	Estate Planning
IRA	Deferred Compensation	
Keogh Plans		

I.   THIRD-PARTY OWNERSHIP

Third-party ownership refers to an arrangement in which a life insurance contract is owned by a party other than the insured. This type of ownership is usually used in business insurance settings and for estate planning purposes.

A.   ESTABLISHMENT OF THIRD-PARTY OWNERSHIP Third-party arrangements need not necessarily be established at the time a contract is applied for but may come about later as a result of a transfer or absolute assignment of the policy. A common example of third-party ownership involves a corporation purchasing a life insurance policy on a director or officer. In addition, wives who own policies covering the lives of their husbands and parents who own policies covering the lives of their children are other common examples of third-party ownership.

B.   INSURABLE INTEREST Any third-party owner must have an insurable interest in the life of the person to be insured.

II.   GROUP LIFE INSURANCE

Group life insurance originated in the early twentieth century in order to provide coverage for a number of persons. Almost 50% of the life insurance in force today involves group life protection. The reasons for its growth in popularity involve the organization of labor (employee benefit plans), tax advantages, and industrialization. The group life concept has expanded from the original employer employee type plan. Now group life policies are issued to cover members of unions, associations, trusts, creditors, and so forth. Group life insurance differs from individual life insurance contracts in many ways including underwriting methods and some policy provisions. This life insurance coverage is concerned with the selection of risks by group factors rather than by individuals. Group life insurance protection differs in another way from individual life insurance in that it involves three parties: the insurance company, the employer, and the employee (although it remains a two-party contract). An individual policy involves only two parties: the insurer and the policyowner. In a group insurance setting, the employer is the policyowner. However, the covered employee receives a **certificate of coverage** that proves that life insurance protection is in existence.

A.   GROUP LIFE INSURANCE CHARACTERISTICS In addition to selecting risks by group characteristics and the involvement of three parties, another characteristic of group life insurance is that it must be incidental to the purpose for which the group has been formed. Group life insurance coverage is generally issued without requiring evidence of insurability by the individuals making up the group (though occasionally, plans do require proof). Because the employer is the policyowner and pays the premium, he receives the master policy.

B.   CONVERSION PRIVILEGE (OPTION) An employee insured under a group plan has the privilege of converting the face amount of his group term life insurance contract to an individual policy of permanent protection. This conversion option is an actual provision found in the contract and states the following.

1. The employee may convert, within 31 days after termination of employment, to one of the insurer's regular permanent forms at standard rates for the employee's attained age.

2. No proof of insurability is required when a conversion takes place.

3. Generally, the death benefit provided under a group life policy is continued during the conversion period. Again, this is the 31-day period from the date of termination of employment during which employees may convert their group coverage to an individual plan. Group life insurance coverage will continue in force for those 31 days, even though the conversion privilege may not be exercised.

C. CONTRIBUTORY VS. NONCONTRIBUTORY PLANS This refers to which party or parties will pay the group life insurance premiums. If the employer pays the entire premium, the plan is referred to as **noncontributory**. If the employee pays part of the premium (the premium is shared by both the employer and employee), the plan is referred to as **contributory**.

1. As mentioned previously, if a plan is noncontributory, the group contract must cover 100% of the eligible persons in the group.

2. If the plan is contributory, at least 75% of the eligible employees must choose to be covered before the plan can become effective. For instance, if 500 employees are eligible for a contributory group plan, at least 375 would have to enroll in the plan for it to be effective.

3. Under contributory plans, the period of time during which the employee may enroll and receive coverage without evidence of insurability is known as the eligibility period.

D. TYPES OF GROUP LIFE INSURANCE Several types of contracts may be used in group life insurance. A group term contract has the same basic characteristics as an individual term life insurance policy. Most group life insurance contracts are issued on a group term basis. Group permanent life insurance is occasionally used in group insurance contracts.

E. ELIGIBILITY OF GROUP MEMBERS Group insurance provides for participation by virtually all members of a given insurance group. Whether individual members choose to participate usually depends on the amount of premium they must pay, if the plan is contributory. If the plan is noncontributory and the employer pays the entire premium, full participation is the general rule.

1. Employers and insurers are allowed some latitude in setting minimum eligibility requirements for employee participants. For instance, employees must be full-time workers and actively at work to be eligible to participate in a group plan. If the plan is contributory, the employee must authorize payroll deductions for their share of premium payments. In addition, a probationary period may be required for new employees, which means they must wait a certain period of time (usually from one to six months) before they can enroll in the plan.

2. The **probationary period** is designed to minimize the administrative expense involved with those who remain with the employer only a short time. The probationary period is followed by the **enrollment period**, the time during which new employees can sign up for the group coverage. If an employee does not enroll in the plan during the enrollment period (typically 31 days), he may be required to provide evidence of insurability if he wants to enroll later. This is to protect the insurer against adverse selection.

F. GROUP LIFE STANDARD PROVISIONS The provisions in a group life contract are similar to those that appear in an individual policy including but not limited to beneficiary, conversion, grace period, assignment, misstatement of age, and so forth.

G. GROUP CREDIT LIFE INSURANCE Group credit life insurance coverage is available to protect a borrower and a lender. For example, if the borrower dies, the amount of the loan is paid by the insurance proceeds. In addition, the lender (creditor) will not be left with an uncollectible debt if the borrower (debtor) should die.

1. The creditor may not require the borrower to purchase coverage from a particular lender. In this case, the creditor may also purchase coverage on the life of the borrower.

2. Credit life insurance may not be written for an amount greater than the total indebtedness.

H. FRATERNALS A fraternal entity is organized for the benefit of its members and not for profit. These entities are able to provide life insurance for their members in the same way commercial companies provide coverage for the public.

1. Fraternal association Some types of fraternals may receive group coverage for the members of its association.

2. Coverage may be provided by fraternal itself for the association members (e.g., Knights of Columbus). Others may be covered by commercial group coverage (e.g., Masons or another form of lodge system association).

I. INDUSTRIAL LIFE Originally designed for low-income families who were not able to afford whole life, these policies are issued in small amounts of generally less than $2,500.

1. Premiums are usually paid on a weekly or monthly basis to a producer who personally visits the policyowner's residence.

2. The basic terms, features, and provisions of industrial life policies are similar to whole life contracts.

3. Industrial health policies are also sold in the same manner and for the same reasons.

III.   RETIREMENT PLANS

Various types of plans are available to individuals who wish to set aside funds for their retirement years. Depending on whether they have been approved by the IRS, these plans are referred to as tax-qualified or nonqualified plans.

A.   TAX-QUALIFIED PLANS Retirement plans that are referred to as tax qualified are those that receive special tax advantages. In general, qualified plans are classified as either defined contribution or defined benefit plans.

B.   TYPES OF QUALIFIED PLANS Qualified plans may be established by an individual and by employers for the benefit of their employees. Some of the more common types are as follows.

1.   **Individual retirement accounts (IRAs)** Any individual who earns wages may participate in an IRA. A person may deduct the maximum contribution if he is a wage earner and does not actively participate in an employer maintained retirement plan or if he is a wage earner who actively participates in an employer-maintained retirement plan but has an adjusted gross income (AGI) of $50,000 or less if single and $70,000 or less if married and filing jointly.

a.   A single person whose AGI is between $50,001 and $60,000 is entitled to a partial deduction based on a formula. Married persons filing jointly whose AGI is between $70,001 and $80,000 are also entitled to a partial deduction. For married taxpayers, the range will increase in 2006 to $75,001 to $85,000.

b.   The maximum annual contribution for any individual to an IRA is $4,000. In 2008, this limit is scheduled to increase to $5,000.

c.   Owners of IRAs must begin to receive payments from their accounts by the time they reach age 70½. In addition, if any withdrawals are made before the owner is 59½ years of age, a 10% penalty based on the amount received will be assessed in addition to income taxes.

d.   Following age 59½, any IRA distribution or payment made to the owner is subject only to ordinary income taxation.

e.   Individuals who are eligible to establish IRAs may create a spousal IRA with a nonwage earning spouse. The limit for a spousal IRA is based on the same schedule as the wage earner or 100% of the earned income of the wage-earning spouse, whichever is less.

f. Individuals who are 50 years old and older may contribute an additional amount in excess of the prescribed limit, up to $500. In 2006, the limit on this additional contribution is scheduled to increase to $1,000.

g. As mentioned previously, any benefits withdrawn from an IRA before age 59½ will be assessed a 10% penalty (note exceptions below). In addition, amounts withdrawn must also be added to the owner's taxable income for the year in which the withdrawals were received. However, if an individual wishes to roll over IRA funds into another IRA, this will be permitted if the proceeds are reinvested in the new IRA within 60 days following receipt of the distribution. Otherwise, the distributions will be taxable in the year received.

h. There are many exceptions to the 10% penalty. They include the following.

   1.) The 10% early withdrawal penalty will not apply if the distribution is used to pay medical expenses that exceed 7.5% of the owner's adjusted gross income.

   2.) Unemployed individuals (those receiving state or federal unemployment compensation for at least 12 consecutive weeks) who take an IRA early distribution to pay health insurance premiums will not be subject to the 10% penalty.

i. Roth IRAs In addition to traditional IRAs, qualifying taxpayers have the option of establishing Roth IRAs. The principal difference between the two is that contributions to Roth IRAs are not deductible but distributions, if taken in the correct manner, are entirely tax free. Features of the Roth IRA include the following.

   1.) Contributions are not deductible; however, qualified distributions are received tax free. To be considered a qualified distribution, the IRA owner must have held the Roth IRA for at least five years *and* the distribution must be made:
   - on or after the date the owner reaches age 59½;
   - to the estate or beneficiary upon the owner's death (within five years of the owner's death);
   - as a result of the owner's disability; or
   - for first-time home buyer expenses, subject to a $10,000 lifetime limit.

   2.) Contribution limits to a Roth IRA are the same as traditional IRA; however, contributions may be made after age 70½. Furthermore, for those 50 years old and older, additional amounts may be contributed. (The additional contribution limit is the same as for traditional IRAs.)

   3.) The maximum contribution amount is reduced for joint filers with adjusted gross income (AGI) between $150,000 and $160,000 and single filers with AGI between $95,000 and $110,000. Taxpayers with AGI exceeding these amounts are not eligible to establish Roth IRAs.

4.) Individuals who set up a Roth IRA can still contribute to a traditional IRA; however, the maximum contribution to all IRAs is limited to the same contribution limit schedule.

5.) The traditional IRA required distribution rules do not apply; distributions need not start at age 70½.

6.) Taxpayers with AGIs less than $100,000 can convert a traditional IRA into a Roth IRA without paying the 10% tax on early withdrawals.

IRA Contribution Limit Schedule (Applicable to both traditional and Roth IRAs)	
Year	Limit
2005	$4,000
2006	$4,000
2007	$4,000
2008 and after	$5,000

j. Education IRAs With this type of IRA, formally known as a Coverdell IRA, a taxpayer can pay for qualified higher education expenses (e.g., tuition, fees, books, and supplies). Nondeductible annual contributions of up to $2,000 per child under age 18 can be made; the $2,000 limit cannot be circumvented by creating more than one IRA per child. (There is a 6% excise tax imposed on excess contributions.)

1.) All buildup of earnings and withdrawals to pay qualified education expenses is tax free.

2.) If the child does not attend college or there are any amounts remaining when the beneficiary (child) reaches age 30, the education IRA may be rolled over into the IRA of another child in the same family without penalty. Distributions not used for higher education expenses are added to the recipient's gross income and are subject to a 10% penalty.

k. Simplified employee pensions (SEPs) SEPs are employer-sponsored IRAs. They offer corporations the opportunity to establish an employer-funded pension plan for eligible employees. Contributions must be made on behalf of employees age 21 or older, who have performed service for the employer during the year for which the contribution is made and for at least three of the preceding five years received a specified amount of compensation.

2. Keogh plans This type of retirement plan is also known as an HR-10 plan. This vehicle is provided for the self-employed individual who wishes to establish a retirement plan that will provide for tax deferral and a reduced tax liability.

a. Like an IRA, annual contributions to a Keogh plan are tax deductible. Contributions may be made to a Keogh plan up to 100% of earned income, or $42,000 per year, whichever is less. (The $42,000 limit is as of 2005. It is indexed for inflation and will increase as time goes by.)

   b. Benefits from a Keogh plan may not be distributed to an owner before age 59½ without penalty, and they must begin no later than age 70½.

3. **Tax-sheltered annuities (TSA) or 403(b) plans** Employees of qualified IRC Sec. 403(b) (tax exempt) organizations are permitted, under the Internal Revenue Code, to contribute funds to annuities with tax-free dollars. Those eligible for tax-sheltered annuities (TSAs) include public, private, and parochial school teachers, school superintendents, college professors, clergymen, and social workers. For example, the pastor or minister of a church would be eligible for a TSA. Government employees are not eligible.

   a. Before-tax dollars are subtracted from the individual's gross income by way of a **salary reduction**. This amount is deposited in an annuity or mutual fund and accumulates on a tax deferred basis. In addition, since the individual's salary has been reduced, his tax liability is also reduced.

   b. The maximum contribution limit for a 403(b) plan will increase to $15,000 in accordance with the following schedule:

Contribution Limits for 403(b) Plans*	
Year	Limit
2005	$14,000
2006 and after	$15,000

   *These same limits also apply to 401(k) plans.

   c. Whereas an IRA and Keogh plan provide for a deferral of income taxation on contributed funds and tax deductions, a tax-sheltered annuity involves tax deferral and a salary reduction (not a deduction).

   d. **Catch-up contributions** TSA plans permit employees with 15 or more years of service to make up for prior contributions that could have been made under the plan, but were not.

   e. Some employees (such a members of the clergy) may be entitled to larger contributions under a number of special provisions found in the Internal Revenue Code.

4. **Section 457 plans** Section 457 plans are similar to TSAs, but they are reserved for employees of other public bodies, such as states, counties, and municipalities. Under these plans, the employer agrees with each employee to reduce salary by a specified amount and invest the deferrals in one or more vehicles that may include insurance products. The principal difference between Section 457 plans and 403(b) plans is that the investments in Section 457 plans are owned by the employer. Those in 403(b) plans are owned by the employee.

5. **Annual premium retirement (tax-deferred) annuities** This type of vehicle is a tax-deferred device but not a tax shelter in its true sense. Tax-deferred annuities provide tax-deferred income. The income earned on the money placed in the tax-deferred annuity is not currently taxable to the owner until it is withdrawn.

   a. Unlike a tax shelter, the owner does not receive a tax deduction in the amount of a contribution (like one would with an IRA or Keogh plan). The owner only receives a deferral of taxation on earned income.

6. 401(k) plans An increasingly popular form of qualified plan, a 401(k) plan allows employees to elect to contribute a portion of their income into an account in their name and instruct their employer to make contributions on their behalf. Amounts the employee elects to contribute (deferring a portion of current income) are treated, for tax purposes, as contributions made by the employer. This makes all monies set aside in the plan deductible by the employer. The contributions plus earnings grow tax-deferred to the employee until withdrawal.

   a. A 401(k) plan provides current and future tax savings since an employee agrees to defer a percentage of his pretax income by way of a salary reduction. The employee's salary is reduced by the amount of the contribution and therefore his tax liability is reduced (since contributions are considered to have been made by the employer). All interest earned on contributions accumulate on a tax-deferred basis.

   b. Employers also save money on unemployment taxes and workers' compensation premiums by contributing to 401(k) plans because these taxes and premiums are, in whole or in part, based upon employee salaries.

   c. Current contribution limits to 401(k) plans are $14,000 ($15,000 in 2006 and later). Those who are 50 years old or older may make additional contributions up to $4,000 ($5,000 in 2006 and later).

   d. The IRS has established strict withdrawal provisions for 401(k) plans including: no withdrawals before age 59½ are allowed except for death, disability, retirement, job change, or proof of financial hardship. Loans, however, are permitted but are limited to the lesser of $50,000 or 50% of the account's vested value.

7. Savings Incentive Match Plans (SIMPLE) A savings incentive match plan (SIMPLE plan) is a tax-favored means for providing a retirement option that does not have to satisfy many of the qualified plan requirements.

   a. Plan assets are not taxed until distributed and contributions are tax deductible by the employer.

   b. SIMPLE plans need not satisfy nondiscrimination requirements.

   c. Eligible employers for SIMPLE plans are those with no more than 100 employees who received at least $5,000 in compensation for the preceding year. The employer must not maintain another employer-sponsored retirement plan to which contributions were made or benefits accrued.

   d. SIMPLE plans can take the form of an IRA plan or a 401(k) plan.

   1.) SIMPLE IRAs SIMPLE plans may be structured as an IRA. An employee may make elective contributions up to a maximum limit annually (this limit is $10,000 in 2005 and thereafter); the employer is required to match the employee contribution, which greatly increases the amount deposited in the plan. There are two employer contribution formulas.

   a. Matching contribution formula Employers must match employee contributions on a dollar-for-dollar basis up to 3% of an employee's compensation for the year. However, the employer may also elect to match contributions for all eligible employees for a given year at a rate lower than 3% but no lower than 1% of each employee's compensation (the employer must notify employees of this before the 60-day election period during which the employees determine whether to participate in a SIMPLE plan).

   b. The alternative formula An employer may choose to make a contribution of 2% of compensation for each eligible employee who earned at least $5,000 (employees must be notified of this before the 60-day election period).

   c. Vesting All contributions to a SIMPLE IRA are nonforfeitable; employees are vested immediately.

   d. Participation requirements A SIMPLE plan must be open to every employee who (1) received $5,000 in compensation during any two preceding years and (2) is expected to receive at least $5,000 during the current year.

   e. Contribution elections Eligible employees may elect to participate in a SIMPLE plan by making elective deferrals during the 60-day period before the beginning of the year or the 60-day period before the employee becomes eligible to participate; contribution amounts elected by the employee may be changed during this period; and participation may be terminated by the employee by simply stopping the contributions.

   f. Taxation of SIMPLE IRA distributions Distributions or withdrawls are taxable upon distribution and includable in income.

   g. Rollovers Distributions from one account may be rolled over into another SIMPLE account; after two years, they may be rolled over from a SIMPLE account into an IRA without penalty.

   h. Early withdrawal penalty Withdrawals before age 59½ are subject to the 10% early withdrawal penalty applicable to IRAs. For early withdrawals made during the first two years of participation, a 25% penalty will be assessed.

8. SIMPLE 401(k) plans An employer that does not employ more than 100 employees or maintain another qualified plan may provide a SIMPLE plan as part of a 401(k) arrangement. The nondiscrimination tests applicable to elective deferrals and employer matching contributions under a 401(k) plan will be satisfied if the plan meets the contribution and vesting requirements applicable to SIMPLE plans discussed above.

a. An employer can take a tax deduction equal to the greater of:

- ■ 15% of the compensation paid or accrued during the tax year to participants in a stock bonus or profit sharing plan; or
- ■ the amount that it must contribute to the SIMPLE 401(k) plan for the year.

b. All eligible employees must be notified that they have right to make or modify an elective deferral during the 60-day period before every January 1.

9. Catch-up contributions for older participants As with older IRA participants, individuals age 50 and older who participate in SIMPLE, 401(k), and 403(b) plans may also increase their elective deferrals in accordance with the following schedule:

Additional Amounts That May Be Deferred		
Year	SIMPLE Plans	401(k) and 403(b) Plans
2005	$2,000	$4,000
2006	$2,500	$5,000

10. Qualified plans Tax-qualified plans may also be divided into defined contribution plans and defined benefit plans.

a. Defined-contribution This type of plan has a separate account for each employee. The plan document states the amount that an employer will contribute to the plan, but it does not promise any particular benefit.

b. Defined-benefit The plan document specifies the amount of benefits promised to the employee at his normal retirement date. It does not specify the amount that the employer must contribute annually to the plan to achieve the benefit.

1.) Special rules for life insurance Life insurance benefits may be included in a qualified pension plan only on a basis that is incidental to the primary purpose of the plan. Life insurance is considered incidental if the cost of insurance is less than 50% of the employer contribution; under a defined benefit plan, the requirement is that it be less than 50% of the employer contributions or that the life insurance death benefit not exceed 100 times the monthly retirement benefit.

2.) The economic benefit of the (cash value) life insurance included in a qualified plan is currently taxable to the employee. The economic benefit is the cost of the pure amount at risk (based on the Internal Revenue Service one-year term insurance rates known as the PS 58 rates), which is the cost of the death benefit only. The total cost of term insurance would be taxable.

C. NONQUALIFIED PLANS Because all retirement plans approved by the IRS are considered qualified, all others are viewed as nonqualified.

1. Nonqualified deferred compensation plans represent an important fringe benefit for executives and other highly paid employees.

2. Nonqualified plans permit the employer to choose the individuals he wants covered by the plan. In other words, the employer may discriminate with a nonqualified plan.

3. These plans are used to provide additional benefits to key employees.

IV. BUSINESS INSURANCE

Life insurance is a useful tool for individuals (personal insurance), charitable organizations, and in the world of business. It helps to assure business continuation and to protect business owners and their dependents. There are various forms of business life insurance which help protect a corporation from economic loss if, for example, a key employee should die prematurely. Some of the more common forms of business life insurance include the following.

A. **KEY-EMPLOYEE (PERSON) LIFE INSURANCE** This type of coverage protects a business against loss of one of its most valuable assets—a **key employee**. A life insurance program would provide the corporation or employer with funds if a key employee were to die and his contribution to the company was terminated. Obviously, the loss of a key employee may not be recovered, but the proceeds of the policy will permit the employer to reduce his financial loss. Policy proceeds may be used to hire a new key person, hire temporary help, or train new employees.

1. Various types of key employees include directors and officers of a firm, key sales or marketing personnel, supervisors, and foremen.

2. The primary purpose is to indemnify a business for financial losses caused by the death of a valuable employee.

3. Key employee life insurance also receives favorable tax treatment. In most cases, the death proceeds of key employee life insurance are not taxable. However, premiums are not deductible for business income tax purposes. However, in cases where premiums are deductible, benefits received are usually taxable to the recipient.

B. **BUY AND SELL AGREEMENTS** Buy and sell agreements help with the orderly continuation of a business where survivors receive a fair cash settlement for a decreased owner's interest. The most common way in which to fund such an agreement is through the use of life insurance. This agreement guarantees that cash will be available if the owner should die prematurely. It allows another individual to purchase the deceased owner's interest so the business will continue without further disruption.

1. Legal contracts are drawn that set a predetermined value on each person's portion of ownership in the business.

2. Buy-sell arrangements may be used in any form of business whether it is a sole proprietorship, partnership, or corporation. There are two basic types of such agreements: entity plans and cross-purchase plans. The entity plan involves a partnership owning a

policy on the life on each partner. For example, if there are three partners, there will be three policies purchased and owned by the partnership. The cross-purchase plan involves a plan where each partner owns a policy on the life of each of the other partners. For example, if there are three partners, each one will own a policy covering the life of each of the other partners. Therefore, six policies will exist in a cross-purchase plan.

3. When a buy-sell agreement is funded by permanent life insurance, the plan may also call for a transfer of ownership should the proprietor prefer to retire at some future time. The employee would use the policy's cash value to make a substantial down payment on the purchase price of the business.

C. SPLIT-DOLLAR INSURANCE   Split-dollar life insurance is a special form of life insurance agreement used in business and family situations to provide life insurance for a minimum cash outlay.

1. This plan requires a cash value type of permanent life insurance.

2. For example, assume a key or valued employee has a definite need for life insurance protection but lacks the necessary funds to purchase it. With a split-dollar plan, the employer contributes to the premium each year an amount equal to the increase in the policy's cash value and the employee pays only the balance of the premium. If the policy is surrendered at any time, the cash savings value amount is returned to the employer. If the insured dies, the employer gets back the money paid out for the premiums and the balance is paid to the deceased's beneficiary.

3. A split-dollar plan involves a single contract that utilizes cash savings value and term insurance protection to guarantee the return of premiums paid by one party and assures a death benefit to be paid to a named beneficiary. Split-dollar is not a type of policy.

D. BUSINESS CONTINUATION AND LIFE INSURANCE   Life insurance plays an important role in helping small businesses continue operating upon the death of their owners or shareholders. The appropriate plan for continuation depends on the type of business involved.

1. Sole proprietorship   This type of entity ends when the owner/proprietor dies. The business can be continued if an appropriate buy-sell agreement (funded by the appropriate amount of life insurance) is created. Otherwise, the business will terminate and be distributed to the proprietor's heirs.

2. Partnership   Any change in the membership of a partnership, such as one partner dying, will dissolve the partnership. The remaining partner(s) must then liquidate the business (almost always at a less than market rate) and distribute the deceased partner's share to his heirs.

    a. Some sort of buy-sell or income-continuation arrangement can be utilized to prevent this forced liquidation and continue the business.

    b. For example, physicians or attorneys may utilize a personal-service partnership with an income continuation agreement. This allows the business to continue for a specified number of years and then an amount will be paid to the deceased partner's heirs.

    3. Corporate entity Close corporations are similar to partnerships. The corporation does not dissolve, however, when a stockholder dies.

    a. Buy-sell agreements funded by life insurance bind the remaining stockholders to purchase the stock of the deceased stockholder at a prearranged price stipulated in the agreement.

    b. The estate of the deceased is also obligated to sell the stock to the remaining stockholders.

E. EXECUTIVE BONUS (SECTION 162) PLAN Section 162 plans involve the purchase of a life insurance policy on one or more employer-selected employees. The employee purchases, owns, and names the beneficiary; the employer retains no policy rights. The employer either pays the premium directly to the insurance company or to the employee who then pays the premium. Under the terms of IRC Section 162, the premium paid to the employee as a bonus is deductible by the business and the amount paid to or for the employee is reportable as taxable income to the employee.

F. USES OF ANNUITIES Annuities may also be utilized in the business realm as well as the personal. Annuities may be used to provide retirement benefits or supplemental income to employees.

V.   SOCIAL SECURITY BENEFITS

Social Security (also referred to as OASDI—old age, survivors, and disability insurance) benefits are determined by a formula based on earnings. The Social Security Administration is responsible for administering benefits and collecting "premiums." Benefits provided under this federal program include death benefits, retirement benefits, and benefits in the event of disability.

A. SOCIAL SECURITY DEATH BENEFITS There are several types of death benefits provided under Social Security.

    1. Lump-sum death benefit A one-time payment of $255, this benefit helps the deceased's survivors pay for funeral costs. Payment is made to a surviving spouse who was living with the deceased. If no surviving spouse is present, the benefit is payable to the children of the deceased.

2. **Surviving spouse's benefit** The eligible surviving spouse of a fully insured worker is entitled, at the spouse's normal retirement age, to a monthly life income equal to the worker's primary insurance amount (PIA) at death. Or, if the spouse wishes to receive these benefits early, she can elect reduced benefits, starting as early as age 60.

   a. If the surviving spouse has a dependent child under age 16 (or age 22, if disabled), and the child was a dependent of the deceased worker, an additional benefit of 75% of the worker's PIA is payable, regardless of the spouse's age, until the child reaches age 16. Disabled children will entitle the surviving spouse to this benefit indefinitely, as long as the child remains disabled and under the care of the surviving spouse.

   b. The **blackout period** is the period of years during which no Social Security benefit is payable to the surviving spouse of a deceased, fully insured worker. It is between the time the youngest child of the worker (in the spouse's case) attains the age of 16 and the spouse's age 60.

3. **Child's benefit** A child who is under age 18 (or disabled before age 22) whose parent is a deceased worker may receive a benefit equal to 75% of the worker's PIA until the child turns age 18 (age 19 if still in high school). If the child marries before age 18, the benefit ends.

4. **Other death benefits** Death benefits may also be provided for parents of a deceased child if the child provided at least half of the parents' support.

B. **SOCIAL SECURITY DEFINITIONS** There are several definitions that are relevant to Social Security benefits, including the following.

   1. **Quarter of coverage** This is a unit of coverage credited to a worker for each portion of a calendar year's covered wages or a self-employed income that equals or exceeds an amount specified for that year by law.

   2. **Fully insured** A person must be fully insured in order to qualify for retirement benefits. A person becomes fully insured by acquiring a sufficient number of quarters of coverage to meet either of the following two tests.

   a. A person is fully insured if he has 40 quarters of coverage (10 years of covered employment). Once a person has acquired 40 quarters of coverage, he is fully insured for life, even if he spends no further time in covered employment (or covered self employment).

   b. A person is fully insured if (1) he has at least six quarters of coverage and (2) he has acquired at least as many quarters of coverage as there are years elapsing after 1950 (or, if later, after the year in which he reaches age 21) and before the year in which he dies, becomes disabled, or reaches, or will reach age 62, whichever occurs first. A person can also become fully insured after retirement age if he acquires quarters of coverage after age 62.

3. **Currently insured** A person is currently insured if he has acquired at least six quarters of coverage during the full 13-quarter period ending with the calendar quarter in which he (1) died, (2) most recently became entitled to disability benefits, or (3) became entitled to retirement benefits.

   a. The six quarters of coverage need not be consecutive, but they must be acquired during the 13-quarter period.

   b. For example, Tom, who reached age 21 in 1988, died in March 2005. He had started to work in covered employment on November 1, 2002, and worked until his death. During that period, he acquired nine quarters of coverage. Tom was currently insured at death because he had more than the required six quarters of coverage in the 13-calendar quarter period.

4. **Primary insurance amount (PIA)** The primary insurance amount is equal to the worker's full retirement benefit at his or her normal retirement age.

C. **GOVERNMENT LIFE INSURANCE PROGRAMS** In addition to Social Security, the federal government operates several programs that provide life insurance, including the following.

   1. **Servicemen's Group Life Insurance (SGLI)** This program provides group life insurance for full-time members of the military while on active duty. The program is administered through a primary insurer that is licensed in all 50 states. Premiums paid by covered service members cover peacetime mortality costs while the costs connected with military hazards (i.e., armed conflicts) are paid by the federal government. Eligible members are covered for up to $100,000 of group term life without providing insurability. Members will be covered unless they elect not to have coverage.

   2. **Federal Employees Group Life Insurance (FEGLI)** This plan was established by the federal government in the 1950s to provide group life for all federal employees (unless they choose not to be covered). It functions in a manner similar to SGLI but is provided for a different segment of government employee (i.e., civil service).

VI. TAX TREATMENT OF INSURANCE PREMIUMS AND PROCEEDS

For the most part, life insurance has been granted favorable tax treatment by the Internal Revenue Service. Death benefits are usually excluded from a beneficiary's gross income.

A. **PREMIUMS** Premiums paid on an individual plan of life insurance are viewed as a personal expense and are not deductible. Those paid on group life plans are deductible by the employer if a noncontributory type plan is involved. These premiums are viewed as a business expense. If the group plan is contributory, premiums paid by the employee are usually not deductible.

   1. The premium for first $50,000 of coverage under a group life insurance plan (noncontributory) is not included in the employee's income for tax purposes. When an individual's group coverage exceeds $50,000, the value of the premiums on the additional

face amount is reportable as income by the employee. The economic benefit of coverage in excess of $50,0000 is calculated on a monthly basis and taxable to the employee.

B. PROCEEDS Life insurance policy death proceeds are generally exempt from income taxation, even though they may exceed the cost of the insurance (the premiums paid).

1. As a general rule, death benefits paid to a beneficiary are not subject to income taxation, except when part of those benefits are composed of interest payments. Such would be the case when an insurance company pays benefits under one of the installment settlement options: part of each payment is considered a nontaxable death benefit and part is treated as taxable interest income.

2. An exception to the general rule of beneficiaries receiving proceeds tax free would be in a case of a **transfer for value**—that is, when a policy is sold to another party. For example, assume Ann purchases an existing $20,000 policy on Bob's life from Bob for $6,000. If Bob dies, Ann would be taxed on the $14,000 "gain."

3. Life insurance proceeds are included in an insured's estate and are generally subject to federal estate taxation.

4. Dividends received are not taxable since they are considered a return of overpaid premiums.

C. CASH VALUES Cash value increases within a life insurance policy are not currently taxable to the policyowner. The investment gain (the extent to which cash values exceed premiums paid) is taxed at the termination (surrender) of the policy before death. This is known as the **cost recovery rule**.

1. Receipt of a portion of the policy's cash value in the form of a policy loan is not a taxable event; as a general rule, interest paid on a policy loan is not tax deductible. However, receipt of a portion of a policy's cash value (partial surrender) lowers the amount of the policyowner's investment (cost basis) in the policy.

2. If a policy loan is still outstanding when a policy is surrendered, the borrowed amount becomes taxable at the time of surrender to the extent the cash value exceeds the policyowner's investment (cost basis) in the contract.

D. 1035 EXCHANGE This involves Section 1035 of the Internal Revenue Code regarding exchanges of insurance contracts and affords the postponement of tax on certain exchanges. The law states that:

■ an ordinary life contract may be exchanged tax free for another life contract or for an endowment or annuity contract;

■ an endowment may be exchanged tax free for another endowment; and

■ an annuity may be exchanged tax free for another annuity contract.

E. TAXATION OF ANNUITIES Investment income earned on annuities during the accumulation phase is deferred until distributed to the annuity owner. Distributions (which represent a withdrawal of both interest and principal) are taxed to the extent that payments exceed the investment in the contract. A 10% penalty is imposed on "premature withdrawals" made before age 59½. Cash surrenders of annuities are taxed the same as life insurance policy surrenders.

1. **Exclusion ratio** Because each annuity payment an annuitant receives consists partly of nontaxable basis and taxable interest, a formula is used to determine the amount of each. This formula, known as the **exclusion ratio**, is:

$$\frac{\text{Investment in the annuity contract}}{\text{Expected return}}$$

The investment in the contract is the total of premiums or contributions paid by the owner into the annuity; the expected return is the total benefit amount that is anticipated will be paid to the annuitant. The resulting percentage is the amount of each payment that is excluded from tax.

2. An annuity's expected return or total benefit amount to be paid to the annuitant can be calculated by multiplying the sum of one year's payments by the life expectancy of the annuitant (or the life expectancy of two or more lives, if the contract is a joint annuity).

3. For example, John contributed $20,000 to his fixed deferred annuity over the years. At age 62, he annuitizes his contract and begins to receive benefits of $350 a month. John's life expectancy (based on IRS tables) is 16.9 years. His expected return from the contract is $70,980 ($350 × 12 × 16.9). Applying the formula to determine John's exclusion ratio, we see that 28% of each monthly annuity benefit ($98) will be excluded from tax; 72% ($252) will be taxed.

$$\frac{\$20,000 \text{ (investment in the contract)}}{\$70,980 \text{ (expected return)}} = 28\%$$

4. **Distributions at death** The tax treatment of annuity benefits upon the death of the annuitant depends on whether death occurs before or after annuitized payments begin.

   a. **Death after annuity start date** If an annuitant dies before receiving the full amount under a refund or period certain annuity, the beneficiary receiving the balance of the guaranteed amount will have no taxable income unless the amount received by the beneficiary plus the amount received tax free by the deceased annuitant exceeds the investment in the contract.

   b. **Death prior to annuity start date** Amounts payable under a deferred annuity contract at the death of an annuitant before annuitization will be taxed as ordinary income to the beneficiary to the extent that the death benefit exceeds the premiums paid. Beneficiaries can elect to annuitize the death benefit over their lifetimes and be taxed in accordance with the annuity exclusion ratio. (This election must be made within 60 days of the annuitant's death.)

5. **Estate taxation of annuities** If the annuity contractholder dies during the deferral period (before annuity payments begin), the entire account value is included in the gross estate (the basis for determining estate tax). If death occurs after annuity payments have begun and payments are to continue to a beneficiary (such as under the terms of an

annuity certain), the present value (discounted to today's dollars) of the future payments are included in the gross estate. If death occurs under a life-only arrangement where no payments continue after death, there is no value for estate tax purposes.

6. **Taxation of corporate-owned annuities** The tax-free (deferred) cash buildup within an annuity applies only to natural persons; income earned by a corporation that owns an annuity is treated as ordinary income for tax purposes and is taxable for the year earned. Therefore, annuities owned by an employer are not appropriate funding vehicles for nonqualified deferred compensation agreements.

7. Lump-sum cash distributions may result in a significant tax burden since income averaging is not available.

VII. OTHER INSURANCE CONCEPTS

One of the most important functions an insurance agent or producer performs is providing information to prospects and clients. In this regard, producers identify client insurance needs, ensure delivery of all required disclosure materials, show clients how different policies can be compared, and help determine how much insurance is called for, based on client needs.

A. **MARKETING LIFE INSURANCE** The start of an insurer's marketing function begins with home office input. Areas of coordination in the home office involve product development, underwriting, claims administration, service, public relations, and others.

1. **Considerations in selecting contract and options** A person should establish his primary life insurance needs when selecting a life insurance plan. This can be done with the help of a producer after an insurer has been selected. Examples of life insurance needs include cash value accumulation, emergency fund, education, retirement, and final expenses. Once a person determines the specific need(s), he can then carefully choose which insurer to purchase life insurance from.

   a. **A.M. Best** This organization provides financial, solvency, claims, and service information to help people in selecting a competent life insurer.

2. **Disclosure requirements** Most states require policy cost and benefit disclosure to prospective life insurance purchasers. Almost every state mandates that the prospect be provided with the following.

   a. **Buyer's Guide** This contains an explanation of life insurance products and how to shop for them.

   b. **Policy Summary** This contains pertinent data about the particular policy the prospect is considering, such as the premium, death benefit, cash values, dividends, etc. In addition, the effective policy loan interest rate must be stated and the 10- and 20-year surrender cost and net payment cost indices must be included.

   c. Policy illustrations Policy illustrations are financial projections of what could happen with a policy's value (cash values, death benefits) if the actual experience mirrored all of the assumed factors used to calculate the illustration. Policy illustrations are not an adequate tool for comparing costs of policies from different companies. Illustrations do not create accurate projections of future performance. Illustrations are not part of the contract and the values projected beyond guaranteed minimums are not guaranteed.

3. Life insurance policy cost comparison methods The primary objective of any method used to compare the cost of one life policy with another is to guide a prospective policyholder to a competitively priced policy. Two of the methods used are the following.

   a. Interest-adjusted net cost method This approach considers the time value of money in comparing life insurance costs by applying an interest adjustment to yearly premiums and dividends. Two versions of the interest-adjusted method are as follows.

      1.) The **surrender cost index** is an analysis conducted over a set time period (10 and 20 years typically) and considers a policy's premiums, death benefits, cash values, dividends, and an assumed interest rate (generally 5%).

      2.) The **net payment cost index** is an estimate of the average annual out-of-pocket net premium outlay (premium less annual dividend), adjusted by interest to reflect the point in time when premiums and dividends are paid during a 10- or 20-year period.

   b. Comparative interest rate method Also known as the Linton Yield Method, the comparative interest rate (CIR) is the rate of return that must be earned on a side fund in a buy term/invest the difference plan so that the value of the side fund will be equal exactly to the surrender value of the higher premium policy at a designated point in time. The higher the CIR, the less expensive the higher premium policy (e.g., whole life) relative to the alternative plan (e.g., term plus a side fund).

4. Overview of consumer considerations With help from the producer or agent, a buyer must determine his needs, the amount of insurance required, and the type of policy to be purchased. Before that, however, the buyer must choose an insurance company and a producer. Criteria applied to these decisions include:

- determining if the producer places the client's interest first;
- determining if the service provided is adequate; and
- determining the solvency and financial standing of the insurer.

B. **HUMAN LIFE VALUE (HLV) APPROACH** A means to gauge the amount of life insurance needed, human life value (HLV) is a measure of an individual's actual future earnings. (Human capital, which is closely related, is the production potential of a person.)

   1. HLV involves the measure of the value of benefits a deceased's dependents may expect from him throughout a normal working life. HLV also exists in any business entity whether it involves a partner, key person, or stockholder.

   2. HLV must be carefully appraised in order to determine the appropriate amount of life insurance needed.

   3. HLV has qualitative and quantitative characteristics.

   4. Life insurance can capitalize and indemnify a human life value.

   5. The HLV approach involves capitalizing (or converting to a single sum) that part of an individual's earning capacity that is devoted to the maintenance of survivors and dependents through the utilization of a life insurance contract. This helps to arrive at the amount of protection to purchase. Estimating this economic value involves several steps:
   - Arriving at the amount of earned income devoted to the family unit
   - Arriving at the working expectancy of the person (insured)
   - Selecting an appropriate capitalization rate
   - Capitalizing the amount of earned income at the selected rate for the working life expectancy

C. **NEEDS APPROACH** This method of determining the amount of needed insurance involves analyzing the numerous family needs that exist if the breadwinner were to die prematurely.

   1. Compared to HLV, this approach is probably more practical from a sales standpoint. A variety of factors are considered, including the individual's income, marital status, presence of children, the employable skills of dependents, and lifestyles.

   2. The specific **cash needs** that should be considered include:
   - an amount to cover costs associated with death, such as funeral expenses;
   - debt cancellation needs (an amount necessary to pay off debt rather than passing it along to heirs);
   - the determination of an appropriate amount to establish an emergency reserve fund (recommended by financial planners as being three to six months of living expenses);
   - an amount necessary to establish a retirement fund;
   - an amount necessary to make any desired bequests (a transfer of property through the operation of a will provision) to heirs at death; and
   - an amount necessary to establish an education fund for children; future educational expenses must be projected based on current tuition costs plus a factor for the anticipated rate of inflation.

3. When planning for the income needs of survivors, factors that should be considered include:

■ the death benefit required to replace the lost salary or the cost of service provided by the deceased person;

■ an amount necessary to provide income during the Social Security blackout period. This is the period from the time the youngest child in a family reaches age 18 until the spouse's Social Security retirement benefits begin at age 60 or 62 (no Social Security income benefits are paid to the surviving spouse during the blackout period); and

■ an amount necessary to retain a capital asset (such as a home) rather than forcing liquidation.

D. PROGRAMMING LIFE INSURANCE One of the more common tools used to determine the amount of life insurance needed involves a process known as **programming**. This process consists of a study of the individual's needs for capital resources and includes an assessment of the person's present financial position and future obligations and the life insurance used to meet these obligations.

E. ESTATE PLANNING This process involves all aspects of creating and liquidating a person's assets. It is hybrid of tax planning, asset distribution, and more.

1. Objectives of estate planning There are several objectives of estate planning including:

■ reducing the cost of asset (e.g., property) transfers;

■ arranging for the best method by which to pay transfer costs; and

■ finding the most efficient way in which to accomplish transfers.

2. Parties to estate planning Several individuals may be and should be involved in this process including a financial planner, an attorney, an insurance agent or producer, an accountant, and a bank trust officer.

3. Estate planning needs There are several needs that a family has following the death of a breadwinner. Some of these include food, clothing, and shelter (e.g., monthly mortgage payment) expenses; education costs; family maintenance; and so forth. The purpose of estate planning is not to provide funds for the maintenance of an insured since he is deceased.

F. UNISEX LEGISLATION IN LIFE INSURANCE The push toward unisex insurance rates has become stronger in recent years. Even though premium rates for life insurance covering females are less per $1,000 of coverage than that for males, the social issue involved may cause this to be altered. Many insurers have begun to utilize unisex rates in life (and disability) insurance.

UNIT QUIZ

1. Which of the following involves a third-party life insurance policy ownership situation?

   A. A wife owning her husband's contract
   B. A policyowner paying premiums on his own policy
   C. An insured's son who purchases his first life policy
   D. An employee who buys life insurance through an employer's plan

2. All of the following statements are true concerning group life insurance EXCEPT

   A. evidence of insurability is not required
   B. individuals covered by the plan are not parties to the contract
   C. a covered employee is the policyowner
   D. group coverage must be incidental to the formation of the group

3. In a contributory plan, what percentage of employees must participate in the plan before a policy will be issued?

   A. 50%
   B. 75%
   C. 90%
   D. 100%

4. A conversion privilege is an element of all group life contracts. An insured employee has how many days to convert to an individual plan once employment is terminated?

   A. 10
   B. 20
   C. 28
   D. 31

5. A group life insurance plan where an employer pays the entire cost is known as a

   A. contributory plan
   B. noncontributory plan
   C. credit life plan
   D. risk sharing plan

6. All of the following statements are correct regarding individual retirement accounts (IRAs) EXCEPT

   A. up to 100% of income may be contributed annually, subject to an annual limit
   B. income limits apply to those who establish traditional IRAs; age limits apply to those who establish Roth IRAs
   C. contributions accumulate tax-deferred and may be deductible in the year contributed
   D. proceeds may not be withdrawn, without penalty, before age 59½

7. Keogh plans are designed for and available to a(n)

   A. employer with more than 100 employees
   B. self-employed professional
   C. business owner who becomes disabled
   D. employee without a qualified plan

8. Bill is a school teacher who is participating in a TSA. Bill's contribution will be treated as a

   A. tax deduction
   B. tax credit
   C. salary reduction
   D. nontaxable income

9. Which of the following statements concerning split-dollar life insurance is TRUE?

   A. This type of plan does not require a permanent policy with a cash value.
   B. It is useful to the key employee who needs protection but has insufficient funds to meet this need.
   C. A split-dollar plan provides pure protection only.
   D. Split-dollar life provides pension benefits in addition to temporary protection.

10. Premiums paid on an individual life insurance policy are generally

    A. not deductible
    B. deductible
    C. contributory
    D. treated as an overpayment

DISCUSSION QUESTIONS

1. Discuss some of the important characteristics of group life insurance.

2. Compare contributory and noncontributory plans.

3. Briefly describe the purpose of group credit life.

4. Briefly describe the following:
    A. IRA
    B. Keogh plan
    C. TSA

5. Compare and contrast a defined benefit and defined contribution plan.

6. Why would a buy and sell agreement be important to a key employee? What is the best way in which to fund this agreement?

7. Provide an example illustrating how split-dollar life insurance works.

8. List several types of death benefits provided by Social Security.

9. Compare fully and currently insured status.

10. Compare the deductibility of premiums payable and proceeds receivable on individual and group life insurance plans. How are dividends on individual policies treated?

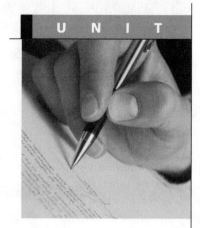

6

Life Insurance Practice Final Examination

Following your thorough study of Units 1 through 5 in this text, take this 50-question practice final on life insurance principles. Grade your performance using the answer key provided. Carefully review the information in this book pertaining to those questions answered incorrectly.

PRACTICE FINAL

1. Which of the following types of life insurance policies is designed to cover an entire family under one contract?

   A. Decreasing term
   B. Family income policy
   C. Family policy
   D. Multiple protection policy

2. John buys a $25,000 policy. John's agent tells him that as long as he is approved the coverage goes into effect immediately. What did John's agent give John?

   A. Consideration
   B. Conditional receipt
   C. Return of premium
   D. Binding receipt

3. The primary purpose of an annuity is to

   A. liquidate the separate account of an investment portfolio
   B. provide income for an individual's retirement
   C. provide income for a beneficiary
   D. create an estate immediately

4. Under what circumstances would an insurance applicant be asked to submit a signed statement of continued good health?

   A. When the initial premium is not submitted with the application
   B. When the policy is underwritten as substandard
   C. In order to receive a preferred rating
   D. When an inspection report is ordered

5. When a firm establishes a contributory group term life insurance contract, what percentage test must be met for the participation?

   A. 50%
   B. 60%
   C. 75%
   D. 100%

6. Vern owns a $10,000 term life policy. He paid the $200 annual premium on February 1. Vern fails to pay the second annual premium and dies on February 28 of the following year. How much will the beneficiary receive from Vern's insurance company?

   A. 0
   B. $8,000
   C. $9,800
   D. $10,000

7. All of the following statements are true with regard to the 10-day free look provision in a life insurance policy EXCEPT

   A. the 10-day free look period begins when the insured receives the contract
   B. an insured who returns the policy within the 10-day free look period will receive a full refund of premiums paid
   C. if a conditional receipt was issued, a pro rata refund will be made if the insured returns the policy within the free look period
   D. to get a refund, the policyholder must return the policy within 10 days from the date the policy was received

8. All of the following are common life insurance policy provisions EXCEPT

   A. entire contract clause
   B. insuring clause
   C. free look period
   D. premium deductibility option

9. Which of the following statements is TRUE concerning the Fair Credit Reporting Act?

   A. It provides that credit life insurance will be available to an applicant on an attained age basis.
   B. It provides additional funding for the cash savings value of a whole life policy.
   C. It provides that the applicant for insurance coverage will be informed if a consumer report is requested.
   D. It provides protection against creditors if the applicant defaults on a loan.

10. The underwriting department of a life insurance company acquires information on an applicant for life insurance coverage from all of the following sources EXCEPT

    A. agent's report
    B. the life insurance application
    C. Department of Motor Vehicles records
    D. Medical Information Bureau

11. To cover the contingency of a family breadwinner's death, all of the following would be appropriate applications for a decreasing term insurance policy EXCEPT

    A. to ensure that the family's 5-year-old son will have a source of funds for his college education
    B. to cover the family's mortgage
    C. to cover the family's car payments
    D. to ensure that the family's home improvement loan is covered

12. Pearl takes out a $100,000 permanent insurance policy on her life, naming her daughter, Juanita, as beneficiary. Five years after the policy was issued, Pearl dies and Juanita submits a claim to the insurer for the death benefit. Upon reviewing the claim, the insurer discovers that Pearl made a number of misstatements on the original application. The insurer will

    A. deny the claim entirely
    B. pay the full $100,000 to Juanita
    C. calculate any additional costs the company incurred due to the misstatements, deduct them from the death proceeds, and pay Juanita the balance
    D. require Juanita to substantiate the misstatements in order to be paid the full $100,000

13. An insured may receive protection against the unintentional lapse of his life insurance contract by requesting the

    A. cash savings amount
    B. extended term option
    C. "at interest" option
    D. automatic premium loan

14. Under a group life insurance policy, an employee demonstrates his evidence of participation by producing a

    A. master policy
    B. certificate of insurance
    C. group policy
    D. premium receipt

15. Ken takes a loan from the cash value of his life policy and then dies. The insurance company will typically pay

    A. face amount minus the interest and loan amount
    B. the death benefit of the policy
    C. not less than $10,000
    D. the death benefit after receiving the loan balance from the beneficiary

16. An individual engaged in a hazardous occupation who applies for a life insurance policy may be treated by the insurer in which of the following ways?

    A. The application will be rejected.
    B. Dividends normally paid will be withdrawn.
    C. The policy will be issued but rated up.
    D. A fixed period option must be implemented in order for the policy to be issued.

17. A retired person purchases an annuity for $90,000. One month later, he starts to receive payments. Based solely on these facts, what type of annuity does he have?

    A. Immediate
    B. Cash payment
    C. Life only
    D. Interest only

18. An agreement to purchase a deceased partner's share of a business that is usually funded by life insurance best describes a

    A. Keogh plan
    B. split-dollar plan
    C. buy and sell agreement
    D. key employee life insurance

19. Jay owns a $100,000 whole life insurance policy with an additional $100,000 accidental death rider attached to it. While driving to work Jay suffers a massive heart attack and dies instantly. His auto then runs off the road and crashes down an embankment. How much will his policy pay to the beneficiary?

    A. $0
    B. $100,000
    C. $150,000
    D. $200,000

20. Darren owns a $50,000 whole life policy. He wants to stop paying premiums, but wants to continue having insurance protection for the remainder of his life. Which of the following options should he select?

    A. Reduced paid-up insurance nonforfeiture option
    B. Contract's policy loan option
    C. Extended term nonforfeiture option
    D. Paid-up additions dividend option

21. Kevin submits his initial premium to his agent. Kevin's agent gives Kevin a conditional receipt. When will Kevin's policy go into effect?

    A. When his check is received by the insurance company's home office
    B. When the policy is delivered to Kevin
    C. When Kevin's check clears his bank
    D. When Kevin takes his required medical exam, premium is received, and the policy is approved by underwriting

22. Linda is 27 years old. She wants to take advantage of market-linked interest rates, and she wants to be able to make additional premium contributions throughout the year. What would be the best type of policy for Linda?

    A. Modified endowment
    B. Straight whole life
    C. Variable universal life
    D. Current assumption whole life

23. An applicant for a whole life insurance policy applies for an accidental death provision in addition to the basic contract. The underwriting department lists this applicant as a standard risk. Assuming that coverage is issued, all of the following statements are correct with regard to the benefits that will be paid by the policy in the event of the applicant's death EXCEPT

    A. if the insured dies in an accident at age 60, the accidental death benefit is payable
    B. the accidental death benefit amount is usually twice the face amount of the policy
    C. the benefit will be paid even if death resulted from an act of war
    D. death must occur within 90 days of the accident

24. Which of the following is accurate with regard to the misstatement of age provision?

    A. If an applicant unintentionally misstates his age on the application no action will be taken by the insurer
    B. Any misstatement of age on an application will result in a benefit adjustment
    C. If a misstatement of age occurs on an application for life or health insurance, a pro rata refund of premium will be made to the insured or be paid to the insurer
    D. All of the above

25. Guy purchases a whole life contract with a face amount of $100,000. Guy may name which of the following as a beneficiary?

    A. His wife
    B. His niece
    C. A favorite charity
    D. All of the above

26. If an insured understated her age and this error is discovered upon her death the insurer will

    A. refund all past premiums paid with any accumulated interest
    B. refuse to pay the face amount of the contract
    C. pay an amount equivalent to that which the premium would have purchased at the correct age
    D. pay the face amount of the contract with a deduction for the amount of the under paid premium

27. The most common method for the payment of life insurance death benefits is the
    A. fixed-amount option
    B. life income option
    C. fixed-period option
    D. lump-sum cash option

28. Fred, age 39, buys an endowment at age 65 policy and names his wife as his only beneficiary. His wife dies 10 years later. Fred dies at age 61, leaving a 32-year-old son and a 30-year-old daughter. The policy proceeds will go to
    A. Fred's son, who is the first-born child
    B. both children, who share equally on a per capita basis
    C. Fred's wife or her estate
    D. Fred's estate

29. Alex owns a $50,000 whole life policy. At age 47, Alex decides to cancel his policy and exercise the extended term option with the policy's cash value. He will receive a term policy with a face value of
    A. $25,000
    B. $50,000
    C. $100,000
    D. the face amount cannot be determined from the information given

30. The insuring clause found in a life insurance contract states which of the following?
    A. The promise that the insurer will pay a stated amount to a named beneficiary after receiving proof of death of an insured
    B. The location where the insurer is domiciled
    C. The date coverage is to take effect
    D. That coverage is effective with payment of the first premium

31. The term used to indicate that a policy's beneficiary cannot be changed is
    A. tertiary
    B. contingent
    C. irrevocable
    D. permanent

32. If a primary beneficiary predeceases an insured, the individuals to whom the proceeds are paid are referred to as the
    A. contingent beneficiaries
    B. collateral beneficiaries
    C. revocable beneficiaries
    D. subsequent beneficiaries

33. The waiver of premium provision in a life insurance policy applies
    A. if the insured becomes disabled
    B. if the policyowner becomes disabled
    C. if the policyowner suffers a financial hardship
    D. when premiums paid exceed the policy's face amount

34. The settlement option that provides for payments to be made in regular installments to a beneficiary until the principal and interest are exhausted best describes
    A. life income
    B. interest only
    C. fixed income
    D. fixed amount

35. Which of the following statements is NOT correct regarding taxation of life insurance?
    A. Dividends themselves are not taxable, but any interest paid on the dividends is taxable as received.
    B. The interest paid on policy loans is tax deductible in the year or years paid.
    C. A lump-sum benefit received by a beneficiary upon death of the individual insured is not taxable as income.
    D. Upon surrender of a policy, the policyowner is taxed on the amount by which the cash value exceeds the sum of premiums paid.

36. In order to reinstate a lapsed life insurance policy, all of the following may be required EXCEPT
    A. all back premiums must be paid
    B. all cash values taken from the lapsed policy must be repaid
    C. the insured may have to provide proof of insurability
    D. a new contestable period may apply to the reinstated policy

37. All of the following statements regarding a 403(b) plan are correct EXCEPT

    A. employees of nonprofit organizations qualify for this type of plan
    B. this type of plan involves a salary reduction rather than a deduction
    C. government employees are eligible for this type of plan
    D. parochial school teachers qualify for participation

38. In a policy insuring the life of a child, which of the following allows the premiums to be waived in the event of the death or disability of the person responsible for premium payments?

    A. Waiver of premium provision
    B. Reduction of premium option
    C. Payor provision
    D. Reduced paid-up option

39. An insured died during the grace period of her life insurance policy and had not paid the required annual premium. The insurance company is obligated to pay which of the following to the beneficiary?

    A. The cash value of the policy, if any
    B. The full face amount of the policy
    C. The face amount of the policy less the annual payment
    D. A refund of any premium paid

40. All other factors being equal, which of the following lists from the largest annual premium to the smallest annual premium?

    A. 20-pay life, 20-year level term, 20-year decreasing term, 20-year endowment
    B. 20-year endowment, 20-year level term, 20-year decreasing term, 20-pay life
    C. 20-year endowment, 20-year decreasing term, 20-year level term, 20-pay life
    D. 20-year endowment, 20-pay life, 20-year level term, 20-year decreasing term

41. A 20-year family income policy was purchased effective April 1, last year. The insured died on August 1, last year. The beneficiary receives monthly income for

    A. 20 years
    B. 10 years
    C. 19 years and 8 months
    D. 9 years and 8 months

42. Generally, premiums paid on an individual life insurance policy are

    A. deductible
    B. not tax deductible
    C. assignable
    D. nonqualified

43. Andrew is the insured under a $150,000 life insurance policy. He has designated his wife as the primary beneficiary of the policy, his two children as contingent beneficiaries, and his alma mater, Homestead U., as tertiary beneficiary. Which of the following correctly describes how the proceeds will be distributed at his death?

    A. Wife, $50,000; children, $25,000 each; Homestead U., $50,000
    B. Wife, $100,000; children, $12,500 each; Homestead U., $50,000
    C. Wife, $100,000; children, $25,000 each
    D. Wife, $150,000

44. Under what type of life insurance policy will the death benefit vary, based on the performance of an underlying portfolio of securities?

    A. Variable life
    B. Universal life
    C. Current assumption whole life
    D. Term life

45. All of the following are typical requirements imposed on those who participate in a group life insurance plan EXCEPT

    A. submitting to a medical exam
    B. full-time employment status
    C. contributing to any premium requirement through a payroll deduction arrangement
    D. satisfying a probationary waiting period before enrolling in the plan

46. If the beneficiary of a life insurance policy predeceases the insured 2 hours before his death and the insured has named no other beneficiary, the common disaster clause would

    A. prevent the proceeds from going into the estate of the beneficiary
    B. provide that the proceeds go directly to the estate of the beneficiary
    C. allow the probate court to decide where the proceeds should go
    D. provide that the proceeds be shared equally between the insured's estate and the beneficiary's estate

47. Which of the following statements is CORRECT regarding a renewable term life insurance policy?

    A. An insurer must renew a renewable term policy at the policyowner's request regardless of the insurability status of the insured.
    B. When a renewable term insurance policy is renewed, the statements on the application once again become contestable for a 2-year period.
    C. Renewal premiums are based on the insured's age at the time of the original application.
    D. The cost of this type of term policy is lower due to a decrease in the chance of adverse selection.

48. Which of the following statements is CORRECT regarding a revocable beneficiary?

    A. A revocable beneficiary may not be changed by the policyowner without the consent of that beneficiary.
    B. A revocable beneficiary receives policy proceeds in the event that the primary beneficiary predeceases the insured.
    C. All policy rights are relinquished when a revocable beneficiary is named.
    D. The policyowner may change the beneficiary without his knowledge or approval.

49. Debbi has decided to cash in her $50,000 life insurance policy and use the $15,000 in surrendered cash values to purchase a single premium annuity. Which of the following descriptions of the income tax treatment of this transaction is CORRECT?

    A. Under Section 1035, the transaction will require Debbi to recognize $15,000 as taxable income in the year the transaction takes place.
    B. Under Section 1035, the transaction requires Debbi to recognize $15,000 as taxable income, but allows her to spread the tax liability over the next five years.
    C. Under Section 1035, the transaction requires Debbi to recognize $15,000 as a capital gain in the year the transaction takes place.
    D. Under Section 1035, the transaction is considered a nontaxable event.

50. Regarding the agent's duties and responsibilities at the time of the application, which of the following is NOT correct?

    A. To probe beyond the specific questions if he feels the applicant is misrepresenting or concealing information
    B. To check to make sure that there are no unanswered questions on the application
    C. To change an incorrect statement on the application by personally initialing next to the corrected statement
    D. To explain the nature and type of any receipt he is giving to the applicant

ANSWERS AND RATIONALES

1. **C** A family policy is designed to cover an entire family under one contract. Whole life coverage is provided to the primary wage earner (either husband or wife) and term insurance is used to cover the spouse and children.

2. **B** Under a conditional receipt, coverage becomes effective on the date the application is approved for the plan applied for, the amount of coverage applied for, and the premium rate applied for. Coverage may also depend on the results of a medical exam which, if acceptable to the insurer, mark the effective date of coverage.

3. **B** An annuity provides income to a person (the annuitant) while he is alive and thus is an effective way to provide for a person's retirement. It differs from life insurance, which provides income to survivors upon the death of the insured.

4. **A** A signed statement of continued good health is normally required when the initial premium is not submitted with the insurance application. The purpose is to ensure that the insured has remained in good health during the underwriting period.

5. **C** If the premium is shared by the employer and employee, at least 75% of all eligible employees must participate in the plan before the policy may be issued.

6. **C** The grace period in life insurance contracts is usually 31 days. If proceeds are paid during the grace period, any outstanding premium owed to the insurer will be deducted from the face amount of the contract.

7. **C** The free look period is granted whether or not a conditional receipt was issued. Furthermore, if the policy is returned within the period, the insured is entitled to a full refund, not to a pro rata portion of it.

8. **D** There is no provision that allows for the deductibility of insurance premiums. In fact, as a general rule, premiums for individual life policies are not deductible. They may be deductible for certain forms of business-owned insurance, but that is not a clause in the policy.

9. **C** The Fair Credit Reporting Act states that when an applicant is denied coverage due to information obtained from a third-party source, the applicant will be informed of the source.

10. **C** Life insurance companies may draw upon primary sources to compile information on applicants for life insurance coverage. These include the application, medical examinations, inspection reports, and the agent's report.

11. **A** Decreasing term insurance provides for a declining amount of insurance over its term. It is appropriate to cover loans or obligations that decrease over time. It is not appropriate to provide for amounts that will not decrease over time, such as a future amount to cover college tuition.

12. **B** Due to the standard incontestable clause included in all insurance policies, the insurer has only 2 years from issue to dispute the statements in an insurance application. After that time (typically 2 years from issue), the insurer cannot challenge any statements made by the applicant on the application nor require the beneficiary to substantiate any statements.

13. **D** The automatic premium loan provision protects the policyowner against the inadvertent lapse of the contract. If the cash value is sufficient, a loan in the amount equal to premium due is subtracted from the cash value to pay the premium.

14. **B** Since the employer is the policyowner and pays the premium, it receives the master policy. Employees covered by the group life insurance

policy do not receive a policy. They are given a certificate of coverage instead.

15. **A** Any policy loan outstanding at the time of the insured's death reduces the policy proceeds. The outstanding loan is subtracted from the face amount of the contract and the remainder paid to the beneficiary.

16. **C** Substandard risks present the insurer with additional exposures to loss that may be due to adverse health conditions, moral hazards, or hazardous occupations or avocations. These risks are usually issued rated policies (policies that are issued with a higher than standard premium).

17. **A** An immediate annuity will make its first benefit payment one payment interval from the date of purchase.

18. **C** Buy-sell agreements help with the orderly continuation of a business where survivors receive a fair cash settlement for a deceased owner's interest. Life insurance is the most common way to fund these agreements. The proceeds guarantee that the necessary cash to pay for the deceased owner's interest will be available.

19. **B** The accidental death rider pays a benefit if the insured dies from an accident. In this case, Jay died from the heart attack before his auto crashed. Therefore, his estate is entitled only to the $100,000 death benefit of the base policy.

20. **A** Under a life insurance policy's reduced paid-up insurance nonforfeiture option, the cash value of an existing policy is used as a single premium payment to purchase a paid-up permanent policy of a lesser face amount. The paid-up policy will remain in force without any additional premium payments.

21. **D** Under a conditional receipt, coverage becomes effective on the date the application is approved for the plan applied for, the amount of coverage applied for, and the premium rate applied for. Coverage may also depend on the results of a medical exam which, if acceptable to the insurer, mark the effective date of coverage.

22. **C** A variable universal life insurance policy is a hybrid of variable and universal life insurance. It offers a combination of investment options, a flexible premium and expense deduction method, and a guaranteed death benefit. It is considered to be the ultimate interest-sensitive product, in part because it combines the marketable features of both variable and universal life insurance.

23. **C** An accidental death benefit clause or rider will not pay a multiple death benefit if the insured died from certain illegal activities; aviation activities, except as a passenger traveling on commercial airlines; where an accident was involved with illness, disease, or mental infirmity; or from an act of war.

24. **B** Under the misstatement of age provision, if the insured's age is stated incorrectly in the application, amounts payable will be adjusted to an amount that the premium would have purchased at the correct age. An adjustment is involved whether the age was misstated to be higher or lower than the insured's actual age.

25. **D** One of the rights of policy ownership is the right to name a beneficiary. Any person, natural or legal (such as a corporation), may be named a beneficiary of a life insurance policy.

26. **C** Under the misstatement of age provision, if the insured's age is stated incorrectly in the application, amounts payable will be adjusted to an amount that the premium would have purchased at the correct age. An adjustment is involved (benefit or premium) whether the age was misstated to be higher or lower than the insured's actual age.

27. **D** The most common way in which life insurance proceeds are paid is as a single, lump-sum cash settlement.

28. **D** Fred's wife was the sole beneficiary named in his policy. When she died, the policy was left without a beneficiary. Fred would have been wise to name their son and daughter contingent beneficiaries in the event his wife predeceased him. Because he did not, the death benefit will be paid to his estate.

29. **B** As a nonforfeiture option, extended term insurance permits the policyowner to have the insurer use the existing cash value to buy term insurance equal to the face amount of the original policy with a single net premium. Therefore, Alex's cash value will buy a term insurance policy with a face amount of $50,000, the same as the face amount of the whole life policy he cancelled.

30. **A** The insuring clause in a life insurance policy states that the insurer will provide life insurance protection for the named insured that will be paid to a designated beneficiary when proof of death is received by the insurer.

31. **C** When an insured makes a beneficiary designation that is irrevocable, the designation cannot be changed without the consent of the named beneficiary. Regardless of the designation, the policyowner retains all other rights of ownership.

32. **A** The contingent beneficiary receives the face amount of the insured's life insurance policy if the primary beneficiary predeceases the insured. This secondary beneficiary will receive the face amount of the policy if the primary beneficiary is not living at the time the insured dies.

33. **B** The waiver of premium provision in a life insurance policy, available for an additional premium, provides for the discontinuance of premium payments if the policyowner becomes totally disabled for a specific period of time (typically 90 days).

34. **D** Under the fixed amount settlement option, a fixed amount of income is designated to be paid at specific intervals. This amount is continued until the proceeds and any interest earned are exhausted.

35. **B** Life insurance policy proceeds are generally exempt from income taxation, even though they may exceed the cost of the insurance (the premiums paid). Any payment made to a beneficiary out of policy proceeds (such as a death benefit) is not taxable. Any interest accrued and paid is taxable. Policy dividends paid to the policyowner are not taxable since they are considered a return of overpaid premiums. Policy loans are not deductible.

36. **B** In order to reinstate a lapsed whole life insurance policy, the cash values must be intact. If the policy's values had been taken, the policy would not have been cancelled. If the policy is a universal life policy, cash values could have been withdrawn. They do not have to be repaid in order to reinstate the policy.

37. **C** Employees of qualified (tax-exempt) organizations are permitted, under the Internal Revenue Code, to contribute funds to 403(b) plans with tax-free dollars. Those eligible for tax-sheltered annuities include public, private, and parochial school teachers, school superintendents, college professors, clergymen, and social workers. Government employees are not eligible.

38. **C** For an additional premium, the payor benefit, provision, or clause may be added as a rider to a life insurance contract. It provides for the continuance of coverage on the life of a juvenile in the event or total disability of the individual responsible for paying the premiums (a parent or guardian).

39. **C** The grace period continues coverage after the date on which the premium is due. Since coverage continues, the face amount of the policy will be paid to the beneficiary if the insured dies during this period. However, any outstanding premium owed to the insurer will be deducted from the face amount of the policy.

40. **D** A 20-year endowment leaves a relatively short time span in which to endow the policy, and therefore the highest annual premiums. A 20-pay whole life insurance policy similarly requires the insured to pay all of the premiums within 20 years, a relatively short time. A 20-year level term policy provides a straight, level benefit amount for a level premium subject to increase as the insured ages. A 20-year decreasing term policy has the lowest premium due to the fact that the face amount decreases as the rate per unit of insurance increases. The premium remains constant through the term of the policy.

41. **C** Family income policies provide for monthly income payments to the beneficiary, beginning at the death of the insured and continuing to the end of the original policy period. The monthly benefit period is measured from the date on which the coverage began. In this case, the insured died 4 months after coverage began, so the beneficiary will receive monthly income from the policy for 19 years and 8 months.

42. **B** Premiums paid on an individual life insurance policy are considered personal expenses by the IRS and are not deductible from the individual's ordinary income.

43. **D** The primary beneficiary (or beneficiaries) of a life insurance policy stand first in line to receive the proceeds at the insured's death. Only if the primary beneficiary predeceases the insured will the contingent beneficiary receive any proceeds, and only if both the primary and contingent beneficiary predecease the insured will a tertiary beneficiary receive any proceeds.

44. **A** Variable life insurance is a combination of insurance product and securities product whose cash values are invested in an underlying account comprised of securities. The performance of the securities determines the product's values (death benefit as well as cash value).

45. **A** Full-time employment status, satisfying a probationary period and contributing to any premium, if the group plan is contributory, are all common requirements for participating in a group life insurance plan. Submitting to a medical exam or providing proof of insurability are not.

46. **A** The common disaster clause of a life insurance policy stipulates that, in case of death in a common accident, the insured is presumed to have survived the beneficiary. This prevents the payment of the insurance proceeds to the estate of the beneficiary and thus permits the proceeds to be distributed to any contingent beneficiaries or wherever else provided for by the policy. This clause also reduces estate taxes because the proceeds will not be taxed in both estates.

47. **A** A renewable term life insurance policy allows the insured to renew the policy at the end of the term without providing evidence of insurability. Renewal premiums are based on the insured's attained age. An age limitation is usually included, so that the insured may not renew the policy indefinitely.

48. **D** A revocable beneficiary may be changed by the policyowner at any time and for any reason without the beneficiary's knowledge or consent.

49. **D** Section 1035 of the Internal Revenue Code allows for the exchange of the following as nontaxable transactions: a life insurance policy exchanged for another life insurance policy or for an endowment or an annuity; an endowment policy exchanged for another endowment policy; and an annuity exchanged for another annuity.

50. **C** Any changes made to an insurance application after it is completed by the applicant must be initialed by the applicant. Some insurers also require that the agent initial changes made to the application. These signatures protect the insurer in the event a dispute arises and the applicant or the agent does not recall the changes that were made.

UNIT

7

Introduction to Health Insurance and Types of Policies

KEY TERMS

Total Disability	Surgical Expense	PSO
Own Disability	Major Medical	Dental Expense
Partial Disability	Coinsurance	Long-Term Care
Presumptive Disability	Common Accident	Group Health
Commercial Health	Stop Loss	Group Underwriting
Private Health	Comprehensive	Group Disability
Disability Income	HMO	ERISA
Business Overhead	MEWA	HIPAA
Group Credit	Service Organizations	ADEA
Basic Hospital	PPO	

I.   INTRODUCTION TO HEALTH INSURANCE

The primary source of health insurance protection is provided by commercial, for-profit companies that write individual and group health insurance. Health insurance is also offered by nonprofit organizations (Blue Cross) and through government programs (Social Security).

A.   RISK AND HEALTH INSURANCE The same basic principles dealing with risk and health insurance are similar to those in life insurance. Concepts such as the law of large numbers, insurable interest, indemnity, and rate making are also very similar to life insurance. Any difference will be reviewed in the appropriate areas.

B.   PRODUCERS/AGENTS Those who solicit accident and health insurance have the same duties (binding, recordkeeping, etc.) and responsibilities as life producers or agents.

   1. For example, information regarding a producer's binding authority and the types of receipts used (conditional and binding) in health insurance are similar to that found in life insurance.

   2. A producer's underwriting responsibility (field underwriting) and his potential liabilities, loss ratios, and the general nature of underwriting in health insurance is similar to life insurance in many ways. Differences will be reviewed accordingly.

C.   LEGAL CONTRACTS Contract law principles, insurance contract features (e.g., adhesion, aleatory, etc.) reviewed in Unit 1, as well as information regarding representations, warranties, and so forth reviewed in Unit 3 also apply to health insurance.

D.   ECONOMIC VALUE The primary purpose of health insurance, like life insurance, is to protect the individual and the family unit. Families depend upon a breadwinner for their income. As in life insurance, human life values must be taken into consideration. In the health insurance realm, human life is subject to loss due to temporary or permanent disability and medical expenses. Not only will these persons have to be adequately protected in order to meet hospitalization and other medical expenses, but they must also be protected against a loss of earnings or income as well.

E.   COMMERCIAL HEALTH INSURANCE This type of health insurance is provided by life, health, and some casualty insurance companies. These companies offer individual and group policies of health insurance including medical expense and disability income.

   1. Individual and group health Policies such as basic hospital expense, surgical expense, hospital confinement, major medical, basic medical expense, comprehensive medical, and so forth may be purchased on an individual or group basis.

   2. Coverages The scope of coverage provided may involve basic coverages or comprehensive or broad type coverages. Coverages provided by each provider will be discussed in the appropriate sections of this text.

F.   PRIVATE (NONCOMMERCIAL) HEALTH PROVIDERS Plans offered by these companies are created on a profit or nonprofit basis to provide hospital, surgical, and other medical benefits. These types of plans maybe utilized by employers, hospitals, unions, and others.

> **TAKE ✓ NOTE**
>
> Types of health insurance policies include disability income, credit, AD&D, medical expense, dental, and long-term care.

1. The most common type is Blue Cross and Blue Shield.

2. Other forms include but are not limited to health maintenance organizations (HMOs), preferred provider organizations (PPOs), and independent practice associations (IPAs).

G. TYPES OF LOSSES AND BENEFITS There are several types of accident and health losses to be insured, including loss of income, accidental death and dismemberment, medical and hospitalization costs, dental, and other limited health exposures.

II. TYPES OF ACCIDENT AND HEALTH INSURANCE POLICIES AND PROVIDERS

Accident and health insurance refers to the broad field of insurance plans that provide protection against the financial consequences of illness, accidents, injury, and disability. Health insurance claims payments to insureds amount to billions of dollars every year.

Within the health insurance arena, three distinct categories of insurance exist: disability income insurance, medical expense insurance, and accidental death and dismemberment insurance.

A. DEFINITIONS OF DISABILITY

1. Total disability Under individual or group DI policies, insureds are considered to be **totally disabled** if they cannot perform the duties of their own occupation for a specific period of time.

a. In previous years, many disability income contracts specified this period of time as two years. After this two-year period expired, an individual would be considered totally disabled only if he were unable to engage in *any* occupation (nonoccupational definition) for which he was suited by training, education, and experience.

b. Many insurers now offer total disability coverage in an individual's own occupation for up to 5 years, 10 years, to age 65, or life, depending upon the insured's occupation classification. An own occupation definition of total disability entitles an insured to receive benefits even if they are earning an income by working at another occupation.

c. There are varying stages of disability including permanent total, temporary total, permanent partial, and temporary partial.

2. Partial disability According to health insurance contracts, **partial disability** is the inability to perform one or more important duties of an insured's occupation. Partial disability benefits are usually 50% of the total disability monthly benefit.

a. An individual who purchases a disability income contract paying $2,000 per month if disabled would receive 50% of this amount, or $1,000 per month for partial disability.

b. In addition, the maximum benefit period allowed for partial disability is short in comparison to total disability. The most common benefit periods are three and six months.

3. Presumptive disability Many disability income contracts include coverage for other forms of disability known as **presumptive disability**. Forms of presumptive disability must usually be medically defined in the contract and include loss of:

- sight;
- hearing;
- speech; or
- two limbs.

Benefits for these losses are generally provided and payable for the length of the benefit period or lifetime, without the requirement that the claimant no longer be earning income. However, some insurers require a loss of earnings test before benefits are payable.

4. Residual disability A residual disability benefit provides a reduced monthly benefit in proportion to an insured's loss of income when he has begun working again after (or during) a disability, but at reduced earnings. In most policies, this benefit is payable only when the insured has returned to his job (and is engaged in his normal occupation). An additional premium is charged for this benefit.

a. For example, an individual owns a disability income policy with a residual disability rider and incurs a 60% loss of income while disabled. The policy would pay 60% of the insured's specified maximum benefit. If the policy paid $2,000 per month for a total disability, the insured would receive $1,200 per month for residual disability.

b. In most cases, no benefits are paid with a residual benefit if the loss of income is less than 20 or 25%.

B. DISABILITY INCOME INSURANCE Disability income insurance (also referred to as income replacement, loss of income, and loss of time insurance) is intended to replace a portion of the insured's earned income (typically 70%) by providing periodic indemnity payments (monthly benefits) while the insured is disabled due to accident or illness. The determination of total benefits paid is based upon the dollar benefit amount selected by an insured for disability, the elimination period (or waiting period) involved, and the maximum benefit period (the time during which benefits are paid) applied for, such as two years, five years, to age 65, or for life.

1. Individual disability income policy An individual disability income contract is one whose premium is paid by the individual insured. This type of policy protects against economic loss that an individual or family may suffer due to the total disability of the wage earner. Disability has sometimes been termed a "living death" due to the fact that it can create additional expenses for an individual and family.

a. Premiums payable on an individual disability income contract are generally not tax deductible.

b. Premium rates are determined per $100 of monthly income benefit, the waiting period selected, the length of the benefit period, the applicant's age, sex (in some states), occupation, income, and whether the applicant has any other current disability income policies in force.

c. The **elimination** (or waiting**) period** under a disability income policy is the time immediately following the onset of a disability when benefits are not payable. Elimination periods eliminate claims for very short-term disabilities for which the insured usually can manage without financial hardship. These periods vary by policy, from one week to one year. The elimination period under most policies is typically 30 days.

d. Many riders are available that may be added to an individual disability income contract to provide additional coverages such as partial disability, residual disability, guaranteed insurability, nondisabling injury benefits, and cost of living adjustments. (These will be discussed in detail in Unit 8.)

e. **Disability underwriting** Understandably, the disability income underwriting decision process is somewhat unique due to the nature of the product. Some of the more unique aspects include the following.

   1.) Occupational considerations are of significant importance; the less hazardous and more stable the occupation, the better the risk. Occupations are rated by class; the less hazardous occupations such as physicians, attorneys, and other professionals are rated more favorably than the more hazardous occupations such as carpenters, plumbers, and electricians.

   2.) The most hazardous occupations are generally grouped by companies in a class of uninsurable risks that would include window washers, firemen, and roofers.

   3.) Benefit (limits) amounts that may be purchased are based on the applicant's net earned income and are generally limited to a percentage of net earned income (70 to 90%) to control over-utilization and malingering. Rarely will a company cover 100% of an insured's earned income.

   4.) Policy issuance alternatives may be employed to provide coverage for an individual who would otherwise be uninsurable. For example, an individual with a mild heart condition might be issued a disability income policy with an extra premium (rate-up) charged or with an exclusion rider that would eliminate coverage for any resulting disability related to the heart condition.

   5.) Disability income starter plans for professionals are offered by some companies. These plans offer lower premiums to get the younger professional started, either in the form of a low, level premium for a set number of years (usually five) before increasing, or on an annual renewable schedule that starts low and then increases each year.

f. Disability exclusions Common exclusions under disability income contracts include loss (injury or sickness) due to war, intentionally self-inflicted injuries, injuries suffered while committing a felony, loss while engaged as a pilot of an aircraft, injuries sustained while serving in the military, and occupational injuries (which are covered by workers' compensation).

g. Computation of monthly benefit Assume that an individual owns a disability income contract paying $2,000 per month for five years in the event that the insured is totally disabled. This contract also has a 30-day waiting period. The insured becomes disabled for 45 days. He would collect $1,000. In other words, he would collect one half of the monthly benefit because he was disabled for one half of one month following the waiting period.

> **1.)** Most insurers express elimination and benefit periods for accidental injury and illness separately. For example, a contract may indicate a seven-day elimination period for accidental injury and a 30-day elimination period for illness.

h. Rehabilitation benefit The insured is reimbursed for any rehabilitation expenses for a company-approved program in addition to the total disability benefit.

i. Disability income protects against loss of income due to injury or covered illness. Benefits are usually provided on a monthly basis although lump-sum benefits may be provided by presumptive disability and so forth.

j. Coverage benefit periods for individual DI policies are generally the following: 18 months; 24 months; 30 months; 5 years (60 months); 10 years (120 months); up to age 65; and for life. The longer the benefit period selected, the higher the premium.

k. Generally, disability income benefits for illness and accidental injury are only payable when the insured is under a doctor's care.

l. Recognizing that many individuals continue to work after age 65, some companies permit the contract to continue, provided the insured remains actively at work, to age 70 or 72.

2. Business overhead expense policy (BOE) Another form of disability income insurance is a **business overhead expense contract**. This policy does not provide income replacement in the same sense as an individual disability income policy. Its intent is not to replace earned income when an insured is totally disabled. Rather, a BOE policy is designed to provide a mechanism for covering the business overhead expenses that continue when the business owner is disabled.

a. Examples of these business expenses include the reimbursement of actual expenses for rent, employee benefits, utilities, depreciation, and other normal fixed expenses.

b. Most BOE contracts have 30-day elimination periods and benefit periods between one and two years.

    c. Business overhead expense policies are written on a reimbursement basis. This is in contrast to individual disability income contracts that are written on an indemnity basis.

    d. BOE policies provide monthly payments based on the actual expenses incurred by the business.

3. Business health insurance The various forms of business health insurance are closely related to the business uses of life insurance. Some of the more common types are the following.

    a. Key-employee disability insurance When a key employee of a corporation becomes totally disabled, a business may suffer serious economic losses. These loss exposures may be offset by purchasing key-employee disability income insurance. This type of contract is important as it protects the business against the inability to perform by the key employee and eases any economic burden that may exist if the disabled employee's salary and other benefits continue during a period of disability.

        1.) Some companies handle this exposure by instituting salary continuation programs where a company funds the disability income plan out of its earnings. Disability income plans may be funded by individual policies or group disability income contracts.

        2.) Premiums When an employer pays the premium on a disability income contract covering a key employee, the premiums paid are not tax deductible to the employer but benefits received are income tax-free.

    b. Group credit health insurance This type of coverage is also referred to as **group credit disability income insurance**. It is the health insurance equivalent to group credit life insurance. It is primarily used in debtor/creditor relationships where large amounts of funds are borrowed. This health contract will protect a lender in the event that borrowers become disabled and cannot meet their monthly payments. This policy would be issued to and paid for by the lender. The amount of coverage may not be more than the total sum of payments due from the borrower. A debtor or borrower is not required to purchase this coverage. This will usually be done by the creditor or lender.

    c. Disability buy-sell policy Structuring a business buy-sell arrangement in the event of disability is similar to that which covers the eventuality of death. Specific policies have been developed for this purpose that provide a substantial payout either in lump sum or in large monthly amounts over a short period of time (12 to 60 months). For the purposes of the agreement, these policies provide a definition of disability and specify the length of time a person must be disabled before benefits are paid.

4. Disability reducing term policy When a financial obligation is payable over an established schedule of payments (such as a mortgage), this type of policy will reduce the benefit payment period as the debt payments are reduced over time (similar to decreasing term life insurance).

C. ACCIDENTAL DEATH AND DISMEMBERMENT (AD&D) This type of coverage, also known as AD&D, provides protection from the accidental death of an insured or pays a specific benefit if an insured suffers a dismemberment covered under the terms of the contract.

    1. Accidental death This coverage may be purchased as a separate policy or as an added benefit to a health insurance contract. These policies or riders provide a specific amount to be paid to a named beneficiary in the event that an insured dies as the result of an accident. The benefit amount payable as a result of accidental death is referred to as the principal sum.

    2. Accidental dismemberment Accidental dismemberment provides that an insured will be paid a specific benefit amount if he suffers the accidental loss of a limb, sight, speech, or hearing. Coverage refers to the actual severance of limbs such as a hand, arm, or leg. It generally does not apply to the severance of a finger or toe, although some contracts pay a lower percentage of benefit in this event.

        a. Some contracts provide a benefit for the loss of use of a limb as well. The benefit amount payable for an accidental dismemberment is referred to as the **capital sum**. The capital sum is generally a percentage of the principal sum.

D. MEDICAL EXPENSE INSURANCE Unlike disability insurance, which provides income in the event of a disabling illness or injury, **medical expense insurance** is designed to cover the cost of treating an illness or disability by reimbursing the insured, fully or in part, for these costs. Several forms of coverage are available under medical expense insurance policies including hospital expense, surgical expense, miscellaneous medical expenses, major medical expense, comprehensive medical expense, dental care expense, and other limited medical expenses. Today, most health insurance companies provide contracts that include all or most of these coverages.

    1. Basic hospital expense Basic hospital expense coverage provides benefits such as room and board expenses. For example, the contract might pay $100 per day for room charges up to a maximum of 180 days. Also provided is coverage for miscellaneous medical expenses (which are a multiple of the daily hospital benefit) including the cost of x-rays, diagnostic tests, ambulance services, laboratory fees, drugs, medicines, operating room charges, nursing services, and doctor visits in the hospital. Hospital expense coverage may be written on an indemnity basis or on a reimbursement basis.

        a. If a policy is written on an **indemnity basis**, it means that the insurer will pay a specified amount per day as provided by a schedule appearing in the policy (with a maximum number of days paid).

        b. If the coverage is written on a **reimbursement** or **expense-incurred basis**, payment is made by the insurer for all or a percentage (such as 80%), of the expenses incurred, regardless of the daily amount involved.

    2. Surgical expense This coverage helps offset the cost of surgery and is usually covered along with hospital and miscellaneous medical expenses. Surgical expense benefits pay for the charges assessed by a surgeon for an operation. Surgical expense coverage lists a schedule of reimbursable amounts in the contract. The most common approach used by surgical expense coverage is to establish a maximum limit for coverage. The amount of the benefit schedule is typically expressed in terms of the maximum benefit payable. In addition, many other surgical procedures are listed with a dollar amount or a percentage

TEST TOPIC ALERT

Coinsurance is the concept of both the insured and the insurer sharing the costs of the insured's medical care. After a deductible is paid by the insured, the insurer's share of the costs is typically 70 to 80%; the insured pays the remaining 20 or 30%.

of the maximum shown. These listings are referred to as **surgical schedules** and provide payment for the usual and customary charges extended for various surgical procedures.

   a. For example, assume that a surgical expense policy has a $5,000 schedule. The $5,000 figure is the maximum for heart bypass surgery. Furthermore, a schedule may provide a percentage of the maximum for less complicated surgical procedures.

3. Miscellaneous coverages provided by basic medical expense insurance Several types of benefits may be provided by basic medical expense contracts including maternity, mental illness, private duty nursing charges, nursing home care, and physicians expense benefits other than surgical expenses.

4. Basic medical exclusions Exclusions are similar to those found in most health contracts, including; preexisting conditions, injuries sustained during the commission of a felony, intentionally self-inflicted injuries, injury or illness caused by war or acts of war, elective cosmetic surgery, conditions covered by workers' compensation, and conditions covered by government plans such as Medicare.

   a. Basic medical expense coverage limitations Many medical expense contracts limit coverage for certain conditions such as maternity, mental illness, alcohol or drug abuse, or preexisting conditions. For instance, these policies may require that new insureds satisfy an eight-month waiting period before receiving coverage for preexisting conditions.

5. Major medical policies Major medical expense contracts were developed as a result of the increased sophistication and expense involved with medical procedures and techniques. Major medical expense contracts are characterized by high maximum limits, blanket coverage, coinsurance or percentage participation, and a deductible.

   a. High maximum limits This is one of the primary characteristics of major medical expense insurance. High maximum limits such as $250,000, $500,000, or $1 million are provided by the contract.

   b. Blanket coverage This type of coverage provides protection for all types of medical expenses incurred whether the insured is in or out of the hospital.

   c. Percentage participation Also known as coinsurance, this stipulates that after a deductible is satisfied, a certain percentage of costs incurred will be paid by the insurer with the remaining amount being the responsibility of the insured. The most common coinsurance ratio is 80/20. This means that the insurer will pay 80% of incurred expenses after the deductible and the insured is responsible for the remaining 20%. The coinsurance clause motivates the insured to minimize unnecessary care.

1.) For example, if an insured owns a major medical expense policy with a $500 deductible and an 80% coinsurance clause, and he incurs a medical bill of $5,000, the insurer will be responsible for $3,600. This is calculated by subtracting the deductible from the total medical bill ($5,000 – $500 = $4,500) and multiplying this figure by 80%. Thus, the insurer pays $3,600 of the total bill and the insured is responsible for $1,400 (the $500 deductible plus 20% of $4,500 or $900).

d. Deductibles The basic purpose of a deductible in major medical expense contracts is to aid in reducing costs by eliminating small claims. As illustrated by the previous example, to determine the amount of a claim to be paid by the insurer, the deductible must first be subtracted from the total medical bill. The remaining amount will then be multiplied by the coinsurance percentage to arrive at the amount that must be paid by the insurer and the amount that remains the responsibility of the insured. Deductibles are generally expressed as a fixed dollar amount and function on a per individual or per family basis (e.g., $100 per individual per year or $300 per family per year).

1.) Corridor (supplementary) deductible This is a deductible that exists between where basic medical expense benefits leave off and major medical begins.

2.) Initial deductible This is the most common form of deductible used in major medical expense contracts. With this deductible, an insured will pay the first $100, $500, or $1,000 of incurred medical bills.

Initial Deductible

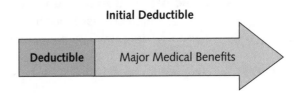

Typically used with comprehensive policies, an initial deductible is a stated amount that the insured must pay before any policy benefits are paid.

Corridor Deductible

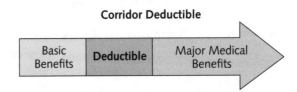

Typically used with supplemental plans, a corridor deductible is the deductible imposed after all basic benefits have been paid but before any major medical benefits will be paid.

e. Internal limitations Major medical policies restrict the amounts payable for specific types of expenses including hospital room and board charges (specific dollar amount per day for semiprivate room), extended care facilities, home health care services, hospice benefits, dental/vision/hearing care (generally, treatment must be necessitated by an injury to be covered), mental/nervous disorders, alcohol/drug treatment, and maternity.

f. Common accident provision This provision may appear in some major medical insurance contracts and is characterized by a single accident deductible. It states that only one deductible will have to be satisfied when two or more persons in the same family are injured in a common (the same) accident.

g. Exclusions Exclusions generally found in a major medical policy include injuries sustained due to war; intentionally self-inflicted injuries; regular dental/vision/hearing care; custodial care; any injuries covered by workers' compensation; in some cases, injuries sustained in private aircraft if an insured is the pilot, copilot, or crew member; cosmetic medical expenses; injuries sustained during military duty; and care rendered in a government facility (unless the insurer is legally required to pay for confinement and services).

h. Stop-loss feature Several major medical policies have a stop-loss provision that states that an insurer will pay 100% of covered expenses after the insured's out of pocket payments for eligible expenses reach a certain level.

i. Benefits under major medical are expressed as a percentage of eligible expenses. The amount paid for medical expenses is based on what is considered a reasonable and customary charge for the service performed. A benefit period begins only after a specified amount of expenses have been accrued during the accumulation period.

j. There are actually two types of plans that provide major medical coverage: (1) supplemental plans and (2) comprehensive plans. A supplemental plan covers expenses that are not included under the basic coverages. For example, if the basic coverage provides room and board but only for 60 days, the cost of room and board will be covered by the (supplemental) major medical plan beginning on the 61st day. In other words, the supplemental plan picks up where the basic ends on specific coverages. The comprehensive major medical plan is simply a single major medical contract covering all expenses.

6. Comprehensive major medical policies This type of contract is similar to major medical insurance, although it provides broader benefits. It combines all of the basic medical expense benefits into a single package ranging from hospital and surgical expense through major medical type coverages.

a. Comprehensive medical expense insurance also provides large maximum benefits.

b. This type of policy is characterized by a deductible and coinsurance provisions. It is generally sold on a group basis.

c. The deductible involved is generally a single deductible per person and per family. All bills incurred above this amount are covered on a percentage participation basis up to the policy limit. For example, this policy may have a $50 per person, $250 per family annual deductible. After these amounts are satisfied, the policy then pays 80% of all covered costs up to a maximum of $250,000. Other types of deductibles, such as a corridor deductible, may be found in these policies.

E. DENTAL EXPENSE A fast growing form of health coverage, dental insurance is typically offered as an additional benefit through group plans for an additional premium and is not sold individually. Providers of coverage include insurance companies, dental service plans (often called Delta Plans), Blue Cross/Blue Shield, and dental maintenance organizations (DMOs) and dental PPOs.

1. **Basic (scheduled) plans** These are similar to surgical expense plan schedules where benefits are paid for listed procedures up to the amount shown on the schedule. Most plans provide first-dollar benefits with no coinsurance or deductibles. Maximum benefits are often lower than the usual and customary charges of dentists; this forces the participant to bear a portion of the cost.

2. **Comprehensive (nonscheduled) plans** These plans resemble major medical coverage because benefits are paid on a reasonable and customary basis and are subject to deductibles and coinsurance. Dental services are divided into three broad categories: diagnostic and preventative services (generally not subject to coinsurance or deductibles), basic services (fillings, oral surgery, periodontics, and endodontics), and major services (inlays, crowns, dentures, and orthodontics).

3. **Combination plans** These combine features of both the basic and comprehensive plans; they typically cover diagnostic and preventive services on a usual-and-customary basis but use a fee schedule for other dental services.

4. **Dental coverage exclusions** Plan exclusions typically include cosmetic services (unless necessitated by accidental bodily injury), replacement of lost dentures, duplicate dentures, oral hygiene instruction, occupational injuries covered by workers' compensation, services furnished by government agencies, and certain services that began before the coverage effective date (crown work that began before coverage).

5. **Dental coverage limitations** To help control costs and eliminate unnecessary care, dental plans contain numerous limitations in addition to deductibles and coinsurance. Such limitations would include calendar year maximums ($500 to $2,000); large lifetime maximums ($1,000 to $5000); limiting routine exams and cleaning to once every six months; full-mouth x-rays to once every 24 or 36 months; and the replacement of dentures to once every five years.

6. **Predetermination of benefits** Also known as precertification or prior authorization, most contracts require a pretreatment review of certain nonemergency services (or when treatment will exceed a specified amount such as $300) by an insurance company. This procedure is not mandatory, but if it is not followed, neither the dentist nor patient will know in advance what benefits will be paid.

7. **Minimizing adverse selection** Probationary periods are used because members of a group who had no prior dental coverage are likely to have a large number of untreated dental problems or treatment was postponed in anticipation of future coverage. Limitations on benefits for late enrollees is used to minimize the problem of an employee enrolling simply to have coverage for an existing need. (Limitations may include a reduction in benefits for up to one year, reducing the maximum benefit for one year, or excluding some benefits for a certain period.) Finally, rarely do dental plans provide a conversion privilege following termination of the group coverage; however, dental coverage is subject to COBRA continuation rules.

8. Additional dental insurance information

a. Coinsurance of 80/20 generally applies after annual deductibles are satisfied.

b. Dental expense integrated with other health insurance benefits such as a major medical contract. Dental plans are sometimes easier to manage when they are separate (stand-alone plans) from other forms of medical coverage.

c. Maximum amounts of coverage are generally less during the first policy year to control losses due to preexisting conditions.

d. Most dental plans have a six-month to one-year waiting period before coverage becomes effective.

e. If an employer provides coverage on a contributory basis, at least 80% or 85% of the employees must participate. For example, an employer with 1,000 employees must have at least 800 to 850 participate in the plan. (This helps reduce adverse selection.)

F. LIMITED POLICIES These types of contracts protect against specific accidents or sickness. Each contract specifies the type of sickness or accident covered and benefits paid may be on a reimbursement or indemnity basis. The limited perils (i.e., accident only) and amounts of coverage are listed in the policy. The following are examples of limited contracts.

1. Dread disease/cancer policy This policy protects only against the disease specified in the contract (e.g., heart disease, cancer).

2. Accident only policy This policy indemnifies an insured for injuries resulting from accidental causes.

3. Travel accident policy This policy indemnifies an insured for accidental injuries arising during travel on a common carrier (bus, train, airline).

4. Credit disability policy This policy covers installment loan transactions only.

5. Hospital indemnity policy This policy provides an indemnity for an insured who is confined to a hospital. Benefits are payable on a per-day basis ($50 per day while in the hospital). These policies may cover accident or sickness.

6. Blanket coverage This coverage covers a group of persons whose status makes it difficult to identify by name. Persons covered are constantly changing, which makes it difficult, such as students of a school, volunteer firemen, passengers of a common carrier, and so forth.

7. Prescription drugs This coverage may be provided as a supplementary benefit or as an individual policy; the insured may obtain prescription drugs at participating pharmacies.

TAKE NOTE

Levels and types of care covered under an LTC policy include skilled nursing facility care, rehabilitation facility care, nursing home facility care, home health care, and respite care.

---

8. **Vision care** A vision care policy will typically cover expenses for testing, lenses, frames, contact lenses, and other prescription glasses. The coverage may be scheduled with dollar amounts for specified services or nonscheduled (paying a percentage of the reasonable and customary charges for the service performed) with service-type plans. Note that most hospital expense and major medical policies (both individual and group) do not cover vision care expenses. Limited policies are required to display prominently on the face page of the policy the fact that only limited coverage is provided.

G. **LONG-TERM CARE (LTC)** A long-term care plan is an individual health policy designed to provide benefits on an expense-incurred, indemnity, or prepaid basis for necessary care or treatment of an injury, illness, or loss of functional capacity provided by a certified or licensed health care provider in a setting other than an acute care hospital, for at least one year after a reasonable elimination period. Long-term care includes medical services and nonmedical assistance for personal care. While acute care consists of medically intensive care for a limited duration, long-term care provides coverage over an extended period of time for chronic or disabling conditions that require nursing care or constant supervision. LTC may be provided in a skilled nursing facility (which is the most expensive and highest level form of care), intermediate (rehabilitation) care facility, or custodial (nursing home) care facility. Most LTC contracts do not require prior hospitalization for admission to a nursing home; the inability to perform some of the activities of daily living (ADLs) is sufficient. (ADLs include mobility, dressing, personal hygiene, and eating.) Benefits generally vary from $40 to over $100 per day and may last from one year to an individual's lifetime.

1. Policy provisions common to an LTC policy include but are not limited to: guaranteed renewability provisions; elimination or waiting period; preexisting condition provision; waiver of premium; and the normal mandatory accident and health provisions found in most health insurance policies.

   a. Long-term care plan services include necessary diagnostic, preventative, therapeutic, curing, treating, mitigating, and rehabilitative services, as well as personal care services required by chronically ill people.

2. Benefits paid under a long-term care policy are income-tax free, up to specified limits, as long as the policy meets the IRS definition of *qualified*. Standards for qualification include:
   - only insurance protection is provided under the contract—the contract cannot contain any cash values;
   - the contract must be guaranteed renewable;
   - the contract does not cover services that are covered under Medicare; and
   - the limit on tax-free benefits is subject to change every year; in 2005, it is $240 per day.

3. Levels of care provided by LTC insurance include the following.

   a. **Home health care** This is care received in the individual's own home such as nursing services, speech and physical therapy, and other home care services.

    b. Respite care Respite care allows family members a reprieve or break from their caregiving responsibilities.

    c. Hospice care Hospice care is provided at home or in a facility for terminally ill individuals with six months or less to live.

    d. Skilled nursing This is care that is supervised by a doctor or registered nurse in a facility that provides lodging, recording of health information, dietary needs, etc.

4. Individual and group LTC contracts Individual LTC contracts provide coverage for one person, who is responsible for paying a premium. The cost of an individual plan is higher than a group plan; since underwriting is performed on an individual basis, it is more stringent. A **group LTC** premium is less expensive and a group plan permits individuals to be insured (i.e., group underwriting) when they may not ordinarily be insurable. Group plans normally include conversion privileges like these found in other accident and health contracts.

5. Integration with other health policies Many Americans have been misinformed about long-term care coverage offered to them by Medicare and other plans. Medicare pays for only a small percentage of charges when an individual requires long-term care. Medicare provides some limited nursing home benefits and some home health care. The benefits offered are of the post acute care (i.e., hospital) type. The skilled nursing care benefit (100 days) is provided by Medicare but was never intended to be a long-term care benefit.

    a. Most private health insurance plans do not provide any long-term care benefits although many are considering this coverage. Many insurers are just beginning to develop and market long-term care plans. These plans are separate from and sold in addition to major medical health plans. Therefore, the cost is also separate from other health plans.

    b. Medicaid does provide significant coverage for nursing home care. According to government statistics, Medicaid pays more than 40% of the country's nursing home care expenses. However, in order to become eligible for Medicaid benefits, individuals must not possess assets greater than specified amounts, which are very low. Nursing home residents receiving Medicaid must contribute most of their income, other than a small personal needs allowance, to the cost of their care.

    c. Due to the lack of benefits provided for long-term care by social insurance (i.e., Medicare, Medicaid) and private health plans, there is a tremendous need and market for this coverage.

6. Optional LTC benefits The following optional benefits are available with long-term care policies.

    a. Inflation protection provides daily and lifetime maximum benefit increases that are guaranteed and automatic. This benefit is generally expressed as an annual percentage based on a simple or compound interest rate.

b. Return of premium option is a form of nonforfeiture option that provides a lump sum cash payment to the policyowner, upon lapse or surrender of the policy, which is equal to a percentage (50%, 75%, 90%) of the total premiums paid (prior claims payments would normally be deducted from the amount returned).

c. Guarantee of insurability provides the policyowner with the option of purchasing additional insurance amounts within specified parameters regardless of insurability (claims history or existing conditions).

III. OTHER TYPES OF HEALTH INSURANCE PLANS AND PROVIDERS

In addition to health insurance plans offered by commercial insurers, consumers can turn to various **service providers**. As opposed to offering coverage that reimburses the insured for medical expenses, service providers actually provide the medical care in exchange for the payment of premiums. The most common types of service providers include health maintenance organizations, preferred provider organizations, point-of-service plans, and Blue Cross and Blue Shield plans.

A. HEALTH MAINTENANCE ORGANIZATIONS (HMOs) HMOs are a comparatively recent development in the financing and delivery of physician and hospital care. An HMO provides a wide range of comprehensive health care services for members who are enrolled on a group basis and who pay a fixed periodic type premium in advance for the services of participating physicians and hospitals. HMOs are characterized as providing service to a limited geographical area and offering a limited choice of health care providers (through recent innovations have challenged these characterizations).

1. HMOs emphasize preventive medicine with early treatment and diagnosis by way of prepaid routine physical examinations and diagnostic screening techniques.

2. These organizations are basically prepaid group practice plans that have an agreement with one or more hospitals for admission of enrolled members on a service type basis.

3. HMOs may be community sponsored or sponsored by hospital employees, government, medical schools, insurance companies (stock companies), producer cooperative, Blue Cross and Blue Shield plans, labor unions, and other types of organizations. HMOs may be structured as either nonprofit or for-profit organizations.

4. An HMO functions on a prepaid basis rather than the traditional methods for delivering health care. The traditional system is based on a fee for service concept. Under an HMO, health care is provided in return for a prenegotiated lump sum or periodic payment.

5. Basic health care benefits Health care services provided by an HMO generally include physicians services, emergency health services, inpatient hospital care, outpatient medical services, diagnostic laboratory services and therapeutic services, and preventive health care services.

6. Supplemental (optional) benefits Some of the common supplemental benefits that may be offered by HMOs include prescription drugs, vision care, dental care, home health care, intermediate and long-term care, mental health care, physical therapy, podiatric care, and alcohol and drug abuse or addiction treatment.

7. **Exclusions** Many of the customary health insurance exclusions apply such as intentionally self-inflicted injuries, injuries or illnesses covered by workers' compensation, and care provided in a government facility.

8. **Primary care physician (gatekeeper)** This is the contracting physician who is responsible for rendering routine or remedial care to the HMO member. The HMO generally requires that all members select a primary care physician. If medical care requires a specialist, the primary care physician must generally authorize the treatment (this is often referred to as the gatekeeper function of the primary care physician).

9. **Copayment** This is the amount of money the member must pay for service. The member pays the copayment directly to the provider of services and is classified as an out-of-pocket expense.

10. **Dual-choice provision** If an employer has 25 or more employees and if an HMO operates in the area, employers that provide health insurance to their employees must be offer at least one HMO option.

11. **Annual open enrollment** An HMO must hold an annual open enrollment period (usually 30 days) for the individual (nongroup) market where it must accept all who apply, regardless of their health status. This should not be confused with the open enrollments for employers when employees may elect to change their health coverage or remain with their existing plan.

12. HMOs offer services primarily for group plans although individual subscribers are accepted.

13. **Types of HMOs** There are three basic types of HMO plans: group practice plans, individual practice association plans, and open-ended plans.

    a. **Group practice** Also known as **closed-panel plans**, this type accounts for about 80% of HMO subscribers. Under this arrangement physicians are either employees of the HMO which pays their salary or employees of another legal entity that has a contract with the HMO to provide medical service for its subscribers. Subscribers must use physicians employed by the plan, thus the title closed panel.

    b. **Individual practice association** Also referred to as **open-panel plans**, in this type participating physicians practice individually or in small groups at their own offices. These physicians accept non-HMO patients as well on a fee-for-service basis. Subscribers choose from a list of participating physicians, thus the title open panel.

    c. **Open-ended HMO** Created by the Health Maintenance Organization Act of 1988, up to 10% of an open-ended HMO's services may be provided by physicians who are not affiliated with the HMO.

B. **BLUE CROSS AND BLUE SHIELD (BLUE PLANS)** The most common types of service organizations include Blue Cross and Blue Shield organizations. These entities have been organized under special legislation and established at the state level by hospitals and other medical professionals as a means of providing health care to the public. The "Blues" offer virtually the same coverages as commercial insurance companies. Benefits include basic medical expense, major medical, and dental coverages.

   1. Blue Cross and Blue Shield organizations operate on a nonprofit basis (although some do function today on a for-profit basis) and are exempt from many state regulations. They have contractual agreements with hospitals and participating physicians that provide services to subscribers (the insureds). Coverage is offered on both a group and individual basis. Blue Cross and Blue Shield plans may offer open enrollment and competitive rates, benefits, and other coverages.

   2. Blue Cross and Blue Shield organizations are not the same as private insurance companies, are not federally sponsored, and are not owned by hospitals and physicians.

   3. **Blue Cross** Blue Cross provides coverage for hospital benefits. Under such a plan, the insured is billed only for services not covered by the particular plan, while the member hospital providing the services is paid directly by Blue Cross. Blue Cross plans were originally organized by individual hospitals to permit and encourage prepayment of hospital expenses.

   4. **Blue Shield** Blue Shield insurance provides coverage for physician's expenses, including surgical expense. Blue Shield pays its benefits either to the hospital or directly to the physician. Assessed charges are usually made on a "usual, customary, and reasonable basis" (UCR) rather than using a benefit schedule employed by private insurers.

   5. **Service vs. indemnity approach** Blue Cross and Blue Shield operate on a service approach where an insured receives the benefits stipulated in the contract, such as "coverage for daily room and board." Under an indemnity approach (used by commercial insurance companies), an insured is provided with a specific dollar amount of coverage for each benefit, such as "$125 per day for daily room and board charges." Group premiums are based on experience rating; premiums for smaller employers are based on community rating.

      a. **Service approach** The insured receives the service; no cost is mentioned in the contract.

      b. **Indemnity approach** The insured receives a dollar amount to cover the costs of covered services.

C. **PREFERRED PROVIDER ORGANIZATION (PPO)** PPOs are groups of health care providers such as physicians and hospitals that contract with employers, insurers, or third-party organizations to provide medical care services at a reduced fee.

   1. PPOs may be organized by the providers themselves or by other organizations such as insurers or groups of employers.

2. Like HMOs, they may take the form of group (closed-panel) practices or specific individual (open-panel) practices. The PPO member is not locked in to a specific panel of providers (as in an HMO) even though the member must pay more if treatment is sought outside the PPO panel; in this respect PPOs offer both an open-panel and a closed-panel option.

3. PPOs provide a large range of services as opposed to comprehensive care; they may also impose limitations such as hospital care in only one hospital.

4. PPOs differ from HMOs in two ways: (1) They do not provide benefits on a prepaid basis. Participants are paid (physicians) on a fee-for-service basis (as in the "old" doctor's office visit style); (2) Employees (subscribers) are not required to use the practitioner, physician, or facility of the PPO that contracts with their group insurer or employer. However, incentives are provided to use the PPO such as lower or reduced deductibles.

5. PPOs are utilized by commercial insurers, Blue Cross/Blue Shield, employer self-funded groups, and so on.

   a. Commercial carriers utilizing PPOs may be organized on a mutual or stock basis. They also offer individual or group type plans.

   b. With employer partially self-funded plans, group plans for employees and dependents are utilized. They are generally administered by third party administrators. Self funding arrangements may also be used by a union trust fund. In any event, the employer or union trust fund assumes a portion (or all) of the financial risk rather than transferring it to an insurer.

6. Utilization review establishes control over providers of service in the PPO. This involves areas such as second surgical opinions, precertification of patients, concurrent review, and ambulatory services.

D. POINT-OF-SERVICE (POS) PLANS A **point-of-service plan** shares similarities with a PPO and an HMO. It is like a PPO in that the employee retains the right to use any service provider but will pay a higher proportion of the costs if the provider is outside the network. (This penalty for using a non-network provider is typically higher than with a PPO). A POS is like an HMO since care received through the network is managed by the primary care physician (or gatekeeper). The use of the gatekeeper approach is to provide greater cost control than with a PPO.

E. MULTIPLE OPTION PLANS Until recently, employers that wanted to offer an HMO, a PPO, and an indemnity plan of coverage would be required to enter into separate agreements with each type of provider. **Multiple option plans** sponsored by a single provider offer employers the opportunity to provide employees the choice of a variety of plans without the administrative costs associated with the establishment of separate agreements.

> **TAKE NOTE**
>
> **Experience rating** is a system of modifying a group's premium rate based on its claims and losses (i.e., its actual experience).

IV. GROUP HEALTH INSURANCE

Like group life insurance, group health is a plan of insurance that an employer (or other eligible sponsor) provides for its employees. The contract for coverage is between the insurer and the employer. The employees are the individual insureds under the contract. Trade associations, labor unions, and customer groups such as creditors and debtors can also sponsor a group health insurance plan.

A. CHARACTERISTICS AND CONCEPTS OF GROUP COVERAGE As in group life insurance, employees covered by group health do not receive a policy. The employer is the policyowner and receives the master group contract. The employee receives a certificate of coverage. There are three parties involved in this situation: the insurer, the employer, and the employee.

1. Group plans may be contributory or noncontributory.

    a. If noncontributory (employer pays premium), 100% of the eligible employees must be covered under the plan.

    b. If contributory (employer pays part and employee pays part), at least 75% of the eligible employees must participate before the group policy can be put into effect.

2. Group underwriting A group health plan requires no medical examination or statement concerning a person's health. There is no individual underwriting since it is accomplished on a group basis. However, if a person declines coverage under a group plan and later changes his mind, the insurer may require proof of insurability. The concept of group health insurance underwriting reduces adverse selection because of the larger number of persons covered by the plan.

3. Experience rating Group health insurance rates are based upon the actual loss experience of the group. **Experience rating** is considered the most cost-effective way to reflect the general health of a group in the premium charged, thus enhancing competition among insurers. The use of **community rating**, employed by Blue Cross/Blue Shield plans for smaller groups, applies the same rate structure to all groups in a community (based, in part, on the costs of providing medical care) and is not competitive with experience rated plans.

4. A group of persons cannot band together for the sole purpose of purchasing group health insurance coverage. The coverage must be incidental to the group.

5. Benefit eligibility To be eligible for group health benefits, employees must be in a covered work classification, satisfy any probationary period, be full-time, and actively at work. Dependents of a covered employee become eligible when coverage is provided to the employee. If coverage is not elected within a specified period of time (generally, 30 or 31 days after the dependent becomes eligible), future coverage is available only during open enrollment periods or when proof of insurability is provided.

6. Coordination of benefits This provision contained in most group health contracts is designed to prevent individuals from receiving benefits that exceed their actual expenses. Coverage as an employee is primary (pays first) to coverage as a dependent, which is secondary (pays last); policies without a coordination of benefits provision are primary to those with a provision.

7. Change or loss of coverage If an employer changes group insurance providers, consideration should be given to the impact of coinsurance provisions and deductible carryover provisions that permit the application of expenses incurred during the last three months of the year to the next year's deductible.

    a. Coverage for employees generally terminates when employment is terminated, eligibility ends, when the master contract is terminated, when maximum benefits are received, or when required employee contributions are not made.

    b. Coverage for dependents generally terminates when the employee's coverage ceases, the dependent no longer meets the definition of a dependent, when maximum benefits are received, or the required employee contribution is not made.

    c. When coverage is terminated, most plans extend benefits for any covered employee or dependent who is totally disabled at the time of termination.

8. Group conversion Group policies contain a conversion privilege permitting the employee to convert his coverage to an individual health plan when that person's employment is terminated. Typically, the employee has 30 or 31 days to convert to an individual plan once employment is terminated without providing evidence of insurability. This privilege is not available to employees who are retiring.

B. MULTIPLE EMPLOYER WELFARE ARRANGEMENTS (MEWAs) The multiple employer welfare arrangement (also known as a multiple employer trust or MET) has become a popular method by which to market group benefits to employers who have a small number of employees. MEWAs are legal entities that may be sponsored by an insurance company, an independent administrator, or some other organization, and they are established for the purpose of providing group benefits to participants.

    1. Each MEWA must have an administrator. The administrator may be an insurance company or a professional administrator.

    2. MEWAs may provide either a single type of insurance or a wide range of coverages. It may provide benefits on a self-funded basis or fund benefits with a contract purchased from an insurance company.

3. **Categories of MEWAs** MEWAs may be categorized according to how they are administered, whether by an insurer or a third party administrator. There are three basic categories.

   a. **Fully insured MEWA** Here benefits are insured and the MEWA is administered by an insurance company.

   b. **Insured third-party administered MEWAs** Benefits are insured and the MEWA is administered by a third party.

   c. **Self-funded MEWA** With this type, benefits are self-funded and the MEWA is administered by a third party.

C. **TAFT-HARTLEY TRUSTS** These are formed as a result of collective bargaining over benefits between a union and the employers of union members. The Taft-Hartley Act prohibits employers from paying funds directly to a labor union for the purpose of providing group insurance coverage to members, but payments may be made to a trust fund established for the purpose of purchasing insurance. The group insurance contract is issued to the trustees of the fund, who must be made up of equal numbers of representatives from the employers and the union. Trusteeships generally provide benefits for the employees of several employers.

D. **OTHER GROUP INFORMATION** Again, group insurance coverage must be incidental to the forming of the group. Other criteria are also taken into consideration by an insurer when writing group insurance such as the following.

   1. **Size of the group** This is a significant factor in the underwriting process. Large groups have prior experience that helps to determine the premium; generally large group employers have enhanced administrative capabilities to assist the insurer with plan administration that could reduce plan expenses. Small groups have less or no experience and can pose an adverse selection problem.

   2. **Composition of group** The ages, sex, and income of the members will affect the premium charged as well.

   3. **Persistency** The length of time that a group case stays "on the books" is a concern to underwriters. Initial acquisition expenses (e.g., commissions) are higher for an insurer. If the business is not kept for three to four years, the insurer does not make any money.

   4. **Benefits (maximum coverage)** Benefits provided must not be more than needed since this could encourage malingering or overutilization.

   5. **Flow of persons** A steady flow of persons through the group allows the business to be more stable.

   6. **Eligibility of the group** Individual employer groups, multiple-employer groups (MEWA), associations (trade, professional, alumni, etc.) groups, and customer groups (such as depositors, debtor-creditor) are all eligible if the health coverage is incidental to the formation of the group.

> **TAKE NOTE**
>
> DI = disability income • STD = short-term disability • LTD = long-term disability

7. **Regulatory jurisdiction** Under the doctrine of comity (by which states recognize the laws of other states), it is generally accepted that the laws of the state in which the policy was delivered to the policyowner have jurisdiction. (The state of delivery must have some relationship to the group such as the policyowner's place of incorporation or location of the principal office.)

E. **INDIVIDUAL AND GROUP HEALTH DIFFERENCES** One primary difference between these two types of health plans is that group insurance provides benefits for nonoccupational illnesses and injuries. Individual policies cover both occupational and nonoccupational. Other differences include the following.

1. An individual contract is a two-party contract between insurer and insured. Group coverage is also a two-party contract (between insurer and employer), but a group policy involves three parties: the insurer, the policyowner, and the individual insureds.

2. An individual insured may have his policy cancelled if it is an optionally renewable or cancellable contract. Under group insurance, an individual cannot be cancelled unless the contract for the entire group is cancelled.

F. **GROUP DISABILITY INCOME** Disability income coverage is available to those who desire it. Group long-term disability (LTD) or short term disability (STD) is available. The definitions of disability (in group DI) are generally more restrictive than those found in an individual policy. The cost of LTD or STD policies is less due to the larger number of insureds.

1. Coverage periods available under STD plans are generally six to 18 months. Coverage periods for LTD plans are similar to those available under and individual plan (i.e., two years, five years, 10 years, to age 65, life).

2. Benefits payable by group disability plans are generally reduced by any benefits received from social insurance plans (e.g., Social Security, workers' compensation, etc.).

G. **TYPES OF GROUP FUNDING AND ADMINISTRATION** There are a variety of ways in which group health insurance plans are may be funded and administered.

1. **Conventional fully insured plans** This is the traditional approach to funding and administering a group health plan in that the insurer assumes the full amount of claims risks and premiums are calculated annually.

2. **Modified fully insured plans** This approach is structured to allow employers to reduce the cost of their group health insurance benefit by modifying the premium payment arrangement. This can be done in the following ways.

   a. **Premium delay arrangement** Employers pay postpone premium payments for a stated period of time (usually 60 to 90 days) beyond the grace period. This gives the employer an opportunity to use the funds during the delay period for investment or other business purposes.

b. Reserve reduction arrangement Generally, this arrangement, available only after a plan has been in force for a year or more, permits the employer to retain a percentage of its annual premium in an amount equal to the insurer's claim reserve for the employer's policy.

c. Retrospective rating arrangement An employer may qualify for an adjustment in premium or a premium refund if the group's actual annual claims experience is lower than the insurer's estimate. On the other hand, if the policyowner's claims experience exceeds the insurer's estimate, an additional premium must be paid.

3. **Partially self-funded plans** Under these types of plans, the employer assumes the risk of covering some or all of the potential claims under the policy.

   a. Stop-loss coverage A large employer may utilize this approach to coverage under which it covers the claims of the insureds up to a certain predetermined level of loss. After that level has been reached, the insurer is responsible for covering the claims.

   b. Administrative-services only (ASO) arrangement Under this arrangements, an employer will purchase the insurance expertise of a third-party administrator to perform administrative functions only, such as handling claims, maintaining records, and projecting costs. No insurance coverage is provided.

   c. 501(c) trust arrangement Unlike conventional self-funded plans (described below), these arrangements permit the immediate deduction of contributions to a plan with any accumulated earnings on trust assets tax deductible.

4. **Fully self-funded (self-administered) plans** Under this approach, the employer assumes full responsibility for covering all costs. Typically, the employer makes periodic contributions to a fund, as opposed to making premium payments to an insurer. Payments to cover employee health expenses are made from the fund.

   a. Since these plans are exempt from state regulatory oversight, they are not subject to payment of state premium taxes or guaranty fund and high-risk pool assessments. Employers also report cost savings due to lower administrative expenses than those charged by insurers. Many employers have also been very successful in negotiating directly with providers for discounted services. Rather than pay insurers to establish networks and process claims, employers have found that they can often save money by performing those services themselves or by contracting with third party administrators.

   b. By funding employees' actual medical costs on a pay-as-you-go basis rather than paying premiums in advance for services that may or may not be used, employers believe they are saving even more money, particularly when the money previously used to pay premiums is earning interest for the employer instead of an insurer.

   c. Employers with multistate locations find self-funding particularly beneficial. Because state insurance laws vary from state to state, employers would have to purchase separate health insurance plans for employees in each state under

TAKE NOTE

Conditions suitable for self-funding would include when costs can be predicted and when the employer has the financial strength to cover the costs of higher-than-expected claims.

state-regulated insured plans. Establishing a self-funded health plan avoids multistate regulatory provisions and allows all employees to be covered under the same benefit plan. Employees moving from one state location to another remain under the same insurance program.

H. REGULATION OF EMPLOYER GROUP INSURANCE PLANS The Employee Retirement Income Security Act of 1974 (ERISA) is a federal law that sets minimum standards for most voluntarily established pension and health plans in private industry to provide protection for individuals in these plans.

1. **ERISA requirements** ERISA requires plans to provide participants with plan information about plan features and funding; provides fiduciary responsibilities for those who manage and control plan assets; requires plans to establish a grievance and appeals process for participants to obtain benefits from their plans; and gives participants the right to sue for benefits and breaches of fiduciary duty. There have been a number of amendments to ERISA, expanding the protections available to health benefit plan participants and beneficiaries. One important amendment, the Consolidated Omnibus Budget Reconciliation Act (COBRA), provides some workers and their families with the right to continue their health coverage for a limited time after certain events, such as the loss of a job. Another amendment to ERISA is the Health Insurance Portability and Accountability Act (HIPAA), which provides important new protections for working Americans and their families who have preexisting medical conditions or might otherwise suffer discrimination in health coverage based on factors that relate to an individual's health. Other important amendments include the Newborns' and Mothers' Health Protection Act, the Mental Health Parity Act, and the Women's Health and Cancer Rights Act.

2. **Fiduciary responsibilities** ERISA protects group plan assets by requiring that those persons or entities who exercise discretionary control or authority over plan management or plan assets, have discretionary authority or responsibility for the administration of a plan, or provide investment advice to a plan for compensation or have any authority or responsibility to do so be subject to fiduciary responsibilities. Plan fiduciaries include, for example, plan trustees, plan administrators, and members of a plan's investment committee.

    a. The primary responsibility of fiduciaries is to run the plan solely in the interest of participants and beneficiaries and for the exclusive purpose of providing benefits and paying plan expenses.

    b. Fiduciaries must act prudently and must diversify the plan's investments to minimize the risk of large losses.

> **TAKE NOTE**
>
> COBRA is a federal act that amended ERISA, the Internal Revenue Code, and the Public Health Service Act to provide continuation of group health coverage that otherwise might be terminated.

    c. In addition, they must follow the terms of plan documents to the extent that the plan terms are consistent with ERISA.

    d. They also must avoid conflicts of interest. In other words, they may not engage in transactions on behalf of the plan that benefit parties related to the plan, such as other fiduciaries, services providers, or the plan sponsor.

3. Reporting and disclosure ERISA requires plan administrators—the people who run plans—to give plan participants in writing the most important facts they need to know about their retirement and health benefit plans including plan rules, financial information, and documents on the operation and management of the plan.

    a. One of the most important documents participants are entitled to receive automatically when becoming a participant of an ERISA-covered retirement or health benefit plan or a beneficiary receiving benefits under such a plan, is a summary of the plan, called the Summary Plan Description (SPD). The plan administrator is legally obligated to provide to participants, free of charge, the SPD. It provides information on when an employee can begin to participate in the plan, how service and benefits are calculated, when benefits becomes vested, when and in what form benefits are paid, and how to file a claim for benefits.

    b. If a plan is changed, participants must be informed, either through a revised summary plan description, or in a separate document, called a Summary of Material Modifications, which also must be given to participants free of charge.

    c. In addition to the summary plan description, the plan administrator must automatically give participants each year a copy of the plan's Summary Annual Report. This is a summary of the annual financial report that most plans must file with the Department of Labor.

I. CONSOLIDATED OMNIBUS BUDGET RECONCILIATION ACT (COBRA)

COBRA was created in 1985 and stipulated that employers must offer continuation of group health coverage for a specified period of time to qualified employees and their beneficiaries who would not otherwise be eligible for continued coverage because of a particular qualifying event involving the covered employee. Such events would include death, divorce, or termination of employment.

    1. Qualified beneficiaries Qualified beneficiaries under COBRA include the spouse and dependent children of an employee entitled to coverage under the terms of a group health plan.

2. Employer penalties An employer that fails to meet the continuation requirements may not take a federal income tax deduction for its group health plan contributions.

   a. For example, if an employer has 1,000 employees and the cost per employee for group health coverage is $2,000, the employer will lose a $2 million business expense deduction if it does not comply with COBRA.

   b. In addition, if an employer fails to meet the requirements, highly compensated employees must include in their income the cost of employer group health plan contributions (e.g., the cost per employee of $2,000) made on their behalf. These "at-risk" employees are usually those who are in the top 25% of the highest-paid employees.

3. Type of coverage under COBRA The continued health coverage provided for plan beneficiaries must be identical to that being provided under the plan for similarly situated beneficiaries.

4. Maximum period of continuation coverage A qualified beneficiary (e.g., surviving spouse) may have more than one qualifying event that entitles the beneficiary to continued coverage, but in no event may the coverage period generally exceed a 36-month period. If an individual is laid off from a job, he may continue coverage for a period not to exceed 18 months.

   a. Continuation coverage may terminate once a beneficiary becomes covered by another plan or Medicare. Continuation coverage does not apply if the employer terminates the entire health plan.

5. Notification required Each covered employee or qualified beneficiary is responsible for notifying the plan administrator of the occurrence of qualifying events within 60 days after the event in order to take advantage of continued coverage.

6. Premiums COBRA allows employers to charge those who elect to continue coverage 102% of the premiums the employer (company) pays for each employee. The additional 2% covers administrative duties and paperwork required of the employer.

   a. A grace period exists for the failure to pay premiums. It is the longest of (1) 30 days; (2) the period the plan allows employees for failure to pay premiums; or (3) the period the insurance company allows the plan or the employer for failure to pay premiums.

J. HEALTH INSURANCE PORTABILITY AND ACCOUNTABILITY ACT (HIPAA) In 1997, Congress passed the Health Insurance Portability and Accountability Act. In part, the purpose of the act was to improve portability and continuity of health insurance coverage in the group and individual markets and to improve access to long-term care services and coverage. Major provisions of the legislation include the following.

1. Exemption from the 10% penalty on premature IRA withdrawals if they are used to pay medical expenses in excess of 7.5% of adjusted gross income. Also exempt from the 10% penalty are early IRA withdrawals to pay for medical insurance if an individual has received unemployment compensation under federal or state law for at least 12 weeks. (The latter is without regard to the 7.5% floor.)

2. Qualified long-term care insurance for chronically ill individuals will be treated as accident and health insurance contracts so that amounts received under contracts issued are generally excludable from income. As noted earlier, the excludable amount is capped at a certain amount per day on per diem contracts and will be adjusted for inflation. (In 2005, this amount was $240.) Furthermore, expenses for qualified long-term care services provided to a taxpayer, the taxpayer's spouse or dependents that are not reimbursed as well as long term care insurance premiums that do not exceed specified dollar limits, will be treated as medical expenses for which itemized deductions may be claimed, subject to the 7.5% of adjusted gross income floor.

3. Accelerated death benefits that are paid to an insured who is chronically or terminally ill under a life insurance contract, or through sales or assignment of a death benefit under a life insurance contract, to a viatical settlement provider may be excluded from gross income. The excludable amount for a chronically ill individual is also capped at a certain daily amount, which is adjusted for inflation. (In 2005, this amount was $240 per day.)

4. Portability of health insurance coverage has been enhanced by placing restrictions on certain group health plans' ability to exclude individuals from coverage based on preexisting conditions or health status. The term *portability* refers to "credible coverage" certificates. These certificates must be issued by employers, upon request, to previously covered employees, to establish the employees' prior creditable coverage for purposes of reducing the extent to which a group health plan can apply a preexisting condition exclusion. To qualify, any individual (including family members) must have been covered under another group plan with no gaps in coverage greater than 63 days. These certificates can be submitted to a new employer to reduce the preexisting waiting period (i.e., one month of credible coverage will count toward satisfying one month of preexisting waiting period).

5. Another health insurance innovation introduced by HIPAA was the **medical savings account (MSA)**, which enabled small businesses, self-employed persons, their employees, and their families who were covered by a high deductible health insurance plan to create qualified trusts for the purpose of accepting contributions to pay for medical expenses. (MSAs were made available on a pilot basis with the number of accounts limited. The cut-off year for new accounts under the pilot program was 2003.)

   a. MSAs are available to smaller employers, or those who employ an average of 50 or fewer people.

   b. Contributions to an MSA must be in cash and cannot exceed a specified percentage of the highest annual deductible as it applies to the covered participant. (For individual-only coverage, this limit is 65%; for family coverage, it is 75%.) Within these limits, the contributions if made by the individual participant are tax deductible; if made by the employer on behalf of the individual, they are not included in the participant's income.

   c. For MSAs, a high deductible health insurance plan is one that has the following annual deductibles and required out-of-pocket expenses:

	Individual Coverage	Family Coverage
Minimum annual deductible	$1,750	$3,500
Maximum annual deductible	$2,650	$5,250
Required annual out-of-pocket expenses	$3,500	$6,450

(The above thresholds were for 2005 and are subject to adjustment for inflation.)

d. Withdrawals taken from an MSA for medical purposes are tax free. If a withdrawal is not used to pay for medical costs, it is included in the participant's gross income and subject to a 15% penalty. After the participant reaches the age of Medicare eligibility (or becomes disabled or dies), the penalty tax is not applicable; however, any withdrawals not used exclusively to pay for medical expenses are still included in the participant's gross income.

6. The allowable deduction for health insurance costs of self-employed individuals and their spouses and dependents is now 100% of those costs.

7. Other key provisions of HIPAA include:

- limiting the period for which a group health plan can deny coverage for a preexisting medical condition to 12 months (18 months in the case of a late enrollee);

- generally prohibiting a group health plan from establishing eligibility for enrollment based on an individual's health status, medical condition (physical or mental), claims experience, receipt of health care, medical history, genetic information, evidence of insurability, and disability;

- guaranteeing availability of health coverage for small employers;

- guaranteeing availability of health coverage in the individual market for all eligible individuals, which include those who

  — have had at least 18 months of aggregate creditable coverage,

  — have been under a group health plan, a governmental plan, or church plan (or health insurance offered in connection with such plans) during the most recent period of creditable coverage,

  — are not eligible for coverage under a group health plan, Medicare, or Medicaid, and do not have other health insurance coverage,

  — have not had their most recent coverage cancelled for nonpayment of premiums or fraud, and

  — have elected and exhausted any option for continuation of coverage (COBRA coverage) that was available under the prior plan;

- guaranteeing renewability of health coverage for all group health plans, unless the plan has failed to pay premiums, committed fraud, violated participation or contribution rules, terminated coverage, moved outside the service area, or ceased association membership; and

- guaranteeing renewability of health coverage in the individual market for all individuals, unless the individual has failed to pay premiums, committed fraud, terminated the plan, moved outside the service area, or ceased association membership.

K.   HEALTH SAVINGS ACCOUNTS (HSAs)   The Medicare Prescription Drug and Modernization Act of 2003 established a new way for consumers to pay for medical expenses: health care savings accounts (HSAs). An HSA is a tax-favored vehicle for accumulating funds to cover medical expenses.

1. Eligibility   Individuals under age 65 are eligible to establish and contribute to HSAs if they have a qualified high-deductible health plan. For an individual, a qualified high-deductible health plan is one with a minimum deductible of $1,000 and a $5,000 cap on out-of-pocket expenses (indexed annually). For a family, a qualified health plan is one with a minimum deductible of $2,000 and a $10,000 cap on out-of-pocket expenses (indexed annually).

2. **Contribution limits** Annual contributions of up to 100% of an individual's health plan deductible can be made to an HSA. For 2005, the maximum annual contribution was $2,650 for individual coverage and $5,250 for family coverage (indexed annually), provided the insured has a deductible at least that high. Individuals who are 55 to 65 years old can make an additional catch-up contribution. Individuals with HSAs who are age 55 and older may make additional annual contributions of $600 (as of 2005), increasing by $100 each year to a maximum additional calendar year contribution of $1000 in 2009 and thereafter.

3. **Tax treatment** Earnings in HSAs grow tax free, and account beneficiaries can make tax-free withdrawals to cover current and future qualified healthcare costs.

   a. Qualified healthcare expenses include amounts paid for:
      - doctors' fees;
      - prescription and nonprescription medicines;
      - necessary hospital services not paid for by insurance;
      - retiree health insurance premiums;
      - Medicare expenses (but not Medigap);
      - qualified long-term care services; and
      - COBRA coverage.

   b. Qualified medical expenses are those expenses incurred by the HSA owner, the spouse, and dependents. Nonqualified withdrawals are subject to income taxes and a 10% penalty tax. HSAs are fully portable and assets can accumulate over the years. Upon death, HSA ownership may be transferred to a spouse tax free.

L. **AGE DISCRIMINATION IN EMPLOYMENT ACT (ADEA)** Signed into law in 1967, the Age Discrimination in Employment Act extends specific protections to employees and job applicants age 40 or older. The act prohibits employers from using age as a basis for refusing to hire an otherwise qualified individual, or for discriminating against a person in compensation, terms, conditions, or privileges of employment. An employer cannot reduce anyone's wages in order to comply with the act or deny an employee or a spouse over age 65 the same health care coverage offered to employees and their spouses under age 65.

   1. **Applicability** The act applies to employers with more than 20 employees, including federal, state, and local government employers. Its purpose and intent is to "promote the employment of older persons based on their ability rather than age; to prohibit arbitrary age discrimination in employment; and to help employers and workers find ways of meeting problems arising from the impact of age on employment."

      a. The act makes it unlawful to discriminate against a person because of age with respect to any term, condition, or privilege of employment, including benefits.

      b. The act makes it unlawful to retaliate against an individual for opposing employment practices that discriminate based on age or for participating in any action or proceeding under the ADEA.

2. **ADEA standards** If an employer provides fringe benefits to its employees, it generally must do so without regard to an employee's age. Employers may, however, provide lower benefits to older than to younger workers:

■ for certain types of benefits, if the employer is spending the same amount, or incurring the same cost, for the benefit for older and younger workers; or

■ if the older employees can receive, from the employer or other sources, a total benefit that is no less favorable than the benefit provided to younger employees.

3. **Benefits subject to different costs** Some employee benefits become more costly with age; some do not. Paid vacation days and sick days are no more expensive for older workers than younger workers. However, the cost of some insured benefits may become more expensive with age. Because the likelihood of death, illness, or disability increases with age, the cost of insuring against these events rises correspondingly.

   a. It is not considered unlawful for an employer to reduce benefits if it can demonstrate that the particular reductions are cost-justified—that is, that the benefit provided to older workers is no lower than is necessary to achieve equivalency in costs.

   b. While an employer may thus reduce these benefits, it must show that the reduction is no greater than is necessary to equalize its costs.

4. **Employee-funded benefits** When employees contribute to the cost of their benefit plans, the rules apply where the premium for those benefits increases with age.

   a. An older employee may not be required to pay more for the benefit as a condition of employment. Where the premium has increased for an older employee, employees must be offered the option of withdrawing from the benefit plan altogether or reducing their benefit coverage in order to keep their premiums the same.

   b. Older employees who choose to participate in a voluntary plan can be required to pay more for the benefit, but only if they do not pay a greater percentage of their premium cost than younger employees do.

   c. Older employees may be offered the option of paying—or paying more—for the benefit in order to avoid otherwise justified reductions in coverage. Where the employees choose to pay more, they can be charged no more than the amount that is necessary to maintain full coverage.

M. CIVIL RIGHTS ACT/PREGNANCY DISCRIMINATION ACT An amendment to the 1964 Civil Rights Act, the Pregancy Discrimination Act requires that pregnancy, childbirth, and conditions related thereto must be treated as similar to other medical conditions.

1. **Applicability** Where an employer offers benefits for any sort, including retirement, health insurance, or disability benefits, it must cover pregnancy and related medical conditions in the same way and to the same extent that it covers other medical conditions.

2. **Guidelines** Women who are pregnant or are affected by related conditions must be treated in the same manner as other applicants or employees with similar abilities or limitations.

   a. An employer cannot refuse to hire a woman because of her pregnancy-related condition as long as she is able to perform the major functions of the job.

   b. An employer may not single out pregnancy-related conditions for special procedures to determine an employee's ability to work.

   c. If an employee is temporarily unable to perform her job due to pregnancy, the employer must treat her the same as any other temporarily disabled employee; for example, by providing modified tasks, alternative assignments, disability leave, or leave without pay.

   d. Employers must hold open a job for a pregnancy-related absence the same length of time jobs are held open for employees on sick or disability leave.

   e. If a health insurance plan excludes benefit payments for preexisting conditions when the insured's coverage becomes effective, benefits can be denied for medical costs arising from an existing pregnancy.

   f. Employers must provide the same level of health benefits for spouses of male employees as they do for spouses of female employees.

   g. Employers must permit women who are on pregnancy leave to accrue seniority in the same way as those who are on leave for other reasons.

   h. To cover pregnancy, childbirth, and related medical conditions on the same terms as other medical conditions, an employer's health plan must provide for the same:
      - deductibles;
      - level of coinsurance payments;
      - choices of physicians and hospitals;
      - basis for reimbursement; and
      - apportionment of premium charges between employee and employer.

UNIT QUIZ

1. With regard to disability income insurance, the determination of whether an individual is disabled is based on
   A. the insured's condition matching those specifically set forth in the policy
   B. the diagnosis of the insured's primary physician
   C. the inability of the insured to perform duties of his job
   D. a "reasonable person" standard

2. A benefit of 50% of the monthly total disability benefit for up to 6 months is typical of what type of disability benefit?
   A. Residual disability
   B. Recurrent disability
   C. Partial disability
   D. Total disability

3. With regard to health insurance, which of the following best describes the elimination period?
   A. The period following the onset of a disability income policy during which no benefits will be paid
   B. The period following the onset of a disability during which no benefits from a disability income policy will be paid
   C. The period following the effective date of a group health insurance policy during which no benefits will be paid for preexisting conditions
   D. The underwriting period for a group health insurance policy during which all those with preexisting conditions are eliminated from coverage

4. All of the following are true concerning major medical insurance EXCEPT
   A. benefits have high maximum limits
   B. benefits are expressed as a percentage of eligible expenses
   C. it is characterized by percentage participation
   D. deductibles are usually of a variable nature

5. John owns a major medical policy with an 80/20 co-insurance provision. This policy also has a $500 deductible. If John incurs medical expenses of $3,700, for how much will he be responsible?
   A. $1,140
   B. $1,850
   C. $2,560
   D. $2,960

6. Amy is the insured under an accidental death and dismemberment policy, which provides for a principal sum of $50,000 and a capital sum of $25,000. She suffers the loss of her right arm in a car accident. Which of the following statements is CORRECT?
   A. She will be paid an amount equal to half the capital sum.
   B. She will be paid $50,000.
   C. She will be paid $25,000.
   D. She will be paid an amount equal to twice the capital sum.

7. Bill has a disability income policy paying him $4,000 per month. The contract also has a 30 day waiting period. Bill was disabled for 75 days. How much will his policy pay?
   A. $4,000
   B. $6,000
   C. $8,000
   D. $10,000

8. A disability income contract that pays the expenses of a firm if the owner becomes disabled best describes
   A. key-employee disability
   B. business overhead expense
   C. residual disability
   D. business health expense

9. The benefit amount payable under an accidental death policy is known as the
   A. death amount
   B. capital sum
   C. dismemberment sum
   D. principal sum

10. Deductibles found in a major medical policy are usually expressed as a(n)

    A. variable amount
    B. fixed dollar amount
    C. deferred amount
    D. indexed amount

11. Intentionally self-inflicted injuries are generally excluded from coverage under all of the following EXCEPT

    A. disability income policies
    B. major medical policies
    C. medical expense policies
    D. dental plan policies

12. Which of the following best describes a health maintenance organization?

    A. Prepaid practice plan
    B. Plan providing traditional health care
    C. Health coverage provided on a fee for service basis
    D. A plan providing death and dental benefits

13. Which of the following may function as a nonprofit organization providing health care benefits?

    A. HMO
    B. MEWA
    C. Blue Cross and Blue Shield
    D. Business overhead expense association

ANSWERS

1. C   2. C   3. B   4. D   5. A   6. C   7. B
8. B   9. D   10. B   11. D   12. A   13. C

DISCUSSION QUESTIONS

1. Define total disability.

2. Contrast partial and presumptive disability.

3. Describe disability income insurance.

4. Briefly describe the coverages provided by a business overhead expense contract.

5. Discuss the purpose of credit disability insurance.

6. Compare the coverages provided by an accidental death contract and those of a dismemberment policy.

7. What coverages are provided by a basic hospital expense plan?

8. Identify four main characteristics of a major medical policy.

9. Discuss the purpose of a Multiple Employer Welfare Arrangement (MEWA).

10. Briefly describe the coverages and other characteristics of Blue Cross and Blue Shield plans.

11. Discuss the basic benefits provided by dental expense insurance.

12. What are the basic differences between group health and individual health policies?

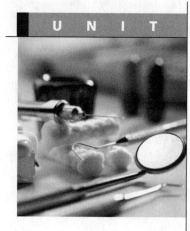

8

Accident and Health Policy Provisions and Riders

KEY TERMS

Uniform Provisions

Entire Contract

Reinstatement

Notice of Claim

Change of Occupation

Cancellation

Insuring Clause

Consideration

Probationary

Elimination

Waiver of Premium

Preexisting

Recurrent

Riders

Noncancellable

Cancellable

Guaranteed Renewable

Conditionally
  Renewable

Optionally Renewable

Case Management

Second Surgical

Preadmission

Concurrent Review

TEST TOPIC ALERT

With health insurance policies, there is some uniformity in that all states require, at a minimum, the same 12 provisions be included in all accident and health policies. Additional provisions are also available to insurers to include in their policies as they desire or as required by state law.

I.   POLICY PROVISIONS, CLAUSES, AND RIDERS

Health insurance is characterized in part by the diversity of contract forms: medical expense, disability, long-term care, etc. However, all are subject to certain minimum policy provision requirements. These provisions were prescribed in the NAIC's Uniform Individual Accident and Sickness Provisions Law, developed in 1950, and subsequently adopted by all 50 states and jurisdictions.

A.   UNIFORM MANDATORY PROVISIONS
There are 12 mandatory, or required, uniform policy provisions that must be included in every accident and health contract issued. The mandatory provision laws were developed to achieve a standardization of general provisions for the protection of the public. In addition, mandatory provisions were adopted to prevent insurers from including restrictive provisions in accident and health contracts that result in legitimate claims being denied. The 12 mandatory provisions are the following.

1. **Entire contract** The application, all endorsements or riders, waivers, and any attached papers make up the entire contract.

2. **Time limit on certain defenses (incontestable clause)** This is the accident and health insurance equivalent to the incontestable clause found in a life insurance contract. It states that after a policy has been in effect for more than two years, claims may not be denied by the insurer due to any misinformation or misstatements made on the application. The time period for this provision may vary by state.

3. **Grace period** As in life insurance, a specific grace period is allowed under accident and health contracts for premium payments. If a premium is not paid on the due date, coverage will remain in effect during the grace period. If the premium is not paid by the end of the grace period, the policy will lapse. The grace period in most accident and health contracts is 31 days (seven days for policies paid weekly and 10 days for policies paid monthly).

4. **Reinstatement** This provision outlines the procedures involved regarding reinstatement of coverage following the lapse of a policy. The insurer will usually require the completion of a reinstatement application to ensure that the insured has not become disabled nor contracted any illness during the lapse period. The insurer may also require the evidence of insurability be provided.

   a. Once a policy has been reinstated, coverage for any accidents sustained is effective immediately and coverage for sickness begins following a 10-day waiting period.

   b. If an insured has submitted a reinstatement application to an insurer and has received no word from the company that it was rejected, coverage will be automatically reinstated 45 days after the reinstatement application was submitted.

5. **Notice of claim** This provision specifies the amount of time an insured has to notify the insurer concerning a claim. Typically, an insured is required to send written notice to the insurer within 20 days of sustaining a loss.

6. **Claim forms** This provision specifies the procedures that an insured must follow to obtain claim forms from the insurer. Once an insured requests claim forms from an insurer, the company must furnish the forms to the insured within 15 days of receipt of the notice.

7. **Proof of loss** Written proof of loss must be supplied to an insurer within 90 days after the date of a loss. If an insured fails to provide written proof within the time required, the claim will be honored if it was not reasonably possible to provide proof within the time limit allowed.

8. **Time of payment of claims** This provision requires an insurer to pay benefits immediately upon receipt of an acceptable written proof of loss submitted by an insured. Periodic payments are usually made at least once a month, such as in a disability income contract.

9. **Payment of claims** This mandatory provision states that all indemnities will be paid to an insured by the insurance company. It also specifies any other benefits to be paid to a named insured or a named beneficiary, such as an accidental death benefit or a dismemberment claim.

10. **Physical examination and autopsy** The insurer has the right to request a physical examination and/or an autopsy of the insured prior to paying any benefits. This provision is most commonly utilized when an insurer requires that a disabled individual submit to a physical examination to prove continued disability.

11. **Legal actions** The insured may not bring any action at law or equity to recover on the policy prior to the expiration of 60 days after written proof of loss has been furnished. An insurer may not be sued later than three years after the time that the proof of loss is required to be filed.

12. **Change of beneficiary** This provision states that an insured has the right to change a beneficiary unless the beneficiary is irrevocable.

B. **OPTIONAL UNIFORM POLICY PROVISIONS** There are numerous optional uniform policy provisions available to all insurers. Insurers may include any or all of these optional provisions as it deems necessary. Some of the more common optional provisions are:

1. **Change of occupation** This provides for a change in benefits or premiums if an insured changes his occupation. For example, if the insured changes from a more hazardous to a less hazardous occupation he will experience a premium reduction. However, if the insured changes from a less hazardous to a more hazardous occupation, he will experience a benefit reduction.

2. **Misstatement of age** This is similar to the misstatement of age provision found in life insurance contracts. All amounts or benefits payable under the contract shall be such as the premium paid would have purchased if the correct age had been stated originally.

3. **Illegal occupation** An insurer will not be liable for any loss if a contributing cause to the illness or injury was as a result of the insured being involved in any illegal activity or occupation. For example, an insurer will not be liable for any loss experienced by an insured if he is injured while committing a felony.

4. **Relationship of earnings to insurance** This provision refers to disability income and restricts the amount of DI insurance that may be issued to an insured based upon that individual's average earnings. Insurers wish to prevent an insured from securing amounts of disability income insurance that are equal to or greater than their salary. This provision helps decrease the chance for malingering.

5. **Conformity with state statutes** This provision amends any policy provision to conform with state laws.

6. **Intoxicants and narcotics** No coverage is provided by an insurer while an insured is intoxicated or under the influence of any narcotic unless the substances have been administered by or taken on the advice of a physician.

7. **Unpaid premiums** Upon payment of a claim any premium due and unpaid may be deducted from the benefits. This provision is usually utilized by an insurer when an insured experiences a loss during the grace period.

8. **Cancellation (refusal to renew)** An insurer may cancel the contract at any time by providing written notice to an insured stating the reasons for cancellation. Any claims pending at the time of cancellation will not be affected by an insurer's action.

9. **Insurance with other insurer** If an insured has duplicate coverage on an expense incurred basis (as opposed to a service type benefit) with other companies and does not notify the insurer of the other policy, the insurer is liable only for its proportionate share of the expenses. Premiums for the unused portion of the coverage are returned to the insured.

10. **Insurance with other insurer** This is a separate provision that applies to coverage provided on an "other than expense incurred basis;" the other conditions of this provision are the same as the previous provision.

11. **Other insurance with this insurer** If an insured already has coverage with the insurer that, with the additional policy, provides benefits exceeding the company's allowable maximum benefits, only the maximum is payable and the excess premiums will be returned to the insured.

12. Some contracts include a **loss of time benefit** provision as well. This benefit generally pays a flat amount per month if an insured is unable to engage in his normal activities due to a covered accident or illness. Additional policy provisions required by state insurance regulations are presented in Unit 13.

TAKE NOTE

As with life insurance policies, the free look period for a health insurance policy begins when the policy is delivered to the policyowner.

C. OTHER PROVISIONS AND CLAUSES

1. **Insuring clause** This clause is generally located on the first page of an accident and health contract. It defines the exposure or risk as loss as result of accident or sickness. It also stipulates that any covered loss must occur in a manner specified in the policy. For example, the insuring clause of an accident and health contract may stipulate that injuries sustained must be due to accidental bodily injury suffered following a probationary period and occurring within the policy period.

2. **Free look** This provision is included in many accident and health contracts today and permits a new policyowner to review a policy, once it has been delivered, for a period of up to 10 or 20 days. If the insured wishes to return the contract to the insurer to receive a full refund of premium, it must occur within the stipulated time frame. The free look period must be noted on the first page of the policy. In addition, the free look period begins when the insured receives the policy.

3. **Consideration clause** The premium paid by an insured in addition to the statements made on the application are the insured's **consideration**. If an application is submitted to the underwriting department and the first premium has not been paid, a necessary consideration is missing.

4. **Probationary period** This is a stipulated period of time, which may apply to a disability income or medical expense contract, following the issuance of a policy during which no benefits will be provided nor coverage afforded. The purpose of the probationary period is to enable the insurer to avoid providing benefits for illnesses that an insured may have contracted before the date of policy issuance.

    a. The length of the probationary period may vary by policy and is usually stated in the insuring clause.

    b. A probationary period is a one-time occurrence that applies only to sickness or illness. Any injuries sustained as a result of an accident are covered immediately.

5. **Elimination (waiting) period** This is the period of time that must elapse before monthly benefits will begin under a disability income contract. It may also be described as a **waiting period**. Where a probationary period is a one-time event, an elimination period must be satisfied for each new disability incurred.

    a. Generally, the most common elimination or waiting period found in disability income contracts is 30 to 90 days. (The specific period is set forth in state law.) If an insured chooses a longer waiting period, he will save premium dollars. An elimination or waiting period is the equivalent of a deductible under other forms of health insurance.

    b. Separate elimination periods apply to loss of income due to sickness and loss due to an injury; generally, insureds select the same waiting period for both sickness and injury.

6. **Waiver of premium** This provision functions in much the same way as the waiver of premium provision in a life insurance contract. It provides that premiums will be waived if an insured is totally disabled for some period of time (usually 90 days or longer). Following 90 consecutive days, all future premiums will be waived as long as disability continues; any premiums paid during the first 90 days of disability will be refunded to the insured. In a life insurance contract, an additional premium must be paid for this benefit; however, with an accident and health policy, there is no additional charge.

7. **Exclusions** Several exclusions are listed in accident and health contracts. Some of the more common exclusions are:

   ■ injury or illness due to war, whether declared or undeclared;

   ■ injuries sustained while an insured is a member of the armed services. The same types of clauses are found in life insurance contracts including the status clause and the results clause;

   ■ intentionally self-inflicted injuries;

   ■ illness as a result of preexisting conditions;

   ■ injuries sustained while an insured is serving as a pilot, co-pilot, or crew member of an aircraft; and

   ■ other exclusions include losses resulting from suicide, riots, use of drugs or narcotics, injuries sustained while committing a crime, or hernia (note that hernia is usually covered as a sickness but not as an accidental injury).

8. **Preexisting conditions** Preexisting conditions are health conditions that have already manifested before the insured's application for health insurance coverage. They are frequently excluded from coverage. Probationary periods have helped to reduce claims for preexisting conditions. Some insurers will issue a policy to an insured knowing that there is a preexisting condition. However, the policy may be issued with a rider excluding coverage for this condition for a specified period of time, such as one or two years.

       a. This provision helps to protect an insurer when an applicant for coverage knows, or suspects, that he may be in need of medical treatment.

9. **Recurrent disability** This provision is utilized when an individual suffering total disability apparently recovers and in subsequent weeks or months the disability reoccurs. This provision will help the insurer determine how and when benefits are payable under certain circumstances. For example, if a previously disabled worker returns to his job and within six months of his return becomes disabled once again due to the original cause of the disability, the insurer will view this as a recurrent disability. If this is the case, a new elimination period is not needed and the original benefit period will continue as if the disabled insured had not returned to work. However, if the insurer determines that a *new* disability has occurred, the insured must satisfy a new elimination period before benefits begin.

TAKE NOTE

Amount of medical bill – [deductible] – [insured's coinsurance portion] = amount insurer pays

---

10. **Coinsurance** Most medical expense, major medical, and comprehensive medical expense contracts include **coinsurance provisions**. This provision provides that an insured will be responsible for a certain percentage of the medical bills incurred after a deductible amount is satisfied. Though some health insurance contracts pay 100% of all eligible expenses up to a high maximum limit, most provide coverage on a 80/20 basis. For example, after a deductible has been satisfied, the insurer will pay 80% of the remaining covered expenses the insured will pay 20%. Coinsurance provisions—that which the insurer covers—do not usually fall below 75%.

   a. **Coinsurance computations** Assume that Mr. Brown owns a comprehensive medical expense policy with a $100 deductible. The contract also includes a co-insurance provision of 80/20. Mr. Brown is hospitalized for injuries sustained in an automobile accident. Mr. Brown incurs a bill during his hospital stay of $6,000. To determine how much of this amount the insurer will be responsible for, subtract the deductible ($100) from the total bill ($6,000). Multiply the remaining $5,900 by 80%, which equals $4,720 paid by the insurer. The insured, Mr. Brown, is responsible for $1,280 (the $100 deductible and 20% of $5,900).

11. **Benefit clause (provision)** This clause establishes the eligibility for payment and the nature of the benefit payment.

12. **Reductions in coverage** Once issued, most health insurance policies do not reduce coverage after a loss although some medical expense contracts have aggregate lifetime benefits. Therefore, policies contain a clause that states that the amount of coverage will not be reduced following a loss (and payment of that loss).

13. **Military suspense provision** If a policy contains a military service exclusion or a provision that suspends coverage during military service and if the premiums are either reduced or refunded during military service, these provisions must be clearly stated. The following apply to policies that are other than noncancellable and guaranteed renewable and guaranteed renewable:

   a. If the policy contains a status exclusion, it shall provide for a pro rata refund of premium upon receipt of a written request.

   b. If the policy contains a results (causation) exclusion, premium refunds are not necessary because the policy would cover losses nor resulting from military service.

   c. A voluntary suspension of coverage may be used; when requested in writing, premiums must be refunded on a *pro rata* basis.

D. RIDERS Several types of riders are available that may be added to various accident and health contracts to add or limit coverage (most often to disability income policies).

1. **Impairment rider** When an impairment rider is added to an accident and health contract (whether it is a medical expense or disability income contract), it may be an indication that the underwriting department has not been able to adequately determine the degree of risk involved and elects to exclude coverage for the particular impairment involved. For example, with a disability income contract, an exclusion rider is the most traditional way to treat disability impaired risks.

    a. These riders may be attached to accident and health contracts to exclude coverage for the life of the contract. Other riders are attached that exclude coverage for specific periods of time, such as one, two, or five years.

    b. Insurers also handle impairments by only agreeing to issue a contract (disability income insurance) if the applicant accepts a longer elimination period, a reduced benefit period, or reduced benefit amount.

    c. Some insurers handle impairment situations by adding additional premiums (referred to as "rating up" the risk).

2. **Future increase (income) option (guaranteed purchase option)** This is an optional benefit that permits an insured to add to his coverage at specified periods in specified amounts without providing evidence of insurability. This is similar in nature to the guaranteed insurability option provided with life insurance contracts.

    a. This option is provided to applicants for disability income contracts.

    b. The guarantee offered may be contingent upon an insured meeting an earnings test before purchasing additional amounts.

    c. In most cases, this option must be exercised by an insured before age 50.

3. **Multiple indemnity rider (double, triple)** This rider may be added to accident and health contracts to provide double or triple indemnity in the event of an insured's accidental death or disability. These riders may also be added to life insurance policies.

4. **Social Security rider (social insurance supplement)** Some disability insurers offer this optional rider as a benefit for total disability that is payable while an insured is not receiving benefits under Social Security.

    a. Some insurers offer a social insurance supplement that encompasses not only Social Security but workers' compensation as well as other state and federal programs.

    b. Under this rider, an insured selects a specific amount of monthly indemnity up to the amount he expects to receive as a benefit from Social Security.

    c. Insurers provide that if Social Security (or social insurance) benefits that have been paid cease or are reduced, the monthly indemnity of the insurance policy will immediately be payable (or increased by a predetermined additional monthly benefit amount if benefits are reduced) if the maximum benefit period of the policy has not ended (and the insured continues to be disabled as defined by the policy).

d. An additional premium is required for this benefit.

5. Cost of living adjustment (COLA) For an additional premium, policyowners can opt for a COLA rider that will adjust monthly disability benefits at the end of each year of a continuing disability to reflect any change in the cost of living from the time the claim started.

  a. Benefits can increase or decrease each year depending upon whether the cost of living increases or decreases.

  b. Benefits can never be reduced to an amount less than the amount specified in the policy on the date of issue.

6. Hospital confinement benefit With this rider, an additional monthly indemnity benefit is paid along with the basic disability policy monthly benefit when the insured is hospitalized.

7. Lifetime extension rider Disability benefits for sickness usually end at age 65 or two years, whichever is longer. With the purchase of this rider (permitted only under certain ages such as 45, 50, or 55), payments will continue for life. Some policies reduce benefits after age 65 by 10% for each year from the inception of the disability after age 55. For example, if a disabling illness began at age 59, the insured would receive full benefits to age 65 then 60% for the rest of her life.

8. Medical reimbursement benefit This rider indemnifies the insured for medical expenses incurred for specific accidents, or in some cases illnesses, where hospitalization is not required.

9. Return of premium (refund provisions) Two types of return of premium rider are generally available: the **cash value type** (cash surrender value), where all premiums paid are refunded at age 65, less all benefits received; and the type that returns a substantial portion of the premium at the end of any 10-year period during which either no claims at all or a minimal amount that total no more than 20% of premiums paid, the insured will receive a refund of 80% of all premiums paid during the 10-year period.

10. Annual renewable term Annually renewable term disability income riders provide supplemental coverage to more traditional contracts; premiums increase on an annual basis.

11. Residual disability This benefit provides reduced monthly indemnity in proportion to an insured's loss of income when he has begun working again but at reduced earnings (income). In most policies, this benefit is payable only when the insured has returned to his job or engaged in his normal occupation. An additional premium is charged for this benefit.

  a. For example, if an insured owns a disability income policy with a residual disability rider, and experiences a 60% loss of income while disabled, the policy would pay 60% of his specified maximum benefit. If the contract paid $2,000 per month

---

TAKE ✓ NOTE

The less restrictive a contract's renewability provision for the insured, the more expensive it is.

---

for total disability, this individual would be paid $1,200 per month for residual disability.

   b. In most cases, no benefits are paid with a residual benefit if the loss of income is less than 20 or 25%.

E. RIGHTS OF RENEWABILITY Accident and health policies may be classified according to their renewability provisions. There are several classifications including noncancellable, cancellable, guaranteed renewable, conditionally renewable, and optionally renewable.

   1. Noncancellable A noncancellable contract may also be referred to as "noncancellable and guaranteed renewable." This type of contract provides an insured with the right to renew his policy up to a specified age (such as age 65), as long as premiums are paid prior to the expiration of the grace period. In addition, the insurer may not cancel, alter the policy terms, or increase the premium charged.

   2. Cancellable A cancellable contract is one that may be terminated or "cancelled" by an insurer at anytime. This type of contract is not advantageous to an insured since the company may cancel at any time, for any reason.

   3. Guaranteed renewable This type of policy permits an insured to renew his coverage up to a specified age (such as age 65). An insurer may not cancel a contract nor alter any of its provisions as long as the insured pays the premium within the grace period. However, according to the right to increase the premium provision, the insurer does reserve the right to increase the premium at policy renewal on a class basis. This means that the insurer may not increase an individual's premium, but can increase premiums for classes (i.e., all firemen or welders, etc.) of insureds.

   4. Conditionally renewable (limited continuance) An insured has the conditional right to renew the policy up to a given age, date, or for his lifetime. With conditionally renewable contracts, the insurer may choose not to renew the contract for specific circumstances such as the insured's retirement, but it may not nonrenew the contract due to a covered individual's deteriorating health. In addition, the insurer also has the right to increase premiums and modify benefits.

   5. Renewable at the option of the insurer This type of contract the insurer reserves the right to terminate or cancel coverage at any policy anniversary or premium due date. The insurer is prevented from cancelling the contract at any other time. In addition, premiums and benefits provided may be altered or modified by the insurer.

II.   COST-SAVING SERVICES

In the past number of years, usage of health care services and the cost of those services have been steadily increasing. Insurers, regulators, and consumers alike understand the need to contain these costs without affecting quality of service. The concept of **managed care**, which can be defined as systems and techniques used to control the use of health care services, has been a crucial aspect of the health care and health insurance industry for years. Managed care is a broad term and encompasses many different types of organizations, payment mechanisms, review mechanisms, and collaborations and is most often practiced by organizations and professionals that assume risk for a defined population (e.g., health maintenance organizations). The following are examples of cost containment measures common to managed care.

A.   PREVENTATIVE CARE Wellness programs encourage individuals to attain healthier life styles and discover a medical problem early so treatment may begin before it becomes an advanced condition that requires extensive and costly attention.

B.   HOSPITAL OUTPATIENT BENEFITS Costs can be controlled by utilization of certain outpatient benefits such as preadmission testing to determine to need for inpatient care, the use of emergency room treatment as an alternative to hospital admission, and performing minor surgery on an outpatient basis.

C.   ALTERNATIVES TO HOSPITAL SERVICES Utilization of a variety of alternatives will help control costs. These include use of a skilled nursing facility as opposed to a prolonged hospitalization; use of home health care services when part-time nursing is prescribed; use of birthing centers that provide a homelike atmosphere and are separate from hospitals; ambulatory surgical centers that are separate from hospitals and less expensive than inpatient surgery, and use of hospice care for terminally ill patients.

D.   UTILIZATION MANAGEMENT PROVISIONS

1. Mandatory second surgical opinions Second opinion programs represent a type of preadmission review. Mainly involving surgery, these programs recognize that unusually high levels of unnecessary surgery have occurred in the past. Second opinion programs have been classified as either **generalized** or **focused**. Generalized second opinions are those that may be required for all elective surgeries. Focused second opinions involve a select set of conditions found to be frequently abused. At times, these programs may be costly and more expensive in a generalized program where one or more second opinion may be given. In the majority of cases, second opinion programs have demonstrated a definite cost savings potential that justifies its inclusion in health care programs. (Especially true where elective surgery is concerned, health care providers are requiring that second opinions are mandatory before benefits will be paid; otherwise, only a reduced amount of the cost is covered.)

2. Preadmission certification This is basically a screening process that filters out those patients for that inpatient services are not required. The purpose of preadmission certification is to make sure that those individuals hospitalized require the intensive and costly services provided by the hospital. This certification process is usually applied to all elective hospital admissions. It is a step-by-step process that usually involves an individual patient's physician and a reviewing body (other physicians). In the cases where admission is not certified by the review organization, the physician is encouraged to use outpatient services as a means for providing medical care to the patient. This is the most efficient and effective process in controlling medical care expenses.

3. **Reductions in coverage** Most plans that require second surgical opinions and/or preadmission certification will reduce benefits if these requirements are not met by insureds.

4. **Concurrent review** This procedure is an evaluation and monitoring process that attempts to insure that a patient's length of stay in a hospital (for medical treatment he is receiving) is of the shortest possible duration, but appropriate for his medical condition. The sequence of patient care is coordinated and alternatives to hospital care are explored. This type of review is a continual process that occurs while the patient is receiving treatment. In many cases, following a concurrent review, a retrospective review will occur that is an "after the fact" process and is designed to determine whether care provided to the patient previously was appropriate.

5. **Ambulatory services** In recent years the development of ambulatory care centers has occurred (often called surgical centers). These centers, designed for the purpose of outpatient surgery, are separate from hospitals. Since these facilities usually fail to meet the definition of a hospital, benefits for their use are not included under hospital expense coverage. Consequently, some basic medical expense plans provide benefits for ambulatory services. To encourage the use of these facilities as a less expensive alternative to hospitals, benefits may be paid at a higher level or even in full. Benefits cover any charges for use of the facility as well as other charges, such as medical supplies, x-rays, and diagnostic tests.

U N I T   Q U I Z

1. Which of the following is a mandatory, or required, uniform health policy provision?

   A. Conformity with state statutes
   B. Change of occupation
   C. Relation of earnings to insurance
   D. Entire contract

2. The grace period found in most accident and health contracts is

   A. 5 days
   B. 20 days
   C. 28 days
   D. 31 days

3. Within how many days of sustaining a loss must an insured send written notice of claim to the insurer?

   A. 5 days
   B. 10 days
   C. 20 days
   D. 30 days

4. An insurer must send claim forms when requested by a claimant within

   A. 5 days
   B. 10 days
   C. 15 days
   D. 20 days

5. Written proof of loss must be sent to an insurer within how many days of the date of loss?

   A. 30
   B. 60
   C. 90
   D. 180

6. Which of the following provisions involve either a benefit or premium reduction?

   A. Change of beneficiary
   B. Relation of earnings to insurance
   C. Cancellation
   D. Change of occupation

7. The free look period in a health insurance policy begins upon completion of

   A. an application
   B. the underwriting process
   C. the delivery
   D. the statement of continued good health

8. A period of time that is satisfied for each new disability incurred best describes the

   A. probationary period
   B. elimination period
   C. recurrent period
   D. residential period

9. Which of the following is CORRECT concerning a guaranteed renewable health policy?

   A. Policy may not be cancelled in any instance
   B. Policy terms may not be altered
   C. Premiums may never be altered
   D. Benefits increase periodically along with inflation

10. All of the following are commonly excluded from coverage under a health policy EXCEPT

    A. intentionally self-inflicted injuries
    B. illness or sickness that is genetically inherited
    C. illness due to drug use
    D. injuries sustained while serving in the armed forces

ANSWERS

1. D	2. D	3. C	4. C	5. C
6. D	7. C	8. B	9. B	10. B

DISCUSSION QUESTIONS

1. Identify the 12 uniform policy provisions.

2. What will occur when a person changes from a more hazardous to a less hazardous occupation and vice versa?

3. Identify several optional provisions that may appear in accident and health policies.

4. Briefly describe the importance of the free look period and when it begins.

5. Discuss the difference between a probationary and elimination period.

6. How does the waiver of premium provision under a disability income policy differ from the same provision found in a life insurance policy?

7. Identify several common exclusions that appear in accident and health contracts.

8. How do noncancellable and guaranteed renewable contracts differ from guaranteed renewable policies?

9. Briefly describe each of the following:
    A. Noncancellable policy
    B. Guaranteed renewable policy
    C. Conditionally renewable policy
    D. Optionally renewable policy

10. Briefly discuss the significance of the concept of recurrent disability.

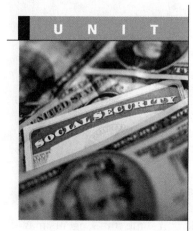

9

Government Health Programs and Social Insurance

KEY TERMS

Medicare	Medicaid	Medicare Supplement
Hospital Insurance	Fully Insured	NAIC Standards
Supplementary Medical	Currently Insured	CHAMPUS
	Disability Offset	State Disability

I.   SOCIAL INSURANCE

Through a number of programs, federal and state governments provide health insurance and health care to select segments of our society: generally, those who are elderly, poor, or disabled. Significant among these programs are Medicare, Medicaid, and the disability benefits portion of Social Security.

A.   MEDICARE This is a two-part federal health insurance program. It provides medical benefits for the aged and for qualified persons who are disabled. It is comprised of Part A, Basic Hospital Insurance and Part B, Supplementary Medical Insurance. In some states, agents may be required to provide individual and group health insurance clients with notification of their eligibility for Medicare benefits.

1. Part A—hospital insurance All persons age 65 or older who are entitled to federal Social Security or Railroad Retirement benefits are automatically eligible for Medicare (on the first day of the month the individual turns 65). In addition, individuals under age 65 who have qualified for Social Security disability payments for at least two years and those who have end stage renal disease are eligible. Eligible insureds do not have to pay any premiums for this coverage.

a. Other elderly persons not covered by Social Security may elect to participate voluntarily by paying a monthly premium.

b. Part A covers inpatient hospital services (subject to a deductible) for up to 90 days in each benefit period. All charges are paid (over the deductible) during the first 60 days; from the 61st through the 90th days, Part A pays for all covered services except for a coinsurance amount. The benefit period begins on the day of admittance to a hospital or extended care facility and ends after the insured has been released for 60 consecutive days. Benefits include payment for prescription drugs only while in the hospital. No coverage is provided for the first three pints of blood.

c. Skilled nursing care is provided for up to 100 days. All covered services for the first 20 days are fully paid after the insured pays the annual deductible ($912 in 2005). The next 80 days are subject to a daily coinsurance amount.

d. Home health services provided by Part A cover medically necessary home health visits including part-time skilled nursing services.

e. Hospice care benefits are designed for the terminally ill, with emphasis on pain reduction and quality of life. Medicare recipients who elect hospice benefits must forego all other Medicare benefits except for physician services and treatment for conditions not related to the terminal illness.

f. Psychiatric hospital care is covered for up to 190 days during the individual's lifetime.

g. Payment of bills under Part A is made directly to the hospital or provider of the service on a reasonable cost basis.

h. Medicare Part A is financed primarily by employment-related tax funds provided through the Social Security (FILA) program. It is financed on a contributory basis, shared equally by employer and employee.

i. If an individual is covered by both private and social insurance (such as an HMO and Medicare), the private insurance is considered primary and will pay benefits first; Medicare would then pay the balance of eligible expenses.

j. Part A has a lifetime reserve of 60 days. Reserve days may be used when more than 90 days of inpatient hospital care in a benefit period are needed (a daily coinsurance amount applies). Once used, reserve days are not renewed.

2. **Part B—supplementary medical insurance (SMI)** Medicare Part B is voluntary medical insurance plan available to all who are entitled to, or have purchased, Part A, which pays benefits for physician and surgeon fees, related medical services and supplies, medically necessary outpatient hospital services, x-rays and laboratory tests, and other health services such as ambulance services and durable medical equipment (hospital beds and wheelchairs).

    a. Individuals pay a monthly premium, an annual deductible (currently $110), and coinsurance of 20% of all remaining covered expenses. After the deductible is satisfied, Part B pays 80% of approved charges.

    b. The Medicare-approved amount for physician services is based upon a national fee schedule; physicians who accept assignment on a Medicare claim agree to take the Medicare-approved amount as payment in full. The patient is responsible for amounts in excess of the Medicare-approved amount for unassigned claims.

    c. Limitations include 50% of approved charges for outpatient mental health treatment and no coverage for the first three pints of blood.

    d. Part B is financed by monthly contributions (premiums) of those who choose to participate, as well as tax revenues. In other words, the cost for SMI is paid by the enrollee and the federal government. The latter pays approximately 75%.

    e. **Exclusions** Medical services not covered under Part B include eye and hearing examinations, routine physical exams, foot care, immunizations, and private nurses.

    f. Individuals are automatically enrolled in Part B following Medicare eligibility. This may be delayed for individuals who are covered under an employer's group health plan. Once individuals leave the group, they then must enroll within seven months of that date.

    g. **Medicare Part B premiums** Currently all Medicare recipients pay 25% of the Part B premium and Medicare covers the remaining 75%; beginning in 2007, the Part B premium will be linked to income.

1.) Individuals earning $80,000 to $100,000 will pay 35%, those earning $100,001 to $150,000 will pay 50%, those earning $150,001 to $200,000 will pay 65%, and individuals with incomes over $200,000 will pay 80%.

2.) Income levels for taxpayers filing jointly will double; recipients with incomes of less than $80,000 will continue to pay 25%.

3.) The Part B deductible increases in 2005 from $100 to $110, and then it will be indexed to the program's per capita cost.

3. **Part C—Medicare Advantage plans** Federal law allows Medicare-eligible participants to opt out of the traditional program (Parts A and B) and enroll in one of the plans described below. These plans constitute the Medicare Advantage option (previously called Medicare+Choice.)

   a. **Coordinated-care plans**

      1.) Health maintenance organizations HMOs of various types, but all requiring services to be rendered by its own providers, except in an emergency.

      2.) Preferred provider organizations PPOs allow beneficiaries to receive services from providers outside the plan, but with higher cost sharing.

      3.) Provider-sponsored organizations PSOs are similar to PPOs except that they are operated by a group of physicians and hospitals.

   b. **Private-fee-for-service plans** These are similar to PSOs, except that they may pay providers more than Medicare recognizes and can charge beneficiaries additional premiums and cost-sharing payments.

   c. **Medicare+Choice MSAs** This was a pilot program that enables senior citizens to establish a special Medical Savings Account. As with regular MSAs, individuals with Medicare+Choice can apply their contributions to their MSAs for health care expenses; however, this kind of MSA must be used in conjunction with a high-deductible (up to $6,000 per year) MSA health plan.

      1.) Annual contributions are limited to 75% of the individual's deductible under the required MSA health plan. For example, if the deductible was $5,000, contributions could not exceed $3,750.

      2.) All earnings on MSA accounts are excluded from taxable income for the current year.

      3.) Distributions to pay for qualified medical expenses are not included in the participant's income; however, distributions for purposes other than medical expenses must be included in taxable income.

      4.) Medicare+Choice has largely been replaced with a Medicare option that provides for health savings accounts (HSAs).

4. Medicare Prescription Drug, Improvement, and Modernization Act of 2003 This law is considered by many to be the most comprehensive change to the federal Medicare program since it was enacted in 1965. Its intent is to provide seniors and the disabled with a prescription drug benefit as well as more choices under Medicare.

   a. Health savings accounts (HSAs) Commonly known as Medicare Advantage, this option allows individuals under 65 to establish and contribute to an HSA if they have a qualified health plan. It provides a tax-favored way to accumulate finds to cover medical expenses.

   1.) A **qualified health plan** for an individual is defined as one with a minimum deductible of $1,000 and a cap of $5,000 on out-of-pocket expenses; for a family, the minimum deductible is $2,000 with a $10,000 cap.

   2.) Annual contributions can be made up to 100% of an individual's health plan deductible. In 2004, the maximum contribution (subject to the health plan deductible limit) for an individual insured $2,600 and $5,150 for a family; these limits are indexed annually.

   3.) Catch-up contributions can be made by individuals age 55 to 65 starting in 2004 in the amount of $500. This amount can be increased by $100 per year up to $1,000 in the year 2009 and each year thereafter.

   4.) HSA earnings grow tax-free. Tax-free withdrawals can be made to cover expenses such as retiree health insurance premiums, Medicare expenses, prescription drugs, long-term care services, and COBRA coverage.

   5.) Nonqualified withdrawals are subject to income tax as well as a 10% penalty. HSA assets can accumulate and are portable. At death, ownership may be transferred tax free to a spouse.

   6.) HSAs may be offered by employers through a cafeteria plan; employer contributions are made on a pretax basis and are not taxable to the employee.

   b. Medicare Part D—prescription drug plan (PDP) Beginning in 2006, Medicare recipients can elect a prescription drug plan for an additional monthly premium. The provisions of this option include the following.

   1.) For the standard benefits under the PDP plan, Medicare beneficiaries will pay a projected monthly premium of $35 and assume an annual deductible of $250. Beneficiaries will then pay 25% of the first $2,250 of prescription drug costs and Medicare will pay the 75% balance; after this limit is reached, coverage stops completely until total drug costs exceed $5,100 (initial $2,250 plus another $2,850). After that, coverage starts again and beneficiaries contribute a copayment of $2 for generic drugs and $5 for brand name medications or 5% of total costs, whichever is higher. (Note that these dollar thresholds are scheduled to increase each year.)

TAKE NOTE

Medicare Part A Hospital expenses
Medicare Part B Physician, surgeon, and other medical expenses
Medicare Part C Optional coordinated health care plan, fee-for-service plans, or MSA
Medicare Part D Prescription drug plan (PDP)

   2.) Benefits will be available through PDPs, which are private plans that will contract with Medicare, and through Medicare Advantage.

   3.) A six-month enrollment period begins on November 15, 2005. The law provides for federal subsidy payments to employers and unions that sponsor qualified retiree prescription drug plans.

   4.) Medicare supplement (Medigap) policies Currently, three of the standardized Medicare supplement plans provide prescription drug coverage. Starting in 2006, the law prohibits the inclusion of prescription drug coverage in these policies. However, Medicare supplement policyholders who have the prescription drug coverage and do not enroll in Medicare Part D will be able to renew their policies.

   a.) Policyholders who elect to enroll in Part D may keep their current Medigap policy without the prescription drug coverage and their premium will be adjusted or they may change to another Medigap plan if they elect Part D during the initial enrollment period.

   c. Medicare-endorsed prescription drug discount cards To bridge the gap between now and the implementation of Medicare Part D in 2006, Medicare-endorsed prescription drug cards will be available to Medicare beneficiaries. Cards are anticipated to cost approximately $30 per year and will offer discounts of between 10 and 25% off the price of prescription drugs (this program will expire December 31, 2005).

5. Employer group health plans Individuals who are participating in an employer group health plan and are Medicare participants are subject to the following:

   a. Special rules apply to working people age 65 and over. Medicare may be the secondary payor to any employer group health plan (employer plans pays hospital and medical bills first); if the employer plan does not cover all expenses, Medicare becomes the secondary payor for eligible expenses.

   b. Special rules apply to certain disabled Medicare beneficiaries who have group coverage provided by an employer with 100 or more employees. Medicare would be the secondary payor of benefits (with the exception of those with permanent kidney failure).

   c. Medicare is the secondary payor for up to 21 months for beneficiaries with permanent kidney failure; following this period, the employer group health plan becomes the secondary payor and Medicare becomes primary.

B. MEDICAID Created in 1965, Medicaid substantially expanded the role of the federal government in health care financing by permitting states to receive matching funds to expand their public assistance programs to individuals with insufficient income to pay for medical care. Medicaid is financed by both federal and state governments and is administered by the individual states.

1. Medicaid is a form of welfare that provides assistance to the needy. It is not funded by Medicare.

2. The extent of covered costs varies among states.

3. It provides supplemental medical care for low income and needy individuals who are aged, blind, disabled, or under 21 years of age. It provides aid to families with dependent children (ADC).

C. SOCIAL SECURITY DISABILITY BENEFITS In addition to retirement and survivor benefits, Social Security provides benefits for disabilities.

1. Social Security disability income coverage extends to any employment where an individual works for salary or wages as well as most self-employed persons.

2. **Benefits** The amount of disability benefits paid by Social Security depends upon the insured status of the individual worker and the Primary Insurance Amount (PIA). The worker must be fully insured in order to receive this benefit.

    a. **Fully insured** A person becomes fully insured by acquiring a sufficient number of quarters of coverage to meet either of the following two tests:

        1.) A person is fully insured if he has 40 quarters of coverage (10 years of covered employment). Once a person has acquired 40 quarters of coverage, he is fully insured for life, even if he spends no further time in covered employment (or covered self employment).

        2.) A person is fully insured if: (1) he has at least six quarters of coverage, and (2) he has acquired at least as many quarters of coverage as there are years elapsing after 1950 (or, if later, after the year in which he reaches age 21) and before the year in which he dies, becomes disabled, or reaches, or will reach age 62, whichever occurs first.

3. **Definition of total disability** The definition of disability under Social Security is much more restrictive than that found in individual or group plans. It states that a person is totally disabled if he "cannot perform the duties of any gainful employment and that the disability is expected to last at least one year or result in death."

4. **Waiting period** There is a five-month waiting period for Social Security income benefits; payments start in the sixth month.

5. **Disability offset** In many cases, group disability (LTD) income benefits are reduced or offset by any amount received from Social Security (or other social insurance such as workers' compensation). However, if a person owns and pays the premium on an individual disability income policy, any benefits received are not reduced by amounts collected from social insurance plans.

D. MEDICARE AND HMOs Health maintenance organizations may be sponsored by the government to provide benefits for those persons eligible for Medicare. There are two basic ways for an HMO to cover Medicare members.

1. **Risk contract** In this situation, an HMO enters into a contract with the federal government to be liable (at risk) for all medical expenses incurred by a Medicare enrollee for covered services. As a result of this exchange of coverage, the government pays the HMO a monthly sum per covered person. Therefore, Medicare is no longer liable to provide coverage for that person. Enrollment in an HMO by a recipient of Medicare is voluntary.

2. **Wrap coverage** Here an HMO is not required to enter into a contract with the government. Medicare continues to pay for all of the member's Medicare eligible expenses. The HMO, however, provides excess (additional) services in comparison to Medicare and is responsible for the cost. Therefore, the HMO coordinates benefits with Medicare and sends it a bill for the amount Medicare should cover. The HMO pays the balance. An HMO's risk is less under Wrap Coverage, that means it costs less.

3. HMO options for Medicare recipients include the following.

   a. **Medicare risk plans** are paid a per capita premium set at approximately 95% of the projected average expenses for fee for service beneficiaries in a given county. Risk plans assume full financial risk for all care provided to Medicare beneficiaries. Risk plans must provide all Medicare covered services, and most plans offer additional services, such as prescription drugs and eyeglasses. With the exception of emergency and out of area urgent care, members of risk plans must receive all of their care through the plan. However, as of January 1, 1996, risk plans can provide an out of network option that, subject to certain conditions, allows beneficiaries to go to providers who are not part of the plan.

   b. **Medicare cost plans** are paid a predetermined monthly amount per beneficiary based on a total estimated budget. Adjustments to that payment are made at the end of the year for any variations from the budget. Cost plans must provide all Medicare covered services but do not provide the additional services that some risk plans offer. Beneficiaries can also obtain Medicare covered services outside the plan without limitation. When a beneficiary seeks care or services outside the plan, Medicare pays its traditional share of those costs and the beneficiary pays Medicare's coinsurance and deductibles.

   c. **Medicare health care prepayment plans (HCPPs)** are paid in a similar manner as cost plans but only cover part of the Medicare benefit package. HCPPs do not cover Medicare Part A services (inpatient hospital care, skilled nursing, hospice, and some home health care) but some do arrange for services and may file Part A claims for their members.

E. MEDICARE SUPPLEMENT (MEDIGAP) POLICIES Medicare supplement policies are policies sold by private insurers that provide benefits (for both accident and sickness) for specific expenses not covered under Medicare that result from deductibles, exclusions, or coinsurance. As such, they are not social insurance but are used to supplement or augment the social insurance benefits offered by Medicare.

1. The National Association of Insurance Commissioners (NAIC) set standards for 12 levels of coverage under Medicare supplement or Medigap policies, designated A through L. Plan A is the most basic policy. Plan J is the most comprehensive in coverage. Others offer various combinations of benefits. All 12 plans include a core package of basic benefits that cover the following coinsurance and deductible features of Medicare.

    a. The insured's share of hospital charges (coinsurance) under Medicare Part A for 61 days through 90 and 91 days through 150 (lifetime reserve).

    b. 90% of charges for 365 additional days in hospital.

    c. The insured's 20% share of expenses covered under Part B.

    d. The Part A blood deductible (three pints) and Part B blood deductible (three pints).

    e. Other coverages maybe added by the policyholder to the basic core coverage (Plan A) in different combinations.

2. High deductible plans The Balanced Budget Act of 1997 authorized new high deductible versions of Plans F and J. These versions begin paying benefits after the high deductible is paid. Expenses that can be applied to the deductible are expenses that would usually be paid by the policy, such as Medicare coinsurance and deductibles for Parts A and B. However, they do not include the plan's separate foreign travel emergency deductible. A separate deductible must be met before these expenses can be applied to the overall plan deductible.

    a. Two new Medigap benefit packages have been designated by the NAIC as Plan K and Plan L. These plans have higher copayments and coinsurance contributions from the Medicare beneficiary and have a limit on annual out-of-pocket expenditures incurred by a policyholder.

        1.) Once the out-of-pocket limit on annual expenditures is reached, the policy covers 100 percent of all cost-sharing under Medicare Parts A and B for the balance of the calendar year.

        2.) For 2006, the out-of-pocket limit for Plan K is $4,000 and $2,000 for Plan L.

        3.) A Medigap policy does not pay cost-sharing for expenses incurred under Medicare Parts C and D.

    b. All Medigap policies must include a free-look period. In most states, this period is 30 days, though some states may provide for a longer period.

    c. The accompanying table outlines the provisions of the standard Medicare supplement plans.

12 Standard Medigap Plans

A	B	C	D	E	F**	G	H	I	J**	K	L
Basic Benefits*	Basic Benefits*	Basic Benefits*	Basic Benefits*	Basic Benefits*	Basic Benefits*	Basic Benefits*	Basic Benefits*	Basic Benefits*	Basic Benefits*	Basic Benefits***	Basic Benefit***
	Part A Deductible	Part A Deductible	Part A Deductible	Part A Deductible	Part A Deductible	Part A Deductible	Part A Deductible	Part A Deductible	Part A Deductible	50% Part A Deductible	50% Part A Deductible
		Skilled Nursing Coinsurance	Skilled Nursing Coinsurance	Skilled Nursing Coinsurance	Skilled Nursing Coinsurance	Skilled Nursing Coinsurance	Skilled Nursing Coinsurance	Skilled Nursing Coinsurance	Skilled Nursing Coinsurance	50% Skilled Nursing Coinsurance	50% Skilled Nursing Coinsurance
		Part B Deductible			Part B Deductible				Part B Deductible		
					Part B Excess (100%)	Part B Excess (80%)		Part B Excess (100%)	Part B Excess (100%)		
		Foreign Travel Emergency	Foreign Travel Emergency	Foreign Travel Emergency	Foreign Travel Emergency	Foreign Travel Emergency	Foreign Travel Emergency	Foreign Travel Emergency	Foreign Travel Emergency		
			At-Home Recovery			At-Home Recovery		At-Home Recovery	At-Home Recovery		
							Basic Drugs ($1,250 Limit)***	Basic Drugs ($1,250 Limit)***	Extended Drugs ($3,000 Limit)****		
				Preventive Care Not Covered by Medicare					Preventive Care Not Covered by Medicare		
					Annual Deductible**				Annual Deductible**	Annual Deductible*****	Annual Deductible*****

*The Basic Benefits policy covers 100% of the Part A hospital coinsurance amount for each day used from the 61st through the 90th day in any Medicare benefit period and 100% of the Part A hospital coinsurance amount for each Medicare lifetime inpatient reserve day used from the 91st through the 150th day in any Medicare benefit period; 100% of the Part A-eligible hospital expenses for 365 additional days after all hospital benefits are exhausted; Part B coinsurance amount (generally 20% of Medicare-approved expenses) after the annual deductible is met, and the cost of the first three pints of blood each year.

**Plans F and J have a high deductible plan option that pays the same benefits as Plans F and J after one has paid a calendar year deductible. Benefits from high deductible Plans F and J will not begin until out-of-pocket expenses exceed the deductible. Out-of-pocket expenses for this deductible are expenses that would ordinarily be paid by the policy. These expenses include the Medicare deductible for Part A and Part B, but do not include the plan's separate foreign travel emergency deductible.

***The basic benefits under Plans K and L provide for different costsharing for items and services than Plans A through J. Plan K pays 100% of Part A hospitalization coinsurance plus coverage for 365 days after Medicare benefits end, 50% of hospice cost-sharing, 50% of Medicare-eligible expenses for the first three pints of blood, and 50% of Part B coinsurance, except 100% coinsurance for Part B preventive services. Plan L pays 100% of Part A hospitalization coinsurance plus coverage for 365 days after Medicare benefits end, 75% of hospice costsharing, 75% of Medicare-eligible expenses for the first three pints of blood, and 75% of Part B coinsurance, except 100% coinsurance for Part B preventive services.

Once a person reaches the annual limit, the plan pays 100% of the Medicare copayments, coinsurance, and deductibles for the rest of the calendar years. The out-of-pocket annual limit does not include charges from a provider and that exceed Medicare-approved amounts. Such charges are called "excess charges," and the policyowner is responsible for paying them.

****These prescription drug provisions will be removed after December 31, 2005.

*****These out-of-pocket annual limits increase each year for inflation.

F. CHAMPUS This is the Civilian Health and Medical Program of the Uniformed Services. It provides health benefits for armed services families—more specifically, families of active duty, retired, and deceased members, and retirees of the armed services. It is intended to supplement benefits from a military hospital or clinic. Those not eligible include active duty personnel, dependent parents, parents-in-law, and most persons eligible for Medicare Part A. CHAMPUS pays for only medically necessary care and services.

   1. In addition, former spouses of active or retired military personnel are covered as long as they do not remarry, are not covered by another health plan, or are not eligible for Part A of Medicare.

G. WORKERS' COMPENSATION Workers' compensation provides coverage for loss of income (and other benefits) due to employment-related injuries or illness to eligible individuals (employees, their survivors, and dependents).

   1. Income payments are made for disabilities that are determined to be permanent total, permanent partial, temporary total, or temporary partial.

   2. Other benefits provided by this coverage include medical expenses, rehabilitation expenses, survivor benefits, and noneconomic benefits.

UNIT QUIZ

1. Which of the following is NOT correct regarding Medicare?

   A. Benefits provided may continue beyond the hospitalization period.
   B. Payments are made directly to the provider of services.
   C. Part A is financed by tax funds.
   D. It provides hospital benefits only.

2. Which of the following statements is CORRECT regarding PART B of Medicare?

   A. A coinsurance feature of 75%/25% is present after the deductible is satisfied.
   B. An annual deductible is required.
   C. It provides coverage for hearing examinations.
   D. Part B is mandatory.

3. Which of the following is CORRECT with regard to the hospital insurance (Part A) plan of Medicare?

   A. The insured must satisfy a deductible.
   B. The insured must pay all premiums.
   C. Part A functions like an HMO.
   D. There is no deductible.

4. Social Security disability benefits will begin following a waiting period of

   A. 2 months
   B. 5 months
   C. 6 months
   D. 12 months

5. Disability benefits will be paid by Social Security to a party who is

   A. partially insured
   B. primarily insured
   C. fully insured
   D. still working

6. Disability benefits paid under Social Security begin in the

   A. 1st month
   B. 3rd month
   C. 5th month
   D. 6th month

7. Which of the following statements is NOT correct concerning Medicaid?

   A. It provides benefits for needy and low income individuals.
   B. The extent of covered costs varies by state.
   C. Medicaid is not funded by Medicare.
   D. It is funded entirely by the federal government.

ANSWERS

1. D   2. B   3. A   4. B
5. C   6. D   7. D

DISCUSSION QUESTIONS

1. Briefly describe the benefits provided by Part A and Part B of Medicare.

2. To what party are payment of bills made under Basic Hospital Insurance?

3. Briefly describe the purpose of Medicaid and how the program is financed.

4. Discuss the difference between fully insured and currently insured status.

5. How long is the waiting period under Social Security before disability benefits are paid?

6. How will benefits be affected if a person owns an individual disability income policy and is eligible for Social Security benefits?

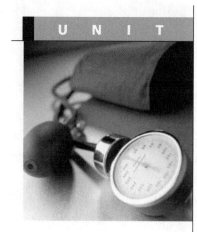

10

Other Health Insurance Concepts

KEY TERM

Owner's Rights

Dependent Coverage

Beneficiaries

Premium Payments

Nonduplication

Coordination

Occupational

Nonoccupational

Taxation

Marketing

COBRA

I.   OTHER HEALTH INSURANCE CONCEPTS

The field of health insurance is broad. Other important concepts as they relate to beneficiaries, taxation, and marketing are briefly reviewed in this section.

A. POLICYOWNERS' RIGHTS Accident and health policyowners have a variety of contractual rights. These include:

- the right of renewal;
- incontestable provision;
- the right to name and change beneficiaries;
- the right to cancel a policy;
- reinstatement provisions;
- the grace period; and
- the right of assignment.

B. DEPENDENT COVERAGE BENEFITS Under an individual health policy, dependent children may also be covered. For this purpose, children must be unmarried and under 19 years of age. Stepchildren and legally adopted children are included in this group.

   1. Coverage ends on the policy renewal date following the attainment of age 19 or marriage, unless the child is handicapped.

   2. Coverage continues for handicapped children as long as they remain unmarried and the incapacity continues.

C. PRIMARY AND CONTINGENT BENEFICIARIES The benefits provided by health insurance contracts are usually payable to an insured, hospital, physician, or dentist for services rendered. However, there are situations where beneficiaries must be named in the event of accidental death. Beneficiary designations in a health insurance contract are as follows.

   1. Primary beneficiary This is the individual who is first in line to receive the policy's death benefit.

   2. Contingent beneficiary This is the individual who will receive benefits if the primary beneficiary dies before the insured. The most common contingent beneficiaries are the children of a breadwinner. For example, a husband will name his wife as primary beneficiary and list his children as contingent beneficiaries.

   3. Tertiary beneficiary This is the beneficiary who will receive death benefits if the primary beneficiary and no contingent beneficiaries survive the insured.

D. MODES OF PREMIUM PAYMENTS Applicants for health insurance have a choice as to how they wish to pay their health insurance premiums. As in life insurance, health insurance premiums may be paid annually, semiannually, quarterly, monthly (check-o-matic), or weekly.

1. Premiums that are not paid on an annual basis are subject to a small additional charge due to the added expense of collecting premiums two, four, or 12 times a year instead of only once. In situations where premiums are paid other than annually, the insurer experiences a loss of interest since less money is collected at the beginning of the policy term.

E. NONDUPLICATION AND COORDINATION OF BENEFITS One of the primary concerns of health insurers centers on avoiding overinsurance and providing duplicate benefits to insureds. Duplicate benefits would enable an insured to profit from purchasing health insurance. Insurers providing duplicate coverage or protection that is too liberal find that it is not in the best interest of the public. This would not only contribute to higher premiums charged but also increased health care costs.

1. Methods an insurer employs to control overinsurance involve the use of deductibles and percentage participation (coinsurance). In addition, in the area of disability income insurance, insurers also help to control overinsurance or duplication of benefits by restricting coverage to a percentage of an insured's average earnings.

2. Group health insurance policies also include a coordination of benefits provision to avoid duplicate coverage. This provision limits total benefits payable to 100% of covered expenses, regardless of the number of group policies involved. Under this provision, each insurer, following the primary carrier, pays in a specified order so that the combined benefits paid will not be greater than the total allowable expenses. For example, an individual's primary insurer would be the company providing group health insurance benefits through his employer. The secondary insurer might be his spouse's group insurer.

F. OCCUPATIONAL VS. NONOCCUPATIONAL CONTRACTS

1. Occupational An occupational contract is one that provides coverage both on and off the job. Generally, only nonhazardous occupations qualify for coverage.

2. Nonoccupational Nonoccupational health insurance policies are those that cover off-the-job accidents or illnesses. These policies provide accident and sickness coverage that excludes employment-related injuries or illness. An individual who works in a coal mine, for example, would only be eligible for a nonoccupational policy since the insurer would not want to provide coverage for such a risk "on the job."

G. TAX TREATMENT OF PREMIUMS AND PROCEEDS The tax treatment of health insurance premiums and proceeds will depend upon the type of policy in question.

1. Individual health insurance premiums and proceeds Premiums paid on personal or individual health insurance policies are generally not deductible. The basic reason for this is that the Internal Revenue Service considers these premiums as a personal expense.

a. Premiums paid on an individual disability income policy are not deductible.

b. Incurred medical expenses that are reimbursed by insurance may not be deducted from an individual's federal income tax. Furthermore, incurred medical expenses that are not reimbursed by insurance may only deducted to the extent they exceed 7.5% of the insured's adjusted gross income. For example, an individual who has an adjusted gross income of $35,000 would be able to deduct only the amount of unreimbursed medical expenses over $2,625. Self-employed individuals may deduct all amounts paid for medical care, including insurance premiums.

c. The proceeds or benefits received from an individual disability income contract are income tax-free. The proceeds received from medical expense insurance are also free of income taxation because they are considered a reimbursement for expenses incurred.

2. Business health insurance premiums and proceeds

a. With a disability income policy, an employer paying the premium on a policy covering the life of a key employee will not be able to deduct the premium if the monthly benefit is payable to the employer or corporation. The benefits received from the policy are income tax free.

b. With a disability income contract where the employer pays the premium and monthly benefits are paid to the key employee, the premiums will be deductible to the employer. However, the monthly income benefits received by the employee are taxable (subject to both income tax and FICA). If an employee contributes any portion of the premium, the benefit will be tax free in proportion to the employee's contribution.

c. With a medical expense insurance plan where a key employee is covered, the premiums paid by an employer are usually deductible since they are considered a customary and usual business expense (group insurance). Benefits received are usually not taxable since they are a reimbursement of incurred medical expenses.

d. Employer-paid group disability income benefits received by an employee are taxable (income tax and FICA); the premiums paid are deductible by the employer as a business expense.

e. Benefits received by an employee for medical and dental expenses, long term care, and accidental death or dismemberment are not taxable to the employee to the extent that the benefits represent reimbursement of expenses actually incurred (if benefits exceed expenses, the excess is taxable); premiums paid by the employer are deductible as a business expense.

f. Self-employed persons may deduct a percentage (phased up to 100% by 2007) of health insurance costs from their gross income; the remaining amount is lumped together with other medical expenses and is deductible only to the extent that the total exceeds 7.5% of adjusted gross income.

g. Premiums for a Business Overhead Expense disability policy are deductible as a business expense; benefits paid to the business are treated as taxable income but are deductible when paid out to meet the continuing expenses they are designed to cover.

h. Disability buy-sell policy premiums are not deductible by the business; the benefits are received tax free.

H. HEALTH INSURANCE MARKETING Health insurance, whether medical expense or disability income, may be marketed to individuals or groups. When health contracts are marketed to and purchased by individuals, an individual policy will be issued to the insured person. When coverage is marketed to groups of persons, it is impractical to issue individual contracts. Therefore, the sponsor (employer) of the group will be the policyholder and will receive a master policy. Each insured (employees, members, etc.) will receive a certificate as proof of coverage.

1. Types of groups The most typical groups that are issued health insurance coverage involve the employer-sponsored and association-sponsored groups. As discussed in a previous unit describing group health insurance, several provisions are included in policies covering the group. One of the most important provisions in this type of policy is the conversion privilege.

a. The possibility of adverse selection always exists in insurance. Sound group underwriting helps to reduce its effect.

2. Franchise insurance This group type of coverage mechanism offers individual policies of health insurance to employees of a common employer, members of an association, or members of a professional society.

a. Characterized by individual underwriting even though a group type of association is receiving coverage.

b. Employers or organizations will usually be charged with collecting premiums from the covered persons. This saves the insurer a considerable amount in administrative costs.

c. Because of reduced insurer costs, a discount of premium is provided by the insurer. Guaranteed issuance of policies is generally provided by the insurer if a specified number of persons apply for coverage within a given period of time.

d. This coverage is usually limited to groups of 25 or less.

3. Mass marketing Many insurers now market accident and health contracts by direct mail, vending machines, television, radio, newspaper, and other means. Mass marketing is most commonly utilized when an insurer wants to target a specific group of persons (such as credit card holders, senior citizens, etc.)

I. CONSOLIDATED OMNIBUS BUDGET RECONCILIATION ACT (COBRA)

COBRA was enacted in 1986 and stipulated that employers must offer continuation of group health coverage for a specified period of time to qualified employees and beneficiaries who would not otherwise be eligible for continued coverage because of a particular "qualifying event" such as death, divorce, or termination of employment. The cost of the continued coverage is paid by the employee.

1. **Qualified beneficiaries** In addition to the individual covered under the group plan, those eligible for COBRA include the spouse and dependent children of the employee.

2. **Employer penalties** An employer that fails to meet the continuation requirements may not take a federal income tax deduction for its group health plan contributions.

    a. For example, if an employer has 1,000 employees and the cost per employee for group health coverage is $2,000, the employer will lose a $2 million deduction if it does not comply with COBRA.

    b. In addition, if an employer fails to meet the requirements, highly compensated individuals must include in their income all employer group health plan contributions made on their behalf. These "at risk" employees are usually those who are in the top 25% of the highest paid employees.

3. **Type of coverage** The continued health coverage provided for plan beneficiaries must be identical to that being provided under the plan for similarly situated beneficiaries.

4. **Maximum period of continuation coverage** A qualified beneficiary (i.e., surviving spouse) may have more than one qualifying event that entitles the beneficiary to continued coverage, but in no event may the coverage period generally exceed a 36-month period. If an individual is laid off from a job, he may continue coverage for a period not to exceed 18 months.

    a. Continuation coverage may terminate once a beneficiary becomes covered by another plan or Medicare.

    b. COBRA does not apply if the employer terminates the entire health plan.

5. **Notification required** Each covered employee or qualified beneficiary is responsible for notifying the plan administrator of the occurrence of qualifying events within 60 days after the event. Qualifying events include the following.

    a. **For the employee**

        1.) Voluntary or involuntary termination of employment for reasons other than gross misconduct

        2.) Reduction in the number of hours of employment

   b. For spouses Same as the above, plus the following.

        1.) Covered employee has become entitled to Medicare

        2.) Divorce or legal separation from the covered employee

        3.) Death of the covered employee

   c. For dependent children Same as for employee and spouse, plus the following.

        1.) Loss of dependent child status under the plan rules

6. Premiums COBRA allows employers to charge those who elect to continue coverage 102% of the premiums the employer (company) pays for each employee. The additional 2% covers administrative duties and paperwork done by the employer.

   a. A grace period exists for the failure to pay premiums. It is the longest of:

- 30 days;
- the period the plan allows employees for failure to pay premiums; or
- the period the insurance company allows the plan or the employer for failure to pay premiums.

U N I T   Q U I Z

1. All of the following are examples of health insurance policyowner's rights EXCEPT

    A. the right of renewal
    B. reinstatement provisions
    C. the right to cancel a policy
    D. the right to change an irrevocable beneficiary

2. All of the following are common modes of paying health insurance premiums EXCEPT

    A. weekly
    B. monthly
    C. annually
    D. every two years

3. Which of the following provisions may be used by an insurer to prevent a duplication of benefits?

    A. Coordination of benefits
    B. Reduction of claim expenses
    C. Warranty
    D. Waiver of benefits

4. Which of the following best describes the coverage provided to an insured under an occupational policy?

    A. Covers on the job only
    B. Covers on and off the job
    C. Covers off the job only
    D. Covers hazardous jobs only

5. Premiums paid on an individual health insurance policy are

    A. generally deductible
    B. generally not deductible
    C. deductible if they exceed 5% of the insureds gross income
    D. none of the above

ANSWERS

1. **D**   2. **D**   3. **A**   4. **B**   5. **B**

DISCUSSION QUESTIONS

1. Identify a health policyowner's rights under the contract.

2. Identify the various modes of premium paying available to an insured. Which method is the least expensive?

3. How does the coordination of benefits provision prevent overinsurance?

4. Compare the definitions of occupational and nonoccupational health policies.

5. Discuss the tax treatment of premiums and proceeds of a personal health insurance contract and a business policy.

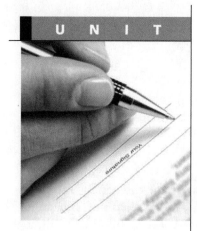

11

Application, Underwriting, and Policy Delivery

KEY TERMS

Underwriting

Producer/Agent's
 Report

Fair Credit

Criteria

Conditional Receipt

Agreement

Consideration

Legal Capacity

Insurable Interest

Warranties

Representations

Claims

Reinsurers

Self-Insurance

Accidental Means

I.   HEALTH INSURANCE UNDERWRITING

The basic purpose of health insurance underwriting is to minimize the problem of adverse selection. Adverse selection involves the fact that those who are likely to have claims are those who are most likely to seek insurance. An insurer who has sound underwriting guidelines and who rarely deviates from those guidelines will avoid adverse selection more often than not.

A principal objective of the underwriting process is to classify risks in specific categories. Numerous items are taken into consideration when attempting to accomplish this task such as the occupation of the prospective insured. The insurer will also wish to achieve a spread of risks. In other words, it is most advantageous to insure a wide range of occupations, associations, or individuals so that possible future losses will be more than offset by underwriting gain (profit).

II.   FIELD UNDERWRITING PROCEDURES AND PRODUCER RESPONSIBILITIES

The term **field underwriting** refers to the role the agent plays in the issue of insurance policies. Insurers would like nothing more than to sell their policies to anyone wishing to buy them. However, they must exercise caution in deciding who is qualified to purchase insurance and they rely on their producers or agents to fulfill many tasks that are vital to the underwriting process and policy issue. These include completing the application thoroughly and accurately, obtaining appropriate signatures, collecting the initial premium, and issuing a receipt.

A.   COMPLETING THE APPLICATION AND OBTAINING NECESSARY SIGNATURES
Before writing a health insurance risk, an insurer underwrites a specific case by utilizing various sources that provide useful information concerning the prospective insured. The greater the loss potential, the greater the number of sources an insurer will use. The primary source of underwriting information is a completed application. It is important that the applicant's name be spelled correctly, especially if inspection reports are ordered. The age and the sex of the applicant are also important, since this will affect rating the risk. A producer should be especially careful when obtaining information on nonmedical applications concerning an applicant's health and medical history. In addition, any existing health insurance policies owned by the applicant should be listed on the application. When discussing disability income insurance, the applicant's occupation must be listed. The underwriting department also obtains information from the producer's report. Additional underwriting information is derived from various medical questionnaires, physical exams, blood tests, and other physician reports.

   1. **Required signatures** Many signatures may be required to complete a health insurance application, so a producer should be aware of their importance. If any of the required signatures are not included, there will be a delay in issuing the policy. Every health insurance application requires the signature of the proposed insured, the policyowner (if different than the proposed insured), and the producer who solicits the insurance. In situations where a corporation is the policyowner, one or more of the partners or officers must also sign the application.

   2. **Producer's report** A producer's report must be completed and signed by the producer only. Forms authorizing an insurer to obtain investigative consumer reports

and medical information from doctors, hospitals, or any investigative agencies, must be signed by the applicant and the producer as a witness. In addition, the Fair Credit Reporting Act notice of disclosure (**Notice to the Applicant**) is also to be completed with the appropriate signatures. If an applicant wishes to pay on a monthly basis and use a check-o-matic plan, he must sign the appropriate forms so that this payment method may be activated.

B. **EXPLAINING SOURCES OF INSURABILITY INFORMATION** It is the duty and responsibility of agents and producers to explain to applicants for health insurance the various sources where the insurer will obtain information regarding the applicant's insurability. Several sources are available to an insurer:

1. **The Medical Information Bureau (MIB) report** The MIB is an intercompany data bank that allows member insurance companies to check applications against the bureau's record of medical impairments. The MIB serves as an aid to underwriting since it will attempt to guide an insurer toward other sources of information if some medical impairment is detected. The MIB also compiles confidential information regarding past applications for health insurance submitted by an applicant. This permits an insurer to compare information on a current application with that found on another application.

2. **Fair Credit Reporting Act** Each insurer and its producers are obligated to satisfy the terms of the federal Fair Credit Reporting Act with regard to information obtained concerning the applicant acquired from a third party.

   a. This law requires that an applicant for health insurance be advised in writing by an insurer that a consumer report may be requested and the general scope of the investigation to be reported.

   b. It is the duty of the producer to obtain the applicant's signature on a disclosure form and explain to the applicant that an investigative consumer report may be required for underwriting purposes.

   c. The Fair Credit Reporting Act also requires that when an applicant is denied coverage because of information obtained from a third-party source, that the applicant be informed of the source.

   d. The insurer is also obligated to permit an applicant to refute any adverse information compiled by the investigative report.

   e. Insurers may use consumer reports or investigative consumer reports to compile additional information regarding the applicant.

    f. A **Notice to the Applicant** must be issued to all applicants for health insurance coverage. This notice informs the health insurance applicant that a credit report will be ordered concerning his past history and any other health insurance they have previously applied for. In addition, the producer must leave this notice with the applicant along with the conditional receipt.

3. Other sources of information

    a. Information from the producer (or agent) in the producer/agent's report

    b. The health insurance application

    c. Attending physician's statement (APS)

    d. Medical questionnaires, examinations, and laboratory tests

    e. Other investigation reports (e.g., Equifax)

C. UNDERWRITING CRITERIA There are several factors evaluated by an underwriting department which affect the health risk. Some of these include the following.

    1. Age The age of the prospective insured will affect annual claim costs differently depending upon the type of benefit involved. Underwriting persons at older ages brings with it a problem of adverse selection.

    2. Sex The sex of an applicant is a major underwriting concern since females are assessed higher rates than males in disability and other forms of health insurance. However, in recent years this has ceased to be a determinant due to state unisex legislation.

    3. Health A person's past and present health is a primary concern as well. Past history provides an insight as to the applicant's possible health in the future. Any person who is presently in poor health will not be able to purchase standard health coverage, if at all.

    4. Physical build Extremes in weight and height (high or low) may affect an applicant's health so an insurer will closely scrutinize this type of risk.

    5. Occupation The more hazardous an applicant's occupation, the more likely the occurrence of an injury or disability. Underwriters seriously evaluate applicant occupations.

    6. Personal habits An applicant with poor habits (e.g., smoking, drug use) would be a concern of the underwriter since they will affect a person's physical and moral state. Avocations (hobbies) are also a consideration. For example, a person who skydives or flies small aircraft is more likely to become injured than someone whose hobby is chess.

    7. Financial status An applicant's financial position is also an underwriting concern because if an individual does not have a stable earning history or is in financial straits, he may be more liable to engage in malingering in order to collect disability income benefits.

D. **UNDERWRITING DECISION** After all the appropriate information is collected, the underwriting department makes its decision. It can:

- accept the risk at standard premium rates;
- accept the risk at preferred (reduced) premium rates;
- accept the risk at substandard rates (by adding an additional premium, altering the coverage, or adding a rider);
- issue coverage with an impairment rider, which excludes coverage for sickness or injury due to a preexisting condition; or
- reject the risk altogether if it fails to meet the insurer's underwriting criteria.

   1. While accepting or rejecting a risk based on specific underwriting criteria is a form of discrimination, it is not considered unfair because the criteria used directly affects the actuarial soundness of the coverage provided.

E. **THE CONDITIONAL RECEIPT** If an applicant for insurance is given an insurability conditional receipt, the insurance coverage becomes effective as of the date of the receipt, as long as the application is approved for the plan applied for, the amount of coverage applied for, and the premium rate applied for. This receipt is generally provided to an applicant when he pays the initial premium at the time of application.

   1. Explanation of the receipt The producer must explain how this type of receipt functions. He may inform the applicant that he is covered immediately, or when the medical examination is completed (if an exam is required), provided the insurer determines that, at the present time (or at the time of the exam), the applicant qualifies for the policy as applied for. If the applicant qualifies, he does not have to wait for coverage until the policy is issued and delivered; protection will begin immediately.

   2. Coverage and the receipt If the applicant fills out the health insurance application and pays the initial premium to the producer, he will be issued a conditional receipt. If the applicant is injured (or suffers illness) as a result of an accident after the date on the receipt and before being issued the policy, the applicant will still qualify for coverage.

F. **SUBMITTING THE APPLICATION** It is the responsibility of the producer to review the application before submitting it to the home office underwriting department. This provides another check to ensure that the application is filled out completely so that there will be no delay in policy issue if the applicant qualifies for coverage. If an initial premium is paid by the applicant at the time of application, it must also accompany the application.

G. **ASSURING DELIVERY OF THE POLICY TO THE CLIENT** Although contract delivery may be accomplished without physically delivering it in the policyowner's possession, a producer should always deliver policies personally.

   1. Possession of a policy does not establish delivery if all conditions have not been met. For example, a policy may be issued with an impairment type rider restricting coverage for a certain health condition. In most cases, the insurer requires that the applicant/insured sign a statement and return it to the insurer verifying that applicant/insured is aware of the addition of the impairment rider. After this has been completed, policy delivery conditions have been satisfied.

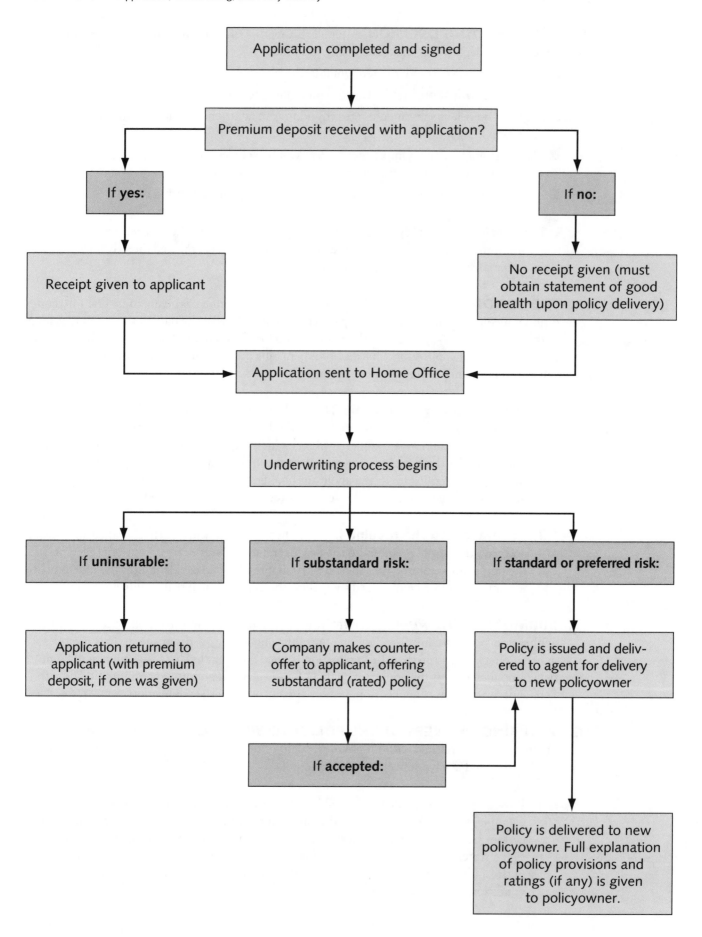

✓
TAKE NOTE

Health insurance policies are legal contracts and must meet the same requirements as life contracts in order to be valid.

2. When a producer delivers the policy, he should again review the applicant/insured's original goals and needs. Any additional questions that an insured may have should also be answered by the producer.

3. Once the delivery of a policy is made, the free look period begins.

H. EXPLAINING THE POLICY AND ITS PROVISIONS, RIDERS, EXCLUSIONS, AND RATINGS TO CLIENTS The majority of applicants/insureds will not remember everything about the health insurance contract after the application has been submitted to the underwriting department for approval. This is the basic reason why a producer should deliver the contract in person. During the policy delivery process, the producer may re explain the policy together with its provisions and exclusions. In addition, the producer should also discuss any riders attached to the contract and any change in premium. This element of service helps avoid any possible misunderstandings, policy returns, or potential lapses.

I. OBTAINING A SIGNED STATEMENT OF CONTINUED GOOD HEALTH In many cases, the initial premium is not paid until the policy is delivered. Most insurers require that when the producer collects the premium, he must also obtain a statement signed by the insured attesting to his or her continued good health (before leaving the policy with the insured).

1. The producer then submits the premium, along with a signed statement of good health, to the insurer.

2. The purpose of this requirement is to make sure the applicant/insured has remained in good health during the underwriting period.

J. CONTRACT LAW This section serves as a review; a more detailed discussion of contract law was presented in Unit 1.

1. Requirements of a valid contract Contract requirements under health policies are the same as the requirements for life contracts. For an insurance contract to be a valid or legal contract, four requirements must be met.

   a. Agreement An agreement must exist between the parties (insured and insurer) based on an offer made by one of the parties and an acceptance of that offer by the other party. Both parties must agree to the terms of the contract.

   b. Consideration For a contract to be valid there must be a valuable consideration involved. In an insurance contract, the insured's consideration is the premium that he pays (and the statements made by the applicant in the application); the insurer's consideration is its promise to pay for covered claims.

c. **Legal capacity** The parties to the contract must be legally capable of entering into a contract. All individuals are considered to be legally capable except for:

- minors;
- insane individuals;
- persons who are intoxicated or under the influence of narcotics;
- persons under duress or forced to enter into a contract; and
- enemy aliens.

d. **Legal purpose** A valid contract must be for a lawful or legal purpose. In other words, the agreement cannot be against public policy. For example, an organized crime contract is not considered lawful.

2. **Insurable interest** All health insurance contracts are subject to the doctrine of insurable interest. This doctrine states than an individual purchasing insurance coverage must have a direct and identifiable interest in the individual to be insured. It must also be clear that the party purchasing insurance coverage has an economic interest of some type in the insured. The purpose of this doctrine is to prevent individuals from profiting from the purchase of health insurance on the lives of others.

3. **Warranties and representations** Statements made by an applicant on an application for health insurance are considered to be representations. **Representations** are statements that are true to the best knowledge of an individual. **Misrepresentations** are statements made that are incorrect. These statements do not have much of an effect on a health insurance contract unless they are of a material nature. **Warranties**, on the other hand, are statements made that are guaranteed to be absolutely true.

K. **CLAIMS** An insured and insurer have various rights and duties when a loss occurs. For example, an insured must provide written notice of claim to the insurer within a specified number of days of the loss. Then, also within prescribed time periods, the insurer must provide claim forms to the insured and the insured must provide written proof of loss to the insurer. The insurer will investigate the claim and verify the loss through attending physician statements (APS) or other documentation. In addition, insurers may not engage in any unfair claim settlements or practices. Claims must be settled as soon as reasonably possible. As determined by state law, any legal action against the insurer in connection with claim may not begin until a certain number of days have passed following the receipt of proof of loss.

L. **CONSIDERATIONS IN REPLACING HEALTH INSURANCE** When accident and health insurance contracts are to be replaced in this state, several policy provisions must be scrutinized to insure that a producer is not engaged in any misrepresentation. Applications shall include a question designed to elicit information as to whether the insurance to be issued is intended to replace any other accident and health insurance presently in force.

1. **Primary provisions to be scrutinized** Several relevant provisions should be scrutinized including but not limited to: preexisting conditions, benefits, waiting periods, exclusions, limitations, and insurer underwriting requirements. For example, many health contracts have a multi-month exclusion for preexisting conditions when a person applies for coverage under a new policy. If a producer is replacing a major medical expense (e.g., major medical policy) contract, he must be aware of this.

2. **Notice regarding replacement** This type of notice must be provided to the applicant by the producer when replacement occurs. Replacement regulations will not apply to: accident-only policies and single premium nonrenewable policies.

3. **Misrepresentation** If a producer engages in misrepresentation during the replacement of health insurance contracts, he may be exposed to errors and omissions liability in addition to license suspension or revocation.

4. **No loss/no gain statutes** Many states have enacted laws that involve the theory of indemnity. They stipulate that the purpose of insurance is not to make a profit. The purpose of insurance is to place the insured (or the beneficiary) in the same economic position as existed prior to the loss.

M. HEALTH REINSURERS Health reinsurance is used to avoid fluctuations in experience that may be disruptive to an insurer's operating results.

1. An insurer places coverage with a reinsurer after the original insurer (ceding company) decides it cannot afford to cover the entire risk.

2. With Quota-Share reinsurance the ceding company and the reinsurance company share in a predetermined percentage of each individual risk (e.g., ceding company 40%, reinsurer 60%). This is a form of treaty reinsurance.

3. Catastrophe reinsurance reimburses an insurer up to a fixed-dollar amount, in excess of a predetermined dollar amount, for multiple losses incurred as a result of an accident or occurrence.

N. MISCELLANEOUS HEALTH INSURANCE INFORMATION

1. **Self-insurance** A self-insurer does not transfer his risk to an outside (commercial) insurer. He generally establishes reserves to cover anticipated losses. Some businesses establish retention programs with excess insurance in order to protect against the impact of large and catastrophic losses. Self-insurance may be contrasted with no insurance. A self-insurer sets aside reserves in order to meet anticipated losses. Someone who carries no insurance is simply assuming or retaining the entire risk of loss.

2. **Accidental means** A policy covering injuries due to accidental means has two requirements that must be satisfied in order for a loss to be covered: the cause of the action and its result must be unexpected and unintended. This is a restrictive definition. For example, if a person decides to jump from a ladder and is injured, the loss would not be covered since the cause (jumping) was intentional even though the result (injury) was unexpected.

3. **Accidental bodily injury** A policy with this definition provides broader coverage since it protects against all accidental injuries (except those that are intentionally self inflicted). In the previous example provided in item 2, the injury suffered would be covered under this more liberal definition.

4. **Sickness** Any loss due to illness is covered by health insurance policies. Sickness or illness loss is generally considered any form of health loss other than an accident.

5. **Peril** A term utilized primarily in casualty (and property) insurance, it is defined as the cause of a possible loss.

UNIT QUIZ

1. Which of the following provides the more restrictive definition that may appear in a health policy?

   A. Accidental dismemberment
   B. Accidental bodily injury
   C. Accidental means
   D. Accidental death

2. Which of the following best describes the MIB?

   A. Computation of medical impairments
   B. Source of application disclosure impairments
   C. Source of producer information
   D. Intercompany data bank of health information

3. The Fair Credit Reporting Act requires that

   A. a producer advise the applicant of the possibility of application declination
   B. the applicant be advised that a consumer report may be requested
   C. the insurer advise the applicant whether coverage is accepted or denied
   D. the applicant be advised of the maximum limit of coverage available

4. With a health insurance policy, the free look period begins

   A. upon the payment of the initial premium
   B. upon receipt of the attending physician statement
   C. when the insurer receives the application
   D. when the policy is delivered

5. All of the following are required to form a valid contract EXCEPT

   A. agreement
   B. insurable intent
   C. consideration
   D. legal capacity

6. A statement guaranteed to be absolutely true best describes

   A. representation
   B. guarantee
   C. warranty
   D. misrepresentation

ANSWERS

1. C   2. D   3. B   4. D   5. B   6. C

DISCUSSION QUESTIONS

1. Why is it important for a health insurance application to be filled out completely and accurately?

2. List several required signatures that must appear on a health insurance application.

3. What type of information is provided to an insurer by the MIB?

4. What can an applicant for health insurance do if he finds that adverse information is included on his consumer report?

5. When must a "Notice to the Applicant" be left with the health insurance applicant?

6. Does possession of a policy by an "insured" constitute full delivery? Explain.

7. When does the free look period begin?

8. Identify the four requirements of a valid contract.

9. Compare a warranty and a representation.

10. Describe those individuals considered to have the legal capacity to contract?

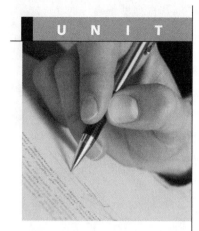

12

Accident and Health Insurance Practice Final Examination

Following your thorough study of Units 1 and 7 through 11 in this text, take this 50-question practice final on accident and health insurance. Grade your performance using the answer key provided. Carefully review the information in this book regarding those questions answered incorrectly.

PRACTICE FINAL

1. Social Security benefits may be payable to a disabled individual after a waiting period of
   - A. 3 months
   - B. 5 months
   - C. 6 months
   - D. 12 months

2. A health insurance contract that does not permit an increase in premiums, modifications to policy provisions, and is not cancellable, best describes a(n)
   - A. noncancellable and guaranteed renewable policy
   - B. guaranteed renewable policy
   - C. optionally renewable policy
   - D. conditionally renewable policy

3. Most Medicare supplement (Medigap) policies have a free look period of how many days?
   - A. 60
   - B. 45
   - C. 30
   - D. 10

4. Which of the following provides the option for an employee to continue to maintain his group health insurance coverage after he is no longer employed by the employer?
   - A. ERISA
   - B. HIPAA
   - C. FICA
   - D. COBRA

5. The mandatory physical exam and autopsy provision found in health insurance policies is most commonly applied by insurers
   - A. to determine the cause and validity of a health insurance claim that exceeds $50,000
   - B. to determine the cause of death when a claim is made under an AD&D policy
   - C. to validate that an individual claiming a disability benefit remains disabled
   - D. whenever benefits are payable to a beneficiary due to the death of the insured

6. Ron has a major medical policy with a $500 deductible and an 80/20 coinsurance provision. If he incurs medical expenses of $4,000, the insurer would pay
   - A. $800
   - B. $2,700
   - C. $2,800
   - D. $3,200

7. All of the following statements are correct concerning the coordination of benefits provision found in accident and health policies EXCEPT
   - A. it guards against duplication of benefits
   - B. it prevents an insured from profiting from an illness or injury
   - C. this provision does not apply to group policies
   - D. premiums would be higher without this provision

8. Assume Hal, the insured under a disability income policy, is severely injured in an accident. He is unable to work for a period of eight months, during which he receives his policy's full benefit. After 8 months, he returns to work, but due to his injury, he can work only on a part-time basis. In order to continue to collect benefits under the policy, the policy must include what kind of provision?
   - A. total disability
   - B. partial disability
   - C. residual disability
   - D. fully insured disability

9. In a disability income policy, an elimination period provision refers to the period
   - A. between the first day of disability and the actual receipt of payment for the disability incurred
   - B. during which any specific accident or illness is excluded from coverage
   - C. between the first day of disability and the day to which the disability must continue before it can result in the insured receiving any benefits
   - D. between the effective date of the policy and the date on which payments under the policy become due

10. Which of the following is commonly and specifically excluded under a medical expense policy?

    A. Loss of income as a result of illness
    B. Self-inflicted injuries
    C. Hospitalization due to mental illness
    D. Injuries caused by accidents

11. The purpose of a grace period in an accident and health insurance contract is to

    A. allow the insurer to determine the deceased's cause of death
    B. permit the beneficiary to establish an insurable interest in the contract
    C. protect the insurer against the adverse selection of policyowners
    D. protect a policyholder against the unintentional lapse of a contract

12. A guaranteed renewable accident and health policy gives the insurer the right to

    A. increase premiums on a class basis
    B. alter policy provisions during the policy term
    C. reduce the amount of insurance after each claim
    D. cancel the policy due to the filing of numerous claims

13. Bob owns a disability income policy paying $1,500 per month in the event that he becomes totally disabled. The policy has a 30-day elimination period. Bob is involved in a traffic accident and is disabled for 105 days. How much will his disability income policy pay?

    A. $2,250
    B. $3,750
    C. $4,500
    D. $5,250

14. The preexisting condition exclusion found in an accident and health policy is designed to protect the insurer against

    A. adverse selection
    B. over insurance
    C. malingering
    D. compliance

15. Which of the following statements is CORRECT regarding surgical expense benefits?

    A. Benefits are typically subject to deductibles of $250 or more.
    B. The amount on the benefit schedule is typically expressed in terms of the maximum benefit payable.
    C. Coverage is usually provided for rehabilitation costs following surgery.
    D. A small amount, usually no more than $350, is provided for incidentals while hospitalized.

16. A comprehensive medical expense insurance policy combines which of the following coverages under one contract?

    A. Major medical coverage and accidental death
    B. Disability income and accidental death
    C. Basic hospital and surgical coverage with major medical coverage
    D. Disability income with basic hospital and surgical coverages

17. Which of the following is an eligibility requirement in order to receive full Social Security disability benefits?

    A. PIA insured status
    B. An individual must have attained fully insured status
    C. An individual must be at least 65 years of age
    D. The recipient must be disabled for at least 12 months before benefits may be received

18. Long-term care insurance provides all of the following coverages EXCEPT

    A. skilled nursing care
    B. private surgical expense
    C. intermediate (rehabilitative) care
    D. custodial care

19. The contractual provision that specifies the time limit that an insured has to return accident and health claim forms to the insurer is known as

    A. payment of claims
    B. claim forms
    C. grace period
    D. proof of loss

20. Which of the following types of health insurance policies provides for a death benefit, payable to the insured's beneficiary?

    A. Disability income
    B. Accidental death and dismemberment
    C. Long-term care
    D. COBRA

21. Which of the following statements regarding participation in Part A of Medicare is CORRECT?

    A. The insured must pay a deductible.
    B. The insured must pay an annual premium.
    C. Benefits are paid directly to the insured.
    D. To participate, an individual must be covered by Social Security.

22. All of the following statements are correct concerning Part B of Medicare EXCEPT

    A. a coinsurance feature of 80/20 is included to cover charges after a deductible is satisfied
    B. benefit payments are subject to an annual deductible
    C. annual physical exams are required to maintain coverage
    D. a premium is charged for Part B participation

23. Walter owns an individual disability income policy paying $800 per month with a 60-day waiting period. If he becomes disabled for 45 days, how much will his contract pay?

    A. $0
    B. $200
    C. $400
    D. $800

24. The period of time that must elapse after the onset of a disability and before monthly disability income benefits begin is referred to as the

    A. probationary period
    B. conversion period
    C. elimination period
    D. holding period

25. An insured must provide written notice of a claim to the insurer within how many days of a loss?

    A. 5
    B. 10
    C. 15
    D. 20

26. After receiving notice of claim from an insured, the insurer must provide claim forms to that insured within how many days of the request?

    A. 5
    B. 10
    C. 15
    D. 20

27. Caleb receives $50,000 from a $100,000 accidental death and dismemberment policy as a result of the loss of his left arm in an accident. Caleb has received the

    A. primary amount
    B. principal amount
    C. capital amount
    D. contributory amount

28. Medicare Part A benefit periods end when a person has been released from a hospital or skilled nursing facility for a period of

    A. 6 months
    B. 60 days
    C. 90 days
    D. 12 months

29. Alice owns a major medical policy with a $1,000 deductible and a provision that provides for percentage participation of 80/20. Due to an illness Alice incurs covered medical expenses of $3,000. How much of this amount will Alice be responsible for?

    A. $400
    B. $1,400
    C. $1,600
    D. $2,400

30. Responses to questions given by applicants on an accident and health insurance application are considered to be

    A. warranties
    B. mandated statements
    C. entitlement
    D. representations

31. Which of the following terms best defines the approach that Blue Cross and Blue Shield organizations use to provide for health care?

    A. Indemnity
    B. Valued
    C. Service
    D. Reimbursement

32. With regard to the reinstatement of a health insurance policy, all of the following statements are correct EXCEPT

    A. evidence of insurability may be required
    B. upon reinstatement, coverage for illness is effective immediately
    C. upon reinstatement, coverage for accidents is effective immediately
    D. reinstatement is automatic unless the insurer informs the applicant within 45 days that he has been rejected

33. Which of the following is a typical benefit period for group short-term disability income coverage?

    A. 1 to 3 months
    B. 6 to 18 months
    C. 12 to 28 months
    D. 18 to 24 months

34. Which of the following statements regarding the change of occupation provision found in a disability income policy is CORRECT?

    A. It sets forth the rights and obligations of the insurer and the insured in the event that the insured engages in a more hazardous or less hazardous occupation.
    B. It voids the policy if the insured suffers an otherwise compensable loss while engaged in an illegal occupation.
    C. It requires that the insurer deny benefits if the insured changes his occupation following the policy effective date.
    D. It provides a formula by which adjustments are made in the elimination period in the event that the insured changes to a higher risk occupation.

35. All of the following are optional uniform health insurance policy provisions EXCEPT

    A. reinstatement
    B. change of occupation
    C. conformity with state statutes
    D. misstatement of age

36. What advantage does the recurrent disability provision provide to the insured under a disability income policy?

    A. It eliminates the imposition of a second elimination period for the same disability.
    B. It provides the insured with lifetime disability benefits.
    C. It eliminates the imposition of an elimination period for a separate disability.
    D. It eliminates the need for the insured to pay a deductible.

37. The amount payable in the event of the insured's death under an accidental death policy is referred to as the

    A. capital sum
    B. principal sum
    C. accidental death sum
    D. dismemberment benefit

38. With regard to the taxation of disability income insurance provided by a business on a key employee, whereby the employer pays the premium and the benefits are paid to the employee, which of the following statements is CORRECT?

    A. Premiums are not tax deductible; benefits are income tax free.
    B. Premiums are tax deductible; benefits are income tax free.
    C. Premiums are not tax deductible; benefits are taxed.
    D. Premiums are tax deductible; benefits are taxed.

39. When added to a health insurance contract, an impairment rider

    A. provides for a discontinuance of premium payments if the policyowner becomes impaired as defined by the rider
    B. defines the criteria for a disability or impairment before benefits are payable
    C. excludes from coverage any loss associated with the defined impairment
    D. identifies specific impairments or disabilities that the contract will cover

40. A medical expense policy's coinsurance provision

    A. specifies the percentage of costs that will be paid each by the insurer and the insured

    B. defines the amount of costs the insured must cover before the policy will pay any benefits

    C. identifies which provider has primary responsibility for benefit payments if the insured is covered by more than one policy

    D. provides that once an insured's costs exceed a specified limit, the insurer pays 100% of covered expenses

41. When Lisa suffered a broken hip, she notified her agent, in writing, within 12 days of the loss. However, her agent did not notify the insurance company until 60 days after the loss. Which of the following statements correctly explains how this claim would be handled?

    A. The insurer may deny the claim since it was not notified within the required 20-day time frame.

    B. The insurer is considered to be notified since the notification to its agent amounts to notification to the insurer, and so the claim will be paid in full.

    C. The insurer may delay the payment of this claim for up to 6 months.

    D. The insurer may settle this claim for less than it otherwise would had the notification been provided in a timely manner.

42. Which of the following statements is CORRECT concerning a Health Maintenance Organization (HMO)?

    A. An HMO provides coverage for overhead expenses in the event that a businessowner becomes disabled.

    B. It is an organization stressing preventive health care and early diagnosis.

    C. Closed-panel plans account for approximately 10% of all HMOs.

    D. Routine physical exams are generally not covered.

43. What is the maximum period of time that group health coverage must be continued for a terminated employee under the COBRA rules?

    A. 12 months

    B. 18 months

    C. 24 months

    D. 36 months

44. A stop-loss provision is common to what kind of health insurance policy?

    A. Major medical

    B. Basic medical

    C. Disability income

    D. Limited risk policy

45. What kind of coverage does a business overhead expense policy provide?

    A. Monthly income payments to a business owner in the event of a key employee's disability

    B. Monthly income payments to cover the operational costs of a business owner if the owner becomes disabled

    C. Disability income payments for a business owner

    D. Medical expense insurance for a business owner

46. Medicare Part A provides coverage for all of the following EXCEPT

    A. hospitalization

    B. home health care services

    C. hospice care

    D. surgeon's fees

47. With regard to health insurance, the Fair Credit Reporting Act

    A. restricts an insurer's review of an applicant's credit history to only those sources the applicant approves

    B. requires the insurer to contact at least one source named by the applicant to gain information on the applicant

    C. requires applicants for health insurance to submit a credit report with the insurance application

    D. requires the disclosure of the third-party source if the applicant is denied coverage due to information provided by a third party

48. Jim's major medical policy contains an annual deductible of $1,000; 50%/50% coinsurance; and a $5,000 stop-loss limit. If Jim incurs $21,000 in covered medical expenses, what will be Jim's total out-of-pocket cost?

    A. $11,000

    B. $10,500

    C. $10,000

    D. $5,000

49. Carl's health insurance policy pays benefits according to a list that indicates the amount that is payable under each type of covered treatment or procedure. Carl's policy provides benefits on a

    A. scheduled basis
    B. reimbursement basis
    C. service basis
    D. cash basis

50. Company X receives a health insurance application from Dilbert with a prepaid premium. One week later, it receives the MIB report indicating a prior heart condition. Company X will most likely

    A. disregard the MIB report
    B. return Dilbert's premium and decline coverage
    C. cover the applicant
    D. cover the applicant excluding the preexisting condition

ANSWERS AND RATIONALES

1. **B** There is a 5-month waiting period for Social Security disability benefits. Payments begin in the sixth month.

2. **A** A noncancellable policy may be referred to as noncancellable and guaranteed renewable. This type of contract provides an insured with the right to renew the policy up to a specified age, as long as premiums are paid before the end of the grace period. In addition, the insurer may not cancel, alter the policy term, or increase the premium charged.

3. **C** Medicare supplement (Medigap) policies must provide a 30-day free look period.

4. **D** Enacted in 1985, COBRA (the Consolidated Omnibus Budget Reconciliation Act) stipulates that employers must offer continuation of group health benefits for a specified time to qualified employees (and their beneficiaries) who would not otherwise be eligible for continued coverage due to certain events such as termination of employment.

5. **C** This provision is most commonly used when insurers require disabled claimants to submit to a physical exam to prove continued disability.

6. **C** The $500 deductible is subtracted from the medical expenses first, leaving $3,500 that is subject to the 80/20 coinsurance provision. Therefore, the insurer will pay $2,800 of the total bill. Ron's total out-of-pocket expense will be $1,200 ($500 deductible plus 20% of the balance, or $700.)

7. **C** Group health insurance policies also include a coordination of benefits provision to avoid duplicate coverage. This provision limits total benefit payable to 100% of covered expenses, regardless of the number of group policies involved.

8. **C** In order to continue to collect benefits after returning to work, Hal's policy must have a residual benefit provision that provides for a (reduced) monthly benefit in proportion to the loss of income experienced after the insured returns to work, but at reduced earnings.

9. **C** The elimination (or waiting) period is the time that must elapse before monthly benefits will begin under a disability income contract. An elimination period must be satisfied for each new disability incurred. The most common period is 30 days.

10. **B** One of the most common exclusions under a health insurance policy is self-inflicted injuries.

11. **D** The grace period follows the date each premium is due and permits the continuance of coverage even though the premium has not been paid.

12. **A** An insurer may not cancel a guaranteed renewable policy or alter its provisions as long as the insured pays the premium within the grace period. However, the insurer reserves the right to increase the premium at policy renewal on a class basis.

13. **B** After the elimination period is satisfied, the disability income policy will pay $1,500 per month while Bob remains totally disabled. Bob's disability continues for 2½ months after the elimination period, so he will receive $3,750 in benefits.

14. **A** Exclusions for preexisting conditions are intended to protect the insurer from adverse selection. Preexisting conditions are usually excluded through the policy's standard provisions or by waiver.

15. **B** Surgical expense coverage lists (or schedules) surgical procedures and the corresponding reimbursable amounts in the policy. The most common approach used by surgical expense coverage is to establish a maximum limit for coverage. The amount of the benefit schedule

is typically expressed in terms of the maximum benefit payable.

16. **C**   Comprehensive major medical expense policies provide broader benefits than major medical insurance. They combine all of the basic medical expense benefits into a single package ranging from hospital and surgical expense through major medical type coverage.

17. **B**   In order to receive disability benefits under Social Security, a person must be fully insured (i.e., having served 10 years in covered employment).

18. **B**   Long-term care insurance is designed to cover services for those who cannot care for themselves (such as custodial or skilled nursing care). It does not provide surgical expense coverage.

19. **D**   Written proof of loss must be submitted to the insurer within 90 days of the date of loss. If an insured fails to provide written proof within the time required, the claim will be honored if it was not reasonably possible to provide proof within the time limit allowed.

20. **B**   Accidental death and dismemberment (AD&D) policies protect against the accidental death of an insured in addition to paying a specific benefit if an insured suffers a dismemberment covered under the policy. Accidental death coverage may be purchased as a separate policy or as an added benefit to a health insurance policy.

21. **A**   Insureds do not need to pay a premium for Part A coverage, though insureds must satisfy a deductible each benefit period. Benefits are paid directly to the medical care provider.

22. **C**   Participation in Medicare Part B is subject to the payment of a monthly premium, 20% coinsurance payments, and an annual deductible. No physical exams are required.

23. **A**   Walter's disability lasted 45 days, well within the 60-day waiting (elimination) period. Because his disability did not last beyond the elimination period, he will not receive any benefits from his disability income policy.

24. **C**   The elimination (or waiting) period is the time that must elapse before monthly benefits will begin under a disability income policy. An elimination period must be satisfied for each new disability incurred. It is the equivalent of a deductible under other forms of health insurance.

25. **D**   An insured is required to submit written notice to the insurer within 20 days of sustaining a loss. Failure to do so within this period may result in the insurer reserving the right to deny coverage.

26. **C**   An insurer must provide claim forms to an insured within 15 days of the insured's request. If it fails to do so, the insured may submit a claim (or proof of loss) in another manner designed to give the insurer notice of the claim or loss.

27. **C**   The benefit amount payable for an accidental dismemberment is referred to as the capital sum. The capital sum is generally a percentage (i.e., 50%) of the principal sum.

28. **B**   The Medicare Part A (hospital insurance) benefit period begins on the day of admittance to a hospital or extended care facility and ends after the insured has been released for 60 consecutive days.

29. **B**   Alice first pays the $1,000 deductible before the 80/20 coinsurance provision is invoked. Then the insurer pays 80% of the $2,000 balance (or $1,600). Ann will be responsible for the remaining 20%, or $400. Therefore, Alice's total cost (including the deductible) will be $1,400.

30. **D**   Statements made by an applicant on an application for health insurance are generally considered to be representations. They are statements that are true to the best knowledge of the individual making them.

31. **C**   Blue Cross and Blue Shield organizations operate on a service approach whereby they actually deliver health care and services, as opposed to insurers that reimburse insureds or health care providers for the cost of care delivered.

32. **B** Once a health insurance policy has been reinstated, coverage for accidents is effective immediately. Coverage for sickness requires a short waiting period, usually 10 days.

33. **B** The typical benefit period for group short-term disability policies is 6 to 18 months.

34. **A** The change of occupation provision, an optional provision, allows for a change in benefits or premiums if an insured changes his occupation. If the insured changes from a more hazardous to a less hazardous occupation, the premium will be reduced. If the insured changes from a less hazardous to a more hazardous occupation, the benefit will be reduced.

35. **A** Reinstatement is one of the 12 provisions required in health insurance policies, as prescribed in the NAIC's Uniform Individual Accident and Sickness Provisions Law.

36. **A** The recurrent disability provision is invoked when an individual suffering from a total disability apparently recovers and subsequently the disability reoccurs. This provision sets the time in which a reoccurrence will be treated as a continuation of the original disability or a new occurrence altogether. This is important to the insured because a new occurrence will require him to satisfy a new elimination period, but a continuation of the original disability will allow him to resume benefit payments.

37. **B** The benefit payable as a result of accidental death is the principal sum. The benefit amount payable for accidental dismemberment is the capital sum and is generally a percentage of the principal sum.

38. **A** Under a disability income policy purchased and paid for by an employer on a key employee, the latter being the recipient of the benefits, the premiums are not tax deductible, but the benefits are not subject to income taxation.

39. **C** The purpose of an impairment rider added to a health insurance policy is to exclude from coverage any loss associated with the specified impairment. Impairment riders enable insurers to provide coverage that might otherwise be denied if the rider were not included.

40. **A** A medical expense policy's coinsurance provision specifies the percentage of costs for which each the insurer and the insured will be responsible. Typically, an insurer's share of costs is 70 to 80%, while the insured is responsible for 20 to 30%.

41. **B** The laws of agency dictate that knowledge of the agent is imputed to the principal. Therefore, Lisa's notice to the agent is deemed to be notice to the insurer.

42. **B** Health maintenance organizations (HMOs) emphasize preventive medicine with early treatment and diagnosis by way of prepaid routine physical examinations and diagnostic screening techniques.

43. **B** The Consolidated Omnibus Budget Reconciliation Act of 1985 (COBRA) stipulated that employers must offer continuation of group health coverage for a specified period of time to qualified employees and their beneficiaries who would otherwise be eligible for continued coverage because of particular qualifying events involving the covered employee. These events include death, divorce, or termination of employment. If an individual is laid off from a job or otherwise terminated from employment, COBRA mandates continued coverage for a period not to exceed 18 months.

44. **A** A stop-loss provision, common to major medical expense policies, provides for 100% payment of costs by the insurer once the insured's out-of-pocket payments for eligible expenses reach a specific level.

45. **B** Business overhead expense insurance is designed to provide monthly income to cover the overhead costs of a business' operation during the business owner's disability.

46. **D** Medicare Part A covers the costs associated with hospitalization, as well as skilled nursing care, home health care, hospice benefits, and limited psychiatric care. Surgeon's fees are covered by Medicare Part B.

47.   **D**   The application of the Fair Credit Reporting Act to health insurance is the same as for life insurance. It requires that an insurance applicant be notified of the source of information if, based on that information, the insurer refuses to issue the requested coverage.

48.   **D**   Jim must first satisfy the $1,000 deductible before the insurer will pay any benefit, subject to the coinsurance provision. Once he pays the deductible, the insurer will pay 50% of the balance ($20,000), or $10,000. Jim is responsible for the other 50% in accordance with the coinsurance provision. This would require him to pay $10,000 in addition to the $1,000 deductible, for a total of $11,000. However, the stop-loss provision limits Jim's expenses to $5,000. The insurer becomes responsible, therefore, for the expenses beyond this limit ($16,000).

49.   **A**   Carl's health insurance policy pays benefits according to a schedule for surgical procedures and the corresponding reimbursable amounts. The most common approach is to set a maximum limit for coverage. The amount of the benefit schedule is typically expressed in terms of the maximum benefit payable. In addition, many other surgical procedures are listed with a dollar amount or a percentage of the maximum limit. These listings are referred to as surgical schedules and provide payment for the usual and customary charges extended for various surgical procedures.

50.   **D**   Preexisting conditions are health conditions that have already manifested themselves before the insured's application for health insurance coverage. They are frequently excluded from coverage. They do not necessarily cause the insurer to reject the application.

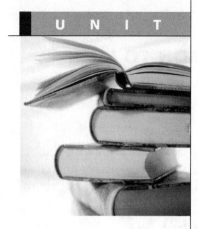

13

New York Life, Accident, and Health Insurance Law

KEY TERMS

Licensing Process

Agents

Brokers

Consultants

Adjusters

Nonresident

Temporary

Renewal

Change of Address

Continuing Education

Cease & Desist Order

Hearings

Penalties

Superintendent's Duties

Certificate of Authority

Solvency

Unfair Claims Settlement

Agent Appointment

Termination

Unfair/Prohibited Practices

Misrepresentation

False Advertising

Defamation

Unfair Discrimination

Rebating

Controlled Business

Sharing Commissions

Fiduciary Responsibilities

Examination of Books

Insurance Frauds

Consumer Privacy

Fair Credit Act

Fraud/False Statements

Licensee Responsibilities

Replacement

Backdating

Marketing Requirements

Genetic Testing

Mandated Benefits

Long-Term Care

Small Employer Plans

Medicare Supplements

I. NEW YORK LAW AND REGULATIONS COMMON TO LIFE, ACCIDENT, AND HEALTH INSURANCE

A. LICENSING PROCESS [SEC. 2103(D-I)]

1. **Types of licenses** In general, any individual or entity that acts as, or claims to be, an insurance producer (i.e., a person who acts as an agent, broker, consultant, adjuster, reinsurance intermediary, or excess lines broker) must be licensed by the state.

   a. **Agents [Secs. 2101(a), 2103; Regs. 22.2, 23.2]** An insurance agent is a person authorized by an insurer, fraternal benefit society, or health maintenance organization (HMO), and any sub-agent of such an agent, to solicit, negotiate, or sell insurance, HMO, or annuity contracts.

      1.) **Agent licensing qualifications** To qualify for a life or accident and health agent's license, an applicant must:
      - be at least 18 years old;
      - apply in writing to the Superintendent using the required forms;
      - fulfill the prelicensing education requirement;
      - pass a written examination; and
      - pay an application fee.

      2.) **Prelicensing education requirement** To qualify for the required written examination, applicants for an agent and broker license must complete a prelicensing study course that has been approved by the Superintendent.

         a.) 40 hours are required for a life and health agent and 90 hours for a property/casualty agent.

         b.) The following providers are acceptable sources of prelicensing education:
         - a college or university that has a curriculum registered with the state education department;
         - any other institution that has had its course approved; and
         - any life or accident and health insurer that maintains equivalent standards of instruction and has been approved by the Superintendent.

      3.) **Exemptions from the written examination** The following individuals do not have to take the written examination to be licensed as agents:
      - representatives of travel carriers (airlines, bus lines, etc.) selling baggage or accident insurance only;
      - applicants who were previously licensed as insurance agents, provided they file applications within two years of the termination of their licenses;

■ licensed individuals applying for additional licenses to represent an insurer other than the insurer who originally appointed them (provided that no additional lines of insurance are to be included in the new license);

■ applicants who are nonresident agents, at the Superintendent's discretion;

■ applicants for licenses to represent a fraternal benefit society;

■ any individual whose license has been suspended or revoked, at the Superintendent's discretion;

■ applicants who are chartered life underwriters (CLUs) or chartered property casualty underwriters (CPCUs), at the Superintendent's discretion; for CLUs and CPCUs, the Superintendent may waive the written examination as well as the prelicensing education requirement; and

■ a nonresident applying for a resident license in New York whose:

— was previously licensed for the same lines of authority in another state;

— has a letter of clearance from his home state that he is in good standing;

— home state grants nonresident licenses to New York residents on the same basis; and

— applies within 90 days of cancelling his resident license.

4.) Lines of authority After qualifying for the license, the applicant may be certified in any of the following lines of authority for which he applied:

a.) Life

b.) Accident and health or sickness

c.) Property

d.) Casualty

e.) Variable life/variable annuity

f.) Personal lines (property and casualty)

b. Brokers [Secs. 2101(c), (h); 2104] An insurance broker is any person, firm, association, or corporation that solicits, negotiates, or sells insurance or annuity contracts for an insured (other than himself) in exchange for a commission.

1.) To be licensed by the Superintendent as an insurance broker, an individual must:

■ be at least 18 years old;

■ apply in writing to the Superintendent using the required forms;

■ complete the applicable prelicensing education requirements;

- have been employed by an insurance company, agent, or broker for at least one year during the three years preceding the date of the application;
- pass a written examination; and
- pay an application fee.

2.) The following applicants are exempt from taking the broker examination:
- persons who have passed the general agent licensing examination within the past two years;
- applicants who are currently licensed as agents;
- chartered life underwriters (CLUs);
- chartered property casualty underwriters (CPCUs;)
- chartered financial consultants (ChFCs); and
- persons who hold a master of science in financial services (MSFS) designation

c. Consultants [Sec. 2107] A consultant is any person who receives a fee for providing insurance counseling or advice. Consultants are compensated by the insured, not the insurer. Insurance consultants, producers who offer advice to the public about the benefits, advantages, and disadvantages of insurance policies for a fee, must be licensed but are not required to complete a prelicensing education course.

1.) No one may conduct business as a consultant unless properly licensed as such.

a.) A consultant is anyone who receives a fee for providing insurance counseling or advice. (Agents and brokers are paid by commission, not by fee, and thus are not required to hold a consultant's license.)

b.) A consultant's license is not required of lawyers, actuaries, and CPAs who are providing information in the course of their professional capacity.

c.) Consulting services include examining, appraising, reviewing, evaluating, and making recommendations on any insurance and profit-sharing contract or plan.

2.) An insurance consultant's license will be issued to a person, firm, association, or corporation complying with the requirements for life insurance or general insurance.

a.) If the license is issued to a firm, association, or corporation, only members, officers, and directors named in the license as sublicensees may act as consultants.

b.) A sublicensee may act only for the firm listed on the license.

3.) To be licensed, an individual must file an application, pass a written examination, and pay the fee.

4.) In lieu of an examination, the Superintendent may accept the results of any previous written examinations given by a certified designation program.

5.) The Superintendent may refuse to issue an insurance consultant's license if the applicant or any proposed sublicensee:

- is not trustworthy or competent;
- has given cause for license revocation or suspension; or
- has failed to comply with the prerequisites for a license.

6.) A licensed insurance consultant may not be an executive in or an employee of, or own stock giving him a substantial interest in any authorized insurance company, nor may a consultant recommend or encourage the purchase of insurance, annuities, or securities from an authorized insurer in which an immediate family member holds an executive position or has a substantial interest.

7.) A consultant's license expires yearly on March 31. However, if an application for renewal has been filed with the Superintendent before April 1, the license continues in force either until renewal is issued or for five days after the Superintendent refuses to issue the renewal license and has so notified the applicant.

8.) Memorandum required for compensation Compensation for agent, broker, and consulting services must be based on a written memorandum stating the amount to be paid. Compensation includes fees, commissions, or anything of value.

- **a.)** The party to be charged for the consulting, agent, or broker services must sign the memorandum and the licensee must retain a copy for at least three years after all services are performed.

- **b.)** Unless specified in the memorandum, a consultant, agent, or broker may not receive compensation for an insurance or annuity sale or for using securities or trusts in connection with pensions if he has received a fee for a related service for the same individual within the preceding 12 months.

- **c.)** Nothing prohibits offsetting a consulting, agent, or broker fee by compensation otherwise payable as the result of a life insurance or annuity sale if the offset is provided for in the memorandum.

9.) When a fee is permitted, no licensee may charge or accept any fee that is not fully disclosed before the service is performed.

a.) The disclosure must be in the form of a dated memorandum signed by the client that contains the terms of the agreement and the amount of the fee.

b.) The fees must be segregated from trust funds and accounted for according to regulations.

d. Adjusters [Secs. 2101(g), 2108] Adjusters must be licensed as independent adjusters or public adjusters.

1.) An independent adjuster is any person, firm, association, or corporation who, for a fee or other compensation, investigates and adjusts claims arising under insurance contracts on behalf of the insurer.

2.) A public adjuster is any person, firm, association, or corporation who, for a fee or other compensation, negotiates or settles claims for loss or damage to property on behalf of an insured.

3.) To be licensed as an adjuster, the applicant must:
- be at least 18 years old;
- file a written application;
- submit fingerprints to the Superintendent along with the written application;
- pass the written licensing examination;
- pay the required fee;
- maintain a $1,000 bond with the Superintendent;
- have at least one year of experience in the insurance business or complete 40 hours of formal training in a program approved by the Superintendent (if applying for a public adjuster's license);
- not have been convicted of a felony or any crime or offense involving fraudulent or dishonest practices (unless the applicant has been pardoned for the offense or received a certificate of good conduct granted by the board of parole); and
- have at least five reputable citizens in the community where the applicant resides or transacts business certify that they have personally known the applicant for at least five years, and believe the application statements to be true, and that the applicant is honest, of good character, and competent.

4.) Adjusters' licenses expire December 31 every two years and may be renewed for additional two-year terms. However, if an application for renewal is filed with the Superintendent before December 31, the license continues in force either until renewal is issued or for five days after the Superintendent refuses to issue the renewal license and has so notified the applicant.

e. Business entities [Sec. 2101(p), 2103(e)] A business entity is a corporation, association, partnership, limited liability company, limited liability partnership, or other legal entity.

1.) Before an original insurance agent's license is issued, there must be on file with the Superintendent an application by the prospective licensee containing information required by the superintendent.

2.) For each business entity, the sub-licensee named in the application will be deemed responsible for the business entity's compliance with the insurance laws, rules, and regulations of New York.

f. Nonresident [Secs. 2101(d), (e); 2103(g)(5)] A nonresident agent or broker is an individual who is licensed or authorized to transact insurance in the state in which he resides or in which he has an office.

1.) An applicant may qualify for a license as a nonresident only if he holds a similar license in another state or foreign country. Licenses issued to nonresidents by the Superintendent grant the same rights and privileges as resident licenses.

2.) Any individual who applies for an insurance agent license in New York who was previously licensed for the same lines of authority in another state does not have to take prelicenisng education or pass a licensing examination provided that:

■ the applicant's home state grants nonresident licenses to residents of New York on the same basis;

■ the person is currently licensed in that state; or

■ the application is received within 90 days of the date of cancellation of the applicant's previous license and the prior state issues a certification that, at the time of cancellation, the applicant was in good standing.

a.) An individual or entity licensed in another state who moves to New York must apply within 90 days of establishing legal residence to become a resident licensee. No prelicensing education or examination shall be required of that person to obtain any line of authority previously held in the prior state except where the Superintendent determines otherwise by regulation.

3.) A nonresident agent or broker's license may be revoked if the individual's home state has revoked, suspended, or denied his license.

a.) The Superintendent must give 10 days' written notice to the nonresident agent or broker before any action is taken.

b.) If the individual submits satisfactory proof that the suspension or revocation has been withdrawn in the home state, the Superintendent will reinstate the nonresident's license in New York.

g. Temporary [Sec. 2109; Reg. 20.1] The Superintendent may issue temporary licenses for up to 90 days if the licensee dies or becomes disabled and may renew the license for additional 90-day terms not to exceed 15 months.

1.) The Superintendent may also issue temporary licenses for up to six months to the designee of a licensed producer entering the armed forces.

    a.) The Superintendent may extend a temporary license for an additional term of six months.

    b.) However, a temporary license issued to the designee of a producer in the military may only be extended for 60 days past the time the absent producer receives his final discharge.

2.) An individual licensee or sublicensee who is unable to comply with license renewal procedures due to other extenuating circumstances, such as a long-term medical disability, may request a waiver. The licensee or sublicensee may also request a waiver of any examination requirement or any other fine or sanction imposed for failure to comply with renewal procedures.

3.) Temporary licensees cannot solicit, negotiate, or sell new insurance.

4.) The Superintendent may issue a temporary insurance producer's license to the following without requiring an examination if the Superintendent deems that the temporary license is necessary for servicing an insurance business:

- the executor or administrator of the estate of a deceased producer;
- the surviving next of kin of a deceased producer, where there is no administrator or executor of the estate;
- an officer or director of a corporation upon the death of the only officer or director who was qualified as a sublicensee or to the executor or administrator of the estate of such person;
- the surviving member or members of a firm or association who at the member's death was a licensed insurance producer;
- the designee of a licensed insurance producer entering the military; or
- the next of kin of a licensed producer who becomes totally disabled.

2. Maintenance and duration Producer licenses issued in New York state are valid for two years.

    a. Renewal [Sec. 2103(j); Reg. 21.2] The following schedule lists the dates on which license renewal forms and fees are due.

        1.) Agent licenses The current license remains in effect until the Superintendent issues or denies the renewal license.

            a.) If a renewal license is denied, the current license will expire five days after the Superintendent notifies the agent of the denial.

            b.) Before the Superintendent denies a renewal application, he must notify the agent of the pending denial and give the applicant a hearing.

If the basis for the denial is the applicant's failure to pass a written examination, the Superintendent does not need to give notice or hold a hearing.

c.) An agent must file an application for a renewal license with the Superintendent by the following dates (if the application is filed after July 1, the agent must pay a late filing fee of $5):
- Life agents—June 30, odd-numbered years
- Accident and health agents—June 30, odd-numbered years
- Property casualty agents—June 30, even-numbered years

2.) Broker licenses Brokers must renew their licenses by the following dates.

a.) Property casualty broker October 31, even-numbered years

b.) Life broker Staggered licensing periods:
- Licenses issued from March 1 to June 30 expire February 28 of odd years.
- Licenses issued from July 1 to October 31 expire June 30 of odd years.
- Licenses issued from November 1 to February 28-9 expire October 31 of odd years.

3.) An individual licensee or sublicensee who cannot renew his license due to extenuating circumstances, such as a long-term medical disability or military service, may request a waiver. The licensee or sublicensee may also request a waiver of any examination requirement or any other fine or sanction imposed for failure to comply with renewal procedures.

4.) Contents of license The license will contain the licensee's name, address, personal identification number, the date of issuance, the licensee's lines of authority, the expiration date, and any other information the Superintendent deems necessary.

b. Change of address [Regs. 21.4, 22.3, 23.5] A licensee must notify the Superintendent of:
- a change of address within 30 days of the change;
- certification from a new home state within 30 days of the change if a nonresident moves from one state to another;
- any administrative action taken against him in any other jurisdiction or by another governmental agency within 30 days; and
- any criminal prosecution taken against him within 30 days of the initial pretrial hearing date.

c. Reporting of actions [Sec. 2110(i)] A licensee must report to the Superintendent any administrative action taken against him in another jurisdiction or by another governmental agency in New York within 30 days of the final disposition of the matter. This report is to include a copy of the order, consent to order, or other relevant legal documents.

d. Assumed names [Sec. 2102(f)] Every licensee must notify the superintendent upon changing his legal name. Except for an individual licensee's own legal name, no licensee may use any name in conducting any business regulated by the state when that name has not been approved by the Superintendent.

e. Continuing education [Sec. 2132] All licensed producers, public adjusters, and consultants must complete 15 hours of approved continuing education courses every two years.

   1.) An instructor of an approved subject is entitled to the same credit as a student taking the course but can only receive the credit once during any two-year licensing period.

   2.) Individuals who earn more credits than required cannot carry them over to the next year.

   3.) Licensed individuals subject to this requirement must file written certification with the Superintendent listing the continuing education classes that were taken and successfully completed.

      a.) The certification must also be signed by the licensee's sponsoring organization.

      b.) Any person failing to meet the continuing education requirements is not eligible to renew his license.

   4.) A nonresident may submit a letter of certification from his home state indicating that the licensee is in good standing and is in compliance with the requirements of that state, including any continuing education requirements.

   5.) Individuals who hold dual residence licenses have the option to complete New York state-approved continuing education courses or submit a letter of certification from the other state.

   6.) Compliance with the continuing education requirements will begin with the first complete two-year licensing period following the issuance of the license.

3. Disciplinary actions

a. Hearings [Sec. 2405] If the Superintendent has reason to believe that a person has committed or is committing an unfair method of competition or unfair and deceptive act, the Superintendent can conduct a hearing on the matter. The Superintendent must give written notice of such a hearing at least 10 days in advance and identify the time, date, location, and purpose of the hearing.

b. Cease and desist order [Sec. 2405] At the hearing, the person has the opportunity to be heard personally or by counsel, and, in the case of a defined violation, to show cause why an order should not be issued by the Superintendent requiring the person to cease and desist from the activity.

1.) Upon good cause shown, the Superintendent can permit anyone to intervene, appear, and be heard at the hearing personally or by counsel.

2.) After the hearing, the Superintendent will write a report on his findings and will deliver a copy of it to the person and any intervenor.

3.) If, after a hearing, the Superintendent determines that a method of competition or an act or practice is unfair or deceptive, the Superintendent can issue an order requiring the person to cease and desist from engaging in the practice or method of competition.

4.) Anyone who violates a cease and desist order may be subject to up to a $5,000 penalty for each violation. The Superintendent may also, through the attorney general, enjoin the person from engaging in the violation.

c. Penalties [Sec. 2127] The Superintendent may, after giving notice and a hearing, order a penalty of up to $500 for each willful violation of the state's insurance laws (unless the law specifically provides for a different monetary penalty).

1.) Failure to pay the penalty within 30 days is itself an offense, unless the order to pay is suspended by a court.

2.) Where the law provides for license suspension or revocation for a violation, the Superintendent may instead impose a fine of up to $500 for each offense, up to a maximum of $2,500. If the licensee fails to pay such penalty within 20 days, and the order to do so is not stayed by the court, the Superintendent may then revoke or suspend the license.

d. Suspension, revocation, and nonrenewal [Sec. 2110] The Superintendent may refuse to renew or revoke, or may suspend the license of any insurance producer, insurance consultant, or adjuster if, after notice and hearing, the Superintendent finds that the licensee or any sublicensee has violated any insurance laws.

1.) Action will be taken if the Superintendent finds that a licensee has:
- violated any insurance law, regulation, subpoena, or order of the Superintendent of insurance or of another state's insurance commissioner, or has violated any law in the course of his dealings in such capacity;
- provided materially incorrect, materially misleading, materially incomplete, or materially untrue information in the license application;
- obtained or attempted to obtain a license through misrepresentation or fraud;

- used fraudulent, coercive, or dishonest practices;
- demonstrated incompetence, untrustworthiness, or financial irresponsibility in the conduct of business;
- improperly withheld, misappropriated, or converted any monies or properties received in the course of business;
- intentionally misrepresented the terms of an actual or proposed insurance contract or insurance application;
- been convicted of a felony;
- admitted to or been found to have committed any insurance unfair trade practice or fraud;
- had an insurance producer license or its equivalent denied, suspended, or revoked in any other state, province, district, or territory;
- forged another's name to an application for insurance or to any document related to an insurance transaction;
- improperly used notes or any other reference material to complete an examination for an insurance license;
- knowingly accepted insurance business from an individual who is not licensed;
- failed to comply with an administrative or court order imposing a child support obligation; or
- failed to pay state income tax or comply with any administrative or court order directing payment of state income tax.

2.) Before revoking or suspending the license of any insurance producer, the Superintendent shall notify the licensee and hold a hearing at least 10 days after giving notice.

3.) The revocation or suspension of any insurance producer's license shall terminate the authority conferred by all sublicensees.

4.) Any individual, corporation, firm, or association whose insurance producer license was revoked must wait for one year before getting a new license. If the revocation was judicially reviewed and the Superintendent's decision was upheld, the licensee must wait one year from the date of the final determination.

5.) No member or officer of a firm or association that had its license revoked is entitled to obtain a new license for the same period of time, unless the Superintendent determines, after notice and hearing, that the person was not personally at fault in the matter for which the license was revoked.

6.) A nonresident insurance producer's license may be revoked in the event that the person's license has been suspended, revoked, or not renewed in the person's home state by a procedure that included the right to a hearing.

   a.) Before revoking the license of any nonresident producer, the Superintendent must give 10 days' written notice.

b.) Upon submission to the Superintendent of proof that a license suspension or revocation issued by a home state was withdrawn, reversed, or voided, the Superintendent will reinstate and restore any licenses revoked in New York.

B. STATE REGULATION

1. Superintendent's general duties and powers [Secs. 201, 2404]
The Superintendent of Insurance, the chief officer of the New York Insurance Department, is appointed by the governor for a four-year term. The Superintendent has the authority to create and implement administrative regulations and rules in order to supervise the Department and enforce the state insurance laws.

a. Whenever there is reason to believe that a person engaged in the insurance business has committed any unfair methods of competition or deceptive acts, the Superintendent is empowered to examine and investigate the affairs of that person.

b. In the event any person does not provide a good faith response to a request for information from the Superintendent within at least 15 days, the Superintendent is authorized, after notice and hearing, to fine the person up to $500 per day for each day he does not respond; however, the penalty may not exceed $10,000.

c. In the event the Superintendent levies five separate civil penalties against any person within five years for failure to comply, the Superintendent is authorized, after notice and hearing, to levy an additional civil penalty of up to $50,000.

d. The Superintendent is also authorized to levy additional civil penalties not to exceed $50,000, after notice and hearing, against the person for every five subsequent violations of this section within a five-year period.

e. Any person may surrender his license in place of paying the civil penalty imposed by the Superintendent.

2. Company regulation

a. Certificate of authority [Sec. 1102] One of the Superintendent's duties is to license all firms, associations, corporations, and joint-stock companies doing insurance business in New York as insurers.

1.) The organization's license, called a certificate of authority, gives the insurer the right to transact insurance business in the state.

2.) Before issuing a certificate of authority, the Superintendent will examine the insurer to determine that it has:
- adequate capital and surplus; and
- fully complied with the required provisions of the insurance code.

3.) To receive a certificate of authority, an insurer must also pay the appropriate fees and have a certified copy of its declaration and charter filed and recorded in the office of the clerk of the county in which the insurer has its principal office.

4.) The Superintendent may refuse to issue a certificate of authority if any proposed incorporator or director of a stock corporation or mutual corporation has been convicted of any crime involving fraud, dishonesty, or moral turpitude, or is an untrustworthy person.

> **a.)** As a part of this determination, the Superintendent is authorized to fingerprint applicants for licensure.

> **b.)** The fingerprints will be submitted to the division of criminal justice services for a state criminal record check and may be submitted to the Federal Bureau of Investigation for a national criminal check.

b. Solvency [Sec. 307] By March 1 of each year, each insurer and fraternal benefit society authorized to do business in New York must file a statement of its financial condition and affairs (as of December 31 of the preceding year) with the Superintendent. Insurers that fail to file an annual statement can be fined up to $250 per day, not to exceed $25,000 total.

c. Unfair claims settlement practices [Sec. 2601; Reg. 216.3-.6] It is illegal to perform any of the following acts frequently enough to indicate a general business practice:

- knowingly misrepresent pertinent facts or insurance policy provisions;
- fail to acknowledge or act promptly upon communications regarding policy claims;
- fail to adopt and implement reasonable standards for prompt investigation of policy claims;
- not attempt in good faith to bring about prompt, fair, and equitable settlements of claims where liability has become reasonably clear; or
- compel policyholders to bring lawsuits to recover amounts due under policies by offering substantially less than the amounts ultimately recovered in suits brought by them.

d. Appointment of agent [Sec. 2103] In order to sell insurance for an insurer, an agent or producer must be appointed by the insurer.

1.) An appointment must be made 15 days from the date an agency contract is executed with the insurance company or the first insurance application is submitted.

2.) The notice of appointment must be filed with the Superintendent.

3.) An appointment is no longer part of an application for an initial agent license.

4.) An agent's license may be issued without an appointment.

e. **Termination of agent appointment [Sec. 2112; Reg. 20.2]** The definition of appointment has been expanded to include employment, contract, and other insurance business relationships. This means that producers as well as companies and others with an insurance business relationship with a producer must submit a written notice of Termination for Cause to the Department if they are terminating a producer for any of the actions listed under suspension, revocation, and nonrenewal.

    1.) Within 30 days of terminating a producer, the party terminating must submit a statement to the Superintendent stating the facts relative to the termination for cause.

    2.) Within 15 days after filing notification with the Superintendent, the party filing the termination for cause must provide a copy of that statement to the producer being terminated.

    3.) Within 30 days after the insurance producer has received the notification, the producer may file written comments about the notification with the Superintendent and send a copy to the insurer at the same time.

    4.) Any supplemental information must be promptly submitted to the Superintendent and then to the producer.

    5.) All information relative to the termination must be kept confidential.

3. Unfair and prohibited practices

a. **Misrepresentation [Sec. 2123; Reg. 216.3]** Misrepresenting or false advertising of a policy or company is illegal.

    1.) No agent or broker may:
- issue or circulate illustrations, circulars, statements, or memos misrepresenting the terms, benefits, or advantages of an insurance policy;
- make misleading estimates or statements as to past or future dividends or surplus to be received;
- misrepresent the financial condition of an insurer or make misleading statements as to the legal reserve system on which an insurer operates; or
- make an incomplete comparison of insurance policies or contracts for the purpose of inducing someone to lapse, forfeit, or surrender a policy. A comparison is considered incomplete if it omits the policy benefits, premium payments, or other provisions that affect benefits.

    2.) A misrepresentation by an insured will not void an insurance contract unless the misrepresentation was material. A misrepresentation is considered material if the insurer, knowing the facts, would have refused to issue the policy.

3.) No insurer may knowingly misrepresent to a claimant the terms, benefits, or advantages of the insurance policy pertinent to the claim.

4.) No insurer may deny any part of a claim on the grounds of a specific policy provision, condition, or exclusion unless the insurer identifies the provision, condition, or exclusion in writing.

5.) Any payment or settlement that, without explanation, does not include all amounts that should be included and are within the policy limits, will be considered to be a communication that misrepresents a pertinent policy provision.

b. False advertising [Sec. 2603] An insurance corporation, its officer, director, or agent may not issue any illustration or statement used to advertise its insurance business unless the corporation or its agent is authorized to transact those lines of authority under its certificate of authority issued by the Superintendent.

c. Defamation of insurer [Sec. 2604] It is illegal to make a false written or oral statement that is derogatory to the financial condition or that affects the solvency or financial standing of an insurer doing business in New York.

1.) No one may counsel, aid, or induce another to start or circulate such a statement.

2.) Anyone who knowingly makes an untrue or inaccurate statement is guilty of a class A misdemeanor.

d. Unfair discrimination [Secs. 2606-2608, 2612]

1.) No individual or entity may, because of race, color, sex, marital status, creed, national origin, or disability:
- discriminate between persons as to the premiums or rates charged for insurance policies;
- require a greater premium from any person than it requires from others in similar cases;
- require any rebate, discrimination, or discount for the amount to be paid or the service to be rendered on any policy; or
- insert into the policy any condition whereby the insured binds himself or his heir to accept a sum less than the full value of the policy except such conditions and stipulations as are imposed upon others in similar cases.

2.) No individual or insurer may, solely because of the applicant's race, color, sex, marital status, creed, national origin, or disability:
- reject an application for an insurance policy;
- refuse to issue, renew, or sell a policy; or
- lower or discriminate in the fees or commissions of producer selling policies.

3.) No person or entity may refuse to issue or renew or may cancel any policy because of any treatment for a mental disability of the insured. However, an insurer may refuse to issue or renew or may cancel a policy based on sound underwriting and actuarial principles related to actual or anticipated loss experience.

4.) The insurer must notify the insured or his physician of its specific reason for refusal to issue or renew or for cancelling a policy.

5.) No authorized insurer who lawfully possesses information derived from a genetic test on a biological sample from an individual may incorporate the information into the records of a nonconsenting individual who may be genetically related to the tested individual; nor may any inferences be drawn, used, or communicated regarding the possible genetic status of the nonconsenting individual.

e. Rebating [Sec. 2324] It is illegal to offer an inducement to a person to encourage the purchase of an insurance policy.

1.) Specifically, agents, brokers, and insurers are prohibited from offering:
- a rebate of premium;
- a rebate of policy fee;
- a rebate of the agent's or broker's commission;
- special favors or dividends; or
- any other inducement.

2.) It also is illegal to make an agreement with an insured for services or benefits not specified in the policy or contract.

3.) No insurer may give, sell, or purchase stocks, bonds, or other securities, or use dividends or profits from these items, as an inducement to purchase a policy or contract.

4.) Insurers may give medical examinations and diagnoses or nursing services to all or some of their policyholders.

5.) Insurers, agents, and brokers may give away items as a form of advertising provided the advertisement is placed conspicuously on the item and the value of the item does not exceed $5.

4. Licensee regulation

a. Controlled business [Sec. 2103(i)] The Superintendent may refuse to issue, suspend, or revoke a license if an applicant receives more than 10% of the aggregate commissions during a 12-month period from insurance sold to a licensee's spouse or other family members or business associates or their immediate family.

b. Sharing commissions [Secs. 2121, 2128] Any insurer who delivers an insurance contract to any insurance broker or to his insured represented will have authorized the broker to receive on its behalf the premium payment that is due at the time of the contract's delivery, provided the payment is received by the broker within 90 days after the premium is due.

1.) No insurance producer or adjuster may receive any commissions or fees in connection with insurance services rendered to the state, its agencies, departments, or other governmental subdivisions unless he actually placed the coverages or rendered insurance services to the state or its agencies.

2.) The Superintendent may require insurance producers and insurance adjusters to file disclosure statements with the Insurance Department and the most senior official of the governmental unit involved, with respect to any insurance services rendered to the state or its agencies.

c. Fiduciary responsibility [Sec. 2120; Regs. 20.3, 20.4] A fiduciary relationship is characterized by special trust and confidence.

1.) Agents, brokers, and reinsurance intermediaries have a fiduciary relationship for all funds they receive in the course of business. Such funds may not be commingled with personal funds without the express written consent of their principals.

2.) The fiduciary laws are easily violated. For example, it is illegal to commingle fiduciary funds (received from clients and intended for the insurer) with personal funds, such as a personal checking account, even for a brief period of time.

3.) The agent who puts an applicant's premium deposit in his own checking account, even with the intention of writing a check to the insurer, has committed a violation.

4.) Premiums collected by agents and brokers but not remitted immediately to insurers must be deposited in an appropriately identified account in a New York bank, referred to as a premium account. An agent or broker who makes immediate remittance to insurers and assureds of such funds need not maintain a premium account of collected funds.

5.) Agents or brokers may make voluntary deposits of their own funds to such premium accounts in order to maintain a minimum balance or to pay premiums due but not collected. Withdrawals from these accounts are allowed only to transfer premiums to the rightful insurers.

6.) No withdrawals from a premium account may be made other than for:
- payment of premiums to insurers;
- payment of return premiums to insureds; and
- transfer to an operating account of:
  - interest, if the principals have consented in writing;

— commissions; or

— withdrawal of voluntary deposits, provided that no withdrawal is made if the balance remaining in the premium account thereafter is less than aggregate net premiums received but not remitted.

7.) An agent or broker may not commingle any funds received or collected as agent or broker with his or its own funds or with funds held by him in any other capacity without the written consent of the person or corporation for whom they are held in a fiduciary capacity. However, deposit of a premium in a premium account is not to be construed as a commingling of the net premium and of the commission portion of the premium.

8.) Every licensee who is required to maintain a premium account must maintain books, records, and accounts in connection with their business to record:

■ all money received in trust for insurers or members of the public;

■ all disbursements out of money held in trust; and

■ all other money received and disbursed in connection with the business.

9.) At a minimum, every licensee required to maintain a premium account must maintain a book or other permanent account record, imprinted with the name and address of the licensee, showing all receipts and disbursement of money, distinguishing among:

■ the receipt of money in trust for insurers and members of the public;

■ disbursements out of money held in trust; and

■ money received and paid by the licensee for general operations, services, sales, and other insurance.

d. **License display [Reg. 34.5]** In a headquarters location and each satellite office, the establishing agent or broker must prominently display the license or licenses of the supervising person or persons responsible for that place of business.

e. **Commissions and compensation [Secs. 2114-2116, 2119; Reg. 20.6]** An insurer or fraternal benefit society may not pay a commission or provide a compensation to a person or organization that is not licensed in New York. If a producer is licensed at the time of the sale, solicitation, or negotiation of an insurance policy, he may receive renewal or deferred commissions even if he is no longer licensed.

1.) Compensation for agent, broker, and consulting services must be based on a written memorandum stating the amount to be paid. Compensation includes fees, commissions, or anything of value.

2.) The party to be charged for the consulting, agent, or broker services must sign the memorandum and the licensee must retain a copy for at least three years after all services are performed.

3.) Unless specified in the memorandum, a consultant, agent, or broker may not receive compensation for an insurance or annuity sale or for using securities or trusts in connection with pensions if he has received a fee for a related service for the same individual within the preceding 12 months.

4.) Nothing prohibits offsetting a consulting, agent, or broker fee by compensation otherwise payable as the result of a life insurance or annuity sale if the offset is provided for in the memorandum.

5.) When a fee is permitted, no licensee may charge or accept any fee that is not fully disclosed before the service is performed.

   a.) The disclosure must be in the form of a dated memorandum signed by the client that contains the terms of the agreement and the amount of the fee.

   b.) The fees must be segregated from trust funds and accounted for according to regulations.

5. **Examination of books and records [Sec. 2404; Reg. 243.0-.3]** Whenever there is reason to believe that a person engaged in the insurance business has committed any unfair methods of competition or deceptive acts, the Superintendent is empowered to examine and investigate the affairs of that person.

   a. Every insurer must maintain its claims, rating, underwriting marketing, complaint, financial, and producer licensing records, and any other records subject to examination by the Superintendent.

   b. In addition, an insurer must maintain a policy record for each insurance contract for six years after the date the policy is no longer in force or until after the filing of an examination in which the record was subject to review, whichever is longer.

6. **Insurance Frauds Prevention Act [Secs. 401 to 407a, 409]** The state legislature has determined that insurance is a business that has the potential for abuse and illegal activities in the issuance of policies and payment of claims. Therefore, it has enacted the Insurance Frauds Prevention Act to combat fraud.

   a. The Superintendent is given broad authority to investigate any activities that may be fraudulent, to halt fraudulent activities, and to develop evidence to be turned over to appropriate authorities for prosecution. The act is particularly concerned with arson for insurance fraud, a damaging crime against society that destroys lives, property, and communities.

   b. The act reinforces the need for an Insurance Frauds Bureau, operating with the Department. Employees of the Bureau may be designated as peace officers in order to carry out their duties to investigate and prevent fraud.

   c. In addition to any criminal liability, the Superintendent may also levy a civil penalty against anyone who commits a fraudulent insurance act in an amount not exceeding $5,000 plus the amount of the claim.

d. All applications for insurance must contain a notice to the applicant regarding the penalties for committing a fraudulent insurance act.

e. Licensees are required to report to the Superintendent any fraudulent acts of which they become aware. This must be done within 30 days of the time the licensee has knowledge that a fraudulent act has taken or is about to take place.

f. The Superintendent must report to the governor and the legislature on an annual basis all activities of the Bureau.

g. The act also requires every insurer that transacts insurance in the state to maintain a special investigations unit (SIU) for purposes of detecting and preventing fraud. This provision applies to insurers who issue:

■ private or commercial automobile insurance;

■ workers compensation insurance; or

■ group or blanket accident and health insurance policies.

7. Consumer privacy regulation [Regs. 420.0 to .24] At least once every year, insurers must give their insureds a notice explaining their privacy policies.

a. The privacy notice must include, in addition to any other information the insurer wishes to provide:

■ the categories of nonpublic personal financial information that it collects;

■ the categories of nonpublic personal financial information that it discloses;

■ the categories of affiliates and nonaffiliated third parties to whom the insurer discloses nonpublic personal financial information;

■ the categories of nonpublic personal financial information that the insurer discloses about its former customers as well as the affiliates and nonaffiliated third parties to whom such information is given;

■ an explanation of the consumer's right to opt out of the disclosure of nonpublic personal financial information to nonaffiliated third parties, including the methods that can be used to exercise such right;

■ any disclosures the insurer makes under the federal Fair Credit Reporting Act; and

■ the insurer's policies that it uses to protect the confidentiality and security of nonpublic personal information.

b. Insurers are also prohibited from disclosing, other than to a consumer reporting agency, a policy number or similar form of access number for a consumer's policy to any nonaffiliated third party for use in telemarketing, direct mail marketing, or other marketing through electronic mail to the consumer.

c. Opt-out rights Consumers and customers have the right to opt out of, or say no to, having their information shared with certain third parties.

1.) The privacy notice must explain how and offer a reasonable way to opt out.

2.) For example, providing a toll-free telephone number or a detachable form with a pre-printed address is a reasonable way for consumers or customers to opt out; requiring someone to write a letter as the only way to opt out is not.

C. FEDERAL REGULATION Although primary responsibility for the regulation of insurance rests with the state, some federal laws also pertain to insurance transactions.

1. Fair Credit Reporting Act [Sec. 15 USC 1681 to 1681d] The Fair Credit Reporting Act, enforced by the Federal Trade Commission, is designed to promote accuracy and ensure the privacy of the information used in consumer reports.

a. Permissible reports A consumer reporting agency may furnish a consumer report only:

- in response to a court order;
- according to the written instructions of the consumer to whom it relates; and
- to a person who is authorized by the consumer to use the information:
  — in connection with a credit transaction involving the consumer and the extension of credit to, or collection of an account of, the consumer;
  — for employment purposes;
  — for the underwriting of insurance involving the consumer;
  — to determine the consumer's eligibility for a license or other benefit granted by a governmental instrumentality required by law to examine an applicant's financial responsibility or status;
  — for legitimate purposes related to a business with the consumer; and
  — in connection with the rental or lease of a residence.

1.) A person may buy a consumer report in connection with an application for credit, employment, insurance, or rental or lease of residences only if:

- the applicant is first informed in writing that a consumer report may be requested; and
- the applicant is informed that a consumer report was requested, and given the name and address of the consumer reporting agency furnishing the report.

2.) If a person applying for credit, insurance, or employment refuses to authorize the preparation of an investigative consumer report, the creditor, insurer, or employer may decline to grant credit, insurance, or employment.

3.) Where an adult applies for insurance on behalf of or to cover his child or a minor, the execution of an authorization and receipt of notice by the parent or adult will be deemed to be receipt of notice and execution of an authorization by the child or minor.

b. Disclosure to consumers Every consumer reporting agency shall, upon request, accurately disclose to the consumer:

- all information on the consumer in its files at the time of the request;
- the sources of the information, except that the sources used solely for prepar-

ing the report and used for no other purpose need not be disclosed, provided, however, that in the event an action is brought, the sources will be available to the plaintiff under appropriate discovery procedures; and

■ who received the consumer report on the consumer, if requested:

— for employment purposes within two years preceding the request; or

— or any other purpose within six months preceding the request.

1.) All consumers must be advised that if they have been denied credit in the past 30 days, they are entitled to receive a written copy of their complete file at no charge.

c. Compliance procedures Every consumer or reporting agency must maintain reasonable procedures designed to avoid violations of this section.

1.) These procedures require that all prospective users of the information:
   ■ identify themselves;
   ■ certify the purposes for which the information is sought; and
   ■ certify that the information will be used for no other purpose.

2.) Every consumer reporting agency must make a reasonable effort to verify the identity of a new prospective user and its use for the report before beginning an investigation. No agency may furnish a report to anyone if it believes that the report will not be used for the proper purposes.

d. Civil liability for willful and negligent noncompliance Any consumer reporting agency or user of information who negligently fails to comply with these requirements is liable to an injured consumer in an amount equal to the sum of:

■ the actual damages sustained by the consumer as a result;

■ the amount of punitive damages the court may allow; and

■ the costs of any suit brought, together with reasonable attorney's fees as determined by the court.

2. Fraud and false statements [Sec. 18 USC 1033, 1034] Anyone who commits an act of fraud; material misrepresentation; embezzlement; misappropriation of monies, premiums, or other property; or makes false statements involving the interstate commerce of insurance, and his actions contribute to the insolvency of the insurer, will be imprisoned up to 15 years.

a. Section 1033 is captioned "Crimes By and Affecting Persons Engaged in the Business of Insurance Whose Activities Affect Interstate Commerce." The section describes certain activities as crimes if they are carried out by individuals engaged in the business of insurance and whose activities affect interstate commerce.

1.) Prohibited activities include:
   ■ knowingly, with the intent to deceive, making any false material statement or report or willfully and materially overvaluing any land, property, or security in connection with any financial reports or documents

presented to any insurance regulatory official or agency for the purpose of influencing the actions of that official or agency;

- ■ willfully embezzling, abstracting, or misappropriating any of the monies, funds, premiums, credits, or other property of any person engaged in the business of insurance;

- ■ knowingly making any false entry of material fact in any book, report, or statement of the person engaged in the business of insurance with the intent to deceive any person about the financial condition or solvency of such business;

- ■ by threats of force or by any threatening letter or communication, corruptly influencing, obstructing, or impeding the proper administration of the law under which any proceeding is pending before any insurance regulatory official or agency; and

- ■ willfully engaging in the business of insurance whose activities affect interstate commerce if the individual has been convicted of a criminal felony involving dishonesty or a breach of trust or has been convicted of an offense under Section 1033.

2.) Punishments for engaging in the prohibited activities specified range from a maximum of one to 15 years of imprisonment plus fines established under Title 18. Under certain provisions, penalties may be more severe if the activity jeopardized the safety and soundness of an insurer and was a significant cause of an insurer being placed into conservation, rehabilitation, or liquidation.

b. Section 1034 is captioned "Civil Penalties and Injunctions for Violations of Section 1033." The section allows the US Attorney General to bring civil actions against a person who engages in conduct constituting an offense under Section 1033. If found to have committed the offense, the person is subject to a civil penalty of not more than $50,000 for each violation or the amount of compensation the person received or offered for the prohibited conduct, whichever is greater.

1.) If the offense contributed to the decision of a court issuing an order directing the conservation, rehabilitation, or liquidation of an insurer, the penalty is remitted to the appropriate regulatory official for the benefit of the troubled insurer's estate.

2.) Imposition of a civil penalty under Section 1034 does not preclude any other criminal or civil statutory, common law, or administrative remedy available by law to the United States or any other person.

3.) The section also permits the Attorney General to seek an order (an injunction) prohibiting persons from engaging in any illegal conduct.

II.   NEW YORK LAW, RULES, AND REGULATIONS PERTINENT TO LIFE INSURANCE ONLY

A.   LICENSEE RESPONSIBILITIES

1. Advertising [Sec. 2122] Agents and brokers who advertise must obey the following rules.

   a. An insurance agent or broker may not make or issue an advertisement or other announcement about the financial condition of an insurer unless it meets the requirements of New York insurance law.

   b. Insurance agents or brokers may not call attention to any unauthorized insurer in their advertisements.

   c. Any advertisement, pamphlet, or card that refers to an insurer must contain the full name of the insurer and the city of its principal office.

2. Prohibited advertising of the Life Insurance Company Guaranty Corporation [Sec. 7718] No insurer, agent, or broker may advertise insurance services or products in a way that uses the existence of the Life Insurance Company Guaranty Corporation to help promote those services or products. Anyone who advertises or uses the existence of the corporation to sell insurance commits an unfair trade practice.

3. Policy summary [Sec. 3209; Reg. 53-2.2] A policy summary must be given to each policyowner when the policy is delivered.

   a. The insurer may charge a reasonable fee to prepare it.

   b. The summary must include the:
   - name and address of the agent or broker and company home office;
   - generic name and annual premium cost of the basic policy and all riders;
   - guaranteed amount payable at death;
   - total guaranteed surrender values;
   - effective policy loan annual percentage interest rate; and
   - life insurance cost indexes for 10 and 20 years or the length of the premium-paying period.

4. Buyer's guide [Sec. 3209; Reg. 53-2.6] Each insured must receive a copy of the insurance buyer's guide and preliminary information at the time of application.

   a. The buyer's guide format is determined by the Superintendent and is based on a model buyer's guide adopted by the National Association of Insurance Commissioners (NAIC). It does not endorse any company or policy but provides information consumers need to evaluate policies and make buying decisions.

b. The buyer's guide provides a consumer-friendly explanation of term, whole life, and endowment insurance. It specifically describes the meaning and use of:

- surrender cost index;
- net payment cost index; and
- equivalent level annual dividend index.

c. Each insured must receive preliminary information at the time of application. Preliminary information includes the:

- agent or broker and insurer's name and address;
- date of the information;
- initial amount of insurance and premium;
- generic name of the policy being considered;
- total guaranteed cash value for the basic policy at the end of the 10th and 20th policy years (can be given on a per-thousand-of-face-amount basis);
- life insurance cost index and the equivalent level annual dividend (where applicable) for years 10 and 20;
- policy loan annual percentage interest rate then in effect and whether this rate is applied in advance or arrears, fixed or variable;
- statement that the insured will receive a complete policy summary when the policy is issued; and
- statement that the insured has 10 days to return the policy for an unconditional refund of the premiums paid.

5. Illustrations [Regs. 53-3.1 to .6] When submitting a policy form for the Superintendent's approval, insurers must give notice as to whether the form will be marketed with or without an illustration. If it is to be marketed without an illustration, the insurer may not use an illustration in a policy using that form in its first year.

a. This requirement applies to policies other than variable life insurance, annuities, credit life, and life insurance policies without illustrated death benefits on any person exceeding $10,000.

b. Illustrations for the sale of life insurance policies must be clearly labeled as such and include the following, among other information:

- insurer's name;
- name and business address of the producer;
- name, age, and sex of proposed insured;
- underwriting or rating classification on which the illustration is based;
- generic name of the policy; and
- initial death benefit.

6. Replacement [Secs. 2123(a)(2,3); Reg. 51.1-8]

a. Replacement occurs when a new life insurance policy or annuity contract is written and an existing one is:

- lapsed or surrendered;

- converted into paid-up insurance or continued as extended term insurance or other form of nonforfeiture benefit;

- converted to reduce the amount of existing insurance or the period it is to continue in force;

- reissued in a reduced face amount so that substantial cash values (more than 50%) are released;

- continued without further premium payments or a reduction in the amount of the premium; or

- assigned as collateral for a loan or subject to substantial borrowing of the loan value (50% or more of the cash values).

b.   Regulating replacement When a policyowner interrupts one life insurance policy or annuity contract and begins to build up values in another, he often suffers financial loss.

1.) The new policy usually has a higher premium rate based on the insured's attained age, and the policyowner must again pay the initial costs of issuing a policy.

2.) In some cases, replacement may be advisable, and these additional costs are acceptable.

3.) In general, however, the interests of life insurance purchasers must be protected zealously. Consequently, New York has issued Regulation 60, which:

- establishes minimum standards of conduct and procedures to be followed in replacing life insurance policies;

- makes available full and clear information so applicants can make decisions in their best interests;

- reduces the opportunity for misrepresentation and incomplete comparisons in replacement situations; and

- precludes unfair methods of competition and unfair practices.

c.   Insurance exempt from replacement These replacement requirements do not apply to:

- new life insurance or annuity provided under a group policy, pension, or other benefit plan;

- a policy or annuity paid for in whole or in part by an employer;

- nonconvertible term insurance policy that will expire within five years and cannot be renewed;

- a policy or annuity distributed through mass merchandising and covering debtors of a creditor or members of an association;

- a contractual conversion privilege being exercised; or

- a policy change customarily granted by the insurer that does not result in additional surrender, expense charges, suicide, or contestable restrictions.

d.   The replacing agent's responsibilities If replacement is involved, the agent must give the prospective insured three documents, in addition to policy information on all proposed and existing coverage affected.

1.) The forms required are:

- the Disclosure Statement (a form that will allow the applicant to summarize and compare the features of his current policy with those of the proposed replacement policy);

- the important Notice Regarding Replacement or Change of Life Insurance Policies or Annuity Contracts (directions on how to analyze whether replacement is in the applicant's best interest); and

- the Definition of Replacement.

2.) Then, the agent is required to complete the following steps.

a.) Obtain a completed Definition of Replacement signed by the applicant and the agent and submit it to the insurer.

b.) Leave a copy of the Definition of Replacement with the applicant.

c.) Obtain a list of all existing life insurance policies or annuity contracts proposed to be replaced.

d.) Submit to the current insurer, whose policy or contract is being replaced:
- a list of all life insurance policies or annuity contracts proposed to be replaced, as well as the policy or contract number for each policy or contract;
- the proper authorization from the applicant; and
- the information necessary to complete the Disclosure Statement; in the event the current insurer fails to provide the required information in the prescribed time, the agent may use good faith approximations based on the information available.

e.) Present to the applicant no later than when the applicant signs the application, the important Notice Regarding Replacement or Change of Life Insurance Policies or Annuity Contracts and a completed Disclosure Statement signed by the agent (the applicant must acknowledge that the notice and the completed disclosure statement have been received and read).

f.) Submit with the application to the replacing insurer:
- a list of all life insurance policies or annuity contracts proposed to be replaced;
- a copy of any proposal, including the sales material used in the sale of the proposed life insurance policy or annuity contract;
- proof of receipt by the applicant of the important Notice Regarding Replacement or Change of Life Insurance Policies or Annuity Contracts; and

■ the completed Disclosure Statement, including the primary reason(s) for recommending the new life insurance policy or annuity contract and why the existing life insurance policy or annuity contract cannot meet the applicant's objection.

e. The replacing insurer's responsibilities

1.) As regards the replacement regulations, each insurer must:

■ inform and train its agents with respect to the requirements regarding replacement transactions;

■ keep the signed copies of the Definition of Replacement for six years; and

■ require with each application a statement signed by the agent as to whether replacement of a life insurance policy or annuity contract is involved.

2.) Where a replacement is likely to occur, the insurer replacing the life insurance policy or annuity contract must:

■ examine all the sales material and the Disclosure Statement, and ascertain that they are accurate and that they meet the requirements of the state insurance law;

■ furnish to the current insurer a copy of any proposal or the sales material and the completed Disclosure Statement within 10 days of receiving the application;

■ submit quarterly reports to the superintendent indicating which insurers have failed to provide the required information;

■ maintain copies for six years of:

— any proposals and sales material;

— a signed receipt by the applicant that he received the important Notice Regarding Replacement or Change of Life Insurance Policies or Annuity Contracts;

— the signed and completed Disclosure Statement; and

— the notification of replacement to the existing insurer;

■ correct any deficits in the form within 10 days of receiving it or reject the application and notify the applicant of the rejection and the reason for it; and

■ treat the proposed life insurance policy or annuity contract as if it were new issuance subject to the same underwriting considerations, including but not limited to:

— premium discount;

— interest rate credit; and

— agent compensation, expenses or bonuses, or other inducements; and

■ in the event that the new policy or annuity issued differs from the one applied for, ensure that the requirements of this regulation are met.

f. Duties of existing insurer Where a replacement is likely to occur, the existing insurer—the insurer whose insurance policy or annuity contract is to be replaced—must:

- keep copies of all notification sent to it for six calendar years; and
- simultaneously furnish all the required information to the agent of record of the existing policy or annuity being replaced and the replacing agent and insurer within 20 days of receiving the request (this information includes the insurer's customer service telephone number, the current status of the existing life insurance policy or annuity contract, and the currently illustrated dividends, interest, and other non-guaranteed costs and benefits).

g. Right to return a replacement policy Any insurer that issues a replacement life insurance policy or annuity contract must provide to the purchaser a 60-day free-look period.

7. Backdating of policies [Sec. 3208] To obtain a lower premium, a life insurance policy may be backdated if the policy is issued to take effect not more than six months before the date of the application. A contract that violates this provision still is valid and can be converted.

III. NEW YORK LAW, RULES, AND REGULATIONS PERTINENT TO ACCIDENT AND HEALTH INSURANCE ONLY

A. LICENSEE RESPONSIBILITIES IN INDIVIDUAL HEALTH INSURANCE

1. Marketing requirements/advertising [Regs. 215.1 to 18] Each insurer must file a certificate of compliance with its annual statements to the Superintendent to certify that its advertising meets these requirements. To ensure the truthful disclosure of all relevant information, all advertisements must meet these requirements.

a. Advertisements must be truthful and must not deceive either in fact or by implication.

b. The form and content of an advertisement must be complete, clear, and easy to understand. Insurance terminology should be kept to a minimum. The Superintendent is authorized to determine whether an advertisement is misleading or deceptive.

c. An advertisement must not state or imply that an insurer or policy is approved or endorsed by a group or organization unless such is the case. Any financial relationship between the insurer and organization must be disclosed.

d. All policy limitations must be disclosed.

e. Deceptive words, phrases, or illustrations are prohibited. For example, words that tend to exaggerate any benefits beyond the term of the policy, such as *no additional cost, savings, minimum, free, special,* or *unlimited* may not be used.

f. Testimonials must be genuine, represent the current opinion of the author, be applicable to the policy being advertised, and be reproduced accurately. If the person making the testimonial has a financial interest in the insurer, that fact must be disclosed in the advertisement.

g. Advertisements may not make unfair or incomplete comparisons and must not disparage competitors, their policies, or their business methods.

h. Introductory, initial, or special-offer policies may not be advertised as offering special advantages unless that is the fact.

2. Individual underwriting by the insurer

a. HIV testing No insurer or its agent may require an applicant for insurance to take an HIV test without first receiving the written informed consent of the individual and without providing information about AIDS and the transmission of HIV infection.

1.) Written informed consent to an HIV test consists of a written authorization that is dated and includes at least:

- a general description of the test;
- a statement of the purpose of the test;
- a statement that a positive test result is an indication that the individual may develop AIDS and may wish to consider further independent testing;
- a statement that the individual may identify on the authorization form the person to whom the specific test results may be disclosed in the event of an adverse underwriting decision;
- the department of health's toll-free telephone number that may be called for further information about AIDS, the meaning of HIV-related test results, and the availability and location of HIV-related counseling services; and
- the signature of the applicant, or if the individual lacks capacity to consent, the signature of a person authorized to provide consent.

2.) In the event that an insurer's adverse underwriting decision is based on the result of an HIV test, the insurer must notify the individual and ask whether to have the test results disclosed directly to the individual or to another person designated by the individual.

If the individual elects to receive the HIV test results directly, the insurer will advise him that he may call the Department of Health's toll-free telephone number for further information.

b. Genetic testing written informed consent No insurer or its agent may require an applicant for insurance to take a genetic test without first receiving the written informed consent of the individual.

1.) Written informed consent to a genetic test consists of written authorization that is dated and signed and includes at least:

- a general description of the test;

- a statement of the purpose of the test;

- a statement that a positive test result is an indication that the individual may be predisposed to or have the specific disease or condition and may wish to consider further independent testing, consult their physician, or pursue genetic counseling;

- a general description of each specific disease or condition tested for;

- the level of certainty that a positive test result for that disease or condition serves as a predictor of such disease;

- the name of the person or organizations to whom the test results may be disclosed;

- a statement that no tests other than those authorized will be performed on the biological sample and that the sample shall be destroyed at the end of the testing process or not more than 60 days after the sample was taken; and

- the signature of the individual subject of the test or, if that individual lacks the capacity to consent, the signature of the person authorized to consent for such individual.

2.) A general waiver that is obtained but that is not in complete compliance with this section does not constitute informed consent.

3.) If an insurer's adverse underwriting decision is based on the results of a genetic test, the insurer will notify the individual and ask him to elect in writing whether to have the test results disclosed directly to the individual or to the individual's physician.

4.) All records and results of any genetic test performed are confidential and may not be disclosed without written authorization.

5.) No authorized insurer who lawfully possesses information derived from a genetic test on a biological sample from an individual may incorporate the information into the records of a nonconsenting individual who may be genetically related to the tested individual; nor may any inferences be drawn, used, or communicated regarding the possible genetic status of the nonconsenting individual.

6.) If the Superintendent determines after notice and a hearing that an authorized insurer or its agent has violated this section, the Superintendent may levy a fine of up to $5,000.

B. NEW YORK MANDATED BENEFITS AND OFFERS (INDIVIDUAL AND/OR GROUP)

1. **Dependent child age limit [Sec. 3216(a)(4)]** All individual accident and health insurance policies that cover dependent children include any children under age 19 except:

   - any unmarried dependent child, regardless of age, who is incapable of self-sustaining employment by reason of mental illness, developmental disability, mental retardation, or physical handicap, subject to any preexisting conditions limitation applicable to other dependents; and

   - any unmarried student at an accredited institution of learning who may be considered a dependent child until attaining age 23.

2. **Newborn child coverage [Sec. 3216(a)(4)(C)]** Policies providing family coverage must cover newborn infants for injury and sickness from the moment of birth. Coverage must include necessary care and treatment of medically diagnosed congenital defects and birth abnormalities, including premature birth. If the policy requires additional premiums for each new family member (whether born or adopted), it can require the policyowner to notify the insurer (and pay the additional premium) within no less than 30 days.

C. LONG-TERM CARE INSURANCE: NEW YORK REGULATIONS AND REQUIRED PROVISIONS

1. **Renewability [Reg. 52.25(b)(1)]** Individual long-term care policies must be guaranteed renewable. **Guaranteed renewable** means that the insured has the right to continue the long-term care insurance in force by timely payment of premiums and the insurer may not change the policy, although premium rates may be revised on a class basis.

2. **Required disclosure provisions [Reg. 52.65]** Disclosure statements are required by the Superintendent in an attempt to give the insured a brief overview of what a policy does and does not cover.

   a. All individual accident and health insurance policies must be accompanied by the completed disclosure form when the policy is delivered. The disclosure form also may be delivered to the applicant at the time of application, as long as the applicant signs a receipt.

   b. In addition to the coverage summary, disclosure forms for individual accident and health insurance include an expected benefit ratio as defined by the superintendent.

   c. Group or blanket certificates for accident and health insurance also must include, or be accompanied by, a synopsis of benefits and the specified disclosure statement. (The specific disclosure statements for individual, group, and blanket policies are different.)

d. A special type of disclosure form must be used with Medicare supplement policies. In addition to stating what the policy does and does not cover, the disclosure form must list each type of service, what Medicare pays, and what the insured is expected to pay.

e. For long-term care insurance policies, insurers must include the following information in or with the disclosure statement:

- a comparison of the benefit levels for at least 20 years of a policy or certificate that increases benefits with a policy or certificate that does not increase benefits; and

- any expected premium increases or additional premiums to pay for automatic or optional benefit increases.

3. Prohibited practices [Reg. 52.16] New York law prohibits the sale of certain policies or coverages. For example, a policy may not provide benefits strictly for specified diseases, or procedures or treatments unique to specified diseases, nor may a policy provide for a return of premium or cash value benefit, except return of unearned premium on termination of coverage for an insured.

a. A policy may not limit or exclude coverage by type of illness, accident, treatment, or medical condition except for:

- congenital anomalies of a covered dependent child, subject to limitations;

- mental or emotional disorders, alcoholism, and drug addiction, except as required by law;

- pregnancy, except for complications and other legal requirements;

- illness, accident treatment, or medical condition arising out of war or act of war, suicide (including attempted suicide or intentionally self-inflicted injury), aviation (other than as a commercial passenger), or coverage with respect to blanket insurance for interscholastic sports;

- foot care in connection with corns, calluses, and flat feet;

- correction of structural imbalance of vertebral column;

- government hospital treatment and benefits provided under Medicare, workers compensation, or employer's liability law;

- dental care;

- eyeglasses or hearing aids;

- rest cures;

- arbitrary cosmetic surgery (except restorative); and

- coverage while the insured is outside the United States, its possessions, or Canada and Mexico.

b. In addition, no policy may have a probationary period longer than:

- 30 days for all specified conditions;

- 30 days for inception of pregnancy (unless otherwise specified by law); and

- zero days for accidents.

c. A group or blanket medical expense policy insuring 300 or more persons, excluding dependents, may not contain a provision excluding or limiting coverage for preexisting conditions for any person electing coverage during the first 30 days of eligibility. This provision does not apply to blanket insurance in which enrollment is voluntary or to dental insurance and association insurance insuring employers with less than 300 employees.

d. Community-rated policies, other than benefits provided through an HMO, and individual policies may not provide benefits that duplicate those recoverable under mandatory automobile no-fault insurance, unless the benefits are purchased as a rider at the policyholder's option and at an appropriate premium.

4. Replacement [Reg. 52.29] Application forms shall include a question designed to elicit information as to whether a long-term care insurance, nursing home insurance only, home care insurance only, or nursing home and home care insurance policy is intended to replace any other accident and health insurance policy currently in force.

a. The application form must require a list of all existing accident and health insurance policies and require identification of those being replaced.

b. The application taken by an agent shall include, or have attached thereto, a statement signed by the agent as follows:

I have reviewed the current accident and health insurance coverage of the applicant and find that the indicated replacement, or the additional coverage of the type and amount applied for, is appropriate for the applicant's needs.

c. Upon determining that a sale will involve replacement, an insurer or its agent shall furnish the applicant, prior to issuance or delivery of a policy, a notice regarding replacement.

1.) One copy of such notice shall be provided to the applicant and an additional copy signed by the applicant shall be retained by the insurer.

2.) A direct response insurer shall deliver to the applicant at the time of the issuance of the policy the notice regarding replacement of accident and health insurance coverage.

5. Permitted compensation arrangements [Reg. 52.25(e)] An insurer may pay commissions to an agent for selling long-term care insurance at a higher level during the first year the policy or certificate is in effect than during the second year.

a. However, all proposed first-year commissions as well as renewal commissions are subject to review and approval to ensure that they are reasonable, not excessive, and consistent with expected loss ratio requirements.

b. When a commission is paid in subsequent (renewal) years, it must be the same as that provided in the second year and must be provided for a reasonable number of renewal years.

6. New York State partnership for long-term care Participation shall be open to residents of New York State and insurers licensed to do business in the state.

a. Qualified policies and certificates sold shall provide that benefits are payable regardless of the insured's residence at the time of eligibility for policy and certificate benefits subject to policy and certificate provisions relating to limitations on coverage outside of the United States.

1.) However, the special eligibility for long-term care protection through the New York State Medicaid program shall be void unless the insured is eligible to receive approved services under the New York State Medicaid program when such special eligibility occurs.

2.) This fact shall be prominently disclosed on the face page of the policy and certificate.

b. Minimum benefit standards for qualified policies and certificates All participating insurers must offer a basic policy and certificate providing minimum coverage under this part. Additional products that exceed the basic policy/certificate minimum coverage will be permitted.

1.) Minimum benefit standards To be approved as a qualified policy and certificate, the policy shall provide coverage on an expense-incurred, indemnity, prepaid, or other basis and provide at least the following benefits.

a.) Nursing home care Nursing home care coverage shall be provided for not less than a lifetime maximum total of 36 months for each covered person.

b.) Home care Home care coverage shall be provided when services are rendered in the insured's place of residence, in a group setting such as an adult day care center, or where human assistance is required by the insured to aid in necessary travel, such as to a physician's office.

c.) Respite care Respite care, meaning nursing home and/or home care services provided in lieu of informal caregiver services, for at least 14 days coverage, shall be renewable annually.

d.) Alternate care Where an otherwise covered person is unable to obtain access to nursing home care or home care services, and the covered person is in a hospital setting awaiting the availability of such services, and has been determined by the attending physician to be in alternate care status, such covered person shall, for the purpose of benefit eligibility including the satisfaction of any elimination period, be deemed to be receiving the nursing home care or home care services for which such covered person is awaiting placement.

e.) Inflation protection Qualified policies and certificates shall provide lifetime inflation protection no less than 5% compounded on an annual calendar or policy year basis. Inflation protection shall be mandatory except if the policy and certificate is purchased at or after age 80.

f.) Level premium Step rate premiums, policy and certificate options to increase benefits, or any premium payment feature where the premium rate rises automatically after issuance shall not be permitted.

- Premiums for qualifying policies and certificates shall be level for the duration of the policy and certificate except where a rate increase is granted by the Superintendent of Insurance for all persons covered by a specific policy and certificate form.

g.) Replacement If a long-term care insurance policy and certificate qualified under the partnership replaces another qualified long-term care insurance policy, the replacing insurer shall waive any time periods applicable to preexisting conditions, waiting periods, and probationary periods in the new long-term care policy and certificate to the extent such time has elapsed under the original policy and certificate.

h.) Elimination periods Elimination periods no greater than 100 days are permitted in qualified policies and certificates. Only a single elimination period for all covered services will be permitted. The commencement of a new elimination period is permitted only when a period of care is separated from another period of care by more than six months.

2.) Medicaid Estate Recovery Act (OBRA 1993) In the Department of Health and Human Services, the Medicaid Estate Recovery Plan was established, as required by the Omnibus Budget Reconciliation Act of 1993, to recover from the estates of recipients of medical assistance an equitable amount of the state and federal shares of the cost paid the recipient.

The amount the Department recovers from the estate of any recipient shall not exceed the amount of medical assistance made on behalf of the recipient and shall be recoverable only for medical care services prescribed.

D. SMALL EMPLOYER MEDICAL PLANS This is an extension of the information presented in Unit 5 and covers New York regulations specifically.

1. Definition of small employer [Reg. 360.2(f)] Businesses that employ between two and 50 eligible employees are considered small employers for insurance purposes. A small employer insurer is an insurance company that offers health insurance plans covering employees of small employers.

2. Benefit plans offered [Reg. 360.2(f)] A small group health insurance policy means a group remittance policy written by an insurer. It does include a policy covering only long-term care benefits, nursing home benefits, home care benefits, dental or vision care services, hospital or surgical indemnity benefits with specific dollar amounts (unless the dollar amounts exceed certain limits), accident-only indemnity benefits, accidental death and dismemberment benefits, prescription drug benefits, disability income benefits, or specified disease benefits.

3. Availability and renewability of coverage [Regs. 360.2(e), .3] Small employers may restrict or limit eligibility based on the number of hours an employee works (no more than 20) or geographical limitations.

   a. Employees and their dependents must be offered a chance to enroll in the employer's group health plan at all times throughout the year.

   b. Once accepted for coverage, an individual or group cannot be terminated due to claims experience.

E. CONTINUATION OF COVERAGE UNDER COBRA AND NEW YORK CONTINUATIONS CONVERSION PRIVILEGE [SEC. 3216(c)(5)] In family policies providing hospital or surgical expense coverage (but not accident only), insured family members who become ineligible because they are no longer within the policy's definition of family are entitled to conversion policies as long as they have not reached the policy's terminating age.

   1. The conversion privilege also must be available to a policyowner's former spouse by divorce or annulment. Conversion policies must contain certain minimum benefits and be available without evidence of insurability.

   a. Written notice of this conversion privilege must be given to the policyowner by the insurer at least 15 days and not more than 60 days before termination of a covered dependent's coverage because of a limiting age.

   b. Application for the conversion policy must be made within 31 days after coverage terminates under the original policy.

   c. The insurer is not required to issue a conversion policy if it appears that the applicant has other hospital and medical expense coverage in force or is eligible for other group benefits that, together with the converted policy, would result in over-insurance.

   d. The individual conversion policy must meet several requirements.

   e. The premium must be determined by the insured's class of risk and age as well as the type and amount of insurance.

   f. The policy must provide the same or substantially the same benefits as those provided in the family policy or those provided in a designated individual conversion policy approved by the Superintendent.

   g. The benefits must become effective on the date coverage under the family policy terminates.

   h. The individual policy may exclude conditions excluded by the family policy.

   2. The individual policy may not exclude any preexisting conditions other than those excluded in the original policy. However, its benefits may be reduced by the amount of benefits paid for preexisting conditions payable under the family policy after it terminates. In addition, benefits payable during the first year of the conversion policy may be reduced so as not to exceed those payable if the family policy had remained in force.

F. NEW YORK STATE DISABILITY BENEFITS LAW New York is one of just a few states that mandates benefits for employees who suffer nonoccupational disabilities.

   1. The New York State Disability Benefits Law (DBL) was established pursuant to Article 9 of the Workers Compensation Act.

   a. It mandates disability benefits for eligible employees who lose their wages because of a disability caused by a nonoccupational injury or illness. (Workers compensation covers accidents and sickness arising during the course of employment.)

   b. The DBL is administered by the chairman of the Workers Compensation Board of the State of New York.

   c. In general, employees compensated for services and working under an employer-employee relationship are covered by this law. Unemployed workers may also be eligible for benefits if they become disabled while unemployed.

   d. The following types of employees, however, are excluded under the plan:
   - a domestic or personal worker in a private home who is employed for less than 40 hours per week by any one employer;
   - the spouse or minor child of the employer;
   - farm laborers;
   - licensed ministers, priests, rabbis, and certain other religious personnel;
   - those in a professional or teaching capacity in a religious, charitable, or educational institution;
   - independent contractors;
   - persons in casual employment for less than 45 days in a calendar year;
   - an executive officer of a corporation who at all times during the period involved owns all of the corporate stock;
   - an executive officer of an incorporated religious, charitable, or educational institution;
   - golf caddies;
   - employees covered under the General Maritime Law or the Federal Railroad Unemployment Insurance Act;
   - employees of the state, another municipal corporation, local government agency, or other political subdivision, unless such employer unit has elected to be a covered employer;
   - elementary or secondary school students regularly attending classes (workers compensation is excluded for both part-time and employment during vacation periods); and
   - licensed real estate brokers or sales associates if most of the person's compensation is related to sales and there is a written contract between the person and the employer as specified in the law.

2. Definitions

a. An employer includes a person, partnership, corporation, or legal representative of a deceased employer, or a receiver, assignee, or trustee who has persons employed.

    1.) Excluded are the state, a municipal corporation, local government agency, or other political subdivision, unless such units elect to be classified as covered employers.

    2.) An employee is defined as an individual performing services for compensation or valuable consideration for a covered employer, provided a legal employer-employee relationship exists. Superintendents, managers, and other administrative personnel are considered employees.

b. **Disability during employment** is the inability of an employee, as a result of injury or sickness not arising out of employment, to perform his regular duties or the duties of any other employment that the employer may offer at the person's regular wages that the injury or sickness does not prevent the individual from performing.

c. **Disability during unemployment** is the inability of an employee, as a result of injury or sickness not arising out of employment, to perform the duties of any employment for which he is reasonably qualified by training and experience. Disability caused by or in connection with pregnancy is included.

3. Employee eligible for benefits
To be eligible for benefits, an employee must have been in the employ of a covered employer at least four consecutive weeks before the disability.

a. Benefits are not payable for any disability that begins during this four-week period.

b. An employee who has satisfied the four-week period continues to be eligible for benefits for a period of four weeks after employment terminates.

4. Benefit payments
Disabled workers whose employment was terminated and who meet the eligibility requirements will receive up to one-half of their average weekly wage during the period of disability.

a. The first payment is due on the 14th day of disability and must be paid directly to the disabled employee within four days.

    1.) Benefits are payable on a biweekly basis thereafter, but the chairman may authorize a different benefit payment schedule in order to conform with the employee's regular pay schedule.

    2.) Benefit payments may not extend beyond 26 weeks in any 52-week period.

b. If a worker is disabled during employment, benefits begin on the eighth consecutive day of disability.

1.) Benefit payments may not extend beyond 26 weeks in any 52-week period.

2.) The worker receives a weekly benefit equal to one-half of his weekly wage, but no more than $170. If the weekly wage is less than $20, the benefit will equal the weekly wage.

c. Written notice (and proof of disability) must be furnished by disabled employees to their employers within 30 days after the start of a disability.

1.) As long as the disability continues, subsequent proof may be required, but no more frequently than once a week.

2.) If requested by the employer or the insurer providing the disability coverage, disabled employees can be required to undergo a medical examination by a practitioner selected by the employer or insurer.

3.) Refusal by an employee to submit to an examination may be grounds to refuse benefits. In cases where benefits are refused, the employer or insurer must send, within 45 days and by first-class mail, notice of the rejection to the disabled employee.

d. Employees entitled to unemployment insurance benefits A person whose employment with a covered employer is terminated and who loses unemployment benefits because he becomes disabled is entitled to receive disability benefits. The individual will receive disability benefits every week for which he would have received unemployment insurance benefits if not disabled.

5. Appeal of benefit rejection An employee who is denied benefits may file an appeal with the chairman.

a. The appeal must be filed within 26 weeks of the notice of the rejection, but the chairman may excuse this time limit if the employee can demonstrate a reason for the delay.

b. In considering the appeal, the chairman may request copies of relevant attending physicians' statements, wage and employment data, and all other papers in the possession of the employer or insurer with respect to the claim.

6. Exclusions and exemptions An employee is not entitled to benefits for:

- more than 26 weeks during a period of 52 consecutive weeks or any one period of disability;
- any period of disability during which the employee is not under the care of an authorized physician, podiatrist, chiropractor, or dentist, as specified by law;
- any period of disability caused by pregnancy except any such period occurring after a return to work for two consecutive weeks after termination of such pregnancy;
- any disability caused by a willful or illegal act on the employee's part;
- any day of disability during which the employee performed work for remuneration or profit;

- any day of disability for which the employee received from the employer, or a fund to which the employer has contributed, remuneration in an amount equal to or greater than the benefits payable under the statutory plan;

- any period during which the employee's unemployment insurance benefit rights have been suspended, except for reasons of disability under this plan;

- disability resulting from an act of war, declared or undeclared, occurring after June 30, 1950; and

- payment of benefits prohibited by the nonduplication of benefits provision.

7. **Contribution to premium cost** Employee contributions are calculated at .5% of wages paid, not to exceed $.60 per week. Employers must contribute the remainder of the premium.

8. **Methods of providing coverage** Under the disability benefits law, an employer is held responsible for providing disability benefits by:

- insuring the payment of benefits through the special state fund;

- insuring the payment of benefits with an insurer authorized to transact accident and health insurance business in New York; or

- self-insuring the benefits under a plan approved by the chairman of the Workers Compensation Board.

9. **Inalienable rights** No employee may be required or permitted to waive his rights to benefits under this plan, except for employees who are receiving Social Security retirement benefits. Social Security retirement benefit recipients may waive coverage under this plan and will be excused from the employee contribution requirement.

10. **Penalty** An employer failing to provide for disability benefits as required by law within 10 days after the employee becomes a covered employee is guilty of a misdemeanor.

G. **MEDICARE SUPPLEMENTS** This is an extension of the information presented and covers New York laws and regulations that govern this type of coverage.

1. **Open enrollment [Reg. 52.22]** An issuer may not deny or condition the issuance or effectiveness of a Medicare supplement policy, nor discriminate in pricing policies, because of the applicant's health status, claims experience, receipt of health care, or medical condition.

   a. Applicants must be accepted at all times throughout the year for Medicare supplement insurance benefit plans available from an issuer.

   b. Preexisting conditions may not be excluded for more than six months after the effective date of coverage.

2. **New York regulations and required provisions [Reg. 52.22(i)]** Insurers, either directly or through their producers, must:

- establish marketing procedures to assure excessive insurance is not sold or issued;

- establish marketing procedures to assure that policy comparisons made by their agents or other representatives will be fair and accurate;

■ display promininently on the first page of the policy a notice to the buyer, stating that the policy may not cover all of the buyer's medical expenses;

■ make every reasonable effort to identify whether the prospective applicant for Medicare supplement insurance already has accident and health insurance and, if so, identify the types and amount of the insurance;

■ establish auditable procedures for verifying compliance with these marketing standards.

3. **Permitted compensation arrangements [Reg. 52.22(h)]** An insurer may pay its agent for the sale of a Medicare supplement policy only if the first-year payment is no more than 200% of what was paid for selling or servicing the policy in the second year.

   a. The payment provided in later years must be the same as that provided in the second year and must be provided for no fewer than five renewal years.

   b. If an existing policy is replaced, no issuer may pay its agents and no agent may receive more payment than the renewal amount payable by the replacing insurer.

4. **Appropriateness of recommended purchase or replacement [Reg. 52.22(f)(4)]** When recommending the purchase or replacement of a Medicare supplement policy, an agent must make a reasonable effort to determine the appropriateness of the recommended purchase or replacement.

   a. Any sale of Medicare supplement coverage that will provide an individual with more than one Medicare supplement policy or certificate is prohibited.

5. **Replacement [Reg. 52.22(f),(g)]** Application forms must include a question to elicit information as to whether the proposed insurance is intended to replace another Medicare supplement or accident and health policy presently in force.

   a. If replacement is involved, an insurer other than a direct response insurer or its agent must give the applicant, before issuing or delivering the policy, a notice regarding replacement of coverage.

   b. One copy of the notice is to be retained by the applicant. An additional copy signed by the applicant is to be retained by the insurer.

6. **Disclosure statement [Reg. 52.63]** The disclosure statement used by insurers issuing policies and certificates of Medicare supplement insurance shall consist of four parts: a cover page, premium information, disclosure pages, and charts displaying the features of each benefit plan offered by the issuer.

   a. The disclosure statement shall be in the language and format prescribed below in no less than 12-point type.

   b. All benefit plans A through J (presented in Unit 7) shall be shown on the cover page, and the plan(s) offered by the issuer shall be prominently identified.

    c. Premium information for plans offered shall be shown on the cover page or immediately following the cover page and shall be prominently displayed.

        1.) The premium and mode shall be stated for all plans offered to the prospective applicant.

        2.) All possible premiums for the prospective applicant shall be illustrated.

7. Renewability [Reg. 52.22(b)(1)(i)] Every Medicare supplement policy must be guaranteed renewable, meaning that the insured has the right to continue the policy by paying the premiums on time. The insurer cannot change any provisions of the policy except to:

- change benefits designed to cover cost-sharing amounts under Medicare to coincide with changes in the Medicare deductible amount and copayment percentage factors;
- change the policy to meet minimum standards for this insurance; or
- change premium rates on a class basis.

8. Medicare Select [Reg. 52.14] Medicare Select is a special program that includes restricted network provisions. Insurers wishing to offer a Select plan must agree to meet minimum standards and must be approved by the Superintendent before actually offering such plans.

    a. Such policies will pay benefits for medical care only when the insured obtains the care or services from health care providers belonging to the network.

    b. The network of providers encompasses a geographic service area within which the Superintendent has authorized an insurer to offer Medicare Select policies or certificates.

    c. To qualify as a Medicare Select plan, the insurer must arrange for a sufficient number and variety of medical care providers in its network area.

        1.) The plan must cover emergency care 24 hours a day, seven days a week.

        2.) A map of the service area, list of network providers, description of the grievance procedure to be used, and description of the quality assurance program must be given to the Superintendent.

N E W   Y O R K   I N S U R A N C E   L A W   P R A C T I C E   F I N A L

Student Instructions: Following your thorough study of New York Life, Accident, and Health Insurance Law in Unit 13, self-administer this 50-question sample examination. Grade your performance using the answer key provided. Carefully review the topical information pertaining to those questions answered incorrectly.

I. General insurance

1. An applicant may qualify for a license as a nonresident only if he

   A. is 15 years old
   B. is willing to take the licensing examination
   C. holds a similar license in another state or foreign country
   D. has complied with all the national requirements for licensure

2. If convicted of violating the Fraud and False Statement Act, an agent may be imprisoned for a maximum term of

   A. 6 months
   B. 10 years
   C. 15 years
   D. 20 years

3. Which of the following may an insurer or agent offer in connection with the sale of life or accident and health insurance?

   A. A premium rate discount
   B. A 2-week, all-expense-paid trip to Hawaii
   C. Free medical diagnoses
   D. A separate agreement to provide mortgage funds to the policyowner

4. Which of the following actions by life and health insurance agents is prohibited by New York insurance law?

   A. Comparing similar policies
   B. Agreeing to provisions not included in the policy, but which the insured specifically requests
   C. Citing dividends currently being paid by an insurer on a specific type of policy
   D. Circulating brochures listing advantages of a certain kind of policy

5. Which of the following statements pertaining to the fiduciary responsibility of insurance agents is CORRECT?

   A. Withdrawals from premium accounts are not specifically limited by regulation.
   B. Premium money not remitted immediately to insurers is to be deposited in an appropriately identified account in a New York bank.
   C. Insurers, not agents, are responsible for premiums collected.
   D. Premiums collected and deposited in a bank by an agent are known as voluntary deposits.

6. What is the purpose of the Fair Credit Reporting Act?

   A. It prohibits insurance companies from obtaining reports on applicants from investigative agencies.
   B. It protects credit companies during the course of their investigations.
   C. It gives consumers the right to question reports made about them by investigative agencies.
   D. It guarantees that credit reports will remain confidential and not accessible to businesses that do no sell insurance.

7. Which of the following statements pertaining to the licensing of insurance consultants is CORRECT?

   A. A person posing as a consultant without being properly licensed as such is guilty of a felony.
   B. To be licensed as a consultant, a person must pass a written examination as prescribed by the superintendent and pay a fee.
   C. The licenses of insurance consultants expire annually on December 31.
   D. An executive of an authorized insurance company automatically qualifies as an insurance consultant.

8. The Superintendent must examine the affairs of every authorized domestic insurance company at least once every

   A. year
   B. 2 years
   C. 3 years
   D. 5 years

9. Keeping premium money separate from personal accounts is part of the

   A. fiduciary responsibility of the agents
   B. reinsurance regulations
   C. duties of the Superintendent
   D. replacement requirements

10. The Superintendent of Insurance is

    A. elected by the public
    B. appointed by the Governor
    C. appointed by insurers
    D. elected by the legislature

11. Before an agent or producer may sell insurance for an insurer, he must first

    A. be appointed by the insurer
    B. pay a fee to the insurer to represent it
    C. find a suitable applicant for the insurer's policy
    D. have been licensed as an agent for over 1 year

12. An insurance consultant's compensation must be based on

    A. the amount of insurance being purchased
    B. how long the agreed-upon service is to be continued
    C. the amount of commissions generated by the client's purchases of insurance in the preceding year
    D. a written memorandum signed by the party to be charged

13. The Superintendent may, after proper notice and a hearing, order a penalty of up to which of the following for a willful violation of New York insurance law?

    A. $5,000 per willful violation
    B. 6 months in jail for a misdemeanor violation
    C. $1,000 or 6 months in jail
    D. $500 per willful violation

14. All of the following are violations of New York insurance law EXCEPT

    A. setting different premium rates for individuals in the same class
    B. offering a rebate to a person in return for purchasing a policy
    C. assuring a new policyowner that his new policy, if lapsed inadvertently for nonpayment of premium, could be reinstated under the terms of the contract
    D. having an interdependent arrangement to sell stock to a person contingent on the purchase of a life or health insurance policy

II. Life insurance

15. Which of the following is an eligible class for employer-employee franchise insurance?

    A. All employees with at least 1 year's service
    B. A group of no fewer than 2 nor more than 25 employees, except that in contributory cases, 75% of the number eligible may not exceed 25
    C. All employees grouped according to salary-range categories
    D. A group of no fewer than 5 nor more than 25 employees when policies are issued individually

16. Which of the following indexes is useful for comparing the costs of a policy's death benefits?

    A. Surrender cost index
    B. Net payment cost index
    C. Equivalent level annual dividend index
    D. Traditional cost index

17. If a life insurance policy is lapsed or surrendered so the insured can take out a new policy, the transaction is said to involve a
A. realignment
B. trade-off
C. conversion
D. replacement

18. In general, annuity benefits that are paid periodically are deemed safe from
A. income tax
B. inflation
C. creditors
D. debtors

19. Which of the following people may share in the commission from the sale of a life insurance policy?
A. Licensed agent with a different insurance company who referred the insurance prospect
B. Licensed attorney employed by a different insurance company
C. Licensed life insurance agent of the same insurer
D. Unlicensed trainee who is making a joint call with a licensed supervisor who closes the sale

20. A life insurance policy may be backdated not more than how long before the date of the application?
A. 3 months
B. 6 months
C. 9 months
D. 1 year

21. When replacing a life insurance policy, a policyowner must be allowed a free-look period of how many days?
A. 10
B. 15
C. 30
D. 60

22. With limited exceptions (such as accidental death benefits), a savings and insurance bank may not obligate itself to pay an insurance death benefit per insured in excess of
A. $5,000
B. $20,000
C. $25,000
D. $50,000

23. A variable annuity is based on
A. the bond market
B. the Dow Jones Industrial Average
C. equity-type investments
D. nonlevel premiums

24. In New York, once premiums have been paid on a life insurance policy for 3 years, policyowners may borrow on the cash value at a specified rate of interest. If interest is payable in advance, the maximum allowable life insurance policy loan interest rate in newly issued policies in New York is
A. 6%
B. 7.4%
C. 8.4%
D. 10%

25. The traditional method of illustrating life insurance costs is considered misleading because it does not take into account
A. the insured's principal objectives
B. the amount of premiums versus the death benefit
C. a time element of when premiums are paid, when dividends (if any) are received, and when cash values are assumed to be paid
D. company practice in crediting premiums and the cash value at a policy's anniversary date

26. When a replacement occurs, the insurer replacing the policy or annuity must do all of the following EXCEPT
A. furnish to the current insurer a copy of any proposal
B. obtain a list of all existing life insurance policies proposed to be replaced
C. examine all the sales material and the signed Disclosure Statement and ascertain that they are accurate
D. maintain copies for 6 years of the signed receipt by the applicant that he received the IMPORTANT Notice Regarding Replacement

27. Which of the following is NOT a required provision of an individual life insurance policy issued in New York State?
A. Entire contract
B. Certificate provision
C. Misstatement of age
D. Grace period

28. If a New York insurer does not prepare a policy summary before delivering a life insurance policy to the policyowner and the policyowner then requests one, the insurer may

A. charge a reasonable fee for the summary
B. charge the policyowner up to $50 for a policy summary
C. charge a reduced premium for a policy without a policy summary
D. refuse to issue the policy

29. Representatives of fraternal benefit societies must be licensed if, during the previous year, they sold life insurance in excess of

A. $100,000
B. $200,000
C. $500,000
D. $1 million

30. All of the following values of a life insurance policy are protected by law from an insured's creditors EXCEPT

A. death benefits
B. cash dividends paid to the insured
C. cash surrender values
D. policy loan values

31. In situations where the sale of a life insurance policy will result in the replacement of an existing policy, the replacing agent is responsible for all of the following activities EXCEPT

A. obtaining a completed and signed Definition of Replacement
B. notifying the existing policy's agent that a replacement is about to occur
C. obtaining the applicant's signature on a Notice Regarding Replacement of Life Insurance
D. submitting to the insurer, with the application, copies of any proposal, sales illustration, and related sales material

32. Participating life insurance policies must allow policyowners to apply their dividends to any of the following options EXCEPT

A. cash payment
B. reducing future premium payments
C. purchasing paid-up permanent life insurance additions
D. purchasing 1-year term insurance

33. If a policy provides an accelerated death benefit provision, all of the following requirements must be met EXCEPT

A. applications must clearly explain that receipt of an accelerated death benefit may affect eligibility for public assistance programs
B. the policy must define a terminal illness as one that is expected to result in death within 12 months
C. the policy must provide a minimum lump-sum benefit of at least the lower of 25% of the policy face amount or $50,000
D. the policy must require policyowners to repay benefits in the event the insured survives beyond the expected date of death

34. All the following statements regarding the life insurance policy summary are correct EXCEPT

A. it must be given to each new policy owner no later than on policy delivery
B. it must present the generic name of the policy as well as the company's name for it
C. it must illustrate all guaranteed cash surrender values
D. it must illustrate all guaranteed policy dividend values

III. Accident and health insurance

35. Which of the following is a mandatory minimum benefit for Medicare supplement policies?

    A. Supplemental coverage for 80% of all eligible hospital expenses not covered by Medicare
    B. Coverage of Part A Medicare eligible hospital expenses to the extent not covered by Medicare from the 61st through the 90th day in any Medicare benefit period
    C. Coverage of the 30% coinsurance amount under Part B Medicare, subject to a calendar year deductible of $100
    D. A $1,000 death benefit

36. Which of the following statements regarding the conversion provision of a family's health insurance policy that provides hospital or surgical expense coverage is CORRECT?

    A. Application for a converted policy must be made within 120 days after the original policy terminates.
    B. A converted policy must be available without the applicant's having to show evidence of insurability.
    C. A policyowner's divorced spouse is not eligible for a converted policy.
    D. The insurer must give the policyowner written notice of the conversion privilege within 5 days before termination of the dependent's coverage.

37. How many days must pass after the onset of a disability before employees covered under the New York Disability Benefits Law can expect their first benefit payment?

    A. 10
    B. 14
    C. 21
    D. 30

38. The maximum percentage of wages allowed in calculating benefits under the New York Workers Compensation Act is

    A. 50%
    B. 60%
    C. 66-2/3%
    D. 75%

39. Which of the following statements regarding maternity and pregnancy coverage in accident and health insurance policies is CORRECT?

    A. Maternity coverage must begin within 90 days from the policy's effective date.
    B. Pregnancy coverage, other than for a pregnancy complication, may be limited to reimbursement of covered expenses during 4 days of in-hospital care.
    C. Pregnancy coverage usually is listed as an exclusion.
    D. Maternity coverage applies only to pregnancy complications.

40. A blanket medical reimbursement may be used to cover

    A. accidental injury expenses up to a stated limit
    B. disabilities caused by sickness
    C. accidental injuries without limit
    D. dependents beyond the limiting age through conversion options

41. Which of the following statements pertaining to the renewability of hospital, surgical, and medical-expense policies is CORRECT?

    A. Policies must be renewed at the request of the insureds if premium payments accompany such requests.
    B. After 2 years from the date of issue or reinstatement, an insurer may not refuse to renew a policy because of a change in the physical or mental condition of the insured.
    C. After a policy has been in force for 2 years or more, the insurer has the right to cancel the policy.
    D. Insureds have 60 days after expiration of their policies in which to renew them.

42. Which of the following benefits is a minimum standard for basic hospital insurance in New York?

    A. Coverage of at least $240 per day for a period of no fewer than 60 days for any continuous hospital confinement
    B. A straight $100 deductible and coverage for no less than a 31-day hospital stay
    C. A daily room and board rate of not less than $40 per day
    D. Coverage for miscellaneous hospital services of not less than 50% of reasonable charges

43. The minimum standard for major medical insurance includes

    A. copayment by the insured not to exceed 35%
    B. total maximum coverage of not less than $100,000
    C. 70% to 30% coinsurance provision
    D. deductible provision based strictly on a per-family basis

44. Which of the following provisions could legally apply to an individual major medical policy that was converted from a group major medical plan?

    A. Maximum coverage of $25,000 for all covered expenses during a calendar year
    B. A hospital room and board charge limited to $90 per day
    C. Maximum coverage of $30,000 for each unrelated injury or sickness
    D. Surgical benefits limited to the lesser of 75% of the prevailing reasonable and customary charges or the benefit payable according to a $4,500 maximum surgical benefit schedule

45. Under the New York Disability Benefits Law, which of the following statements pertaining to disability benefits payable to an insured is CORRECT?

    A. No employee can be required or permitted to waive rights to benefits under the New York Disability Benefits plan.
    B. Such benefits may be denied at the discretion of the employer.
    C. Employees may opt out of the New York Disability Benefits plan if they prefer not to contribute to premium cost.
    D. An employer can request exemption from the New York Disability Benefits plan.

46. An employer may use all of the following methods to provide benefits under New York's Disability Benefits Law EXCEPT

    A. insuring benefits through the special state fund
    B. helping employees to obtain individual coverage with insurers of their choice
    C. insuring benefits with an insurer authorized to transact accident and health insurance business in New York
    D. self-insuring the benefits under a plan approved by the chairman of the Workers Compensation Board

47. All of the following statements regarding Medicare supplement insurance policies are correct EXCEPT

    A. they may duplicate benefits provided by Medicare
    B. they must conform to one of 10 standardized plans, labeled A through J
    C. they must provide a minimum of 30 days from the date of delivery during which the policyowner may return the policy for a full premium refund
    D. they must provide coverage for at least 90 days of nursing home care but may require a copayment of up to $25 per day

48. A type of long-term care insurance benefit designed to provide nonprofessional family caregivers a short rest period by paying for short-term professional home health care is called

    A. custodial care benefit
    B. chronic care benefit
    C. adult day care
    D. respite care benefit

49. The purpose of the Long-Term Care Security Demonstration Project is to

    A. determine if a need exists for long-term care insurance
    B. provide free long-term care insurance for New York residents who fall below minimum income levels
    C. provide New York residents with affordable long-term care insurance and the possibility of qualifying for Medicaid protection under favorable terms
    D. provide New York residents with Medicaid protection for the same cost as a typical long-term care insurance policy

50. Under accident and sickness policies providing family coverage, newborns are covered beginning

    A. at the moment of birth
    B. 7 days after birth
    C. 14 days after birth
    D. 30 days after birth

ANSWERS TO NEW YORK LAW PRACTICE FINAL

1. **C**	11. **A**	21. **D**	31. **B**	41. **B**
2. **C**	12. **D**	22. **A**	32. **D**	42. **A**
3. **C**	13. **D**	23. **C**	33. **D**	43. **B**
4. **B**	14. **C**	24. **B**	34. **D**	44. **D**
5. **B**	15. **B**	25. **C**	35. **B**	45. **A**
6. **C**	16. **B**	26. **B**	36. **B**	46. **B**
7. **B**	17. **D**	27. **B**	37. **B**	47. **A**
8. **D**	18. **C**	28. **A**	38. **C**	48. **D**
9. **A**	19. **C**	29. **B**	39. **B**	49. **C**
10. **B**	20. **B**	30. **B**	40. **A**	50. **A**

Glossary

A

Accidental Bodily Injury Bodily injury resulting from an accident.

Accidental Death and Dismemberment Insurance (AD&D) A form of insurance providing benefits in the event of accidental death or the accidental loss of sight (or the loss of a member(s), such as an arm or a leg).

Accidental Death Benefit A lump-sum payment for loss of life due to an accident that was the direct cause of death. The cause of the mishap must be accidental for a benefit to be payable under the policy.

Accidental Means An unforeseen, unexpected, unintended cause of an accident that results in an injury. The cause of the action and the result must not be intentional or there will be no coverage.

Accumulation Provision A percentage increase made in the benefits available under the policy. It is intended as a bonus to the insured for continuous renewals. (It is not usually included in policies issued currently.)

Adverse Selection The tendency of a disproportionate number of poor risks to purchase life insurance or maintain existing insurance in force (e.g., the selection against the insurer).

Agent An authorized representative of an insurance company(ies) who solicits, negotiates, or countersigns life insurance and/or annuity contracts (in many companies he also sells health insurance). An agent represents the company.

Aggregate Amount The maximum dollar amount that can be collected under any policy for any disability or period of disability.

Annuity A contract providing periodic income payments for a fixed period of time or during the lifetime of an annuitant. It may be defined as the systematic liquidation of an estate.

Annuity, Cash Refund A life annuity contract that provides that upon the death of the annuitant, the beneficiary (or his estate) will receive a lump sum payment, which represents the difference between the amount the annuitant paid to the insurance company and the total income payments received by the annuitant.

Annuity, Certain Payable for a minimum specified period and continuing thereafter throughout the lifetime of the annuitant.

Annuity, Deferred Payments commence more than one year after the payment of the first (or single) premium to the insurance company, usually at a selected retirement age.

Annuity, Immediate The income commences one, three, six, or 12 months after its purchase.

Annuity, Installment Refund Similar to a cash refund annuity, except that money is refunded in installment payments and the insurance company makes payments to the designated beneficiary until the total of the payments made to the annuitant and the beneficiary equals the consideration paid.

Annuity, Joint and Last Survivor An annuity issued on the lives of two or more persons, which is payable as long as one of them survives.

Assignee A person, firm, or corporation to whom the rights under a contract are assigned in their entirety or in part.

Assignment The legal transfer of the benefits or rights of a policy by the insured to another party.

Association Group Individual policies written to cover members of a trade or professional association (e.g., American Medical Association or the Ohio Association of Hat Manufacturers).

Attained Age An age that a person or an insured has attained on a given date. For life insurance purposes, the age is based on either the nearest birthday or the last birthday, depending upon the practices of the insurance company involved.

Automatic Premium Loan (Automatic Premium Advance) A provision in a life insurance policy that states that if an insured fails to pay a premium by the end of the grace period, the amount of the premium due will be loaned to the insured automatically. However, the loan value of the policy must be sufficient to cover the loan plus interest. Generally, the insured must request that this clause be made a part of the policy at the time of application.

Average Earnings Clause (Relation of Earnings to Insurance) A provision in the policy that allows the insurance company to reduce the monthly income disability benefits payable if the insured's total income benefits exceed either his current monthly earnings or his average monthly earnings during the two-year period immediately preceding the disability.

Aviation Clause A clause that limits the liability of the insurance company if the death of an insured is caused by certain types of aviation accidents.

B

Beneficiary A person(s) designated to receive a specified payment(s) in the event of the insured's death.

Beneficiary, Contingent (Secondary) A person who is entitled to benefits only after the death of a primary beneficiary.

Beneficiary, Irrevocable The insured may not change the designated beneficiary without the beneficiary's consent.

Beneficiary, Primary A person who is entitled primarily to benefits upon the death of an insured.

Beneficiary, Revocable The designated beneficiary may be changed at the insured's request without the consent of the beneficiary.

Beneficiary, Tertiary The person entitled to policy benefits if the primary and contingent beneficiaries predecease the insured.

Binding Receipt Insurance becomes effective on the date of the receipt and continues for a specified period of time or until the company disapproves the application.

Blanket Accident Medical Expense Entitles the insured, who suffered a bodily injury, to collect up to a maximum established in the policy for all hospital and medical expense incurred, without any limitation on individual types of medical expenses.

Blanket Policy Coverage of a number of individuals who are exposed to the same hazards, such as members of an athletic team who are passengers on the same plane. The covered persons need not be identified individually.

Blue Cross An independent, nonprofit (for the most part) membership association providing protection against the costs of hospital care in a limited geographical area. Provides coverage for hospital costs.

Blue Shield An independent, nonprofit (for the most part) membership association providing protection against the costs of surgery and other items of medical care in a limited geographical area. Provides coverage for doctor's fees.

Broker An insurance solicitor, licensed by the state, who represents various insureds and who is permitted to place general insurance coverages with any insurance company authorized to transact business in the state in which he is licensed.

Business Insurance A policy whose principal purpose is to provide reimbursement to an employer for the time lost by a key employee who is disabled.

C

Cancellable Policy A policy that may be terminated either by the insured or the insurance company by notification to the other party in accordance with the terms of the policy.

Capital Sum This is the amount payable under accidental dismemberment coverage. It may be the amount payable for accidental loss of two members or both eyes (or one of each). An indemnity for the loss of one member or the sight of one eye is usually a percentage of the capital sum.

Cash Surrender Value The amount (stated in the policy) that is available in cash upon the surrender of a policy for cancellation before or after the policy matures (as a death claim or otherwise). This is one of three nonforfeiture options.

Catastrophe Insurance Health policies that provide substantial benefits for serious, prolonged, or expensive disabilities that cause enormous financial problems for the insured. This is generally referred to as Major Medical Expense Insurance.

Coinsurance (Percentage Participation) A provision that specifies that the insurance company will pay only part of a loss and requires the policyholder to pay the balance himself. For example, in the case of Major Medical Expense Insurance, the insurance company may be obliged to pay 75% of an insured's expenses in excess of the deductible amount, if any, and the insured is required to pay the other 25% himself.

Common Disaster Clause This clause defines the method of the payment of the proceeds of the policy by the insurance company if the insured and the named beneficiary die simultaneously in a common disaster. It protects the contingent beneficiary since it would consider that the primary beneficiary predeceased the insured.

Comprehensive Major Medical Insurance A policy designed to give the protection offered by both a basic and a major medical policy. It is characterized by a low deductible amount, coinsurance clause, and high maximum benefits, usually $5,000 to $10,000. This policy is generally referred to by the shortened term of "Comprehensive Insurance."

Compulsory Health Insurance A plan of insurance under the supervision of a state or the federal government that requires protection for medical, hospital, surgical, and disability benefits. Statutory Disability Benefit Laws are in effect in the states of New York, New Jersey, Rhode Island, California, Puerto Rico, and Hawaii (as of January, 1979). In the state of New York, the law requires the maintenance of an approved program of loss of time benefits (income benefits).

Concealment Failure by an applicant to disclose in his application for insurance a fact that is relevant to the acceptance or the rejection of his application.

Conditional Receipt A receipt given for the payment of the initial premium (accompanying the application) that makes coverage effective under the contract if the risk is approved as applied for, subject to the other conditions set forth in the receipt.

Consideration One of the elements of a valid contract. The premium and the statements made by the prospective insured in the application are construed as the insured's consideration. The insurance company's consideration is its promise to pay a valid claim.

Contributory Plan A term applied to employee benefit plans (such as group insurance or group annuities) under which both the employees and the employer contribute.

Conversion Privilege The right granted to the insured to change his coverage from a group policy to an individual policy. If a member of a group resigns from the group, he is given an opportunity to secure an individual policy within a specified period regardless of whether or not he is in good health at that time. This term is also applied to the right of an insured to convert from a convertible term policy to a permanent form of insurance.

Credit Life Insurance Life insurance designed to pay the balance of a loan (usually repayable in installments) if the insured dies before the loan has been repaid in full. Generally, credit life insurance is handled by a bank, department store, or a finance company. Usually, this form of insurance is written on a group basis, but it may also be written on an individual basis.

D

Deductible The amount of loss or expense that must be incurred by the insured before benefits become payable. The insurance company pays benefits only for the loss in excess of the amount specified in the deductible provision. There are various types of deductible provisions.

Disability A physical condition that makes an insured incapable of performing one or more duties of his occupation, or, in the case of total disability, prevents him from performing any other type of work for remuneration. (This wording varies from one insurance company to another.)

Disability Benefit A feature added to some life insurance policies that provides for the waiver of premiums upon the furnishing of proof that an insured has become totally and permanently disabled and/or for the payment of monthly income benefits to the insured.

Dividend A refund of part of the premium under a participating policy or a share of policyholder surplus funds apportioned for distribution. They are derived from savings in mortality and expenses and interest earned in excess of the assumed rate used in the calculation of the premium in the policy reserves.

Dividend Options The insured is given the option to apply dividends as follows: he may receive the dividend in cash, apply the dividend toward the payment of any premium due on the policy, apply the dividend to the purchase of paid up additional insurance, or leave the dividend with the insurance company to accumulate an interest.

Double Indemnity A clause providing payment of twice the face amount of the policy if loss of life is due to an accident.

Duplicate Coverage A term usually applied to benefits (other than loss of time) where an insured is covered by several policies with one or more insurance companies providing the same type of benefits, and often resulting in overinsurance.

E

Elective Indemnity Fixed lump-sum payments that an insured may elect to receive instead of accepting the weekly or monthly indemnity provided for the policy. Usually, such payments are made for sprains, dislocations, fractures, or for the loss of fingers or toes.

Elimination Period A period of time after the inception of a disability, during which benefits are not payable. An elimination period must be satisfied for each separate disability that occurs. *See also* waiting period.

Endorsement An attachment to the policy by which the scope of coverage is altered (e.g., restricted or increased). The terms of such endorsement (rider) take precedence over the printed portions of the policy which are in conflict with the endorsement.

Endowment Insurance A policy that (after a specified number of years) pays a stated amount to the insured. If the insured dies during the endowment period, the face amount of the policy is paid to the designated beneficiary. An endowment pays at the earlier of death or a specified period.

Evidence of Insurability Any statement or proof of a person's physical condition that may affect acceptance for insurance.

Exclusions Provisions in the policy that eliminate coverage for specified losses or causes of loss.

Experience Rating (Group Insurance) The premium is computed on the basis of past losses and expenses incurred by the insurance company in the settlement of claims and other expenses involving a particular group of risks.

Extended Term Insurance A nonforfeiture option, under which the face amount of the policy is continued in force for a specified additional period of time after default in the payment of a premium.

F

Face Amount The amount of insurance stated on the face of the policy that will be paid upon the death of the insured (or in some cases at the maturity of the policy). It does not include any amount that has been added through dividend additions or additional insurance payable in the event of accidental death, etc.

Facility of Payment Clause A provision in a policy that permits the insurance company to pay insurance proceeds to persons other than the insured, the designated beneficiary, or the estate of the insured.

Family Expense Policy A policy that insures both the policyholder and his immediate dependents (usually his spouse and children).

Family Income Benefits Under this form of life insurance, on the death of the insured, a monthly income is payable to the beneficiary(ies) to the end of the family income period stipulated in the policy in addition to the lump sum payment (face amount). For example, it could run for a period of 10 years starting with the inception date of the policy, or it could run for 15 years, 20 years, or to age 65. Usually, it is a decreasing term insurance provision that is combined with whole life insurance. If the insured survives the family income period, the family income protection ceases. The policy reverts to the face amount (usually, payable in a lump sum upon the death of the insured).

Family Maintenance (Family Protection) Policy This type of policy combines ordinary life insurance and level term insurance. It affords the payment of a monthly income during a stated period of 10, 15, or 20 years or to age 65 as preselected by the insured. The monthly income is payable from the date of death to the end of the preselected period. The payment of the face amount of the policy is payable at the end of such preselected period.

Franchise Insurance An individual policy written to cover a group of persons that does not qualify for true group insurance. The benefits may vary slightly within the group.

Fraternal Insurance A cooperative type of insurance provided by a social organization for its members (e.g., life insurance offered by the "Knights of Columbus").

G

Grace Period A specified period after a premium payment is due, during which the protection of the policy continues even though the payment for the renewal premium has not as yet been received.

Group Insurance Policy A policy protecting a group of persons, usually employees of a firm. Generally called a "master policy."

Guaranteed Renewable The option of renewal to a specified age, or for a lifetime, vested solely in the insured. However, the insurance company has the right to increase the premiums applicable to an entire class of policyholders.

H

Health Insurance A broad term covering the various forms of insurance relating to the health of persons. It includes such coverages as accident, sickness, disability, and hospital and medical expense. This term is used instead of Sickness and Accident Insurance.

Hospital Benefits Benefits payable for charges incurred while the insured is confined to, or treated in, a hospital, as defined in the policy.

Hospital Expense Insurance Benefits subject to a specified daily maximum for a specified period of time while the insured is confined to a hospital, plus a limited allowance up to a specified amount for miscellaneous hospital expenses such as operating rooms, anesthesia, laboratory fees, etc. Also known as hospitalization insurance.

I

Incontestable Clause A clause that makes the policy indisputable (except for nonpayment of premium and the operation of the war clause exclusion) regarding the statements made by the insured in the application after a specified period of time has elapsed (usually one, two, or three years).

Indemnity The payment of a benefit for a loss insured under a policy. The insured is indemnified for a specified loss, or part thereof.

Individual Insurance Policies that afford protection to the policyholder and/or his family (as distinct from group insurance). Sometimes it is referred to as personal insurance.

Industrial Policy A policy providing nominal indemnities for a short period of time and characterized by premiums (collected in person by an agent) that are usually payable weekly or monthly.

Inspection Report A report that contains general information regarding the health, habits, finances, and reputation of an applicant made by a firm that specializes in rendering this type of service.

Insurable Interest Substantial economic interest of the beneficiary in the insured due to blood relationship, marriage, or economic dependence.

Insurance Protection in accordance with a written contract against the financial hazards (in whole or in part) of the happening of specified fortuitous events. May also be defined as the transfer of risk from one party to another.

Insuring Clause A clause that defines and describes the scope of the coverage afforded and the limits of indemnification.

J

Joint Life Insurance Insurance on the lives of two or more persons with the face amount payable in the event of death of either (or any one) of them.

Juvenile Insurance Life insurance policies written on the lives of children within specified age limits (e.g., a jumping juvenile policy).

K

Key-Employee Insurance An individual policy designed to reimburse an employer for the loss of a key-employee's service due to his death. Usually, the employer pays the premium and is the beneficiary.

L

Lapse Termination of a policy because of the policyholder's failure to pay the premium within the time required.

Legal Reserve Life Insurance Company An insurance company that operates under insurance laws that specify the minimum amount of reserves that the insurance company must maintain on its policies.

Level Premium A premium that remains unchanged throughout the life of a policy.

Level Term Insurance A term contract whose face amount remains level throughout the life of the contract but whose premiums increase according to the age of the insured.

Life Expectancy The average number of anticipated years of life remaining for individuals who are the same age (e.g., 35) in accordance with the mortality table indicated in the policy.

Life Insurance Insurance upon the lives of human beings that creates an immediate and guaranteed estate at the death of an insured.

Limited Pay Life Insurance A plan of permanent life insurance under which the premiums are payable for a specified number of years (e.g., 10, 15, 20, or 30 years, or to age 65) after which the policy can continue to remain in effect for life without it being necessary for the insured to make any additional payments.

Limited Policies Those that restrict benefits to specified accidents or diseases, such as travel policies, dread disease policies, ticket policies, accident only policies, and so forth.

Loss-of-Income (Time) Benefits Income benefits payable to the insured because he is unable to work due to an insured disability.

Loss-of-Income Insurance Policies that provide benefits to help replace an insured's earned income lost or curtailed as a result of an illness or an accident.

Loading An amount that is added to net premiums in order to cover the insurance company's operating expenses and possible contingencies. The cost of acquiring new business, collection expenses, and general management expenses constitute loading.

Loan Value The amount specified in a policy that the insurance company will lend to an insured at the rate of interest that the insurance company may charge for such loans (as indicated in the policy).

M

Major Medical Expense Insurance Policies especially designed to help offset the heavy medical expenses resulting from catastrophic or prolonged illnesses or injuries. Generally, they provide benefits payments of 75–80% of all types of medical expense above a certain amount first paid by the insured, and up to the maximum limit of liability provided by the policy, usually $5,000 or $10,000.

Maturity The date on which a policy becomes payable due to the death of the insured or as a result of an insured's living to the end of an endowment period.

Medicaid A state medical assistance program for eligible needy or blind persons.

Medicare A program of health insurance and medical care for persons who are 65 years of age or over, operated under the provisions of the Social Security Act. It is comprised of two parts: Part A, Hospital Insurance; and Part B, Supplementary Medical Insurance (this part is optional).

Miscellaneous Expenses Hospital charges other than room and board (e.g., x-rays, drugs, laboratory fees, etc.). These are provided under hospital expense insurance.

Misrepresentation A false statement that the prospective insured makes in an application for a policy. An omission of a material fact can also be construed as a misrepresentation. A misrepresentation is material if the insurance company, having known the true facts, would have refused the policy as applied for by the prospective insured. Statements on applications are considered representations, not warranties.

Moral Hazards Habits, morals, or financial practices of an insured that increases the possibility or extent of a loss.

Morbidity Table Shows the incidence and extent of disability that may be expected from a given large group of persons. This table is used in the computation of rates. It is comparable to a Mortality Table used in connection with life insurance.

Mortality Table A statistical table that indicates the probability of death and survival at each age.

Mutual Life Insurance Company A life insurance company owned and controlled by its policyholders. Mutual Life Insurance Companies issue participating policies.

N

Noncancellable A policy that an insurance company is not permitted to terminate or amend during its term (except for nonpayment of a premium). Usually, the renewal of the policy is guaranteed at the option of the insured to a specified age at a fixed premium. Also written as "noncancellable and guaranteed renewable."

Noncontributory Plan A group employee benefit plan under which the employer pays for the full cost of the benefits for his employees.

Nonforfeiture Values (Options) Benefits required by law to be made available to the insured (or his beneficiary) in the event that he discontinues his premium payments. These provide that he does not forfeit or lose all that he has invested in the policy.

Nonmedical Life Insurance Insurance that is issued without requiring the applicant to submit to a medical examination. The insurance company relies on the applicant's answers to the questions regarding his physical condition, personal references, and inspection reports. However, the insurance company retains the right to require a medical examination, if an investigation indicates a need for one.

Nonparticipating Insurance Insurance that does not pay dividends to the policyholders.

O

Optional Renewal Policies Policies that are renewable at the option of the insurance company.

Ordinary Life Insurance Insurance policies of $1,000, or multiples thereof, that provide coverage for the entire life of the policyholder and for which the premiums are payable until death. It is also referred to as whole life insurance or straight life insurance and is different from term insurance in that it includes a cash value buildup.

Overinsurance An excessive amount of insurance carried by an insured that might tempt him to prolong his period of disability, remain in a hospital longer than necessary, etc.

P

Paid-Up Additions An additional amount of insurance purchased through dividends (single premium insurance) that increases the amount of protection afforded.

Paid-Up Insurance Life insurance on which future premium payments are not required. Frequently, the term is used to identify a 20-payment life insurance policy on which 20 annual premiums have been paid. Fractional paid-up insurance is the term applied to the policy that is issued under the nonforfeiture option (i.e., when the insured does not wish to pay further premiums on his policy and elects this option).

Partial Disability An illness or injury that prevents an insured from performing one or more of his occupational duties. Usually pays 50% of the total disability benefit.

Participating Insurance Insurance that entitles the policyholder to share in the divisible surplus of the insurance company through dividends.

Payor Clause A clause that provides for the waiver of premiums on a child's policy following the death or the total disability of the adult applicant for the child's policy.

Policy The printed document issued by the insurance company to the insured that is the insurance contract.

Policy Loan A loan made by an insurance company to an insured under his policy (not in excess of its cash value). Policy loans may be assessed a fixed interest rate or an adjustable rate.

Policy Term That period for which the premium is paid and coverage is provided.

Preexisting Condition Any injury occurring, sickness contracted, or physical condition that existed before the issuance of a health policy.

Premium The initial payment and the subsequent periodic payments required to keep a policy in force.

Presumptive Disability These are forms of disability involving loss of hearing, sight, speech, or limbs.

Principal Sum The amount payable for loss of life due to accidental death.

Probationary Period A specified number of days after the date of issuance of the policy, during which coverage is not afforded for sickness. Sickness contracted during the probationary period is not covered regardless of the duration of such disability. This is a one time event whereas an elimination period may occur upon each separate disability.

Proceeds The net amount of money that is payable by the insurance company at the death of an insured or when the policy matures.

Q

Qualified Plan A retirement or employee compensation plan established and maintained by an employer that meets specific guidelines set by the IRS and consequently receives favorable tax treatment.

Quarantine Indemnity A monthly benefit payable while the insured is involuntarily quarantined by a location health department because of exposure to a contagious disease.

R

Rating A method under which an insurance company can issue a policy for a subsequent risk by increasing the premium based on the increased risk involved.

Rebating Paying, offering, or giving anything of value (or any valuable consideration not specified in the policy) to any person as an inducement to purchase a policy of insurance. Rebating is illegal and both parties are guilty of it when it is done knowingly.

Recurrent Disability Clause A provision that specifies a period of time during which the recurrence of a condition is considered a continuation of a prior period of disability or hospital confinement.

Reduced Paid-Up Insurance A nonforfeiture value (option) in a policy that provides for the continuation of the insurance but at a reduced amount. (It is sometimes called "Fractional Paid-Up Insurance.")

Reinstatement The resumption of coverage under a policy that lapsed.

Reinsurance The underwriting by one insurance company (called the reinsurer) of part or all of an individual risk written by another insurance company.

Renewable Term Insurance Insurance that may be renewed at the end of the term for another term(s) without evidence of insurability. The rates increase at the end of each term and are based on the attained age of the insured at that time.

Reserve A sum (required by law) set aside by an insurance company to assure the payment of future claims.

Rider A legal document amending a policy. Additional benefits or a reduction in benefits are often incorporated in policies by an endorsement (rider). A waiver for a health impairment may also be effected by a rider.

Risk (Impaired or Substandard) An applicant whose physical condition does not meet the normal minimum standards.

S

Schedule A list of specific maximum amounts payable, usually for surgical operations, dismemberments, and so forth.

Schedule Type Policy Includes a listing and a complete text of the provisions of each of several benefits, most of which are optional, and some of which may be omitted at the election of the applicant.

Service Benefits Those benefits that are received in the form of specified hospital or medical care rather than in terms of cash amounts.

Settlement Options Methods (other than immediate payment in lump sum) by which an insured (or beneficiary) may choose to have the proceeds of an insurance policy paid.

Special Class Risk An applicant who cannot qualify for a standard policy, but may secure one with an endorsement (rider) waiving the payment for a loss involving certain existing health impairments. He may be required to pay a higher premium or to accept a policy of a type other than the one for which he had applied.

Stock Life Insurance Company A life insurance company owned and controlled by its stockholders who share in its divisible surplus. Generally, stock insurance companies issue nonparticipating life insurance. however, some of them also issue participating life insurance.

Substandard Risk A risk that is less than the standard risk an insurer looks for.

Suicide Clause A provision specifying that in the event the insured commits suicide within two years from the date the policy was issued, the insurance company's liability is limited to the payment of a single sum equal to the premium(s) actually paid (less any indebtedness due the insurance company).

Supplementary Contract An agreement between an insurance company and an insured under which the insurance company retains the lump sum payable (under a life insurance policy) and makes payments to the insured or the beneficiary in accordance with the settlement option selected by the insured.

Surgical Expense Insurance A policy that provides benefits to pay for the cost of operations.

Surgical Schedule A list of cash allowances that are payable for various types of surgery, with the respective maximum amounts payable based upon the severity of the operations.

Surplus The amount by which the assets exceed the liabilities.

Systematic Premium Plan (Check-O-Matic Plan) A plan under which the insured authorizes a bank to deduct the necessary funds from his account each month to pay a premium that is forwarded to his insurance company by the bank.

T

Term Insurance Insurance that is generally designed to afford coverage for a limited number of years. Usually, no provision is made for cash values. It can be described as "pure protection."

Total Disability An illness or injury that prevents an insured from continuously performing every duty pertaining to his occupation or from engaging in any other type of work for remuneration. (This wording varies from one insurance company to another.)

Travel Accident Insurance Provides benefits for accidental injury while traveling, usually a common carrier. A type of limited policy.

Twisting Inducing an insured to cancel his present insurance and replace it with insurance in the same or another insurance company by misrepresenting the facts or by presenting an incomplete comparison.

U

Unallocated Benefit Reimbursement up to a maximum amount for the cost of extra hospital services, but not specifying the exact amount to be paid for each charge. (This is often referred to as a blanket benefit.)

Underwriting The analysis of information pertaining to an applicant that was obtained from various sources and the determination of whether the insurance should be: (a) issued as requested, (b) offered at higher premium, or (c) declined.

W

Waiting Period The duration of time between the beginning of insured's disability and the commencement of the period for which benefits are payable. *See also* elimination period.

Waiver An agreement that waives the liability of the insurance company for certain disabilities or injuries ordinarily covered in the policy.

Waiver Endorsement An agreement that waives the liability of the insurance company for a loss that would normally be covered under the policy.

Waiver of Premium A provision included in many policies that waives the payment of premiums after an insured has been totally disabled for a specific period of time (usually six months).

War Clause A clause in a policy that limits an insurance company's liability if a loss is caused by war.

Warranties and Representations Most state laws specify that all statements by the applicant in the application (or to the medical examiner) are considered (in the absence of fraud) to be representations and not warranties. A warranty must be literally true. A breach of warranty may be sufficient to void the policy whether the warranty is material or not and whether such breach of warranty had contributed to the loss. A representation need only to be substantially true. Generally, a representation is considered to be fraudulent if it relates to a situation that would be material to the risk and that the applicant made with fraudulent intent.

Whole Life Insurance *See* ordinary life insurance.

Wholesale Insurance Group insurance written for small groups of employees, usually less than 50. Each employee applies for and receives an individual policy. Usually, this type of insurance is written without a medical examination and the premiums are on a renewable term basis, but higher than on regular group insurance.

Appendix

This appendix contains a sample whole life participating life insurance policy and sample application, as well as a sample health insurance policy and application. These documents are representative of typical policies and applications issued by insurance companies in the United States and contain the standard language and provisions found in actual forms.

LONG LIFE INSURANCE
COMPANY OF AMERICA

WHOLE LIFE POLICY

• We pay the face amount on death of the insured

• Premiums payable as shown on page 3

• Nonparticipating (no annual dividends payable)

We agree to pay the face amount to the beneficiary when the insured dies. We must receive proof that the Insured died while the policy was in force.

Be sure to read this policy. It includes promises, rights, and benefits. These are subject to policy terms.

If you are not satisfied with this policy, return it within 10 days to us or to the representative or agent you bought it from. We will cancel it and return any premium paid.

This policy is a legal contract between you and us.

READ YOUR POLICY CAREFULLY!

Policy Number:	
Insured:	
Face Amount:	
Date of Issue:	
Policy Date:	
Age of Insured:	
Premium Class:	

DEFINITIONS

When we use the following words this is what we mean:

THE INSURED

The person whose life is insured under this policy as shown on page 3.

YOU, YOUR

The owner of this policy, as shown in the application, unless subsequently changed as provided for in this policy. The owner may be someone other than the insured.

WE, OUR, US

The Life Insurance Company

POLICY DATE

The effective date of coverage under this policy and the date from which policy anniversaries, policy years, policy months, and premium due dates are determined.

DATE OF ISSUE

The date the policy is issued and also the date used to determine the start of the suicide and incontestability periods.

POLICY ANNIVERSARY

The same day and month as your policy date for each succeeding year your policy remains in force.

WRITTEN REQUEST

A request in writing on a form acceptable to us signed by you. We also may require that your policy be sent in with your written request.

PROCEEDS

The amount we are obligated to pay under the terms of this policy when our policy is surrendered or matures or when the insured dies.

IN FORCE

The insured's life remains insured under the terms of this policy.

LAPSE

A premium is in default, and the insured's life is no longer insured except as may be provided for in the Policy Values section of this policy.

TERMINATE

The insured's life is no longer insured under any of the terms of this policy.

INDEBTEDNESS

Unpaid policy loans, unpaid policy loan interest, and unpaid premium.

AGE

The insured's age at the insured's nearest birthday.

BENEFICIARY

A beneficiary is any person named in our records to receive insurance proceeds after the Insured dies.

MODE

The manner of premium payment such as monthly, quarterly, semiannually, or annually.

GENERAL PROVISIONS

THE CONTRACT

This is your policy. We issued it in consideration of your application and your payment of premiums. This policy and the attached application make up the entire contract. We agree not to use any statements other than those made in the application in challenging a claim or attempting to avoid liability under this policy.

CHANGE OF PROVISIONS

No Representative or Agent or other person except our President, a Vice President, our Secretary, or an Assistant Secretary has authority to bind us, to extend the time in which you can pay your premiums or to agree to change this policy.

INCONTESTABILITY

This policy is incontestable, unless you do not pay the premium, after it has been in force during the lifetime of the Insured for two years from its Date of Issue, except for any rider which has a separate incontestability clause. This means that we cannot use any misstatement to challenge a claim or avoid liability after that time.

MISSTATEMENT OF AGE OR SEX

If the Insured's age or sex is misstated, we will adjust any proceeds payable to the amounts which the premiums paid would have purchased at the correct age and sex.

EXCLUSIONS

SUICIDE EXCLUSION

If the Insured commits suicide within two years from the Date of Issue, we will limit our payment to a refund of premiums paid, less any Indebtedness.

OWNERSHIP AND BENEFICIARY

OWNERSHIP

This policy belongs to you. The Owner is the Insured unless otherwise designated in the application or unless changed as provided under the Change of Ownership or Beneficiary provision. Unless you provide otherwise, you may exercise all rights and privileges granted by this policy during the Insured's lifetime.

BENEFICIARY

Unless you change the Beneficiary as provided under the Change of Ownership or Beneficiary provision, the Beneficiary will remain as designated on the application.

Any reference to a Beneficiary living or surviving means that the person must be living on the earlier of:

1. the day that we receive due proof of the Insured's death; or
2. the 15th day after the Insured's death.

The legal rights of a Beneficiary are subject to the legal rights of any person to whom the policy has been assigned.

ASSIGNMENT

You may assign this policy. We assume no responsibility for the validity of any assignment, and we will not be considered to have knowledge of it unless it is filed in writing at our Home Office. When it is filed, your rights and those of any Beneficiary will be subject to it.

CHANGE OF OWNERSHIP OR BENEFICIARY

You may change the Owner or Beneficiary of this policy during the lifetime of the Insured. Changes must be requested in writing on a form satisfactory to us and sent to our Home Office. Upon receipt, it is effective as of the date you signed the written request, subject to any payments made or other action taken by us before we received your written request. No change is valid until it is received by us in our Home Office.

You may also name an Owner's Designee in the same manner. The Owner's Designee is the person who will become the Owner if he or she is living and you are still the Owner at the time of your death. This designation may be changed or terminated in writing only.

Transfer to the new Owner is subject to any payment made or action taken by us before we are notified of the prior Owner's death. Notification must be received at our Home Office to be effective.

PREMIUMS

PREMIUMS

The Effective Date is the date from which premium due dates, policy years and policy anniversaries are determined. The first premium is due on the Effective Date. To keep this policy in force during the Insured's lifetime, you must pay each premium for as long as is shown on page 3. You may pay premiums under any mode of payment, subject to our approval. All premiums after the first must be paid by the due date to us at our Home Office.

GRACE PERIOD

All premiums should be paid by the due date. (You do have 31 days after the due date to pay each premium.) If you do not pay the premium within the Grace Period, your policy will lapse unless the premium is paid under the Automatic Premium Loan provision. Policy benefits may be continued under one of the options available if you stop paying premiums. If the insured dies during the grace period, we will deduct any premium due from the proceeds.

REINSTATEMENT

If our policy lapses because you did not pay a premium, we will reinstate it if you ask us to on four conditions:

1. your written request is received at our Home Office within five years of the due date of the first premium which you did not pay;
2. you show us that the Insured is still insurable according to our normal rules;
3. you pay all overdue premiums plus 6% compound interest on premiums; and
4. you repay, or agree to continue in effect, any loan made to you under this policy before it lapsed and also pay any interest on that loan.

CASH VALUE

You may surrender, or turn in this policy at any time, in return for its Cash Value less any Indebtedness. You may request instead, within 60 days after the date your premium was due, to have any one of the Paid-Up Insurance Options take effect instead of paying the premium due.

If you do not choose an option within 60 days after the date your premium was due, or if you die after the 31-day grace period without having chosen an option, the Extended Term Insurance option will automatically take effect if this policy is in the standard premium class. Otherwise, the Reduced Paid-Up Insurance option will automatically take effect.

If your insurance is continued under one of the Paid-Up Insurance Options, it will not include any benefits other than the Face Amount of this policy. No additional benefits in any riders attached to the policy are included in the Paid-Up Insurance Options.

CASH VALUE

The Cash values on policy anniversaries are shown in the Table of Values, assuming all premiums have been paid. The Cash Value at any other time will be determined by us with an allowance for the portion of the premiums paid and the time elapsed in the policy year. The basis for determining Cash Value is explained under Basis of Computation. We may delay the payment of the Cash Value for a period of no more than six months after you request payment.

If you do not pay a premium within 60 days of the date it is due, the Cash Value of the policy remains the same as it was on that date. After 60 days, the Cash Value will be used to purchase the appropriate paid-up benefits.

If the policy is being continued under one of the Paid-Up Options, you may surrender it for its Cash Value. That Cash Value may not be less than the Cash Value on the previous policy anniversary if the policy is surrendered within 31 days of that anniversary.

PAID-UP INSURANCE OPTIONS

EXTENDED TERM INSURANCE

This option is available only if this policy is in the standard premium class. This is shown on page 3. The amount of insurance continued in force will be in the Face Amount less any Indebtedness. The period of Extended Term Insurance will begin on the due date of the first premium which you did not pay. This period is calculated using the Cash Value less any Indebtedness as a net single premium for the Insured's sex and age. This period is shown in the Table of Values based on the assumption that there is no Indebtedness.

REDUCED PAID-UP INSURANCE

Instead of having Extended Term Insurance, you may continue this policy as Reduced Paid-Up Insurance. It is payable at the death of the Insured and is effective from the date to which you have paid premiums. The amount of the Reduced Paid-Up Insurance is shown in the Table of Values based on the assumption that there is no Indebtedness. It is calculated by using the Cash Value less any Indebtedness as a net single premium based on the Insured's sex and age. This option has Cash Value which may be used in the same manner as Cash Value while premiums are being paid.

POLICY LOANS

CASH LOANS

You may take a loan against this policy. You may borrow up to the amount of Cash Value available. The Cash Value available on a premium due date, or during a grace period, or on a policy anniversary date if the policy is on a Paid-Up Insurance Option, is the Cash Value of the policy less any Indebtedness. The Cash Value available at any other time is the amount that, together with loan interest, will equal the Cash Value available on the next premium due date or the next policy anniversary date if the policy is on a Paid-Up Insurance Option.

The annual rate of interest on your loan will be 8%, payable on each policy anniversary. If you do not pay the interest when due, the amount will be added to the loan.

You may repay all or any part of the loan at any time during the lifetime of the Insured. We will not terminate the policy if you do not repay the loan or loan interest unless the loan and the interest together are more than the Cash Value of the policy. In that case, we will terminate the policy 31 days after we mail a termination notice to the last known addresses of both you and any assignee of record.

We may delay making a loan for a period of no more than six months after you request the loan. However, we will not delay the making of loans to pay premiums for this policy.

INDEBTEDNESS

Indebtedness means that you owe money including any interest because of a loan on this policy. Any indebtedness at time of settlement will reduce the proceeds. Indebtedness may be repaid in whole or in part at any time before the policy matures. However, if you do not pay a premium within the grace period, any outstanding Indebtedness can be repaid only if the policy is reinstated. If at any time Indebtedness equals or exceeds the policy's value, the policy will terminate, and we will give any assignee 31 days notice. Notice will be mailed to your and any assignee's last known address.

AUTOMATIC PREMIUM LOAN

You may request on the application or by writing to us at our Home Office that the Automatic Premium Loan provision be used to pay premiums. If this provision is used and your policy has enough Cash Value available, any premium you have not paid by the end of the 31-day grace period will be paid by an Automatic Premium Loan.

When two consecutive premiums have been paid by Automatic premium Loans, the applicable Paid-Up Insurance Option will automatically take effect at the next premium due date.

BASIC OF COMPUTATION

The Commissioners 1958 Standard Ordinary Table of Mortality and compound interest at the rate of 4½% per annum for the first 20 policy years and 3½% per annum thereafter are used to calculate the reserves, cash values, net premiums, and reserve values for this policy; except that any such calculations for extended insurance are made using the Commissioners 1958 Extended Term Insurance table and compound interest at the rate of 4½% per annum for the first 20 policy years and 3½% per annum thereafter. In all such calculations death benefits are assumed payable at the end of the policy year of death. Cash values of the policy are shown in the Table of Values and are equal at each duration to the excess of the then present value per the face amount of future guaranteed benefits over the then present value of the non-forfeiture factors for the remainder of the premium paying period. Values for years not shown in the Table are available on request and will be calculated on the same basis as those shown. During any policy year the amount of cash value and paid-up insurance and the period of extended insurance will be calculated with the due allowance for the lapse of time and the payment of any fractional premiums. The cash value at any time of any paid-up or extended insurance will be the reserve at that time on such insurance, except that within 31 days after a policy anniversary it shall not be less than the cash value on that anniversary. All values are greater than or equal to those required by statute.

Any supplementary benefits which may be included in this policy shall in no way change the values of this policy, unless otherwise specified in those benefits.

CHANGE OF PLAN

You may exchange this policy for another policy on the same plan for a lesser amount. You may also exchange it for another on a different plan if we approve it and you meet all requirements and make all necessary payments.

SETTLEMENT OPTIONS

The policy proceeds payable at the death of the Insured will be paid in one sum or will be applied in whole or in part to any Settlement Option elected. You may select a Settlement Option while the Insured is alive. You may also select the use of more than one Settlement Option. Each election of a Settlement Option you make must include at least $2,500 of policy proceeds. The Settlement Options are described below.

If you have not made an election that is still in force when the proceeds become payable, the payee may elect any available option. Any election must be in writing in a form acceptable to us. Before the date the proceeds become payable, you may elect any valuable option or change a previous election by sending your written request to our Home Office on a form satisfactory to us. Your election or change will take effect as of the date you signed the written request, subject to any payments made or other action taken by us before receipt of the written request.

If no election has been made by the date of the death of the Insured, an election may be made by the Beneficiary within one year of the death of the Insured.

Payments under the following options may be made monthly, quarterly, semiannually, or annually, subject to our minimum payment requirement.

OPTION A—INTEREST PAYMENT

We will hold the proceeds as principal and pay interest at the current rate determined annually by us, but not less than 2½% compounded annually.

The proceeds may be withdrawn at any time by the payee in whole or in part (not less than $250 each time) upon written request.

OPTION B—INCOME OF SPECIFIED

We will pay an income of a specified amount until the principal and interest at not less than 2½% compounded annually are exhausted.

OPTION—C INCOME FOR SPECIFIED PERIOD

We will pay an income for a specified number of years in equal installments, as shown in the following table.

OPTION—D LIFE INCOME

We will pay equal monthly payments for a specified period certain and thereafter for life as shown in the following table.

OPTION—E JOINT AND SURVIVOR INCOME

We will pay an income, based on the age and sex of two payees, as long as either or both of the payees are alive. The following table shows sample minimum monthly installment payments under this option. Payments for different combinations of ages and sexes may be obtained upon request from our Home Office.

We will require proof of age and survival of the payee or payees under Options D and E.

OTHER SETTLEMENT OPTIONS

Provisions may also be made for payment of proceeds of this policy in any reasonable arrangement mutually agreed upon.

EXCESS IN INTEREST

We may pay interest in excess of the guaranteed rate on proceeds held under any option. Excess interest will be paid or credited in amounts and manner as we determine.

Settlement option benefits may not be assigned or subject to encumbrance and, as far as allowed by law, are not subject to claims of creditors or legal process.

We may defer the payment of any amount being withdrawn through the exercise of a withdrawal right for up to six months after it is requested.

AMOUNT OF EACH MONTHLY PAYMENT PER $41,000 OF PROCEEDS—OPTIONS C and D

OPTION C		OPTION D													
		Age of Payee		Period of Certain			Age of Payee		Period of Certain			Age of Payee		Period of Certain		
Period (Years)	Monthly Payments	Male	Female	10 Yrs	15 Yrs	20 Yrs	Male	Female	10 Yrs	15 Yrs	20 Yrs	Male	Female	10 Yrs	15 Yrs	20 Yrs
1	$84.28	11*	16*	$2.71	$2.70	$2.70	36	41	$3.48	$3.45	$3.41	61	66	$5.61	$5.21	$4.75
2	42.66	12	17	2.72	2.72	2.71	37	42	3.53	3.50	3.45	62	67	5.74	5.30	4.80
3	28.79	13	18	2.74	2.74	2.73	38	43	3.59	3.55	3.50	63	68	5.87	5.39	4.85
4	21.86	14	19	2.76	2.76	2.75	39	44	3.64	3.60	3.54	64	69	6.01	5.48	4.90
5	17.70	15	20	2.78	2.78	2.77	40	45	3.70	3.65	3.59	65	70	6.16	5.56	4.94
6	14.93	16	21	2.81	2.80	2.79	41	46	3.76	3.71	3.64	66	71	6.30	5.65	4.98
7	12.95	17	22	2.83	2.82	2.81	42	47	3.82	3.77	3.69	67	72	6.45	5.73	5.02
8	11.47	18	23	2.85	2.84	2.84	43	48	3.88	3.82	3.74	68	73	6.60	5.82	5.05
9	10.32	19	24	2.87	2.87	2.86	44	49	3.95	3.88	3.75	69	74	6.76	5.90	5.09
10	9.39	20	25	2.90	2.89	2.88	45	50	4.02	3.95	3.84	70	75	6.91	5.97	5.12
11	8.64	21	26	2.93	2.92	2.91	46	51	4.09	4.01	3.90	71	76	7.07	6.05	5.14
12	8.02	22	27	2.95	2.95	2.93	47	52	4.17	4.08	3.95	72	77	7.23	6.12	5.17
13	7.49	23	28	2.98	2.97	2.96	48	53	4.25	4.15	4.01	73	78	7.38	6.18	5.19
14	7.03	24	29	3.01	3.00	2.99	49	54	4.33	4.22	4.07	74	79	7.54	6.24	5.20
15	6.64	25	30	3.04	3.03	3.02	50	55	4.42	4.29	4.12	75	80	7.69	6.30	5.22
16	6.30	26	31	3.08	3.07	3.05	51	56	4.50	4.37	4.18	76	81	7.84	6.35	5.23
17	6.00	27	32	3.11	3.10	3.08	52	57	4.60	4.44	4.24	77	82	7.98	6.39	5.24
18	5.73	28	33	3.14	3.13	3.11	53	58	4.69	4.52	4.30	78	83	8.13	6.43	5.25
19	5.49	29	34	3.18	3.17	3.15	54	59	4.79	4.60	4.36	79	84	8.26	6.47	5.26
20	5.27	30	35	3.22	3.20	3.18	55	60	4.90	4.69	4.41	80	85	8.39	6.50	5.26
21	5.08	31	36	3.26	3.24	3.22	56	61	5.01	4.77	4.47	81	86	8.51	6.53	5.27
22	4.90	32	37	3.30	3.28	3.25	57	62	5.12	4.86	4.53	82	87	8.63	6.55	5.27
23	4.74	33	38	3.34	3.32	3.29	58	63	5.23	4.94	4.59	83	88	8.73	6.57	5.27
24	4.60	34	39	3.39	3.36	3.33	59	64	5.35	5.03	4.64	84	89	8.83	6.59	5.27
25	4.46	35	40	3.43	3.41	3.37	60	65	5.48	5.12	4.70	85†	90†	8.92	6.60	5.27
		*And under										† And over			

AMOUNT OF EACH MONTHLY PAYMENT PER $1,000 OF PROCEEDS—OPTION E
(Based on the payees' ages at their nearest birthdays on the date the proceeds are settled under the option)

Age	Amount	Age	Amount	Age	Amount
55	$3.92	62	$4.55	69	$5.46
56	3.99	63	4.66	70	5.63
57	4.07	64	4.77	71	5.80
58	4.16	65	4.90	72	5.98
59	4.25	66	5.03	73	6.18
60	4.34	67	5.16	74	6.38
61	4.44	68	5.31	75	6.60

Note: Values shown apply if the payees are a man and a woman of equal ages. Other values for ages 55–75 are available on request.

TABLE OF POLICY VALUES

The cash or loan values of the policy and amounts of paid-up insurance and nonforfeiture factors shown are for each $1,000 face amount. The periods of extended insurance shown are the same for any face amount. The values in the Table are applicable only at the ends of the policy years shown, provided no premium is in default. When an "Age" is shown in the "End of Policy Year" column, the values are those applicable at the policy anniversary nearest the birthday on which the Insured attains that age. The values are applicable to this policy, determined by the age nearest the birthday of the Insured on the policy date, assuming that there is no indebtedness.

| End of Policy Year | Cash or Loan | Paid Up | †Extended Insurance | | Cash or Loan | Paid Up | †Extended Insurance | | Cash or Loan | Paid Up | †Extended Insurance | | Cash or Loan | Paid Up | †Extended Insurance | | Cash or Loan | Paid Up | †Extended Insurance | | End of Policy Years |
| | | | Yrs | Days | | | Yrs | Days | | | Yrs | Days | | | Yrs | Days | | | Yrs | Days | |
	Issue Age M–24/F–30				Issue Age M–25/F–31				Issue Age M–26/F–32				Issue Age M–27/F–32				Issue Age M–28/F–34				
1	0.00	0	0	0	0.00	0	0	0	0.00	0	0	0	0.00	0	0	0	0.00	0	0	0	1
2	2.00	0	0	0	0.00	0	0	0	0.00	0	0	0	0.00	0	0	0	0.00	0	0	0	2
3	0.00	0	0	0	1.00	3	0	138	2.00	10	0	270	2.00	9	0	265	3.00	13	1	25	2
4	9.00	42	3	187	11.00	30	4	91	12.00	53	4	204	13.00	55	4	305	14.00	58	5	21	4
5	19.00	85	7	222	21.00	91	8	65	23.00	97	8	220	24.00	98	8	205	26.00	103	8	277	5
6	30.00	128	11	193	32.00	133	11	143	34.00	137	11	258	36.00	141	11	238	38.00	145	11	190	6
7	41.00	169	14	139	43.00	172	14	97	45.00	173	14	11	48.00	181	13	352	31.00	187	13	295	7
8	32.00	204	16	191	55.00	212	16	132	58.00	217	16	46	61.00	222	15	299	64.00	226	15	168	8
9	64.00	244	18	81	67.00	248	17	314	70.00	253	17	161	74.00	259	17	57	77.00	262	16	240	9
10	76.00	279	19	158	80.00	282	19	35	83.00	200	18	198	87.00	293	18	44	91.00	298	17	241	10
11	89.00	313	20	164	93.00	320	19	357	97.00	324	19	170	101.00	327	18	342	106.00	334	18	185	11
12	102.00	347	21	60	106.00	351	20	216	111.00	357	20	46	116.00	362	19	229	121.00	367	19	42	12
13	116.00	380	21	282	212.00	385	21	87	126.00	390	20	248	131.00	394	20	46	136.00	397	19	190	13
14	130.00	410	22	63	135.00	414	21	206	141.00	420	21	19	146.00	423	20	151	152.00	428	19	317	14
15	143.00	440	22	186	131.00	446	21	345	156.00	448	21	96	162.00	452	20	245	169.00	459	20	57	15
16	160.00	468	22	255	166.00	472	22	28	173.00	478	21	193	179.00	481	20	323	186.00	486	20	113	16
17	176.00	496	22	310	183.00	501	22	96	189.00	503	21	211	196.00	508	20	353	203.00	512	20	128	17
18	192.00	321	22	323	199.00	525	22	91	204.00	329	21	221	214.00	534	21	10	221.00	537	20	133	18
19	209.00	546	22	326	217.00	552	22	106	224.00	554	21	221	232.00	559	20	359	240.00	563	20	129	19
20	227.00	572	22	321	234.00	573	22	39	243.00	580	21	211	251.00	583	20	335	259.00	586	20	92	20
AGE																					AGE
M60	474.00	804	17	142	469.00	796	17	58	465.00	789	16	356	460.00	780	16	276	453.00	772	16	197	60-M
F-65	437.00	792	17	275	453.00	783	17	208	448.00	777	17	123	443.00	768	17	39	438.00	759	16	322	65-F
M65	333.00	849	13	101	530.00	844	13	55	546.00	838	14	359	542.00	832	14	302	538.00	826	14	246	65-M
F-66	474.00	804	17	142	469.00	796	17	58	465.00	769	16	356	460.00	780	16	276	435.00	772	16	197	66F

Years	Nonforfeiture Features	Years	Nonforfeiture Features	Years	Nonforfeiture Features	Years	Nonforfeiture Features	Years	Nonforfeiture Features
1–20	$11.08836	1–20	$11.43719	1–20	$11.80509	1–20	$12.19269	1–20	$12.60181
21–71	$9.62081	21–75	$9.97732	21–74	$10.35254	21–73	$10.74786	21–72	$11.16435

End of Policy Year	Cash or Loan	Paid Up	†Extended Insurance Yrs	†Extended Insurance Days	Cash or Loan	Paid Up	†Extended Insurance Yrs	†Extended Insurance Days	Cash or Loan	Paid Up	†Extended Insurance Yrs	†Extended Insurance Days	Cash or Loan	Paid Up	†Extended Insurance Yrs	†Extended Insurance Days	Cash or Loan	Paid Up	†Extended Insurance Yrs	†Extended Insurance Days	End of Policy Years
	Issue Age M–24/F–30				Issue Age M–25/F–31				Issue Age M–26/F–32				Issue Age M–27/F–32				Issue Age M–28/F–34				
1	0.00	0	0	0	0.00	0	0	0	0.00	0	0	0	0.00	0	0	0	0.00	0	0	0	1
2	0.00	0	0	0	0.00	0	0	0	0.00	0	0	0	0.00	0	0	0	0.00	0	0	0	2
3	4.00	17	1	148	5.00	21	1	262	6.00	24	2	2	7.00	27	2	87	8.00	30	2	150	2
4	14.00	64	5	200	17.00	66	5	218	19.00	72	5	316	20.00	73	5	278	22.00	78	5	317	4
5	28.00	108	8	310	30.00	112	8	214	32.00	116	8	282	34..00	120	8	234	36.00	123	8	172	5
6	40.00	148	11	117	43.00	154	11	104	45.00	157	10	357	48.00	163	10	302	50.00	164	10	167	6
7	53.00	189	13	141	56.00	194	13	47	59.00	198	12	300	62.00	202	12	177	65.00	206	12	47	7
8	67.00	230	15	25	70.00	233	14	233	73.00	236	14	71	77.00	242	13	319	80.00	244	13	144	8
9	81.00	267	16	105	83.00	272	15	325	88.00	274	15	122	92.00	278	14	329	96.00	282	14	165	9
10	95.00	302	17	66	99.00	306	16	250	104.00	312	16	106	108.00	315	15	379	112.00	318	15	84	10
11	110.00	337	17	344	115.00	342	17	172	119.00	344	16	323	124.00	349	16	142	129.00	353	15	324	11
12	126.00	371	18	212	131.00	375	18	14	136.00	379	17	175	141.00	382	16	335	146.00	385	16	126	12
13	142.00	403	19	10	147.00	406	18	152	153.00	411	17	326	158.00	413	17	100	144.00	417	16	267	13
14	158.00	433	19	112	164.00	437	18	268	170.00	441	18	57	176.00	444	17	207	182.00	447	16	356	14
15	175.00	462	19	197	181.00	465	18	335	188.00	470	16	133	194.00	472	17	268	201.00	476	17	62	15
16	192.00	489	19	237	199.00	493	19	22	206.00	497	18	168	213.00	500	17	314	220.00	503	17	93	16
17	210.00	315	19	264	218.00	521	19	59	225.00	524	18	191	233.00	528	17	346	240.00	530	17	113	17
18	229.00	542	19	280	237.00	546	19	59	244.00	548	18	180	252.00	552	17	323	260.00	535	17	100	18
19	248.00	566	19	262	256.00	569	19	29	264.00	572	18	160	273.00	577	17	312	261.00	579	17	79	19
20	268.00	590	19	235	276.00	593	18	356	285.00	597	18	132	294.00	600	17	273	303.00	604	17	50	20
AGE																					AGE
M60	449.00	762	16	101	444.00	753	16	22	438.00	743	15	295	432.00	733	15	205	425.00	721	13	100	60-M
F-65	433.00	751	16	243	427.00	740	16	147	421.00	730	16	32	414.00	718	15	309	407.00	706	15	203	65-F
M65	533.00	818	14	175	528.00	810	14	105	523.00	803	14	34	518.00	795	13	332	512.00	786	13	254	65-M
F-66	449.00	762	16	101	444.00	753	16	22	438.00	743	15	295	432.00	733	15	205	425.00	721	15	100	66F

Years	Nonforfeiture Features	Years	Nonforfeiture Features	Years	Nonforfeiture Features	Years	Nonforfeiture Features	Years	Nonforfeiture Features
1–20	$12.99747	1–20	$13.45368	1–20	$13.93581	1–20	$14.44525	1–20	$14.98462
21–71	$11.60317	21–70	$12.06613	21–69	$12.55471	21–68	$13.07110	21–67	$13.61718

End of Policy Year	Cash or Loan	Paid Up	†Extended Insurance Yrs	†Extended Insurance Days	Cash or Loan	Paid Up	†Extended Insurance Yrs	†Extended Insurance Days	Cash or Loan	Paid Up	†Extended Insurance Yrs	†Extended Insurance Days	Cash or Loan	Paid Up	†Extended Insurance Yrs	†Extended Insurance Days	Cash or Loan	Paid Up	†Extended Insurance Yrs	†Extended Insurance Days	End of Policy Years
	Issue Age M–24/F–30				Issue Age M–25/F–31				Issue Age M–26/F–32				Issue Age M–27/F–32				Issue Age M–28/F–34				
1	0.00	0	0	0	0.00	0	0	0	0.00	0	0	0	0.00	0	0	0	0.00	0	0	0	1
2	0.00	0	0	0	0.00	0	0	0	0.00	0	0	0	0.00	0	0	0	0.00	0	0	0	2
3	10.00	36	2	293	11.00	39	2	312	12.00	41	2	318	13.00	13	2	315	14.00	45	2	307	2
4	23.00	79	5	249	25.00	84	5	253	27.00	88	3	243	28.00	88	5	158	30.00	92	5	133	4
5	38.00	123	8	99	40.00	129	8	20	42.00	131	5	297	44.00	134	7	205	46.00	136	7	110	5
6	53.00	169	10	90	55.00	171	9	312	58.00	175	7	218	60.00	176	9	71	63.00	179	8	335	6
7	68.00	209	11	276	71.00	212	11	135	74.00	215	9	357	77.00	218	10	209	80.00	220	10	61	7
8	84.00	249	13	14	87.00	251	12	197	91.00	255	10	56	94.00	256	11	236	98.00	260	11	88	8
9	100.00	206	13	363	104.00	289	13	189	108.00	292	12	16	112.00	295	12	203	116.00	297	12	26	9
10	117.00	323	14	289	121.00	325	14	88	126.00	329	13	285	130.00	330	13	83	135.00	334	12	276	10
11	134.00	356	15	135	139.00	360	14	309	144.00	363	13	116	149.00	365	13	288	154.00	368	13	95	11
12	152.00	390	15	312	157.00	392	15	100	163.00	396	14	280	168.00	398	14	69	174.00	402	13	248	12
13	170.00	421	16	66	176.00	424	15	229	182.00	427	14	27	188.00	430	14	169	194.00	433	13	354	13
14	189.00	452	16	164	195.00	454	15	311	203.00	456	15	93	208.00	460	14	266	215.00	464	14	73	14
15	208.00	480	16	219	215.00	484	16	11	222.00	487	15	168	229.00	480	14	126	236.00	492	14	120	15
16	228.00	508	16	260	235.00	311	16	39	242.00	513	15	183	250.00	517	14	351	257.00	519	14	135	16
17	248.00	534	16	266	255.00	536	16	35	263.00	539	15	190	271.00	542	14	346	279.00	545	14	138	17
18	268.00	558	16	243	277.00	562	16	41	283.00	565	15	185	293.00	567	14	332	302.00	571	14	132	18
19	290.00	583	16	231	298.00	585	16	1	307.00	589	15	155	316.00	592	14	310	325.00	595	14	103	19
20	311.00	603	16	176	321.00	610	15	336	330.00	612	15	118	339.00	615	14	266	348.00	617	14	53	20
AGE																					AGE
M60	418.00	709	14	361	411.00	697	14	261	403.00	684	14	147	395.00	670	14	33	386.00	655	13	275	60-M
F-65	400.00	693	15	92	393.00	681	14	357	384.00	666	14	227	376.00	652	14	112	367.00	636	13	348	65-F
M65	506.00	777	13	176	500.00	767	13	97	493.00	757	13	6	486.00	746	12	286	479.00	735	12	201	65-M
F-66	418.00	709	14	361	411.00	697	14	261	403.00	684	14	147	393.00	670	14	33	386.00	655	13	273	66F

Years	Nonforfeiture Features	Years	Nonforfeiture Features	Years	Nonforfeiture Features	Years	Nonforfeiture Features	Years	Nonforfeiture Features
1–20	$15.55601	1–20	$16.16216	1–20	$16.80426	1–20	$17.48469	1–20	$18.20570
21–66	$14.19507	21–65	$14.80600	21–64	$15.45194	21–63	$16.13455	21–62	$16.85451

†Extended Insurance is not available if this policy is rated as a substandard class as shown on page 3.
Note: Not all age tables are shown.

LIFE INSURANCE APPLICATION
Long Life Insurance Company

PART I   The following questions relate to the person proposed for insurance

PART I Questions	Right Column
1. Proposed insured—First name, middle initial, last name ☐ Male ☐ Female	**16.** Beneficiary

1. Proposed insured—First name, middle initial, last name   ☐ Male   ☐ Female

2. Date of birth   month   day   year   3. Age nearest birthday   4. Place of birth

5. Telephone numbers   Day: Night:

6. Address for premium notices (bills will be sent to owner at this address)

7. Residence of insured (if different)

8. Social Security number of the insured   9. Amount of existing LL Insurance $

10. Any other name now or previously known by (incl. maiden name, if applicable)

11. Within the last 12 months has the insured smoked: Cigarettes? ☐ Yes ☐ No   (a urine test may be required)   Cigars or a pipe? ☐ Yes ☐ No

12. Insurance amount and plan

   Basic policy $ Plan
   Insured rider $ Plan
   Children rider $ Term to age 22 Insurance (complete Child Rider questionnaire)
   Waiver of Premium   ☐ Yes   ☐ No   (issue ages 15–55 only)

13. Dividends (if selection is missing or not available, #4 will be effective)
   1 ☐ Pay in cash
   2 ☐ Reduce amount due—any excess dividend as ☐ #4   ☐ #3   ☐ #2
   3 ☐ Purchase paid-up life additions (not available on term insurance)
   4 ☐ Accumulate at interest
   5 ☐ Purchase one-year term additions (not available on term insurance)

14. Premium payment frequency   ☐ Annual   ☐ Semiannual   ☐ Quarterly   Automatic Premium Loan Provision to be effective on permanent insurance unless requested otherwise.

15. Owner (if no owner is shown, the applicant will be the owner.)
   Class   Name (please print clearly)   Age   Relationship to insured
   1.
   2.
   3.

---

16. Beneficiary
   Class   Name(s) (please print clearly)   Relationship to insured

   If two or more beneficiaries are named, state the class: 1, 2, 3, etc. Surviving beneficiaries in the lowest class share equally. All decisions made by LL in good faith as to the identity of beneficiaries not designated by name shall be conclusive as to LL's liability, and any payment made in accordance therewith shall, to the extent thereof, discharge LL of its obligation for such payment.

17. Will coverage applied for replace or change any existing life insurance or annuity (other than LL)? If "Yes," submit form A-52.   ☐ Yes   ☐ No

18. If a group insurance conversion:
   Group name: _____
   Date group insurance terminated: _____   ☐ Policy terminated   ☐ Employment terminated
   Note: Part 2 on the reverse side should be completed only if Waiver of Premium is requested in question 12 or #5 in question 13.

19. Conversion or exchange of existing LL insurance (other than group):
   Total face amount: _____   Plan: _____
   Policy numbers:
   _____   _____   _____
   _____   _____   _____
   _____   _____   _____

   The above policies are hereby tendered (1) for endorsement, if a rider insurance conversion, or (2) for surrender, if basic policy conversion or exchange; in consideration for an effective as of the date of issue of the insurance herein applied for. If a surrender, pay any cash or dividend values to me. (The above policies must accompany this application).

   If Term Conversion, Part 2 on the reverse side should be completed only if #5 is selected in question 13 or if Waiver of Premium is requested in question 2.

   For Exchanges, Part 2 on the reverse side must be completed in all cases unless notified otherwise.

20. Special requests

21. How did you hear about LL?
   ☐ Family member has LL   ☐ Newspaper   ☐ Radio   ☐ TV   ☐ Mail insert
   ☐ Bank lobby sign   ☐ Friend or relative   ☐ Other:

22. Changes made by LL

23. Issuing bank:
   No.   Name:

---

1. Under penalty of perjury, I certify that the Social Security number(s) is/are correct and that I am not subject to backup withholding.
2. I hereby certify that the statements above are correct and agree that LL, believing them to be correct, shall rely and act on them.
3. If LL makes a change in space 22, it will be approved by my acceptance of the policy.
4. I agree that the insurance applied for shall not take effect until the first full premium is paid and the policy delivered while each person to be insured is in good health. Once submitted, this application will remain the property of LL.

_____   X _____   X _____
Date   Signature of Insured (if age 15 or over)   Signature of First Owner in question 15, if any

X _____   X _____
Signature of Applicant (if other than Insured)   Signature of First Owner in question 15, if any
If Insured is under 15, check if: ☐ Mother   ☐ Father   ☐ Guardian

Action	Date	By	Agent No.	Agent Signature		
R/R			Agency	Source, if diff.	Initial Premium Rec'd $	Date Received

1

| Name of Proposed Insured (print) | |

PART 2 To be completed by the LL agent if non-medical. (If this is to be a medical application, the examiner will complete this section.)

1. (a) Employer's name and address	Details of "YES" answers. Identify the question number. Include diagnosis, dates, duration, names and addresses of all attending physicians and medical facilities. Give reason for checkup, treatment, and medication.
(b) Job title and exact duties	

(c) Years so employed	(d) Change in occupation contemplated? ☐ Yes ☐ No
	Other occupations last two years? ☐ Yes ☐ No

2. (a) Do you intend to reside or travel outside the United States and Canada except for vacations? ☐ Yes ☐ No

(b) Have you ever made claim for or received any pension or disability benefits? ☐ Yes ☐ No

(c) Have you ever had an application for life or health insurance declined, postponed, modified or offered at other than regular premiums for your age? ☐ Yes ☐ No

3. (a) Do you participate in parachuting, motor racing, or any other hazardous avocations? ☐ Yes ☐ No

(b) Do you own, operate or are you licensed to operate an airplane? ☐ Yes ☐ No

(c) How many flights have you made in the past 12 months in other than commercial airlines/airplanes? ☐ Yes ☐ No

4. Have you ever consulted any doctor or practitioner for, or suffered from any illness or disease of:

(a) The brain or nervous system? ☐ Yes ☐ No

(b) The heart, blood vessels, or lungs? ☐ Yes ☐ No

(c) The stomach or intestines? ☐ Yes ☐ No

(d) The skin, glands, middle ear, hearing, eyes, or vision? ☐ Yes ☐ No

5. Have you ever had or been advised to have an electrocardiogram, Xray, or other diagnostic test? ☐ Yes ☐ No

6. Have you ever had or been treated for rheumatism, bone disease, cancer, syphilis, or other venereal disease, or any disorder of the muscle or bones, including the spine, back, or joints? ☐ Yes ☐ No

7. Have you ever had or been treated for: chest pain, dizziness, fainting, convulsions, allergies, asthma, shortness of breath, persistent cough, repeated headache, paralysis, stroke, or diabetes? ☐ Yes ☐ No

8. Have you even been treated for or had any known indication of:

(a) Alcoholism? ☐ Yes ☐ No

(b) Mental or nervous disorder? ☐ Yes ☐ No

(c) Any deformity or congenital disorder? ☐ Yes ☐ No

9. Have you ever used or dealt in barbiturates, excitants or hallucinogens, narcotics, or other habit forming drugs? ☐ Yes ☐ No

10. Are you now being treated or taking medicine for any condition or disease? ☐ Yes ☐ No

11. Have you ever consulted a doctor or practitioner for, or had any known indication of, any illness, disease, or physical defect or disorder not included in the above question? ☐ Yes ☐ No

12. Other than above, within the past three years, have you had a checkup, consultation, illness, injury, surgery, or been a patient in a hospital, clinic, sanitarium, or other medical facility? ☐ Yes ☐ No

13. Females age 15 and over only:

(a) Ever had any disorder of menstruation, pregnancy, or of the female organs or breasts? ☐ Yes ☐ No

(b) Are you now pregnant? ☐ Yes ☐ No

(c) Ever had a caesarean section? ☐ Yes ☐ No

(d) Are uterine functions now irregular? ☐ Yes ☐ No

(e) Number of children _____

14. Height (in shoes) _____ ft. _____ in. Weight (clothed) _____ lbs.

Has weight changed in the past two years? ☐ Yes ☐ No

If "Yes": Gain _____ lbs., Loss _____ lbs. How long at present weight? _____

15. Family History—Indicate below any diabetes, cancer, high blood pressure, heart or kidney disease, mental illness, or suicide.

Family Member	Age If Living	State	Age at Death
Father			
Mother			
Brothers & Sisters No. Living ____ No. Dead ____			

Date _____ X _____

Signature of Examiner (Agent if non-medical)

I hereby certify that the above answers and statements are correct and I agree that LL, believing them to be correct, shall rely and act on them. I agree that they shall be a part of my application for insurance or policy change request. I acknowledge receipt of the attached Disclosure Notice and MIB Notification.

I HEREBY AUTHORIZE any licensed physician, medical practitioner, hospital, clinic, or other medical or medically related facility, insurance company, the Medical Information Bureau or other organization, institution or person, that has any records or knowledge of the Proposed Insured or his/her health to give to the Medical Director, Long Life Insurance, any such information.

A photographic copy of this authorization shall be as valid as the original.

_____ _____ X _____

Name of Proposed Insured (please print)   Date   Signature of Proposed Insured (parent or guardian if insured under age 15)

PART 3   To be completed by an Examiner authorized by LL. Omit if non-medical.

16. Males only Chest (inspiration) _____ in. Chest (expiration) _____ in. Waist _____ in.	17. Blood Pressure Systolic Diastolic (All sound ceases) If over 138/88, repeat twice 3 minutes apart	18. Pulse Rate _____ Quality _____ Irregularities per minute _____	19. Urinalysis Albumin _____ Sugar _____

20. For question 14 answers Did you measure? ☐ Yes ☐ No Did you weigh? ☐ Yes ☐ No	21. Did you observe any indication of physical or mental impairment or abnormality not indicated in Part 2? ☐ Yes ☐ No If "Yes" explain:

I have personally seen the person whose name appears in Part 2. I am satisfied as to the identity of that person. I certify that the answers in Part 2 were correctly recorded by me.

Paramedic Stamp:

_____ X _____ _____
Date   Examiner

A consumer inspection report, if we request one, may include information obtained through personal interviews with your neighbors, friends or others with whom you are acquainted. This inquiry includes information as to your character, general reputation, personal characteristics and mode of living. You have the right to make a written request within a reasonable period of time to receive additional, detailed information about the nature and scope of this investigation. Please direct any such request to Medical Director, Long Life Insurance.

Information regarding your insurability will be treated as confidential. We may, however, make a brief report thereon to the Medical Information Bureau (MIB), a nonprofit membership organization of insurance companies, which operates an information exchange on behalf of its members. If you apply to another MIB member company for life or health insurance coverage, or a claim for benefits is submitted to such a company, MIB, upon request, will supply such company with the information in its files.

We will not reject your application because of data furnished by MIB; it may simply alert us to the possible need for further information. MIB files do not contain medical reports from doctors or hospitals, nor do they indicate whether any insurance applications have been accepted or rejected.

Upon receipt of a request from you, MIB will arrange disclosure of any information it may have in your file. (Medical information will be disclosed only to your attending physician.) If you question the accuracy of the information in the MIB file, you may contact MIB and seek a correction in accordance with the procedures set forth in the Federal Fair Credit Reporting Act. We may also release information in our file to other life insurance companies to whom you apply for life or health insurance, or to whom a claim for benefits may be submitted.

ERIE HEALTH INSURANCE
COMPANY OF AMERICA

Erie Health agrees, in accordance with the provisions of this policy, to pay the benefits provided in this policy due to injury or sickness.

Twenty-Day Right to Examine Policy   You may return this policy by delivering it to the Home Office or to an agent of the Company within 20 days after receiving it. Immediately on such delivery, the policy will be void as of the date of issue and any premium paid will be refunded.

President

Secretary

Insured:
Policy Number:
Policy Date:

DEFINITIONS

"You," "Your," and "Yours" means the insured named on the Policy Schedule. "Time," "Us," and "Ours" means the Company.

COVERED PERSON

Covered person means the insured and all eligible dependents shown on the policy schedule, or added by endorsement.

CUSTODIAL CARE

Means care given to a covered person if the person:

1. is mentally or physically disabled and such disability is expected to last for an indefinite time;

2. needs a protected, monitored, and/or controlled environment;

3. needs help to support the essentials of daily living; and

4. is not under active and specific medical, surgical and/or psychiatric treatment, which will reduce the disability to the extent necessary for the person to function outside a protected, monitored, and/or controlled environment.

DENTAL SERVICE

Means any medical or surgical procedure that involves the hard or soft tissue of the mouth that requires treatment as a result of a disease or condition of the teeth and gums. Treatment for neoplasms is not considered a dental service.

DISABLED DEPENDENTS

This section amends the Eligible Dependents section. An unmarried child who cannot support himself due to mental incapacity or physical handicap may continue to be insured. This child must be fully dependent upon you for support. The Company may inquire of you two months before attainment by a dependent of the limiting age set forth in this policy, or at any reasonable time thereafter, whether such dependent is in fact a disabled and dependent person. In the absence of proof submitted within 60 days of such inquiry that such dependent is a disabled and dependent person, the Company may terminate coverage of such person at or after attainment of the limiting age. In the absence of such inquiry, coverage of any disabled and dependent person shall continue through the term of such policy or any extension or renewal thereof.

EFFECTIVE DATE OF COVERAGE

A covered person's effective date of coverage is: (1) the policy date, if the covered person is listed on the application and the policy schedule; or (2) the date of policy endorsement, if the covered person is added.

ELIGIBLE DEPENDENTS

Eligible dependents are those dependents shown on the policy schedule or added by endorsement. This may include: (1) Your lawful spouse; and (2) Unmarried dependent children, including step-children and adopted children (or children who are in your custody pursuant to an interim court order of adoption), if they are legally dependent on you for their support and under 21 years of age.

Your newborn children, born while the policy is in force, will be covered for 60 days after birth. For coverage beyond 60 days after birth, written application must be made to the Company within that 60-day period. An additional premium will be required retroactive to date of birth. Other eligible dependents may be added by you upon evidence of insurability satisfactory to the Company. Additional premium will be required.

ELIGIBLE FOR MEDICARE

Means that the covered person is either:

1. covered by both Part A and Part B of Medicare; or

2. not covered for both Part A and Part B of Medicare because of:

    a. a failure to enroll when required;

    b. a failure to pay any premium that may be required for full coverage of the person under Medicare; or

    c. a failure to file any written request, claim or document required for payment of Medicare benefits.

HOSPICE PROGRAM

Means a coordinated interdisciplinary program for meeting the special physical, psychological, spiritual, and social needs of dying covered persons and their immediate families. The covered person must be enrolled in the program by a physician.

HOSPITAL

Means a place other than a convalescent, nursing, or rest home, that:

■ provides facilities for medical, diagnostic, and acute care on an inpatient basis. If these services are not on its own premises, they must be available through a prearranged contract;

■ provides 24-hour nursing care supervised by registered nurses;

■ has x-ray and lab facilities either on its premises or available through a prearranged contract; and

■ charges for these services.

A special ward, floor, or other accommodation for convalescent, nursing, or rehabilitation purposes is not considered a hospital.

IMMEDIATE FAMILY

Means you, your spouse, and the children, brothers, sisters, and parents of either you or your spouse.

INJURY

Injury means accidental bodily injury sustained by a covered person while covered under this policy.

MEDICALLY NECESSARY CARE

Means confinement, treatment or service that is rendered to diagnose or treat a sickness or injury. Such care must be (1) prescribed by a physician; (2) considered to be necessary and appropriate for the diagnosis and treatment of the sickness or injury; and (3) commonly accepted as proper care or treatment of the condition by the US medical community. Medically necessary care does not include care considered to be: (1) experimental or investigative in nature by any appropriate technological assessment body established by any state or federal government; (2) provided only as a convenience to the covered person or provider; and (3) in excess (in scope, duration or intensity) of that level of care which is needed to provide safe, adequate and appropriate diagnosis and treatment. The fact that a physician may prescribe, order, recommend or approve a service or supply does not, of itself, make the service or supply medically necessary.

MEDICARE

Medicare means the Health Insurance for the Aged Act, Title XVIII of the Social Security Act as amended.

MENTAL ILLNESS

Mental illness means a mental or nervous disorder, including neuroses, psychoneurosis, psychopathy, psychosis and other emotional disorders. Affective disorders (including bipolar disorders and major depression), alcoholism, drug addiction and chemical dependency are also included in this definition.

OTHER HEALTH INSURANCE PLAN

This means any plan that provides insurance, reimbursement or service benefits for hospital, surgical or other medical expenses. This includes: (1) individual or group health insurance policies; (2) non-profit health service plans, including Blue Cross and Blue Shield; (3) health maintenance organization subscriber contracts; (4) self-insured group plans; (5) welfare plans; (6) medical coverage under homeowners or automobile insurance; and (7) service provided or payment received under laws of any national, state or local government. This does not include Medicaid.

If coverage is provided on a service basis, the amount of benefits under such coverage will be taken as the cost of the service in the absence of such coverage.

PART A

Means the Hospital Insurance Benefits for the Aged portion of Medicare.

PART B

Means the Supplementary Medical Insurance for the Aged portion of Medicare.

PHYSICAL MEDICINE

Means the diagnosis and treatment of physical conditions relating to bone, muscle or neuromuscular pathology.

PHYSICIAN

A person licensed by the state to treat the kind of injury or sickness for which a claim is made. The physician must be practicing within the limits of his or her license.

POLICY OWNER

The insured shown on the policy schedule unless someone else is designated the owner on the application.

PRE-EXISTING CONDITIONS

A pre-existing condition is a condition not fully disclosed on the application for insurance:

1. for which the covered person received medical treatment or advice from a physician within the six-month period immediately preceding that covered person's effective date of coverage; or

2. which produced signs or symptoms within the six-month period immediately preceding that covered person's effective date of coverage.

   The signs or symptoms must have been significant enough to establish manifestation or onset by one of the following tests:

   a. The signs or symptoms would have allowed one learned in medicine to make a diagnosis of the disorder; or

   b. The signs or symptoms should have caused an ordinarily prudent person to seek diagnosis or treatment.

Pre-existing conditions will be covered after the covered person has been insured for two years, if the condition is not specifically excluded from coverage.

REASONABLE AND CUSTOMARY CHARGE

Means the lesser of:

1. The actual charge;

2. What the provider would accept for the same service or supply in the absence of insurance; or

3. The reasonable charge as determined by the Company, based on factors such as:

   a. the most common charge for the same or comparable service or supply in a community similar to where the service or supply is furnished;

   b. the amount of resources expended to deliver the treatment and the complexity of the treatment rendered; and

   c. charging protocols and billing practices generally accepted by the medical community or specialty groups; or

   d. inflation trends by geographic region.

SICKNESS

Sickness means an illness, disease or condition of a covered person that manifests itself after the covered person's effective date of coverage. For sickness that manifests itself during the first 15 days following the effective date, coverage is provided only for covered expenses incurred after that 15-day period.

SKILLED NURSING FACILITY

Means a nursing home, licensed as a skilled nursing facility, operating in accordance with the laws of the state in which it is located and meeting the following requirements:

1. Is primarily engaged in providing room, board and skilled nursing care for persons recovering from sickness or injury;

2. Provides 24-hour-a-day skilled nursing service under the full-time supervision of a physician or graduate registered nurse;

3. Maintains daily clinical records;

4. Has transfer arrangements with a hospital;

5. Has a utilization review plan in effect;

6. Is not a place for rest, the aged, drug addicts, alcoholics or the mentally ill; and

7. May be a part of a hospital.

COVERAGE DESCRIPTION

DEDUCTIBLE AMOUNT

The deductible amount for each covered person during each calendar year is the larger of:

■ the basic deductible amount shown in the policy schedule; or

■ the amount of benefits paid for covered expenses by any other health insurance plan as defined in the policy.

The deductible amount must be:

■ incurred each calendar year; and

■ deducted from covered expenses.

A calendar year begins on January 1 and ends December 31.

MAXIMUM FAMILY DEDUCTIBLE AMOUNT

A maximum family deductible amount equal to three times the basic deductible amount will satisfy the deductible requirements for all covered persons in a family during a calendar year.

FAMILY CAP MAXIMUM

The maximum expense amount incurred per family for covered expense will not exceed the family cap maximum shown in the policy schedule for any calendar year.

CARRY-OVER DEDUCTIBLE

Any covered expense incurred and applied to a covered person's basic deductible amount during the last three months of a calendar year may also be used to reduce that person's basic deductible amount for the next calendar year.

The maximum family deductible and the carry-over deductible provisions will not apply if the benefits paid by other health insurance are used as the deductible.

RIGHT TO CHANGE DEDUCTIBLE AMOUNT

You may apply for an increase or decrease in the basic deductible amount within a 60-day period after a premium rate change, or during the first 30 days of a calendar year, provided that: (1) the new basic deductible amount is one that is available on this form, (2) a request for the change is made in writing to the Company, and (3) no claims have been incurred during that calendar year.

If you request a decrease in the deductible amount, the Company will require proof of continued insurability of all covered persons.

PAYMENT OF BENEFITS

Benefits for covered expense incurred will be paid in accordance with Sections A and B of the covered expense provision.

If benefits paid by other health insurance are used as the deductible amount, all covered expense will be paid at 100 percent, but payment will not exceed the amount that would have been paid in the absence of other health insurance.

Where applicable, the rate of payment starts again for each covered person each new calendar year after the deductible amount has been met. The Company will pay up to the lifetime maximum benefit shown in the policy schedule for each covered person.

If the payment by other health insurance is used as the deductible amount, the lifetime maximum benefit will be increased. The maximum benefit will be increased by $3 for each $1 paid by other coverage over the basic deductible.

PAYMENT OF BENEFITS WHEN ELIGIBLE FOR MEDICARE

When any covered person is eligible for Medicare, he or she will be deemed to have Part A and Part B Medicare coverage that is primary to the coverage under this policy. Services covered by Medicare will not be covered by this policy to the extent that benefits are payable by Medicare. If there is remaining covered expense after Medicare pays for assigned services, benefits will be paid at 100% up to the amount approved by Medicare; for unassigned services, benefits will be paid at 100% up to our reasonable and customary charge limit. Payment of benefits for services not covered by Medicare will be determined by the terms and limits of this policy.

COVERED EXPENSE

Covered expense means an expense that is (a) incurred for services, treatment or supplies prescribed by a physician and described in Section A below; (b) incurred by a covered person as the result of sickness or injury as defined; (c) incurred for medically necessary care; and (d) incurred while the covered person's coverage is in force. Covered expense does not include any charge in excess of the reasonable and customary charge.

A.   The following items of covered expense are subject to the deductible and rate of payment as described in this policy and shown in the policy schedule.

1.   Room, board and general nursing care while confined in a semi-private room, ward, coronary care or other intensive care unit in a hospital. For confinement in a private room, the covered expense is limited to the hospital's most common daily charge for a semi-private room.

2.   Other hospital services including services performed in a hospital outpatient department or in a free-standing surgical facility.

3.   Physician services and surgical services, including second surgical opinions by board-certified specialists. This does not include services rendered by members of your immediate family.

4.   Reconstructive surgery to restore function for conditions resulting from accidental injury provided the injury occurred while the covered person was insured under this plan. Reconstructive surgery that is incidental to or follows covered surgery performed as the result of trauma, infection or other diseases of the involved part.

   Reconstructive surgery for congenital defects provided the covered person has been insured continuously under this plan since the time of birth.

5.   Hospice programs when (a) the physician projects a life expectancy of six months or less; and (b) the physician enrolls a covered person in the program. Notification is to be made in writing to the Company within seven days of admission to a licensed hospice facility. Covered expense includes up to 30 days of inpatient treatment at a hospice facility. Hospice home care is covered in addition to benefits provided under item 6. Benefits for services that include inpatient hospice services, hospice home care and counselling under the authorized hospice program are limited to $15,000 during the covered person's lifetime.

6.   Up to 40 home health care visits in any 12-month period. One visit consists of up to four hours of home health aide service within a 24-hour period by anyone providing services or evaluating the need for home health care.

For home health care to be a covered expense, the physician must certify that:

a.   hospitalization or confinement in a skilled nursing facility would otherwise be required;

b.   medically necessary care is not available from members of the covered person's immediate family or persons living with the covered person without causing undue hardship; and

c.   the home health care will be provided by a state-licensed or Medicare-certified home health agency.

Home health care does not include:

a.   services not included in the home health care plan established for the covered person by the physician;

b.   services provided by the covered person's immediate family or anyone residing with the covered person;

c.   homemaker services; or

d.   custodial care.

7.   Professional ambulance service to the nearest hospital that is able to handle the sickness or injury. One trip to a hospital for a covered person for each sickness or injury is covered.

8.   X-ray, radioactive treatment, laboratory tests, and anesthesia services.

9.   Outpatient physical medicine benefits to a maximum of $500 for each covered person per calendar year. Physical medicine benefits include but are not limited to: rehabilitative speech, physical, occupational and cognitive therapies; biofeedback; sports medicine; cardiac exercise programs; adjustments and manipulations. The limitation does not apply to the treatment of burns, fractures, complete dislocations; joint replacements or related conditions for which a covered person is hospitalized for surgery and physical medicine that immediately follows hospitalization.

10.   Rental, up to the purchase price, or purchase, when approved in advance by the Company, of (a) a basic wheelchair, basic hospital bed or basic crutches; (b) the initial permanent basic artificial limb, eye or external breast prosthesis; and (c) oxygen and the equipment needed to administer oxygen.

   Casts, orthopedic braces, splints, dressings and sutures.

   Dental braces, dental appliances, corrective shoes, orthotics or repairs to or replacement of prosthetic devices are not covered expenses.

11.   Drugs that require the written prescription of a licensed physician. However, if a prescription drug benefit rider is attached to this policy, covered drugs will be paid under that rider (to age 65 or prior Medicare eligibility) instead of under this policy.

12. Whole blood, blood plasma and blood products, if not replaced.

13. Dental service for an injury to a sound natural tooth when the expense is incurred within six months following the injury.

    "Sound" is defined as:

    a. organic and formed by nature;

    b. not extensively restored or endodontically treated; and

    c. not extensively decayed or involved in periodontal disease.

14. Treatment of mental illness. Expense incurred by a covered person while confined as an inpatient to a hospital or psychiatric hospital for mental illness as defined in the policy. Coverage is limited to a maximum benefit of $2,500 for a covered person during a calendar year. Outpatient treatment, drugs or medications are not covered.

15. Sterilization, if the covered person has been insured on this policy for at least two years.

16. Treatment of temporomandibular joint dysfunction except for: crowns that correct vertical dimension; splints, orthopedic repositioning appliances, biteplates and equilibration treatments (including splint equilibration and adjustments); bite functional or occlusal registration, with or without splints, and kinesiographic analysis; any orthodontic treatment, including extraction of teeth; study models, except for the complete model made necessary when surgical intervention is completed. Surgical charges for correction of orthognathic conditions are covered.

B. The following items 1, 2 and 3 of covered expense will not be subject to the basic deductible amount of the 80 percent rate of payment. Covered expense will be considered for payment under this section before it is considered under any other section of the policy. Covered expense for which a benefit is payable under this section will not be considered for payment under any other section of the policy.

1. Skilled nursing care: Medically necessary care in a skilled nursing facility for up to 30 days provided (a) the covered person enters the skilled nursing facility within 14 days after discharge from an authorized hospital confinement; (b) the skilled nursing facility confinement is for the same condition that required the hospital confinement; and (c) such care is authorized by the Company within seven days following admission to the skilled nursing facility. The daily benefit for confinement in a skilled nursing facility will not exceed one-half of the semi-private hospital room rate for the area.

2. Second and third opinions required by the Company's authorization service. Only an exam, x-ray and lab work, and a written report by the physician rendering the opinion are included. You will be supplied with a list of three recommended physicians from whom the second or third opinion may be sought. The service may allow another physician to be consulted if the physician is (a) a board-certified specialist in the field of the proposed treatment; (b) is not financially associated with the first physician; and (c) does not perform the treatment.

3. Pre-admission testing, x-rays, and lab work performed on an outpatient basis before an authorized hospital admission provided (a) the tests are related to a scheduled admission; (b) the charges for the tests would have been covered expense if the individual was confined as an inpatient in a hospital; and (c) the tests were not repeated in or by the hospital, or elsewhere.

HUMAN ORGAN/TISSUE TRANSPLANT OR REPLACEMENT

Covered expense incurred by a covered person for the following human organ or tissue transplants or replacements if the procedure is authorized as indicated below, to a maximum lifetime benefit of $250,000 for each covered person.

Human organ transplant. The following procedures are covered if the procedure is authorized in writing by the Company prior to the beginning of the donor search and selection:

a. Bone marrow transplant

b. Heart transplant

c. Liver transplant

No benefits will be paid if the procedure has not been authorized by the Company prior to the beginning of the donor search and selection. To begin the authorization process, the physician or the physician's assistant must contact the Company's authorization service.

Tissue transplant or replacement. The following procedures are covered if authorized according to the procedures outlined in the authorization provision:

a. Cornea transplant

b. Prosthetic tissue replacement, including joint replacement

c. Vein or artery graft

d. Heart valve replacement

e. Implantable prosthetic lens in connection with cataracts

Donor Expenses. Expense incurred for surgery, storage and/or transportation service related to donor organ acquisition is also covered, up to a maximum benefit of $10,000 per covered procedure.

If the transplanted organ is from a live donor, expense incurred by the donor that is not paid by any other plan of insurance will be covered as if the donor's expense were the expense of the covered person.

No benefits will be paid for any transplant not authorized in writing by the Company prior to the beginning of donor search and selection or any transplant or replacement procedure not specifically listed above.

Kidney Disease or End Stage Renal Disease. Expense incurred for dialysis, transplantation and donor-related services to a maximum of $30,000 for each covered person during a calendar year. The transplant must be authorized in writing by the Company prior to the beginning of the donor search and selection. No benefits will be paid if the procedure has not been authorized by the Company prior to the beginning of such search.

Together with expense for dialysis and/or transplantation, expense incurred for surgery, storage and/or transportation service related to donor organ acquisition is limited to the $30,000 annual maximum. If the transplanted organ is from a live donor, expense incurred by the donor that is not paid by any other plan of insurance will be covered as though the donor's expense were the expense of the covered person, and included in the $30,000 annual maximum.

The limits in this provision for kidney disease or end stage renal disease provide for coordination with the governmental coverage for end stage renal disease.

COVERED COMPLICATIONS OF PREGNANCY

You, your spouse or a dependent child are covered for complications of pregnancy as defined below. Benefits are provided on the same basis as any covered sickness. Covered complications of pregnancy are limited to:

1. Conditions (when pregnancy is not ended) whose diagnoses are distinct from pregnancy, but are caused or adversely affected by pregnancy. Some examples: acute nephritis, nephrosis and cardiac decompensation.
2. Non-elective caesarean section
3. Ectopic pregnancy that is terminated
4. Spontaneous termination of pregnancy (miscarriage) that occurs before the 26th week of gestation; or missed abortion

Covered complications of pregnancy do not include: high-risk pregnancy or delivery, false labor, premature labor, occasional spotting, physician prescribed rest, morning sickness, pre-eclampsia or placenta previa.

CONGENITAL ILLNESS OR DEFECT OF A NEWBORN CHILD

Congenital illness or defect of a child of the insured born while this policy is in force will not be considered a pre-existing condition. Benefits will be provided on the same basis as any other sickness.

AUTHORIZATION PROVISION

This plan requires pre-authorization of all hospital admissions, inpatient surgeries, outpatient surgeries and transplants. The payment of benefits for covered expense described under the "Coverage Description" section of this policy may be reduced if the authorization procedure described below is not followed.

AN AUTHORIZATION DOES NOT GUARANTEE THAT BENEFITS WILL BE PAID. PAYMENT OF BENEFITS WILL BE DETERMINED BY THE TERMS AND LIMITS OF THE POLICY.

ELECTIVE ADMISSION OR SURGERY

For non-emergency hospital confinement, inpatient surgery, outpatient surgery or day surgery performed in a hospital, you must have the physician ordering the confinement or surgery obtain authorization before the patient is admitted to the hospital or has surgery performed. The authorization is obtained by the physician or physician's assistant from the Company's authorization service. The service can be reached by telephone during normal business hours, each Monday through Friday. A toll-free number and the name of the Company's authorization service is provided on the ID card given to you by the Company. You must instruct the physician to obtain the authorization by using the authorization form provided by the Company.

The service may require a second opinion prior to granting authorization. In such cases, you will be supplied with a list of three recommended physicians from whom the second opinion may be sought. However, the service may allow another physician to be consulted who (a) is a board-certified specialist in the field of the proposed treatment or surgery; (b) is not financially affiliated with the first physician; and (c) does not perform the surgery or provide the treatment. If the second opinion confirms the need for admission, then the admission will be considered AUTHORIZED. If the second opinion does not confirm the need for surgery or treatment, the service may allow a third opinion to be sought from a physician meeting the qualifications described for second opinions.

The physician may proceed with treatment on the basis of verbal authorization from the service. This will be followed by a written authorization sent to you, the hospital and the physician. The authorization remains valid for 60 days from the date of the written authorization. For treatment beginning after the 60-day period, a new authorization must be obtained.

EMERGENCY ADMISSIONS

Emergency admissions are admissions for life-threatening conditions or for a condition for which the absence of immediate treatment would cause permanent disability. An emergency admission must also be authorized in the same manner as an elective admission or surgery, as soon as it is reasonably possible to give notice of such confinement. Otherwise that portion of an emergency confinement occurring beyond 48 hours after admission (excluding Saturdays, Sundays and legal holidays) is considered UNAUTHORIZED.

UNAUTHORIZED ADMISSION, CONFINEMENT, OR SURGERY

If authorization is obtained in accordance with the above procedures, the hospital admission or surgery will be considered authorized; otherwise, it will be considered UNAUTHORIZED. An admission, confinement or surgery for which authorization was obtained shall be considered UNAUTHORIZED if (a) the authorization is no longer valid when confinement begins or surgery is performed; or (b) the type of treatment, admitting physician or hospital differs from the authorized treatment, physician or hospital.

Also, that portion of a hospital confinement, whether non-emergency or emergency, that exceeds the number of authorized days will be considered UNAUTHORIZED, unless an extension is granted. To receive an extension, the physician must call the Company's authorization service at least 24 hours prior to the originally scheduled discharge date and request an extension. The authorization service may or may not authorize an extension. Unauthorized extensions will be considered on the same basis as an unauthorized admission.

REDUCTION OF PAYMENT

The first $500 of covered expense incurred for unauthorized hospital admissions, confinements (or the unauthorized portion thereof) or any surgery shall not be paid by the Company; nor will that $500, or any portion thereof, be applied to the basic deductible amount requirement or rate of payment determination. As described under the Coverage Description section, to be a covered expense, the services, treatment and supplies must be medically necessary and the resulting charges reasonable and customary.

EXCLUSIONS AND LIMITATIONS

EXPENSES NOT COVERED BY THIS POLICY

This policy does not provide benefits for the following:

1. pre-existing conditions during the first two years coverage is in force; except as provided by the policy;

2. expense incurred for a sickness during the first 15 days after a covered person's effective date of coverage;

3. intentionally self-inflicted injury, suicide or suicide attempt, whether sane or insane;

4. care, treatment or services while in a government hospital, unless the covered person is legally required to pay for such services in the absence of insurance;

5. injury or sickness to the extent that benefits are paid by Medicare or any other government law or program (except Medicaid); or any Motor Vehicle No-Fault Law;

6. injury or sickness covered by any Worker's Compensation Act or Occupational Disease Law;

7. war or any act of war; injury or sickness while in the military service of any country (any premium paid for a time not covered will be returned pro-rata);

8. treatment of Temporomandibular Joint Dysfunction except as provided in item 16 of the covered expense provision;

9. dental service including x-rays, care or treatment except as provided under item 13 of the covered expense provision;

10. treatment for infertility; confinement, treatment or services related to artificial insemination; restoration of fertility, reversal of sterilization or promotion of conception; or expense incurred for genetic counselling, testing or treatment.

11. eyeglasses, contact lenses, hearing aids, eye exams, eye refraction or eye surgery for correction of refraction error;

12. normal pregnancy or childbirth (except as may be provided by rider), routine well-baby care including hospital nursery charges at birth; abortion or caesarean section except as provided in the Covered Complications of Pregnancy provision;

13. expense incurred for weight reduction or weight-control programs, including surgery; treatment, medication or hormones to stimulate growth;

14. reconstructive or plastic surgery that is primarily a cosmetic procedure, including medical or surgical complications therefrom; except as provided in item 4 of the covered expense provision;

15. the first $500 of otherwise covered expense incurred during any unauthorized hospital confinement or the unauthorized portion of a confinement or unauthorized surgery (see Reduction of Payment Provision);

16. treatment, removal or repair of tonsils or adenoids during the first six months of coverage, except on an emergency basis;

17. expense incurred due to injury or sickness due to committing a felony or while under the influence of illegal narcotics;

18. sales tax or gross receipt tax;

19. custodial care.

CLAIMS

NOTICE OF CLAIM

If a covered person incurs covered expense, you must give the Company written notice of claim. The notice must be given within 60 days after the claim begins, or as soon as is reasonably possible. The notice must be given to the Company or its agent, and must include your name and policy number.

CLAIM FORMS

When notice of claim is received, the Company will send you claim forms. If you do not receive the forms within 15 days after the giving of such notice, you shall be deemed to have complied with the proof of loss requirements if: (1) you give the Company a written statement of the nature and the extent of the loss for which claim is made; and (2) such statement is given within the time limit stated in the Proofs of Loss provision.

PROOFS OF LOSS

You must give the Company written proof of loss within 90 days after the covered expense is incurred. If written proof is not given in the time required, this will not make the claim invalid as long as the proof is given as soon as reasonably possible. In no event, except in the absence of legal capacity, may proof be given later than one year from the time otherwise required.

PAYMENT OF CLAIMS

Benefits will be paid to you unless you have assigned them to a doctor, hospital or other provider. Any benefits unpaid and unassigned at your death will be paid to the designated beneficiary or your estate.

TIME OF PAYMENT OF CLAIMS

Benefits for covered expense will be paid promptly upon receipt of written proof of loss. If not paid within 30 days of receipt of proof of loss, interest at the rate of 8 percent per annum will be paid, in addition, after the 30th day.

PHYSICAL EXAMINATION

While a claim is pending, the Company has the right to have a covered person examined as often as reasonably necessary. This will be at the Company's expense.

CONTRACT

CONSIDERATION

This policy is issued on the basis of the statements and agreements in the application and payment of the required premium. Premium payment in advance on or before the policy date will keep this policy in force from the policy date until the first renewal date. The premium is set out in the policy schedule. Each renewal premium is due on its due date subject to the grace period. All periods of insurance will begin and end at 12:01 A.M., standard time, at your residence.

ENTIRE CONTRACT; CHANGES

This policy, your attached application and any endorsements constitute the entire contract. No change in this policy is valid unless approved by an executive office of the Company. The approval must be endorsed by the officer and attached to the policy. No agent can change this policy or waive any of its provisions.

TIME LIMIT ON CERTAIN DEFENSES

After two years from the effective date of coverage, no misstatement made in the application (unless fraudulent) will be used to void the policy or deny any claim beginning after the two year period.

No claim for expense incurred by a covered person that begins more than two years from that person's effective date of coverage will be reduced or denied on the grounds that a disease or physical condition (not excluded from coverage by name or specific description) had existed prior to the covered person's effective date.

GRACE PERIOD

There is a grace period of 31 days for the payment of each premium due after the first premium. The policy will stay in force during this grace period. If the premium is not paid by the end of the grace period, this policy will lapse. No coverage will be provided during the grace period if the covered person has similar coverage available through another carrier and does not pay premium to the Company.

NONRENEWAL

The grace period does not apply if the Company has given you written notice that it will not renew the policy. This notice must be sent to you at least 30 days before the premium is due. Notice will be mailed to your last known address in the Company's records. Coverage will continue for any period for which premium has been accepted.

The Company can only decline to renew the policy on the renewal date occurring on, or after and nearest, each anniversary. The anniversary will be based on the policy date or last reinstatement date. This does not apply if premiums are not paid. Nonrenewal will not prejudice any expense incurred while the policy was in force.

LEGAL ACTION

You cannot bring legal action to recover on this policy before at least 60 days have passed from the time written proof has been given to the Company. No action can be brought after three years from the time written proof has been given to the Company. The time limit is five years in Kansas; six years in South Carolina.

TERMINATION OF INSURED'S COVERAGE

Your coverage will end on the date the policy lapses or is nonrenewed.

TERMINATION OF DEPENDENT COVERAGE

Coverage will end for your dependent children on the date the policy lapses or is non-renewed, or on the premium due date following the earliest to occur of (a) the date of their marriage, (b) the date they reach age 21 (or age 25 if the dependent is enrolled in and actively pursuing a full-time course of study at an accredited institution of higher learning), or (c) the date they are no longer dependent on you. Coverage will end on your spouse: (a) on the date the policy lapses or is non-renewed; or (b) on the premium due date following the date of a divorce. Benefits will still be paid to the end of the time for which premiums were accepted.

CONVERSION

A spouse or a dependent child who is no longer eligible for coverage on this policy can obtain a similar policy. No proof of good health will be required, but written application must be made within 60 days after that person's coverage terminates.

MISSTATEMENT OF AGE OR SEX

If any age or sex has been misstated, an adjustment in the benefits payable will be made to recover any past premiums due.

REINSTATEMENT

If you do not pay a renewal premium within the time granted, your policy will lapse. It will be reinstated if the Company or its agent accepts the premium without requiring an application.

If the Company or its agent requires an application for reinstatement, and the application and one modal premium are received within six months of the lapse date, the policy will be reinstated when approved by the Company. The Company has 45 days to act on your application. Your policy will be reinstated unless the Company notifies you in writing of its disapproval.

You will be covered for an injury sustained on or after the reinstatement date. You will be covered for a sickness that begins more than ten days after the reinstatement date.

After the policy is reinstated, you and the Company will have the same rights as existed just before the due date. These rights are subject to any provisions endorsed or attached to the policy. Premium cannot be required for more than 60 days before the date.

CONFORMITY WITH STATE STATUTES

If this policy, on its effective date, is in conflict with any laws in your state of residence, it is changed to meet the minimum requirements of such laws.

EH Health Insurance Company of America
Major Medical Insurance Application

Name _____   Occupation _____   Sex _____
      Last   First   Middle   M/F

Billing Address _____   Height _____   Weight _____
          Street   City   State   Zip Code   Ft. In.   Lbs.

Date of Birth _____   Place of Birth _____   Phone (_____)_____
        Mo./Day/Yr.   City/State   Area Code   Number

Social Security # _____   Phone (_____)_____
                                                          Area Code   Number

1) I am a member actively at work at least 30 hours a week   ❏ Yes   ❏ No

YOUR CHOICE OF DEDUCTIBLE: ❏ PLAN A–$250   ❏ PLAN B–$500   ❏ PLAN C–$1,000

HOW WOULD YOU LIKE YOUR PREMIUM BILLED?   ❏ Monthly   ❏ Quarterly

WHICH PLAN ARE YOU APPLYING FOR?   ❏ Comprehensive   ❏ Basic

If you wish to include your spouse and/or eligible dependent children, complete this section

NAME (First, Middle, Last)	SEX	DATE OF BIRTH	HEIGHT	WEIGHT
Your Spouse				
Your Children				

THE FOLLOWING QUESTIONS ARE TO BE ANSWERED FOR EACH PERSON APPLYING FOR COVERAGE. ANY MISSTATEMENTS MAY AFFECT YOUR COVERAGE—GIVE FULL DETAILS TO ALL "YES" ANSWERS IN THE SPACE PROVIDED.

In the last 10 years, has any person proposed for insurance been diagnosed, treated by or consulted a licensed physician or practitioner for any of the following?

	Yes	No		Yes	No
a. Abnormal blood pressure, chest pain, stroke, heart attack or murmur or any other heart, blood or circulatory disorder	❏	❏	f. Ulcers, colitis, rectal disorder or any disorder of the digestive system, liver or gallbladder	❏	❏
b. Cancer, tumor, growth, enlarged lymph nodes, skin disorder or discolored areas or lesions of the skin or mouth	❏	❏	g. Diabetes, thyroid disorder, speech impairment or disorder of the eyes, ears, nose or throat	❏	❏
c. Emphysema, lung or respiratory disorder	❏	❏	h. Seizures or neurological disorder, mental, nervous or emotional disorder, psychiatric or psychological counseling or treatment	❏	❏
d. Arthritis, or any disorder of the back or neck, muscles, bones or joints	❏	❏			
e. Kidney or urinary system disorder, disorder of the prostate or reproductive system, or breast disorder	❏	❏	i. Alcoholism, drug or chemical dependency or substance abuse	❏	❏
			J. Acquired Immune Deficiency Syndrome or AIDS Related Complex (ARC)	❏	❏

For Office Use Only	Eff. _____	Ren. Date _____	Paid _____
	CC _____	Cert. No. _____	

1

NOTICE OF INSURANCE INFORMATION PRACTICES

TO PROPERLY UNDERWRITE AND ADMINISTER YOUR INSURANCE COVERAGE A CERTAIN AMOUNT OF INFORMATION MUST BE COLLECTED. THE APPLICATION FOR INSURANCE CONTAINS INFORMATION OBTAINED FROM YOU NECESSARY FOR THIS PURPOSE. IN ADDITION, AS PART OF OUR REGULAR UNDERWRITING PROCEDURE, OTHER INFORMATION MAY BE COLLECTED FROM OTHER SOURCES ABOUT YOU OR YOUR ELIGIBLE DEPENDENTS WHO MAY BE PROPOSED FOR INSURANCE.

GENERALLY, DISCLOSURE OF PERSONAL INFORMATION WILL NOT BE MADE TO THIRD PARTIES. HOWEVER, IN SOME CIRCUMSTANCES, THE INSURANCE COMPANY OR YOUR AGENT WILL MAKE DISCLOSURE OF PERSONAL INFORMATION WITHOUT YOUR AUTHORIZATION TO THIRD PARTIES. THIS MIGHT INCLUDE THE DISCLOSURE OF PERSONAL INFORMATION TO PERSONS OR ORGANIZATIONS WHO MAY WISH TO MARKET PRODUCTS OR SERVICES, INCLUDING AFFILIATES OF THE INSURANCE COMPANY, BUT ONLY IF YOU HAVE NOT INDICATED TO US IN WRITING THAT YOU OBJECT TO OUR DOING SO.

YOU HAVE THE RIGHT TO OBTAIN ACCESS TO PERSONAL INFORMATION ABOUT YOU OR YOUR ELIGIBLE DEPENDENTS, IF PROPOSED FOR INSURANCE, COLLECTED BY THE COMPANY OR YOUR AGENT, EXCEPT INFORMATION RELATING TO A CLAIM, CIVIL OR CRIMINAL PROCEEDING. MEDICAL INFORMATION WILL ONLY BE RELEASED THROUGH A DOCTOR, PRACTITIONER, OR OTHER MEDICAL PROFESSIONAL SELECTED BY YOU WHO IS LICENSED TO PROVIDE PROFESSIONAL CARE RELEVANT TO THE NATURE OF THE INFORMATION. YOU ALSO HAVE THE RIGHT TO SEEK CORRECTION OF INFORMATION YOU BELIEVE TO BE INACCURATE.

	Yes	No
2) Are you or any of your dependents currently pregnant? **If yes, list name and due date.**	☐	☐
3) In the last 2 years, has any person proposed for insurance taken prescription medication for more than 30 days? **If yes, state condition, name of medication, dosage and frequency in space provided below.**	☐	☐
4) In the last 5 years, have you or any of your dependents to be insured had any physical disorder, illness, injury, surgery, or check-up, or consultation other than admitted above?	☐	☐

Complete the following for each "YES" answer to questions 1 through 4:

Ques. No.	Name of Person	Date of Treatment From	To	Reason for Checkup, Diagnosis, Illness or Condition Frequency of Attacks	Treatment or Findings, Medication, Recommendations, Hospitalization and/or Surgery Degree of Recovery	Name and Address of Each Physician, Practitioner and Medical Facility

If additional space is needed, use a separate sheet. Sign, date and return it with this form.

	Yes	No
5) Has any person proposed for insurance had health insurance declined, postponed, ridered, rated, cancelled or had reinstatement or renewal refused? **If yes, state the name of the company, action, reason and date in the space below.**	☐	☐
6) Does any person proposed for insurance now carry health insurance or have an application pending with another company? **If yes, state name of applicant, company, type and amount of coverage in the space provided below.**	☐	☐
7) Will the coverage you are applying for replace any coverage listed above? **If yes, give details below.**	☐	☐

_____
_____
_____

I understand and agree that the statements and answers in this application are complete and true to the best of my knowledge and belief and shall form a part of the contract of insurance. I also understand and agree that the insurance applied for, if issued, shall be subject to such statements and answers and will take effect on the effective date stated on the schedule provided the applicable first premium has been paid.

I AUTHORIZE any physician, medical practitioner, hospital, clinic, other medical or medically related facility, insurance or reinsuring company, Medical Information Bureau, consumer reporting agency, employer, or the Veterans Administration, having information available as to advice, diagnosis, treatment, or care of any physical or mental condition concerning me, my spouse, or my minor children, including information about drugs, alcoholism, or mental illness, and any other non-medical information concerning me, my spouse, or my minor children to give to the Company, its affiliates, its legal representative, or its reinsurers any and all such information.

I UNDERSTAND the information obtained by use of the Authorization will be used by the Company or its affiliates to determine eligibility for insurance.

I KNOW that I may request to receive a copy of this Authorization.

I ACKNOWLEDGE having received and read the Notice Regarding Medical Information Bureau and the Notice of Insurance Information Practices (where applicable).

I AGREE that a copy of this Authorization shall be as valid as the original.

I AGREE that this Authorization shall remain valid for two years from the date shown below.

_____	_____	_____
DATE	SIGNATURE OF PROPOSED INSURED	SIGNATURE OF SPOUSE (IF APPLYING)